D1116220

The Option Trader Handbook

Strategies and Trade Adjustments

Second Edition

GEORGE M. JABBOUR, PhD

PHILIP H. BUDWICK, MsF

WILEY

John Wiley & Sons, Inc.

Published by John Wiley & Sons, Inc., Hoboken, New Jersey.
Published simultaneously in Canada.

For general information on our other products and services or for technical support, please contact our Customer Care Department within the United States at (800) 762-2974, outside the United States at (317) 572-3993 or fax (317) 572-4002.

Wiley also publishes its books in a variety of electronic formats. Some content that appears in print may not be available in electronic books. For more information about Wiley products, visit our web site at www.wiley.com.

Library of Congress Cataloging-in-Publication Data:

Jabbour, George (George Moussa)
  The option trader handbook : strategies and trade adjustments / George M. Jabbour, Philip H. Budwick. – 2nd ed.
      p. cm. – (Wiley trading system)
  ISBN 978-0-470-48161-5 (cloth)
  1. Options (Finance)   2. Options (Finance)–Prices.   3. Stock options.   I. Budwick, Philip.
II. Title.
  HG6024.A3J32   2010
  332.64′53–dc22

                                                                                          2009041414

Printed in the United States of America.

10 9 8 7 6 5 4 3 2 1

To our families: Thank you for all your love and support.

Contents

CHAPTER 2   Tools of the Trader   29

CHAPTER 5   Calls and Puts   259

Preface to the First Edition

Option trading is both an art and a science. The science of option trading is very straightforward and mechanical and involves the specific steps in establishing a position, pricing, and understanding how movements in the underlying stock affect your trades. The art of trading, on the other hand, involves the use of your imagination and ingenuity. The market is your canvass and you coordinate different strategies and adjustments to create a unique painting, which is your portfolio. As mechanical as option trading seems, to be truly successful you will need to apply your own artistic style with respect to developing strategies and making trade adjustments. This book is about the art of making trade adjustments.

Making an adjustment to a stock or option position is one of the most overlooked and underutilized skills in trading. Moreover, it is one area where your personal style and imagination are valued over any other quantitative trading skill. Options give you the flexibility to trade markets in any direction, or with no direction at all, and for as long or as short a time period as you want. Just as eight simple musical notes can be combined to make an infinite number of symphonies and songs, calls and puts also can be combined in a number of ways, using different expiration dates and strike prices, to create an almost infinite number of positions and follow-up adjustments.

Using the right trade adjustment can hedge or even boost your profits, limit your losses, and create risk-free trades. Trade adjustments can also be used to repair losing positions. Whether you invest using only stocks, only options, or both, the information in this book is intended to give you the tools you need to improve your trading skills and performance.

The material in this book presents the art of trade adjustments in a logical sequential order. First, we discuss the most important aspect of investing—risk and trade management. Trade adjustments are tools used to implement trade and risk management. Therefore, you cannot understand how to use the tools if you are not aware of the theory behind them.

That is why in the first chapter we present the guiding principles of risk and trade management and describe how to apply them to manage your portfolio. We discuss investment and portfolio themes and how to develop a professional approach to your trading. Finally, we detail our formula for trading success, known as SCORE, which not only teaches you how to incorporate our principles of risk and trade management into your daily trading, but also lays out a complete step-by-step trading and portfolio management system.

After you have learned the theory, you need to know the right tools for effectively putting the theory into practice. Chapter 2 provides an overview of the tools you will need to control your risk, take advantage of the benefits of options, and make adjustments to your positions. This book is not meant for the pure beginner in options; we assume that the reader has a minimal understanding of how options work and a familiarity with the basic strategies. Nonetheless, we provide a quick overview of the most important characteristics of options and various strategies to remind the reader of the terms and strategies that are used throughout the book. The trade adjustments discussed range from basic to quite complex. Therefore, a general background in option strategies is required and presented in Chapter 2. We also discuss implied volatility and time decay, two often overlooked option characteristics, which, if used effectively, can reduce many common mistakes made by most traders.

Once you have learned the theory and the tools to put that theory into practice, you are ready to learn the art of trade adjustments. The remaining chapters discuss how to adjust various trading positions to lock in a profit, hedge against a loss, or boost an overall profit. Each chapter covers a different type of underlying position and all the possible adjustments that can be made to that position, whether the underlying stock moves higher or lower, or even if it moves sideways. We start with long and short stock positions and the various adjustments you can make using options. We also deal with basic and advanced call and put positions and cover adjustments to more advanced strategies such as spreads and combinations.

The strategies and adjustments in the book continually build on information presented in previous chapters. Therefore, you are encouraged to read the book straight through because the strategies and adjustments become more complex and follow a natural progression. However, most traders will probably use the text as a reference handbook and go directly to the chapter or strategy they are interested in reading about. In later chapters you may find references to earlier chapters or find short summaries of position analysis where the relevant background to a specific strategy was presented earlier in the handbook.

We tried whenever possible to make it easy for the handbook users to read up on the specific strategy they are interested in and find all the information they need in one place. However, you will find that all the strategies and adjustments complement each other and you will gain a better understanding of the art of trading by first reading the chapters in order. Thereafter, you can keep the handbook at your side and use it as a trading reference.

Within each chapter, we use numerous examples to demonstrate the different trade adjustments using real stocks. The stocks used as examples are merely for illustrative purposes and in no way are to be construed as an investment opinion on whether to buy or sell such securities. Whenever we quote stock or option prices or specific strategy costs, we are estimating the premiums on the given options based on market prices at the time of writing for purposes of illustrating the given strategies and adjustments. The prices quoted for each option are the assumed prices you would hypothetically buy or sell those options for in each example and we ignore bid/ask spreads.

When calculating the profit and loss for each strategy or adjustment as well as for the risk/reward profile charts contained in each chapter, we assume that the relevant options are at expiration and worth only their intrinsic value, if any. The positions can be terminated at any time prior to expiration either by closing the position or exercising the options. However, the only time we know the exact value of the option is on its expiration day, so we assume all positions are held to expiration. For simplicity, the profit calculations also exclude commissions, taxes, and other transaction costs as well as the effect of the time value of money.

When discussing option pricing in Chapter 2, we present the Black–Scholes option pricing model merely for purposes of explaining the different option pricing factors and how they affect the price of the option. Although the formula assumes that the options are European style, we apply the price sensitivity factors in the Black–Scholes model to American-style equity options discussed in the handbook—to simplify the explanation of how each pricing factor can affect the value of a call or a put.

The number of possible trade adjustments to the positions we cover in the handbook is almost infinite and we could not possibly cover every single trading scenario or contingency. We try to present the best possible trade adjustments given the movement of the underlying stock and even present some adjustments that we do not recommend, for the sake of being as complete as possible. The number of possible adjustments that can be made is limited only by your imagination, so feel free to take what you read one step further whenever practical.

Moreover, there are some strategies to which we did not cover trade adjustments. Because most complex option positions can be broken down into more familiar simple strategies already covered in this handbook, you can easily take the adjustments covered here and apply them to any option strategy. However, you should never overtrade your position or make too many adjustments. Sometimes the best adjustment is closing out a profitable trade to realize your gain or closing out a losing position to limit your loss. Therefore, the handbook is meant to teach you to make appropriate trade adjustments and not overtrade positions by making as many adjustments as possible.

This book is intended to be a tool for both stock and option traders. Whatever strategy you are using, you can find numerous trade adjustments for most situations. Making the right adjustment to your position at the right time can improve your trading skills and performance. However, all skills take time to learn and the same is true with the art of trade adjustments. Let your imagination be your guide, and this handbook will become one of the most valuable assets in your portfolio.

Preface to the Second Edition

The key to being a successful trader is to always improve your skills and never assume you know everything about the markets and the products you are trading. Moreover, you can improve your knowledge by simply reviewing in greater detail what you already know and look at it in a different way. We are always striving to improve ourselves with respect to option trading, and in the years since the first edition of *The Option Trader Handbook*, we have delved deeper into the mechanics of option pricing and trade adjustments to gain a new perspective on the art of option trading. As a result of our efforts, we are proud to present the second edition of *The Option Trader Handbook* with even more tools and tips to improve your understanding of how options work and how to make better trading decisions.

The largest addition to the new edition is in Chapter 2, "Tools of the Trader." We have added a new section dedicated to the option Greeks and risk management. Most people have a general understanding of the different factors that affect the pricing of an option but very little understanding of what the Greeks are and how to read and understand them. More important, how can you use this information to make better trading decisions and avoid making some common mistakes? We focus on the most significant pricing factors, which are time to expiration, stock price, and volatility, and discuss the Greek values used to measure changes in these factors. In addition, we describe their general characteristics to better understand how options move with changes in these pricing factors and what risk we are exposed to in our positions. Finally, after highlighting the key principles of each of these pricing factors, we discuss how to apply these principles to improve your risk management and make better trading decisions.

Specifically, we look at Delta and how sensitive options are to changes in the price of the underlying stock and how those sensitivities change whether you are in the money, at the money, or out of the money. We then look at time to expiration and time decay and understand how fast options can shrink to nothing and ways to reduce those risks. We also discuss implied volatility, its unique characteristics, and how changes in volatility have significant effects on the prices of options. We also discuss the VIX, or market implied volatility index.

To better illustrate the Greeks and their application in trading, we added a Greek profile description under each option strategy. We describe the basic Greek characteristics of each option strategy, as well as the specific risks. Understanding the Greek profile of each strategy will help you to choose the right strategies for different situations.

To show the practical application of the Greeks, we highlight our step-by-step approach to using the Greeks together to make better trading decisions and avoid many common mistakes. We highlight this approach in our Valuable Derivative Traders program, where we develop a three-step approach to analyzing implied volatility, strike selection, and time to expiration to arrive at the most appropriate option strategy and risk management approach. Finally, we provide our detailed theory of trade adjustments and explain why we choose a risk/reward approach to trade adjustments versus looking solely at the Greek values.

In the subsequent chapters, we add some detail to some of the adjustments already discussed. We also add information on credit spreads, butterflies, and short straddles. Our goal is to provide the reader with as much additional detail as possible on the tools of the trader and risk management techniques to ensure a better understanding of how to trade options smarter and with increased awareness of how to manage the risk. You will be able to take better advantage of the adjustments discussed if you are better prepared before you even enter into a trade.

Like the first edition, this book is meant to be a tool that provides you with the necessary skills to improve your trading decisions. We worked to add additional material to ensure that you never stop improving your knowledge about options. Moreover, even if you are familiar with the Greeks, we presented a program to help you see the Greeks in a more practical way so that you can directly apply that knowledge to your trading.

We want to thank our families for putting up with us while we wrote both editions of this book and for their nonstop love and support, not only for us but of our passion for options. More important, we are thankful for this book for giving us a new perspective on options and the opportunity to strengthen our friendship and share our enjoyment of trading options. Finally, we want to thank all of the editorial and production staff at John Wiley & Sons for their support, guidance, and patience during this long process and for all the time they put in to get our book completed.

CHAPTER 1

Trade and Risk Management

INTRODUCTION

When novices begin to learn martial arts or boxing, they invariably want to start by learning how to punch or strike their opponent. To them, that is the most exciting part of learning martial arts, and they are in a rush to learn to attack. However, the trainer or coach will usually start by teaching them how to defend themselves or block an attack. If you cannot defend yourself from getting hit, then you will not last long enough to attack your opponent. Most novices fail to see the importance of defensive techniques. In sports, the motto is that defense wins championships. After all, even if you score points, you cannot win if you let your opponent score more points against you.

The importance of defense is also true in option trading. Beginners and advanced traders alike want to focus on trading strategies and making money. They usually overlook the importance of defense. Of course when trading options, we are not at risk of getting punched or attacked, but the money we invest is under constant attack. We are competing with thousands of traders and investors who want to "take" our money. Investors and traders need to learn to defend their capital against losses just like boxers need to protect their bodies and heads. Allowing too many losses, or "attacks," to your trading capital will leave you with no money, and you will be out of the trading game. Therefore, option investors must also first focus on defense before jumping into the offense of making trades or establishing positions.

The defensive skills that should be studied by any investor before focusing on trading strategies are risk and trade management. Learning how to control and manage the risk of each and every trade, as well as your portfolio on the whole, is vital to protecting your capital. Many investors have had the experience of making money on a series of trades only to see one or two bad trades wipe out all their hard-fought gains. Imagine working hard the first six rounds of a boxing match to weaken and hurt your opponent, only to come out in round seven with your hands at your sides and allow your opponent to knock you out. Ignoring risk and trade management is just like walking into a boxing ring with your hands stuck to your sides, leaving your whole body and face exposed.

We believe that the difference between a good investor and a bad investor comes down to the proper use of trade and risk management. This is not to say that stock picking, market timing, and analytical skills do not play a part in the success of traders. However, it is trade and risk management that allows such qualified investors to keep the fruits of their labor and not give back all their profits. We all have heard many stories of day-trading millionaires in the tech boom of the late 1990s when all it took was going long in anything with .com in the company name to make money. However, most of those millionaires walked into the year 2000 with their gloves at their sides and were systematically knocked out one by one, with many of them losing all of their gains. Again, these traders focused on the techniques of trading without worrying about a good defense—risk and trade management.

Therefore, our first step before learning trading strategies is to review the principles of good risk management. As with any skill, you will not pick it up simply by reading this chapter once. You need to study the principles and practice applying them as you trade. It takes time before it becomes ingrained into your trading style. As human beings, we are susceptible to the emotional stress, anxiety, and excitement that come with trading and making or losing money. The principles of risk and trade management help remove much of the emotion from trading and go a long way toward helping you as much as possible to avoid making costly mistakes.

THE PHILOSOPHY OF RISK

The most misunderstood concept in investments and finance is the concept of risk. However, risk is what investing is all about. Remember the old cliché: It takes money to make money. What this really means is that to make money you need to risk money. You must put some of your capital at risk in order to receive a reward. It is the incentive of the reward that encourages you to take on the risk. Because you must risk money to receive your reward, the science of finance is all about pricing and quantifying that risk to determine whether the reward is worth the risk.

Assume that a 5-year U.S. treasury note is paying 4% interest per year. We often refer to U.S. treasuries as risk-free securities because the odds of the U.S. government defaulting on the note are so infinitesimally small; you are practically guaranteed to receive your interest throughout the life of the note, as well as the return of your principal at the end of the 5 years. Assume that a private corporation is also offering a 5-year note. This corporation is a very strong business entity but there is a small risk that the business could go under and you will not get your principal back. If the corporation is offering to pay 4% interest per year, would you consider purchasing the corporation's note over that of the U.S. government?

Naturally, the answer is no. Why should you purchase a risky security that is paying the same interest, or reward, as a security that technically has no risk? There is no incentive at all to take on the risk of the corporation defaulting and losing your money. The basic theoretical concept of risk/reward is that you should be compensated for taking on additional risk by receiving a higher reward (return). Of course, the theory of risk/reward is more complicated than our simplification, but for our purposes of understanding risk management, it is sufficient to state that investors require higher returns in order to take on increased risk. Therefore, in order for the corporation to induce you to purchase their security, they need to offer you a better reward to compensate you for taking on the additional risk over the risk-free security. Assume that the corporation and the investors decide that, using complex financial models that are beyond the scope of this book, offering an additional 2% interest per year on the note is enough of an additional reward to compensate for the greater risk that exists in the corporation's note. In other words, 6% per year in interest is perceived by the market to be a sufficient reward to encourage investors to purchase that corporation's note.

This example summarizes the basis for all investment decisions. We want to know the risk of the investment and the reward we receive for assuming such a risk. If we have two investment alternatives, the way to select the best choice for our money is to compare the risk and reward of each investment to determine which one gives us the best reward for the amount of risk we must assume. Therefore, before every trade, you should always determine and quantify the risk and reward of the investment.

With respect to options, the quantification of risk and reward is very straightforward and is covered in our first and most basic principle of risk management:

KEY PRINCIPLE

You must be able to determine and quantify the maximum risk (loss) and maximum reward, as well as the breakeven points, of a position before committing any money to that investment.

This principle requires that you calculate the maximum risk, the maximum reward, and the breakeven points for every trade you are considering. Even if you fail to make these determinations prior to entering a trade, you should be able to look at any existing trade and immediately determine the maximum risk, maximum reward, and breakeven points. Deriving these three factors should become second nature. We cannot emphasize enough how important it is for every investor to understand and be able to derive these three factors before entering into any position.

We strongly recommend that you calculate these three factors in the same order as we stated them; that is, first calculate your maximum risk, then your maximum reward, and finally your breakeven points. The reason is that for you to be truly successful, you must understand the next principle of risk management:

KEY PRINCIPLE

You are a risk manager first and an investor or trader second.

Most traders immediately start by thinking of the maximum reward because they are only focused on how much money they could make. They forget that to make that money, they first need to risk something. Greed makes you focus on your reward first and clouds your judgment regarding risk, which leads to costly mistakes. For example, many investors become enamored with the idea of selling options to take in premium because they immediately get a credit. They focus first on how much money they receive and pay little attention to the enormous risk that comes with selling naked options. Unfortunately, the time they eventually learn about that risk is when they have suffered huge losses and are forced out of the game altogether.

Always focus first on how much money you could lose. Focusing on how much money you could lose puts you in the frame of mind of a risk manager. Once you have understood and accepted the amount of money you could lose, you can make a clearer decision on whether you are willing to proceed with the analysis and possibly proceed with the trade. You will begin to make decisions based on how to quantify, control, and limit your risk.

We caution the reader to not take lightly the extent of the maximum risk derived for any trade. For example, some option strategies have unlimited risk. Most traders take the words "unlimited risk" too lightly at times because ego and pride makes them feel that it really is improbable to have unlimited risk. They say things such as, "I will get out of the position if it moves against me long before I suffer any major losses." However, the market can prove us wrong in very costly ways, as the following story demonstrates.

Nick Leeson, a 28-year-old derivatives trader, worked for the 200-year-old Barings Bank out of its Singapore office. In November and December 1994, he began selling naked options on the Nikkei index (Japanese stock market), expecting the Nikkei to trade sideways over the next couple of months. As long as the Nikkei stayed in a tight trading range, Leeson would profit from his naked option positions. On January 17, 1995, an earthquake hit Kobe, Japan, and as a result of the economic aftermath, the Nikkei started to fall sharply. Instead of closing out his positions to cut his losses, Leeson began purchasing futures on the Nikkei index to stop its fall and try to reverse the declining market. The more the Nikkei fell, the more futures Leeson purchased to try to overcome his growing losses.

More and more margin was required for the naked options and growing futures position Leeson amassed until the margin calls became too much for Barings to cover. The magnitude of the losses totaled around $1.3 billion. Leeson was arrested and put in prison because he hid the size of his trades from Barings, which was forced into bankruptcy. The Dutch bank ING stepped in and bought Barings, a 200-year-old bank, for $1.00. Next time you see an advertisement for ING, remember how one trader ignored maximum risk and good principles of risk management and brought down an entire bank.

TRUTH ABOUT REWARD

Before proceeding further with risk and trade management, we clarify some myths related to the rewards of option trading. Breaking down some of the misconceptions of the potential rewards of trading options is imperative for traders to truly understand and appreciate the risk involved. The following principle seems obvious enough, but we find too many traders, both novices and experienced investors, fall prey to this greatest misconception of all:

KEY PRINCIPLE

Options are not a get-rich-quick scheme.

The potential rewards of option trading are significant, but in no way should it be seen as a get rich quick scheme. Traders looking for quick cash end up trading more on emotion and greed than detailed analysis and proper risk management. The desire for money forces investors to look desperately for the next trade. They are more likely to take unnecessary risks to get their return, and those additional risks usually lead to large losses. It is even worse if they happen to have some positive results early. If investors have a string of successful trades, they develop a false sense of invincibility and ego and begin to increase the stakes in their already risky trades until they lose everything very fast.

KEY PRINCIPLE

Investing is a long marathon, not a fast sprint.

The honest truth about rewards is that they take time and effort. It is unrealistic to assume that everyone can start trading options and turn $5,000 into $100,000 in 1 year. You should therefore have a realistic plan about the type of rewards you can earn and in what time frame. Making money in options requires a lot of commitment and discipline. Investing in options is like starting a business. In the beginning, most investors lose money, and it takes a lot of effort, research, experience, and even some luck to be successful and start producing results. Therefore, the beginning stages might be quite frustrating, and you may even feel like the market is out to get you. However, the path to the rewards of investing can be a profitable one if you have the discipline, patience, and determination to do the work.

RISK MANAGEMENT

Risk

Once you have an appreciation and respect for the risks involved in trading and the hard work required to reap the rewards, you can begin to understand how to use risk management to improve your trading performance.

First, the whole point of using options to trade is that they are an excellent tool for controlling and limiting risk. Therefore, your first step is to always trade with the intent to limit or control risk. Once you have a handle on the risk, you can prevent any one trade from significantly reducing your trading capital.

The first step we have already emphasized is to know exactly what your risk is before entering a specific trade. Once you have quantified that risk, that is, say, $400 or $4,000, you need to determine what your plan is if the trade goes against you. It is nice to think that every position you enter into will make money, but you always have to consider what will happen if you are wrong. You need an exit strategy based on the price of the underlying stock or the percentage loss at which you decide to close out the position to prevent any further loss. Thus, the following is an important principle in risk management:

KEY PRINCIPLE

For each and every trade, you must determine your exit strategy for when the trade goes against you.

Assume you purchase 100 shares of ENRON at $70 for a cost of $7,000. You expect ENRON to move higher and therefore are bullish on the stock. However, before you purchase ENRON, you need to develop an exit strategy to decide when you will get out of the trade if the stock moves lower instead of higher. If you develop the exit strategy ahead of time, then you can make the decision before your capital is at risk. By developing your exit plan before your money is at risk, you can make a clear, emotionless decision as to how much loss you are willing to absorb before you decide to close the position. If you wait until the stock starts dropping in price, you may begin to panic, get frustrated, and even freeze up and fail to pull the trigger and close the trade when you should.

You may even utter the words that are the kiss of death in risk management: "The stock has to recover and move back higher; it cannot just keep falling forever!" The reason we call this the kiss of death is because as soon as you utter this phrase, you are practically giving in to the position and letting it control you. You are refusing to close out and limit your loss because of a false hope that the position will recover. So you end up waiting and doing nothing and losing even more money. That phrase is an indication of "trade freeze" where you are unwilling to make a move to limit your risk. We used ENRON as an example because we can bet that many traders held onto ENRON the whole way down until it was worth $0.10, crying the whole way that the stock just has to move back higher.

The stock is under no legal obligation to move back higher simply because you are holding 100 shares. Such thinking violates the following principle:

The market will tell you which way the stock is moving; you cannot tell the market where you want the stock to move.

When the stock is falling, you are in the heat of a battle and it could be too late to try to make a logical decision concerning your risk. Your perception is skewed and becomes biased because you are losing money, and you will look for things that are not there. For example, you will be so desperate for the stock to recover that you will look for any signs of life and hang your hopes on those faint signals.

If the market is telling you that the stock is moving lower, then your desire to not lose money will make you ignore the obvious signs. Therefore, we cannot stress enough that you must make an exit plan before the trade so that if the stock drops in price, you will not freeze up or panic but simply stick to your risk management plan and close out the position. This way, you will prevent any one position from wiping out your other gains or your trading capital. However, establishing a predetermined exit strategy works only if you follow the next principle:

KEY PRINCIPLE

You should have the discipline to stick with your exit strategy plan to cut your losses no matter what happens. Any decision to stray from your exit strategy should be based on sound analysis or as a result of a change in circumstances of the underlying security.

Your exit strategy is based on your personal risk tolerance. It is better to establish a specific exit strategy than a generalized plan to maybe get out of the trade if it moves against you. Assume you did purchase 100 shares of ENRON at $70. You could have decided that you would close out your position if it loses 15%. You could have used a monetary value and decided to close out the trade if it is down by more than $1,000. If you used technical analysis, you may have developed an exit strategy based on the stock price and a technical indicator you found in the price chart of ENRON. For example, if you found that ENRON has support at $67, you could have decided that you will close out the bullish position if ENRON breaks through support at $67 and continues to move lower.

There is no one right answer in developing an exit strategy. Each person has a different risk or loss tolerance or a different assumption of where the stock will move to. Therefore, we recommend that you develop an exit strategy that is comfortable for you. If you put $7,000 of your $200,000 portfolio into ENRON, you may be willing to absorb more of a loss before closing the position than someone who had $7,000 worth of ENRON in a $10,000 portfolio. As long as you are comfortable with the basis for selecting your exit strategy, then your only real concern is that you stick with your plan and act immediately when the stock hits your loss target, whether it is a specific stock price, loss percentage, or loss amount.

This approach is also applicable when trading options, because the underlying security is a stock. For example, if we bought a $70 Call on ENRON instead of 100 shares of stock, we could use the same criteria for determining when to close out our option position, with one notable exception—time. Because options have expiration dates, time affects the value of our long options as well as our short options. Therefore, we may also have an exit strategy based on time. For example, we may determine that we expect ENRON to move higher in the next 30 days or so and purchase a 2-month call. Our exit strategy could be that we close the long call if ENRON has not moved higher in 30 days because that was the time period in which we expected a move.

Therefore, the first part of risk management is determining what our maximum risk is before entering a position and then developing an exit strategy to close out the position if the trade moves against us. You will never have a perfect record when trading; you will have losing positions no matter what you do. However, if you have 10 trades and 9 move against you, you can still have an overall positive return if you practice good risk management by closing out the 9 losing trades before they produce significant losses. Always know the full risk before entering into any investment and always have a plan to get out if you start to lose money.

Reward

We do not just recommend developing an approach for handling the risk of a trade, we also advocate dealing with the reward portion as well. Most investors enter into a trade expecting to make money. They do not really develop clear reasons why they expect to make money except for such standard analysis as "I expect the stock to go up." In addition to understanding the risk involved in a trade, investors should understand the reward they hope to receive as well. Why do you expect the stock to move higher? Do you have an idea of how high you expect it to move? When will you close the position? How long do you expect to hold the stock? Most traders gloss over these types of questions and simply place their money into the trade. However, if you do not consider these questions, how will you know the right time to get out of the trade and pocket your return? How do you prevent trade paralysis, where you watch a winning position turn into a loss right before your eyes because you failed to close it out when you had an unrealized gain?

The tendency by most investors is to simply buy and hold a stock without any clear plan as to when to get out if they have an unrealized profit. For the long-term buy-and-hold investor, this is the right thing to do. The long-term investor (e.g., someone investing for an individual retirement account, pension plan, or college fund) is buying for the long haul, and the strategy is to hold on for years and let the stock move higher over time. However, for all other investors and traders, risk management also involves properly managing rewards based on the following principle:

KEY PRINCIPLE

You should always have an exit strategy for closing out your profitable position.

Most investors ignore this tenet of risk management because they feel that if they are making money, why do they need an exit strategy? Failure to have some sort of profitable exit strategy usually indicates that you do not have a vision going into the trade. You expect the stock or option to go up in price and make money, but stocks and options do not just go up indefinitely. If you have no logical reason for the trade, then you will never know the right time to get out. What usually happens is that you end up cutting profits short or letting winners run too long until they reverse and produce losses. Therefore, you need to manage your gains as much as you need to manage your losses.

Before entering a trade, you need to develop a plan as to what your profit target is. Once that profit target is reached, you can close out the trade and pocket your returns. You do not need to be as strict with profit exit strategies as we recommend you be with exit strategies when the position is losing money. The profit in the position provides additional room to breathe, and therefore you can give the position more time as long as the stock or option continues to show strength in moving in the expected direction. For example, you could close out the position if it earns 25% or if the stock hits a certain price or resistance point. Maybe you have a predetermined dollar value you are looking to make. Another option is to close out half your position when the trade doubles in value (e.g., for option trades) to take your cost off the table and play with "house money."

In addition to an exit strategy, you should also plan potential trade adjustments to enhance the performance of your position. The goal of the subsequent chapters is to teach you various trading adjustments to make to your trading position. Many of these adjustments are meant to reduce your risk, lock in a profit, or hedge against a loss. Making plans on how to adjust a position in the middle of the trade could lead to a rushed decision that is not that well thought out. If the market begins to move quickly, it may cause you to rush into making an adjustment that is inappropriate for your position. Therefore, we recommend that before you enter into a position, you also plan what potential adjustments you can make. You can study the various adjustment strategies covered in this book and become familiar with the ones that best fit your trading style and risk tolerance. Managing risk and reward after you open your position through trade adjustments is just as important as managing your risk and reward before you enter into the position.

Breakeven Points

Every position you enter into may have one or more breakeven points at which you either recover the costs of the position or suffer no profit or loss. When you establish a position for a net debit, the breakeven point is very significant because it tells you how far the underlying security has to move before you recover the cost of your trade. If you establish a net credit trade, the breakeven point tells you at what point you will begin to lose money on the position. Therefore, the breakeven point is a significant part of risk and reward. You should be able to calculate the breakeven point of any trade before you enter the position, as well as the new breakeven point created from any adjustments to the trade.

TRADE MANAGEMENT

Trading Theme

In the previous section we covered risk management and recommended that before every trade you should determine your maximum risk, maximum reward, and breakeven points, and also determine an exit strategy if the position is making or losing money. Taking such steps before the trade is entered into is a way for you to examine the risk, quantify it, and develop a plan on how to control it. The subject of trade management also focuses on dealing with risk in your trades and portfolio as a whole as well as your overall approach to trading.

The best way to teach the lesson of trade management is to use the analogy of chess. When learning chess, the first step you take in improving your game is to learn opening strategies, that is, specific sets of moves made in the beginning of a chess game to establish a certain attack or defensive pattern. Beginners study the moves and memorize the patterns. They learn different variations of the openings so that they can adapt in case the moves occur in a different order than the memorized pattern. Chess openings usually cover the first 10 moves or so but set the stage for the entire game. If you can establish a good position through proper use of an opening strategy, then you will have a strong defensive position from which to attack and gain the advantage.

The problem is that most novice chess players merely focus on memorizing the moves. They look at the picture of where the pieces are supposed to be at the end of the opening stage and work on getting their pieces into the same position. They study the mechanics only and therefore move mechanically without thought. Their analysis is only move to move, and they do not see the bigger picture. Chess is a game of strategy and concentration and is unlike checkers, where both players simply react from one move to the other. What the beginner fails to realize is that every opening strategy has its own theme. For example, one opening has a theme of establishing a strong offensive position in the center of the board while another is focused on establishing a strong defensive position.

Each opening is not just a series of mechanical moves. To have success in executing each opening strategy, you must understand what the theme of the opening is. What is the opening trying to accomplish? Understanding the theme will allow you to move away from simple mechanical moves and force you to play with a goal in mind. As long as you have the overall theme mastered, you can execute your plan no matter what your opponent does. Even if your opponent reacts in an unexpected manner, you can still stick with your overall plan and adjust with no problem. Each move will be made within the context of the opening strategy, and you will be able to calmly execute your plan.

How is this relevant to option trading and trade management? Like chess novices, many new traders focus only on the mechanics of trading. They study the option strategies and concentrate on how to open and close positions; that is, they become mechanical traders. However, every trade has a theme behind it. When you select a stock to invest in, there is an overriding theme to your investment. You have conducted research and analysis on the security and have made a prediction or assumption about the direction you expect the stock to move and how long you think it will take to make such a move.

Another mistake novice chess players make with respect to selecting an appropriate opening strategy is that they fail to choose the strategy that best represents their playing style. For example, players with an attacking style should not choose a passive defensive opening strategy. If they do, then they will attempt to make attacking moves from a position that was not intended for such attacks and will end up weakening their position and opening themselves up for severe counterattacks. This mistake is often made because the players ignore matching the theme or overall strategy of the opening they choose with their playing style and simply focus on the mechanical moves. The difference between chess players and chess experts in this respect is that experts understand the theme and the strengths and weaknesses of the opening they select as well as the strengths and weaknesses of their playing style and focus all their moves on executing that strategy.

Assume you have analyzed and researched the stock of XYZ and have decided that the stock will move higher over the next few months. Your reasons could be based on technical analysis or fundamental analysis or a combination of the two. You have established a theme for your investment in XYZ. Your theme is that you are bullish on XYZ for specific reasons and you wish to make an investment that will profit from the impending rise in price of XYZ over the next few months. In other words, you have developed a plan of attack on XYZ. Most investors do not see trading as developing themes and plans for attack, but investing without any plan or theme is simply throwing money around like a gambler would do at Las Vegas, moving from table to table. Therefore, like expert chess players who select an overall theme to their opening strategy and move each piece in furtherance of this plan of attack, the option trader must also develop a trading plan for each position.

To develop a trading plan or theme, you need to decide what your trading objectives are. Most investors simply say that their objective is to make money. However, this is too vague of an objective and is akin to the chess players simply saying they want to win the game. The more specific objective is focused on how you want to make your money. Do you want to make money buying stock, shorting stock, purchasing calls and puts, selling options, using spreads, using nondirectional strategies, using high-risk or low-risk strategies, picking specific stocks or sectors, trading volatility, picking only one strategy or various strategies, only focusing on indexes (but which ones?), and so on? As you can see, the question of how you want to make your money has numerous answers and can be quite overwhelming to a trader with so many investment choices to choose from.

When chess players are researching openings, they are encouraged to select the openings that best fit their playing style. With an almost infinite list of opening strategies, you can easily find a strategy that best fits your playing style: conservative, aggressive, offensive, defensive, direct attacking, flank attacking, slow development, quick development, and so on. The same process is required of investors. Traders need to determine what their trading style is and their level of risk tolerance.

This self-assessment process is the most important step in developing an effective trade management system. In *The Art of War*, the classic treatise on strategy, Sun Tzu wrote, "If you know the enemy and know yourself, you need not fear the result of a hundred battles." With respect to investments, the enemy is the uncertainty of the market and every trade is a battle. Knowing yourself means that you must put in the effort to classify your trading style. Are you a conservative or an aggressive investor? Is your time frame short term or long term? Do you prefer focusing on a wide array of sectors or indexes or just a few select stocks? If you study and research the market and you know your own trading style, then you need not fear the result of a hundred battles (trades). You will be able to match your trading style with the right investment choices. Although you will not win every battle, your wins will outnumber your losses as long as you always trade within your style.

If you do not know your trading style, then you will simply follow the crowd and invest blindly. You will trade without conviction and be easily swayed by the volatility of the market. Worst of all, you will look for guidance from any source to find trading ideas instead of developing them on your own. This usually results in following the wrong advice. You will never understand what is causing your losing trades to fail and your winning trades to make money, and your luck, because no skill is involved when trading blindly, will run out.

Once you have determined your trading style, you can develop the appropriate trading theme to match your style, just as chess masters select the appropriate opening theme to match their playing style. Then it will be easier to know what trading opportunities to look for. For example, if you are a long-term conservative investor, you will look for stocks of well-established companies with a history of sustained growth. You would then be inclined to select more appropriate option strategies for this type of stock—such as Long-term Equity AnticiPation Securities (LEAPS), covered calls, long calls, and bull spreads. Understanding your trading theme will narrow your focus and make it easier to research investment alternatives.

The Theme of Your Portfolio

Developing your trading theme will assist you greatly in developing a portfolio of investments that are all focused on furthering your goal of positive returns. As much as you need an overall theme for your investment strategy, you need a theme of trade and risk management for your portfolio. For example, if you have a conservative, long-term investment theme, then your portfolio should reflect this theme in your risk and trade management. You will not allow any position to make up a significant portion of your portfolio and thus expose you to too much risk. You might keep a certain amount of cash in reserve so that you always have capital in case a good trading opportunity comes along. Finally, you might decide that because you are a long-term investor, you will not trade your portfolio frequently. Your investment theme will therefore affect the way you balance your portfolio and manage your risk.

If you are aware of your investment theme, you should be able to glance at your portfolio and see that theme reflected in your trades and the structure of your portfolio. To truly understand this principle, let us look at the most basic example, which is prevalent in mutual funds. Assume that you are a fund manager of a small-cap value fund. The investment theme of the fund is to find stocks with small market capitalizations (i.e., $500 million or less) that are relatively cheap based on some criteria such as price-to-book and price-to-sales ratios. You will only investigate and invest in small companies that meet your thematic criteria and select the companies that best represent your trading theme. Of course, you will also be concerned with future growth prospects, earnings, and capital appreciation. If we were to look at the stocks listed in your fund, we should be able to notice that all the stocks you are invested in appear to be small companies; that is, we will not find GE, MSFT, or IBM. Thus, a basic principle of your trading theme will be obvious in your overall portfolio.

You should conduct the same exercise on your portfolio. Do all your trades appear to represent a particular trading theme or are they a hodgepodge of different, unrelated strategies with one thing in common—your capital at risk? If that is the case, then you lack a portfolio theme. This makes it difficult to follow your investment decisions and keep track of why you made each trade, because each position will most likely have its own independent justification.

If you do not have clear guidance on why you entered into each trade, then you most certainly will not be following predetermined exit strategies. Therefore, you will also be ignoring the principles of risk management; when you fail to control your risk, your risk will control you! Investing with this kind of "trade blindness" is akin to gambling in Las Vegas, and remember the old adage in gambling, "The House always wins." If you have never gambled, let us clarify that you are not the House, and eventually you will lose everything when your luck runs out. Therefore, following your investment theme in your portfolio will keep your trades focused and allow you to better manage and control your risk.

Diversification and Flexibility

All the strategies within your portfolio need not be identical simply because they are established under the same trading theme. Diversification is highly recommended in all aspects of investing, including the selection of option strategies. A portfolio theme, for example, does not envision having a portfolio made up entirely of covered calls or credit spreads. There are various option strategies that share common investment themes. Each strategy may work better under certain conditions, and therefore we need to understand the best environment for each one. Golfers have more than 10 clubs to choose from each time they hit the ball, and to be successful they must understand which club is best to use in different situations. The same is true with option strategies.

Avoid falling in love with any one strategy. If the market conditions change, a particular strategy may be inappropriate. As a result, you must be flexible in choosing a more appropriate strategy. Therefore, not only must you diversify your strategy selections, but you must also be flexible and adapt to changes in the market to switch to strategies that are more appropriate. You must adapt to the markets; the markets will not adapt to you.

TRADING AS A BUSINESS

The best way to incorporate all the principles of risk and trade management into your investments is to treat your trading as a new business. Your business is trading, and you are the president and chief financial officer of the company. This is a professional endeavor and not to be taken lightly or treated as a game or hobby—you are risking real money. You should think of trading as a career, and your job is to run the company that controls your investments. The employees of your business are your trading positions, and their jobs are to make you money. Whether you are an investor who merely trades on the side or a professional money manager or trader, you should have the same professional approach to your trading.

Start-Up Phase

At the start-up phase of a new business, there are many sunk costs and expenses required to get the business started as well as much preparation and hard work. As the owner of the new company, you need a detailed business plan, which outlines the purpose of the business and how it will get started and conduct its daily operations and also provides guidance on budgeting issues so that the company can manage its revenues and expenses. You will need to acquire assets to start the business and hire employees. The start-up phase, which usually covers the first year, is the most important and difficult part of starting a new business. Most new businesses take some time to be profitable, and therefore you, as the owner, have to be able to bear the losses until your company can begin turning a profit.

Option trading also has a start-up phase. You will need to invest time and money to learn about options and study the market before you begin to trade. Most traders begin working hard after they start trading and fail to prepare ahead of time. Learning on the run, that is, learning while you trade and lose money, is a very expensive form of education. Of course, you will constantly be learning as you trade, but before you invest the first dollar in your new business, you need to commit yourself to learning everything you can about options.

We have dealt with many option traders, both beginners and experienced investors, who still do not understand the mechanics of options. We are not referring to the complexities of options, which take some time to master, but rather the basic mechanics that every investor must know before risking a single dollar. Investors with a couple of thousand dollars committed in a position with short options have admitted to not knowing about assignment and exercise. Some investors will place $3,000 into a position and then ask for help in how to close the trade after they have made money (imagine putting money somewhere, realizing a nice profit, and having no idea how to get that money out). Others know nothing about time decay. You cannot invest in a security such as options with expiration dates when the security will no longer exist and not understand the role time plays in the value of an option.

If you planned to start a small company, you would not commit capital without a basic understanding of how the business you are entering into operates. Why? It would be too risky. Remember, your goal is to reduce and control risk, not increase risk. Therefore, taking the time to understand the mechanics of options before committing funds will help reduce the risk you are exposed to when trading. Our advice is not just for novice traders only. Many experienced option traders only focus on one type of strategy and therefore only learn what is relevant for that strategy. However, many traders who change their strategies never bother to learn more about the mechanics of the new strategies they are trying, and as a result many experience significant losses. Losing money simply because you do not know a basic characteristic of options is akin to throwing money out the window. When running a business, which is how trading should be treated, you cannot overlook crucial pieces of information and expect to make money.

Therefore, as with starting a new company, you should put in the effort and time before you begin trading to learn the business you are about to enter. Even if you have traded stocks for years, options are completely different. The mechanics of options are not difficult, so there is no reason not to learn them. Do not just learn that you buy a call if you expect the stock to go up and a put if you expect the stock to go down. You should learn about exercise and assignment, time value and time decay, implied volatility, the factors that affect the price of options, open interest and volume, how options are traded, and so on.

If you are an experienced option trader, then give yourself the time now to ensure that you learn as much as you can about options. You may be surprised to learn some things you never knew had a negative or positive effect on your trading. The worst trait of a trader is hubris, or excessive pride. Thinking you know everything about trading may cause you to not learn something very basic that could have helped improve your overall performance.

Just as a new company is based on a business plan, so should trading options. We have already discussed the type of business plan that is required for trading options—an investment and portfolio theme. Developing these themes is, in effect, the business plan for your investments. Therefore, before you begin trading, you should have your trading business plan developed. Write it down so you can refer to it regularly and keep focused on your trading themes. Adjust them as you and your portfolio adapt to the market. Businesses have to adapt to changing market conditions and so do investors. If you are an experienced trader and are investing without a business plan, take the time now to develop your trading and portfolio themes before putting another dollar of your capital at risk.

Remember that the first year of a new business can be difficult and that it sometimes takes a while before the business is profitable. Option trading takes the same time and effort. One of our earlier principles was that options are not a get-rich-quick scheme. You may experience some losses at first as you gain experience and get the feel of how options work. Although we stated that you should learn all you can before beginning to trade, some things can only be learned by actually trading, such as the feel of the market. Therefore, when you start trading, as with any new business, you need to be able to absorb some losses without going under. Start trading with capital you are willing and, more importantly, financially capable of losing. This way, you can learn from any trading mistakes without losing all your money and becoming unable to trade again. We all have our own learning curve, and we always learn more from our trading losses than we do from our successes.

We mentioned earlier that the employees of your new business are the trades whose job is to make you money. A new business usually hires only a few employees when starting out and is very selective about its hires. The first employees play a key role in getting the business started, implementing the business plan, and helping the company generate a profit. Therefore, the company only wants qualified employees who match the philosophy of the new business. Your option trades also have the same responsibilities. You should be very selective with your trades and only choose those candidates that are qualified such that they meet the criteria laid out in your investment themes. Every trade should have some relationship to your investment themes. If you wish to move into a different area, simply adjust your investment themes.

When you are starting out in a new business, you do not want to expand too quickly and be overstaffed because it will be too difficult to keep tabs on so many employees, and this will result in overspending. With trading, you do not want to start off by opening numerous positions and being "overstaffed." As stressful as trading is, you do not want to make it worse by having to follow 15 trades at the same time. It is very difficult to monitor all those positions at once and still apply the principles of risk and trade management. Moreover, having so many trades requires much capital, and you may be spreading yourself too thin. Start small and grow your "company" as your capacity to handle more "employees" grows.

The most important part of hiring "employees" (making trades) is that you have to remember your role as employer. The job of your "employees" is to make you money. Many companies set performance standards that their workers have to meet. If those performance standards are not met, the workers lose either their bonus or their job. If your "employees" produce losses, then they are not performing as expected; consequently, fire them. There are no bonus reductions or letters of reprimand. You have to run a tight business because it is your money at stake. If you have a position that is not performing, then fire it. In other words, close out the position before you lose more money. We discussed exit strategies earlier. These exit strategies are the criteria you establish to fire "employees"—for example, losses greater than 10%, fired! Do not be afraid to fire underperforming "employees," because keeping them on the payroll will just cost you more money.

Growth Phase

When your trading "business" enters the growth phase, your portfolio is growing bigger and your trading theme is more established. You are executing trades in furtherance of your investment and portfolio themes and practicing good risk and trade management. As your portfolio grows, you are not straying from any of your original principles. You have a group of "employees" that are performing, and you routinely fire the ones that do not perform and replace them with new ones. As CEO, you are studying the market and guiding your business through the ups and downs. You have some losing months and some winning months, but you try to manage your capital so that no losses wipe out your company, and try to keep some cash in reserve for insurance and possible trade opportunities that may arise.

This is by far the most exciting phase of your trading "career." But it also requires the most discipline, even more so than in the start-up phase. It is very difficult to get started and actually make money. It is even more difficult to stay profitable. The tendency for most businesses when they begin making money is to think that they are invulnerable and will just continue making more and more money. They begin to stray from the business plan and make riskier choices in the desire to make even more money. They may even try to move too soon into other markets to capture as much of the business as possible and end up expanding too quickly. Once the business gets too overextended, one small slipup or a series of losing months usually has disastrous effects and could bring the business crashing down.

With option trading, once you begin to make money consistently, that is the time where the principles you followed during the start-up phase become even more important. The reason you are making money is because you followed those principles, so why abandon them now when they are more important? The principles of risk and trade management are meant to ensure that you keep the money you earned. The key to the success of wealthy fund managers is that not only did they make money, but they kept it as well.

Mature Phase

After you start your business and work to consistently grow your portfolio over time, you reach the mature phase. You worked very hard at incorporating risk and trade management into your investing, and it allowed you to stay focused on your investment themes. You have some periods where you lose money and some periods where you make money, but overall your return is positive. You use a diversified pool of strategies and because you remain flexible, you adapt to changing market conditions to take advantage of the benefits of using different option strategies.

As a mature investor, the amount of work and discipline required does not diminish. Your focus is still on controlling your risk because you do not want to watch all your hard work disappear in losing trades. Most likely, you have more "employees" than you had in the past, but no more than what you can effectively manage. You have probably adjusted your investment themes over time as you have become a better investor and learned how to use more option strategies or even the same ones you have always used but in different ways. Most important of all, you never stop learning and perfecting your trading style. Because the market is constantly changing, you cannot sit back and expect to always make money doing the same thing over and over. Remember, you always need to remain flexible.

Just Business, Nothing Personal

Treating your trading as a business means accepting the fact that it is just business and you should not take it personally. When you lose money on a trade, it is not a personal attack on your character or a conspiracy by the underlying security to ruin you. Losses are a part of trading, and no matter how successful you become, you will always experience losses. That is why we focus so much attention on risk and trade management, so that those inevitable losses will not hurt you.

Traders who take losses personally turn into emotional investors who resemble vigilantes. They have been wronged by the market and are out for justice. For example, assume an emotional investor purchases a long call on XYZ and instead of XYZ moving higher, it drops in price. The businesslike trader simply fires the underperforming employee and looks for another trade opportunity. Emotional investors wonder how they can make their money back on the position. XYZ has cost them money, and they feel they must make back their losses on that stock. Emotional investors usually take on more risk to get revenge on XYZ and, more often than not, end up losing even more money on a trade that should have been closed out sooner under a predetermined exit strategy.

There is no place for revenge in the business of investing. Taking losses personally is extremely unprofessional and will definitely cloud your judgment. You will trade on anger and resentment and depart from the principles of risk and trade management. We in no way recommend you take losses lightly, but losses are a part of trading; you can either learn from them and improve your performance or embark on a trading vendetta that will cost you even more money than you lost on that one position.

Whether you are a beginner or an advanced trader, at the start-up or the mature phase, you must continue to act like a trading professional. Keep your emotions in check as much as possible by not taking any losses personally. The market is not your enemy; the market is where your business will make money. If a stock does not move as expected and costs you money, then spend the time to analyze why the position did not work so you can make better decisions next time. That is the professional approach.

SCORE—THE FORMULA FOR TRADING SUCCESS

Now that you have developed a basic understanding of risk and trade management, we will provide you with a formula for how to successfully implement these principles in your daily trading. In order to make it easier to remember our formula for trading success, we represent it by the acronym SCORE, summarized as follows:

Select the Investment
Choose the Best Strategy
Open the Trade with a Plan
Remember Your Plan and Stick to It
Exit Your Trade

Select the Investment

Before you can make an option trade, you need to find a good investment candidate. Options are derivatives whose value is derived from the price of an underlying security, which, in our case, is stocks. Therefore, before making any option trade, you have to identify what stock you are going to invest in as the underlying security. The process of stock selection is the most important and most difficult part of investing. Not only do you have to select a stock, but you also have to predict which direction it will move. An added characteristic of options is that you also have to determine the time frame of the anticipated move because options have expiration dates.

Because the value of an option is based on the underlying stock, a working knowledge of the stock market is imperative. If you know nothing about the stock market, you will know even less about how to trade options. For people who have never invested before, starting out in trading by using options is akin to trying to learn math for the first time by starting with calculus. Therefore, you need to know the stock market in order to trade options because you need to know how to pick stocks and make informed and reasonable predictions about the direction the stocks will move. The first step in placing a trade is selecting the underlying stock.

There are numerous stock-screening tools on the Internet using both fundamental and technical analysis criteria, which you can use to narrow your focus. Within these two types of stock analysis techniques are numerous indicators. There is no right answer on what combination of indicators to use. You have to research the different indicators and see which ones you prefer. You may also develop your own approach as to what combination of indicators gives the best signals.

We do not recommend one particular type of analysis over another, but rather emphasize that the selection process should involve some type of analysis to allow an educated prediction of future stock movement. You need a reason to select a particular stock for establishing a position. Part of the analysis of a potential stock candidate should include answers to the following questions:

Which direction do you expect the stock to move? Up, down, or sideways?

Why do you expect the stock to move in that direction?

Do you have an idea of the magnitude of the anticipated move?

Do you have an idea of the time frame of when the expected move will occur?

We are not implying that you should have specific answers to each of these questions. The questions should merely serve as focus points when conducting your analysis. Selecting stocks is not an exact science, but you can improve your chances if you make the effort to choose investments using as much research and analysis as possible.

Remember that the principles of investment themes become extremely important in the stock selection process. The stocks you are selecting and the criteria you are using to select them should be related to your investment theme. That is why we stress the importance of establishing your investment theme. It will provide a narrower focus when searching for stock candidates.

Choose the Best Strategy

Once you have found a stock through research and analysis and made an estimate about the direction, magnitude, and timing (as best as possible) of the future price movement, it is time to choose an appropriate option strategy. Before considering any option strategy, the first step is to look at the implied volatility of the underlying stock. In the next chapter we cover in more detail how to use implied volatility when trading, but we mention it here briefly because it is part of the process of choosing a strategy. Implied volatility helps us determine whether the options of an underlying stock are relatively expensive or relatively cheap. As with stocks, we do not want to buy overpriced options with inflated premiums. That is why the first step before choosing a strategy is to analyze the implied volatility of the underlying stock.

Surprisingly, most option traders ignore implied volatility when trading. Assume that you are looking to buy calls on a stock that you are bullish on and you do not realize that the implied volatility of the options on that stock is at a historical high; that is, the options are extremely overpriced. If you purchase a long call when the options are relatively expensive, you are overpaying for that long call. The more you pay for the call, the higher is your maximum risk and the higher is the breakeven point.

Once you have reviewed the volatility of the options, the next step is to select the best option strategy to match your assumption of where the stock will move to and in what time frame. There are easily more than 20 different option strategies covering bullish, bearish, and neutral positions, and choosing can be overwhelming. In the next chapter we outline most of the basic option strategies and briefly describe the best situation in which to use each one. The more familiar you are with the option strategies, the better you will get at choosing the most appropriate ones.

Finally, once the volatility and direction are determined, you must also estimate the time it will take for the underlying stock to make the expected move. For example, say you expect a stock to move higher and you purchase a 1-month call, and the stock moves sideways for the next 30 days and then starts to move higher. If your call expires, then you will not participate in the upward movement of the stock because you selected too short a time frame for your option. Therefore, when selecting a strategy, do not forget to take into consideration the time to expiration as well as the time you think it will take for the expected move in the underlying stock.

Open the Trade with a Plan

Now that you have selected a stock and the appropriate option strategy, you are ready to establish your position and open the trade. Before opening the trade, however, you must go through your risk management steps. First, you must determine your maximum risk, maximum reward, and breakeven points. Once you have selected your strategy, you should be able to immediately calculate these three factors. Review the risk/reward factors carefully. Make sure that you are comfortable with the risk and are satisfied with the potential reward. If the risk seems too high, or the reward is not sufficient given the risk or anticipated move in the stock, then either pass on the trade or return to the previous step and pick another strategy.

Once you are satisfied with the risk/reward profile of the trade you are considering, you must move on to trade management. Remember that trade management deals with exit strategies. Therefore, you must now determine your exit strategies if the stock moves as expected or moves against you. Based on your analysis of where the stock is expected to move, you can estimate what would be a good point to get out if the stock moves as expected. To limit your risk, determine a point at which you feel it will be better to close out the trade and take the limited loss rather than suffer the maximum loss.

Another part of trade management, and the main focus of this book, is planning possible follow-up trades or adjustment strategies, whether the stock moves as expected or the opposite way. It is not easy to envision every possible adjustment scenario before the trade is entered into, but you can still have a general idea ahead of time as to what kinds of adjustments you can make. This type of preparation is useful because you can think more clearly while there is no money in the trade, and therefore no risk or stress, as opposed to waiting until something happens and possibly making a rushed decision.

Therefore, before you open the position, run through the risk and trade management process so that you are fully aware of the risks, how to control them, and how to manage your trade before any capital is committed. You will find that it is much easier to analyze the risk and plan the trade when there is no money on the line. Once the position is opened, you will have your plan in place, which will take some of the emotion and anxiety out of your trading.

One suggestion that may make this process more meaningful is to keep a trade journal for every position. In the journal you can write your notes about the stock and the fundamental and technical analysis points you used to make your investment decision. Next, you can write the option strategy you are choosing and why. Then you can write out the maximum risk, maximum reward, and breakeven points as well as your exit strategies, including any possible trade adjustments. Writing these things down helps for two reasons. First, it forces you to think out your trade, step by step. Second, it makes the exit plans and adjustments easier to follow because they are written clearly and serve as a daily reminder as to what you can do.

After numerous trades, your journal entries will demonstrate clear investment and portfolio themes. You can add notes to winning and losing trades as lessons learned from each trade to improve your performance. The journal will become a living textbook for you to document your learning process, which you can always refer to for past experiences and insight. Moreover, if you trade in the same stocks again and again, you will have your own history of what works with those stocks and what does not, as well as the relevant analysis, which you can use to find the same profitable opportunities again.

The final step in this process is simply to open the position. Once you have completed the foregoing steps, you are ready to open the trade with your broker. These steps may seem like a lot to do before every trade, and you may feel that by the time you run through this process the investment opportunity will disappear. However, the pretrade process can be done quickly if you are familiar with the various option strategies and how to calculate the risk/reward factors. That is why we stress taking the time and effort to learn all the necessary mechanics before beginning to trade. With some experience, you can run through the outlined process in less than 5 or 10 minutes and still have more than enough time to place your trade. With respect to your trading journal, you can place the trade first and then create your entry.

Remember Your Plan and Stick to It

Once your trade is established, the only thing you have to do is monitor your position and remember your trading plan. Because you put all the thought into planning the trade before you opened the position, your job is simply to remember what your plan is and stick to it. At this stage, you need discipline to follow your plan and not let your emotions bias your judgment. That is why we recommend the use of a trading journal. If you have various trades open at the same time, then your journal is a quick reminder of the trading plan you established for each position. When one of your positions begins to move one way or another, you can check your notes to see what exit strategies or follow-up adjustment you planned or suggested. You should always be prepared to make trade adjustments at any time during the position. These possible adjustments, covered in greater detail in this book, can be used to lock in a profit, hedge against a loss, or improve your overall return.

Although we recommend that you stick with your established trading plan, we also believe in flexibility. Therefore, your risk and trade management parameters can always change as along as you have good cause to adjust them. If you just change them in your head in the middle of a trade for emotional reasons (e.g., greed, anxiety, trade paralysis), then you are disregarding the principles of risk and trade management. If you change your plan, have a good reason for doing so; if you have no good reason for doing so, do not change your plan.

Exit Your Trade

Planning a trade and having it move the way you expected produces unrealized gains. In order to realize those profits, you need to exit the position. This sounds very simple, but sometimes greed and trade paralysis make you stay in trades too long and the position can move against you and wipe out that unrealized profit. Therefore, if you make an exit plan, then you need to execute that plan. Exit strategies are meant to limit your loss and take your profit off the table. This only works if you have the discipline to stick with your exit plan and actually follow through to close out your position.

On the profit side, if the position moves strongly in your favor, then you can adjust your profitable exit strategy if you feel that the trend is likely to continue. The better choice is to use one of the adjustments covered in later chapters to lock in some of that profit and let the position continue to run or to hedge against the position reversing and moving against you. With potential losses, you should not be so flexible because a small losing position can become a large losing position very quickly. In positions with an unrealized loss, either make an adjustment to limit or prevent further losses or get out altogether.

Once the trade is closed and you have limited your loss or collected your profit, we recommend that you follow up in your trading journal with some final notes on the position. If you followed your trading plan exactly and made money on the trade, then it is worth noting in the journal. If you deviated from your trading plan, then you should record what that change was and why. You should learn from your losses and gains alike, and if you close the trade and move on without realizing what made the trade work and what did not, then you will not improve as an investor. Trading is a process in which you are continuously learning and adapting, and the closing of a position should be just as educational as the process involved when you enter a trade.

CHAPTER 2

Tools of
the Trader

INTRODUCTION

There are numerous tools for successfully implementing a trading plan and investment theme, as well as taking advantage of the benefits of using options. In the previous chapter, we discussed risk and trade management and the application of those principles in a successful trading system. Basically, we detailed our theoretical approach to trade management to get you in the right frame of mind to trade. The practical approach—that is, the way the theory is to be applied—is based on the proper use of the tools available to the trader. In this chapter, we review the tools of option trading so that the theory of trade management can be put into practice effectively.

First, we give an overview of some important characteristics of option pricing and explain what factors have an effect on the option premium. We discuss the "Greeks" and why they are important to understand and show you how to use them to develop trading positions with respect to strike selection, choosing time to expiration, and using volatility to select the more appropriate strategies. Finally, we give a detailed summary of all the major options strategies, with information on their risk profiles and Greeks, as well as a general idea of when to use each strategy.

The tools covered in this chapter are extremely important, and your success in using options depends on understanding these concepts and applying them correctly. We also provide you with an easy step-by-step system to apply the Greeks when analyzing a prospective position to make the best investment choices and avoid many common mistakes. Remember that risk management is our primary goal and the Greeks are our primary tools for managing option's risk. Moreover, the tools and trading approach presented in this chapter can be combined with the SCORE trade management formula from the previous chapter to provide you with a detailed and highly effective risk management approach to option trading. Finally, understanding these tools will better prepare you to understand the various adjustment strategies covered in this book.

OPTION VALUE

"Moneyness" is defined as the potential profit or loss that is realized from the immediate exercise of an option. An option can be classified as being in the money (ITM), at the money (ATM), or out of the money (OTM). An option is ITM if it would lead to positive cash flow to the holder if it were exercised immediately. A call is ITM if the stock is trading above the strike price. For example, if XYZ is trading at $45, then an XYZ $40 Call is ITM. A put, on the other hand, would be ITM if the stock is trading below the strike price.

For an option to be OTM, it would have to result in a negative cash flow if it were exercised immediately. For example, if XYZ were at $45, then the $50 Call is OTM. A put is OTM if the stock is trading above the strike price.

An option is ATM when the stock is trading at the same level as that option's strike price. For example, an XYZ $40 Call and an XYZ $40 Put are both ATM if XYZ is trading at $40. We also sometimes refer to options as ATM if the stock is trading very close to the strike price, because stocks rarely trade right at the strike price of an option for very long. Therefore, if XYZ is at $40.50, we can say that the XYZ $40 Call or XYZ $40 Put are ATM.

The option premium consists of time value and intrinsic value. Intrinsic value is the exact amount an option is ITM. For a call, it is the amount by which the stock price exceeds the strike price, and for a put, it is the amount by which the stock price is below the strike price. Time value is simply the amount by which the option premium exceeds its intrinsic value.

Assume that XYZ is at $43 and an XYZ $40 Call is trading at $4.50. The XYZ $40 Call is ITM by $3.00 (the amount the stock price exceeds the strike price), and therefore the XYZ $40 Call has an intrinsic value of $3.00. The remaining $1.50 in the price of the option is time value.

What about an XYZ $45 Call priced at $1.00 with XYZ trading at $43? Because the stock is trading below the strike price of the XYZ $45 Call, the call is OTM. OTM options have no intrinsic value at all and are made up entirely of time value. Therefore, the $1.00 price of the OTM XYZ $45 Call is pure time value.

Intrinsic value is always easy to calculate because it is simply the difference between the stock price and the strike price of the ITM option.

Time value is based on many factors (such as time to expiration, strike price, and volatility of the underlying stock, which are explained in the next section), and as long as there is any time left to expiration, an option always has a time value premium. The only trading day when time value will be close to $0 and the option will either be worth its intrinsic value or $0 (if not ITM) is on expiration day.

OPTION PRICING

Although the mathematics that goes into option pricing is beyond the scope of this book, you should have a basic understanding of the different factors that affect the price of an option. To determine the theoretical price of an option, we use the Black-Scholes option-pricing model. The relevant parts of the Black-Scholes formula for our purposes are the inputs, that is, the factors that influence and affect the price of an option. Those factors are as follows:

Stock price
Strike price
Time to expiration
Volatility
Dividends
Interest rate

For our purposes, we represent how the Black-Scholes formula works in Figure 2.1 and avoid the detailed calculus. We plug the six option price factors into the Black-Scholes formula, which calculates the theoretical value of the call or put.

It is very important that you understand the effect these six factors have on the price of an option. These factors are constantly changing in the market, and you should be aware of how these changes could help or hurt your position. Some option strategies are designed to specifically capitalize on a change in some of these pricing factors during the life of an option. For example, understanding two of these factors—time to expiration and volatility—is very important for many of the option strategies covered in this chapter and in the trade adjustment chapters that follow. Therefore, we cover these two factors in greater detail.

Stock Price

The price of the underlying stock is very important for establishing the value of an option. If the stock moves higher, calls will become more

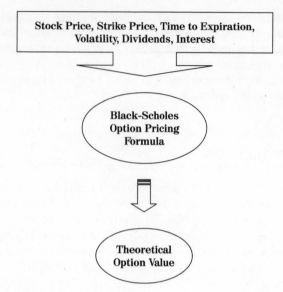

FIGURE 2.1   Black-Scholes Flow Chart

valuable, and if the stock moves lower, puts will become more valuable. Because we are investing in options based on an expectation of where the underlying stock would move, the stock price has a huge influence on the price of options.

Strike Price

The selection of the strike price of your option has a direct effect on the price of that option and whether it is ITM, ATM, or OTM. As we said, the intrinsic value of an option is the amount by which the option is ITM. The more ITM the option is, the greater the intrinsic value and the higher the premium. OTM options have no intrinsic value, are made up entirely of time value, and will be cheaper than ITM options. The further out of the money the option is, the less likely it is to be in the money by expiration. In other words, the potential for deep out-of-the-money options to have any intrinsic value is small. Therefore, options that are further out of the money have less value than OTM options closer to the current price of the stock.

Time to Expiration

In general, the longer the time to expiration, the more valuable the option. For example, an option expiring in 5 months will be worth more than an option expiring in 2 months. With more time to expiration, there is a better chance that the stock will move ITM and stay there by expiration. This may not be true for some European-style puts, which can be exercised only on expiration day.

Volatility

Volatility is a measure that reflects the magnitude of the change in the price of a stock over time. High-volatility stocks have the ability to make large percentage moves up or down. Options on such stocks have a better chance of being ITM, perhaps deep ITM, by expiration and therefore are more expensive than options on lower volatility stocks.

Dividends

When dividends are paid out by a company, they reduce the price of the stock. Therefore, dividends expected during the life of an option increase put premiums and reduce call premiums. However, because most dividends are regularly announced, option premiums already have dividends factored into the price. The effect of dividends on option premiums is therefore negligible unless a special dividend is declared during the life of the option.

Interest Rates

The effect of interest rates on option prices is relatively negligible, especially when you are dealing with very short-term options. Nevertheless, rising interest rates increase the price of calls and decrease the price of puts.

Table 2.1 shows the change in the price of a call or a put due to an increase in each of the factors affecting the price of an option.

TABLE 2.1 Summary Table		
	Call	**Put**
Stock price	+	−
Strike price	−	+
Time to expiration	+	+
Volatility	+	+
Dividends	−	+
Risk-free interest rate	+	−

OPTION GREEKS AND RISK MANAGEMENT

Changes in any of the pricing factors can have an effect on the price of a call or a put, and this represents an element of risk. Of the six pricing factors discussed in the previous section, the most significant are the stock price, time to expiration, and volatility. Understanding the relationship between changes in these pricing factors and changes in the option prices is an important way to measure these risks. For example, if we know that stock price increases will make calls more valuable and cause a decrease in the puts, then understanding exactly how stock price changes will affect the price of options is important to truly understand the risk of our position.

Fortunately, we do have a way to measure the sensitivity of option prices to changes in stock price, time to expiration, and volatility: the Greeks. The Greeks are numeric values that represent how sensitive an option price is to the relevant pricing factors, and they are often derived from the Black-Scholes pricing formula. These Greek values are easily found online for every traded option. Since the Greeks are risk exposure measurements, we need to understand them in detail to practice good risk management. In the next few sections, we cover the Greek measurements for changes in stock price, time to expiration, and volatility, and discuss in detail how to apply that knowledge to make more intelligent trading decisions, better manage risk, and avoid common mistakes. This understanding is crucial to develop a risk manager approach to trading options.

TIME DECAY

Because options expire after a certain period of time, they are considered wasted assets. As each day passes, the time to expiration decreases and the time value premium also decreases. Assume that XYZ is trading at $53 and a 3-month XYZ $50 Call is trading at $6.00. The intrinsic value of this $50 Call is $3.00. The remaining $3.00 is pure time value.

Assume that at expiration of the $50 Call 3 months later, the stock is still at $53 and has not moved at all. At expiration, there is no more time left, so the $50 Call will not have any time value premium and will be valued at exactly its intrinsic value. Therefore, with XYZ still at $53, the XYZ $50 Call will be worth $3.00. The net will be a loss of $3.00. This is the loss of the time value premium because the only factor that has changed (assuming all other variables have not been affected) is the passage of time. As the time to expiration decreases, the time value premium also decreases or decays.

The rate of time decay in an option is not linear. In our example, with XYZ holding at $53 for 3 months, the time value premium did not decay at a constant rate. The rate of decay increases as expiration approaches and is the fastest in the last 30 to 45 days. We can illustrate this with an example using a real stock and hypothetical inputs into the Black-Scholes option pricing model.

Assume that AMZN is trading at $55 and we wish to use a 6-month $55 Call for our example. To price this option using the Black-Scholes formula, we need the six pricing factors defined earlier: stock price, strike price, time to expiration, volatility, dividends, and interest rates. The stock and strike prices are both $55, and we know the time to expiration is 6 months. Assume that the annual volatility is 50% and that the interest rate is 1.5%. AMZN does not pay any dividends, so that factor is not relevant. If we plug these factors into the Black-Scholes formula, we get a theoretical option price for the 6-month AMZN $55 Call of $7.80. If we keep all of the factors constant except the time to expiration, we can see the effect of the change in time on the option premium. Using the same Black-Scholes inputs for AMZN, we calculate the $55 Call price and reduce the time to expiration 1 month at a time until we reach the expiration date. The results are shown in Table 2.2.

As the results indicate, the decay in the time value premium of the AMZN $55 Call is not linear. As the time to expiration approaches, the absolute dollar and percentage changes in the call price increase. The difference in the value of the call price between 6 months and 5 months to expiration, and even between 5 months and 4 months to expiration, is not that significant. However, the difference in the value of the call between 2 months to expiration and 1 month to expiration and in the last month before expiration is quite dramatic. Figure 2.2 shows the value of the $55 Call versus time to expiration.

Figure 2.2 gives us a visualization of the properties of time decay in an option. The further out from the expiration date the option is, the smaller

TABLE 2.2   Time Decay

Time to Expiration	Theoretical Call Price ($)	$ Decrease	% Decrease
6 months	7.80		
5 months	7.15	−0.65	−8.33
4 months	6.40	−0.75	−10.49
3 months	5.50	−0.90	−14.06
2 months	4.50	−1.00	−18.18
1 month	3.15	−1.35	−30.00
1 day	0.50	−2.65	−84.13

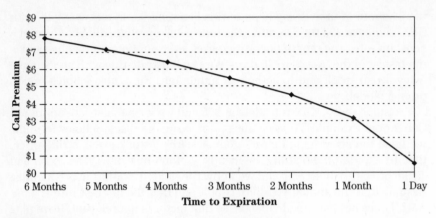

FIGURE 2.2   Time Value Premium of AMZN $55 Call

the effect of time decay, which is greatest in the last 30 days. These characteristics of time decay are extremely important to remember when you are trading options because they can be used to your advantage. Figure 2.2 gives us our first Key Time Decay Principle, highlighted next.

KEY PRINCIPLE

Time decay of an option's premium is greatest in the last 30 days to expiration.

The Greek value used to measure decay in an option is called Theta. For practical purposes and simplicity, we use the calculation of Theta, which expresses how much a call or put premium will decay with the passing of one day of time. Since Theta represents decay, it is always shown as a negative number. Given the nature of time decay (i.e., greatest in last 30 days), we would expect an option's Theta to be greater when there is less time to expiration.

Table 2.3 shows three different ATM GOOG call options, with the same strike price but different expiration dates, and their Greek values. For each option, Theta is highlighted. Notice that the Theta value for the MAY $400 Call is much higher than the Theta for the SEP $400 Call, which is 4 months further out in time. The difference in Theta is quite significant since the MAY $400 Call has less time value premium than the SEP $400 Call. Therefore, the amount of premium lost in time decay in the May $400 Call, holding all other factors constant, is greater in absolute and relative terms than the SEP $400 Call.

TABLE 2.3 GOOG Call Option Greeks—3 Different Months

GOOG@$394

GOOG MAY $400 Call $9.60			GOOG JUNE $400 Call $19.10			GOOG SEPT $400 Call $38.00		
Theoretical Data			**Theoretical Data**			**Theoretical Data**		
Implied Vol.	38.5149	Delta	0.44889	Implied Vol.	38.7464	Delta	0.4992	Implied Vol.	39.4735	Delta	0.5524
Gamma	0.0133	**Theta**	**-0.4421**	Gamma	0.0077	**Theta**	**-0.2693**	Gamma	0.0042	**Theta**	**-0.1631**
Vega	0.0642	Rho	0.3055	Vega	0.5336	Rho	0.2046	Vega	0.9414	Rho	0.6553

37

For instance, the MAY $400 Call is trading at $9.60 with a Theta of −0.4421, and the SEP $400 Call has a price of $38.00 and a Theta of −0.1631. After one day of decay, holding all other factors constant, the MAY $400 Call will decay theoretically by $0.44, or 4.6%, while the SEP $400 Call will decay theoretically by $0.16 or 0.4%. In percentage terms, you can see how much greater Theta is in the front month options, and Theta starts increasing exponentially in the last 30 days. It is easy to see how fast a short-term option's premium can decay down to nothing while a long-term option's premium will only lose a fraction of its value. Based on this example, we can state our next principle with respect to time decay.

KEY PRINCIPLE

Theta is larger in front months and is smaller the further out in time you go. As a result, front month options will decline by a greater value in absolute and relative terms versus long-term options, holding all other factors constant.

Now let us look at Theta across different strikes within the same expiration month for options on GOOG with the stock trading at $405. Table 2.4 shows the call option chain with Theta highlighted. The figure shows that Theta is greatest near the at-the-money options and decreases as you move further in the money or further out of the money. To understand the significance of this distribution, we can look at the time value and intrinsic value premiums of the different strike prices.

TABLE 2.4 GOOG Option Chain—Theta in Same Expiration Month

Strike	Last	Bid	Ask	Delta	Gamma	Rho	Theta	Vega
		GOOG Call Option Chain/Greeks						
GOOG $405						June 2009 (38 days to expiration)		
$ 360.00	$ 50.27	$ 50.40	$ 51.20	0.8923	0.0044	0.3262	**−0.1121**	0.2439
$ 370.00	$ 42.10	$ 42.20	$ 42.80	0.8391	0.0060	0.3107	**−0.1484**	0.3264
$ 380.00	$ 34.48	$ 34.50	$ 35.10	0.7622	0.0074	0.2883	**−0.1814**	0.4054
$ 390.00	$ 27.50	$ 27.70	$ 28.10	0.6810	0.0087	0.2600	**−0.2110**	0.4698
$ 400.00	$ 21.49	$ 21.40	$ 21.70	0.5870	0.0094	0.2274	**−0.2256**	0.5108
$ 410.00	$ 16.50	$ 16.10	$ 16.40	0.4936	0.0097	0.1927	**−0.2321**	0.5234
$ 420.00	$ 11.80	$ 11.70	$ 12.00	0.4013	0.0093	0.1582	**−0.2222**	0.5075
$ 430.00	$ 8.50	$ 8.30	$ 8.50	0.3163	0.0086	0.1257	**−0.2054**	0.4675
$ 440.00	$ 5.69	$ 5.60	$ 5.90	0.2422	0.0075	0.0968	**−0.1781**	0.4105
$ 450.00	$ 3.90	$ 3.70	$ 4.00	0.1778	0.0063	0.0723	**−0.1496**	0.3449

In-the-money options are made up mostly of intrinsic value and, to a lesser extent, time value premium. The deeper in the money the options are, the greater the amount of intrinsic value while time value premium becomes almost negligible because of the extreme moneyness of those options. With so little time value premium, there is not that much to decay away as expiration approaches because the option premium is predominantly intrinsic value. Since an in-the-money option can never be worth less than its intrinsic value, the only decay such an option will experience is the small time value premium, if any, that exists. Therefore, the options further in the money have less and less time value premium to decay off and thus will have much smaller Theta values. As each day passes, the amount of time value premium remaining approaches zero as the option approaches its intrinsic value by expiration.

KEY PRINCIPLE

ITM options are mostly comprised of intrinsic value with little or no time value premium, and therefore have relatively small Thetas.

If we look to the other side of the option chain, we have the options that are far out of the money, which are comprised entirely of time value premium. These out-of-the-money options are also the cheapest since they are only time value premium, and the further out of the money they are, the less likely they are to be in the money by expiration and therefore are worth less. Since these options have relatively smaller premiums than their at-the-money and in-the-money counterparts, and they are 100% time value, they do not have to decay that far before they get to $0, assuming they are still out of the money by expiration. Therefore, the actual Theta value will be small in absolute terms.

Although the out-of-the-money options have smaller Theta values, the actual amount of decay that occurs in these options as a percentage of the actual option price is quite significant. For example, Table 2.5 lists the price and Theta value for a far-out-of-the-money GOOG call with about 1 month to expiration. This example shows a GOOG $500 Call that is extremely out of the money and highlights the high relative decay in out-of-the-money options. Notice that with the call trading at $0.45, it has a Theta value of $0.04, which means that holding all things constant, this call option will theoretically decay by $0.04 for every day that goes by. We know that time decay grows exponentially in the last remaining days prior to expiration, but for illustrative purposes, let us assume that in this example it will be linear over the time period in question, that is, decay by $0.04 for the next days. This actual Theta value seems quite small, but it happens to represent an initial decay of 9% of the option premium in 1 day. Assuming

TABLE 2.5   GOOG OTM Call Theta

GOOG = $405
JUNE $500 Call = $ 0.45   **(38 Days to Expiration)**

Greeks			
Implied Vol.	32.32%	Delta	0.0273
Gamma	0.0015	**Theta**	**−0.0394**
Vega	0.0826	Rho	0.0111

Theta stays at $0.04, with each day that passes, the reduction in the price of the option will be quite substantial. In theory, at that rate, starting at $0.45, the option will decay to nothing in about 10 to 11 days, and each day it will lose an even bigger percentage of its premium. Therefore, although the actual Theta value is small, the amount of decay the out-of-the-money option suffers is substantial relative to its price.

KEY PRINCIPLE

OTM options have small Theta values, but the amount of decay these options suffer as a percentage of their option premium is substantial.

Finally, let us consider at-the-money options and the strikes immediately above and below them. These options mainly consist of time value premium with little or no intrinsic value since their strikes are usually right above or below the actual price of the stock. At-the-money options have a very good chance of being in the money at expiration and therefore have a significant amount of time value premium relative to the out-of-the-money and in-the-money options. As each day passes with little or no movement in the price of the stock, holding all other factors constant, the chances of at-the-money options to be in the money at expiration decrease and thus their time value premiums (which take into account higher chances of finishing in the money) must decrease as well. Since these options have the highest amount of time value premium in absolute dollars compared with the in-the-money and out-of-the-money strikes, their Theta value must be higher as well.

In percentage terms, the amount of decay the ATM options suffer is still less than the OTM options but is more than the ITM. For example, referring back to Table 2.4, we see that the 1 month to expiration ATM $410 Call with a price of $16.40 has a Theta of −0.23 which is a decay of 1.4%. That is much lower than the 9% rate of decay in the previous out-of-the-money example. Therefore, not only are at-the-money options a good balance in price between the cheaper, purely time value premium, out-of-the-money options and the higher priced, mostly intrinsic value, in-the-money options, but also they are a good trade-off between the relatively low Theta of the higher priced in-the-money options and the higher percentage decay of the cheaper out-of-the-money options. In other words, the at-the-money options let you balance out cost with Theta.

KEY PRINCIPLE

ATM options have a higher absolute Theta value but offer a good balance between the higher priced, smaller decay ITM options and the lower priced, higher decay OTM options.

Trading Lessons Learned from Time Decay (Theta)

If we review the key principles with respect to time decay and Theta, we get a better understanding of how options work and what risk management ideas we can use to make more knowledgeable trades. The main principle we have learned is that time decay is greatest in the last 30 days or so to expiration. If you are buying a call or a put position and wish to reduce the risk of time decay, you should only buy options with at least 2 months to expiration. Many times beginners will buy front month calls or puts for a directional position because the front month is cheapest. However, as indicated by Theta, if the underlying stock does nothing within a week or so, those front month options can decay very fast. Trading options is difficult enough without adding more risks such as exponential time decay.

Therefore, not only does buying options at least 2 months out from expiration give you more time to be right but also you are not penalized so heavily while waiting to see if your trade works out. There might be some liquidity issues in buying options further out in time versus the front month (i.e., slightly wider bid/ask spread or less volume traded), but most active stocks and indexes see sufficient activity across the first few expiration months. Even if this is not entirely true, going out an extra month or so to reduce the effects of time decay and give yourself more time to be right is definitely worth it. This will certainly help reduce time decay related losses that many beginners suffer from chasing those relatively "cheaper" front month options.

One exception to this rule would be if you are expecting a move to occur within the next few days to a week. In that case, the time frame of the move is extremely short, and you are expecting the underlying move to happen soon enough to overcome any decay that is likely to occur. Of course, the ability to predict the specific timing of underlying stock moves is quite difficult, so we recommend this approach only when there is some high confidence that a move is about to occur and you are not therefore concerned with decay so much as with directional moves in the very near future. But overall, the best approach is to always give yourself as much time as possible to be right and avoid the risks of time decay as much as possible. Further out expiration options may "cost" more in relative pricing but you lose less in decay, and that is a trade-off that will save you in the long run.

One of the great things about studying the Greeks is learning not only how to avoid certain risks with respect to what factors affect the pricing of an option but also how to use them to your advantage. Although time decay is an enemy to all long option holders, it is a wonderful friend to those who sell options or enter into spreads or combinations, which benefit from time decay. In this instance, we desire time decay to eat away at the premiums of the options we sold, but we still need to know how to use it best to our advantage to make better trading decisions.

Since we know that options decay fastest in the last 30 days to expiration, then we should always try to sell options with 30 days or less to expiration to take the most advantage of that time decay. Options with 2 or 3 months to expiration will certainly bring in more premium when sold, but you are not only giving the position more time to move against you, you are also not getting any significant time decay to act on your behalf. We are not necessarily recommending you sell options short, but if you do, it is better to have time decay work for you.

Another lesson learned from studying Theta is related to out-of-the-money options. As we saw before, the actual Theta value for far-out-of-the-money options in the current expiration month is small, but the amount of the decay as a percentage of the premium is quite large. Beginners are often attracted to far-out-of-the-money options because they seem so cheap, but a very important lesson to learn in the investment world is that things are cheaper for a reason. First, the underlying stock would need to make a significant move for those options to get close to even being at the money, but more important, with each day that passes without any movement, those far-out-of-the-money options will decay fast.

In a matter of days, your position could lose a significant amount, and over time, if you repeatedly choose the premiums of those front month far-out-of-the-money options, you will continually suffer losses due to time decay. Even if you catch a rare stock that makes a significant move to overcome that decay and results in a large profit, the odds are against this happening consistently, and to repeat an important point, these options are cheap for a reason. Therefore, it is best to avoid going after the cheaper out-of-the-money options, as the Theta and relative decay are strong headwinds to go up against and will lead to losses in the long run.

DELTA/GAMMA

The Greek value related to measuring sensitivity of option prices to changes in the price of the underlying stock is called Delta. Delta measures the change in the price of the option for a $1.00 change in the price of the underlying stock. Calls have a positive Delta because as the stock price increases, the price of the call will increase as well. Puts have a negative Delta because a rise in the price of the stock will cause puts to lose value. Delta is always expressed in decimal form, from −1.00 to +1.00, and understanding the characteristics of Delta will explain how options move, as well as assist you in deciding which strike prices to choose.

In addition to discussing Delta, we must also introduce Gamma. Delta is literally the first derivative, that is, how much the price of the option will change for a $1.00 change in the underlying stock; Gamma is the second derivative measuring how much Delta will change for a $1.00 change in the price of the underlying stock. Delta is the speed at which options change in price relative to the stock price, and Gamma is the rate of acceleration. Let's look at some extreme examples. Assume XYZ is at $50 and we are looking at the $80 Call with a month left to expiration. There is a huge price difference between the stock price and the strike price, and the call premium is entirely made up of time value. If the stock moves a little higher, the call premium really does not have to increase in value because it has quite a distance between its strike and the stock price. In other words, it has a very small Delta. Likewise, the Gamma has to be quite small. Since Delta and Gamma reflect the sensitivities of the option premium to movement in the underlying, the Greeks tell us that far OTM calls are not very sensitive to small incremental moves in the price of the underlying.

KEY PRINCIPLE

Deep OTM options are not very sensitive to small price moves in the underlying.

Now let us look at a deep ITM call option. Assume that with XYZ still at $50, we take a look at a $20 Call with a month to expiration. The stock price is well above the strike price, and we know that the $20 Call has to be worth at least $30 of intrinsic value to avoid an arbitrage situation, plus a very small amount of time value premium, since the option is so far in the money with just a month left to expiration. To avoid an arbitrage situation, the call premium has to move pretty much dollar for dollar with the stock price to maintain its intrinsic value/stock price relationship. Therefore, the Delta will be pretty close to 1.00, depending on how much time value premium exists. This will allow the speed of the option premium to move in line with the speed of the stock price.

Since the Delta will be close to its maximum value of 1.00, Gamma will be close to zero, since the speed of the changes in price will not need to accelerate much further as it is already near its maximum value. Based on Delta and Gamma, we see that the far-in-the-money options will have the highest sensitivity to changes in the price of the underlying stock.

KEY PRINCIPLE

Deep ITM options are the most sensitive to price changes in the underlying.

Since we looked at the extremes of far out of the money and far in the money, we can now look at what happens to options between those extremes. Assume that XYZ stock makes a significant move higher. Many of the out-of-the-money calls will move in the money or significantly closer to being at the money, and we would expect those far-out-of-the-money small Deltas to grow as the stock price keeps moving higher to avoid arbitrage situations. The way the Deltas grow is by Gamma, which also has to grow to ensure the Deltas are increasing fast enough to push the call premium higher and keep the same pace as the stock price.

Therefore, as a call goes from far out of the money to being at the money to eventually moving in the money, the Deltas will increase, as will the Gammas. However, we know that at some point, as the Delta keeps getting bigger, Gamma will decrease as Delta approaches 1.00 and cannot increase more in value. Thus Gamma will increase as the far-out-of-the-money call moves to at the money, but then Gamma will decrease as the call moves deeper in the money. Figure 2.3 gives a graphical representation

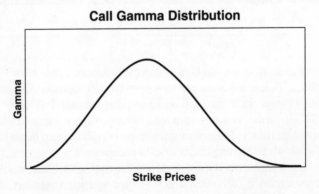

FIGURE 2.3 Gamma Curvature

TABLE 2.6 IBM Option Call Chain with Delta/Gamma Values

Strike	Last	Bid	Ask	Delta	Gamma	Rho	Theta	Vega
IBM $106.28						**JULY 2009 (47 days to expiration)**		
$ 40.00	$ 62.01	$ 66.10	$ 66.70	1.00	0	0.0514	−0.0011	0
$ 45.00	$ 60.80	$ 61.10	$ 61.70	1.00	0	0.0579	−0.0012	0
$ 50.00	$ 55.80	$ 56.10	$ 56.70	1.00	0	0.0643	−0.0014	0
$ 55.00	$ 50.80	$ 51.10	$ 51.60	1.00	0	0.0707	−0.0015	0
$ 60.00	$ 45.80	$ 46.00	$ 46.60	1.00	0	0.0772	−0.0016	0
$ 65.00	$ 40.80	$ 41.00	$ 41.60	1.00	0	0.0836	−0.0018	0
$ 70.00	$ 35.46	$ 36.00	$ 36.60	1.00	0	0.09	−0.0019	0
$ 75.00	$ 30.52	$ 31.10	$ 31.60	1.00	0	0.0964	−0.0021	0.0001
$ 80.00	$ 24.90	$ 26.30	$ 26.70	0.9997	0.0001	0.1028	−0.0023	0.0009
$ 85.00	$ 20.24	$ 21.60	$ 21.80	0.995	0.0015	0.1085	−0.0038	0.0064
$ 90.00	$ 15.40	$ 16.90	$ 17.10	0.974	0.0064	0.1116	−0.0087	0.0255
$ 95.00	$ 12.10	$ 12.40	$ 12.50	0.904	0.0178	0.1082	−0.02	0.0658
$ 100.00	$ 8.30	$ 8.30	$ 8.50	0.7668	0.032	0.095	−0.0338	0.1165
$ 105.00	$ 5.00	$ 4.90	$ 5.10	0.576	0.0413	0.073	−0.0425	0.1493
$ 110.00	$ 2.60	$ 2.55	$ 2.60	0.373	0.0401	0.0482	−0.0408	0.1446
$ 115.00	$ 1.10	$ 1.05	$ 1.10	0.2044	0.0302	0.0272	−0.0305	0.1097
$ 120.00	$ 0.40	$ 0.35	$ 0.45	0.094	0.0179	0.0132	−0.018	0.0673
$ 125.00	$ 0.15	$ 0.10	$ 0.20	0.0365	0.0085	0.0056	−0.0085	0.0343
$ 130.00	$ 0.10	$ −	$ 0.10	0.0122	0.0033	0.002	−0.0033	0.0148
$ 135.00	$ 0.05	$ −	$ 0.10	0.0036	0.0011	0.0007	−0.0011	0.0055

of the "curvature" of Gamma across all strikes within a specific expiration month. This curvature is very important to understand and will help explain a lot of how options move in relation to price moves in the underlying. We now have a sense of the distribution of Delta and Gamma across the strike prices of a specific option chain, and we can look at an actual option chain to confirm our understanding.

Table 2.6 shows an option chain of calls on IBM with 47 days to expiration and with IBM at $106.28. First, let us look at the deep-in-the-money calls. In this example, we consider the $65 Call as a good example of a far-in-the-money call. With an ask price of $41.60, this deep-in-the-money call has an effective purchase price of $106.60 ($65 strike price + $41.60 in premium). Since IBM is trading at $106.28, this in-the-money call has about $0.32 worth of time value premium, with the rest being intrinsic value. The Delta of this $65 call is very close to 1.00 and has a Gamma of almost zero (as with Delta, Gamma here is rounded off in the option chain). For every $1.00 that IBM goes up in price, this $65 Call will move almost in tandem with the stock price.

Let us look at the opposite extreme of this option chain and consider the $130 Call with an ask price of $0.10, a Delta of 0.0122, and a Gamma of 0.003. As expected, these far-out-of-the-money calls have very little Delta and small Gamma, given the large distance between their strikes and the underlying stock. It is important to reiterate that Delta/Gamma is a measure of sensitivity. Therefore, the actual Delta/Gamma values are confirming that the $130 Call is not going to move that much if IBM moves up a little in price, and the Gamma is small enough to confirm that the Delta will also not change that much either.

However, should IBM begin making significant moves, we know the Gamma curvature will cause the Deltas to grow at an accelerated rate. As we move down from the $130 Call to the slightly OTM $110 Call, the Deltas increase from 0.0122 to 0.373, and Gammas also increase, from 0.0033 to 0.0401. As we move closer to the at-the-money calls, Delta approaches 0.50 and Gamma peaks at 0.041 (the top of the curvature). Thus, at-the-money options have a Delta close to 0.5 and a Gamma at its maximum.

KEY PRINCIPLE

ATM options are a good balance of sensitivity and price.

Deep-in-the-Money Options

As noted before, deep-in-the-money options have Deltas that approach 1.00 the deeper in the money they are, and therefore, they will move almost point for point with the underlying stock. If we know the deep-in-the-money option with a Delta close to 1.00 will move in line with the stock, then we can take advantage of this information to use options as a proxy for the stock and participate in the price move of the stock for much less money and with significantly less risk. If we can participate in a stock's price action for less money, then we can put our money to work in more stocks by using options than if we bought the stock outright. Thus, even if you have a small account, you can take advantage of options when you know how to use the Greeks to control your risk.

One significant difference between stocks and options is the fact that options are decaying assets that expire at some point, whereas stocks can theoretically be held indefinitely. Therefore, for you to use deep-in-the-money options as a proxy for stock positions, you must first address the issues of time decay and short-term holding periods for options. The longest time to expiration that exists for regular options is about 9 months, which is certainly a long time, but not long enough for most people who wish to use options as a proxy for stock. This is where LEAPS become very useful. Long-term Equity Anticipation Securities (LEAPS) are simply options with expiration dates 1 to 2 years out in time. LEAPS expire in January of their given expiration year, and most stocks and indexes trading today have LEAPS listed. Therefore, by using deep-in-the-money options with Deltas close to 1.00 and choosing LEAPS to give you a relatively long time to expiration, you can avoid a lot of the option-related problems with respect to time decay and expiration by going out years instead of months and thus use options effectively as proxies for stock positions.

Let us look at an example to see how this would work. In April 2009, IBM is trading at $101.27, and the JAN 2011 $50 Call with almost 2 years to expiration is trading at $52.00 with a Delta of 0.92 and a Gamma of 0.002. Figure 2.4 shows a comparison graph that has both the price of IBM and the price of the JAN 2011 $50 Call over the past 6 months. As the graph indicates, the price of the option has tracked very closely with the price of the stock, with slight discrepancies due to a Delta of less than 1.00. However, for the most part, the long-term call has moved with the price of the stock and allows you to participate in the price action of IBM at a much lower cost. If we purchased 100 shares of IBM, it would cost us $10,127. However, if we purchased the deep-in-the-money LEAPS call, it will cost us only $5,200.

To truly see the benefits of taking advantage of high Delta options, let us look at a portfolio example we developed from a few years ago. Table 2.7

FIGURE 2.4 IBM LEAP Price Graph

TABLE 2.7   LEAP Price Examples for EBAY, SBUX, and MMM

LEAP v. Stock Portfolio

100 Shares of EBAY@	$34.11	$ 3,411.00
100 Shares of SBUX@	$38.79	$ 3,879.00
100 Shares of MMM@	$86.47	$ 8,647.00
		$15,937.00
1 EBAY JAN08 $20 Call@	$16.60	$ 1,660.00
1 SBUX JAN07 $20 Call@	$19.70	$ 1,970.00
1 MMM JAN08 $60 Call@	$29.20	$ 2,920.00
		$ 6,550.00

shows the prices of EBAY, SBUX, and MMM as of April 2006. With EBAY trading at $34.11, SBUX at $38.79, and MMM at $86.47, it would cost you $15,937 total to purchase 100 shares of each (assuming no margin). Also included in Table 2.7 are the prices of deep-in-the-money LEAPS calls on each of the three stocks. If instead of purchasing 100 shares each of the three stocks, you purchased one long-term call option for each, your total cost would be $6,550, significantly cheaper than the $15,937 it would cost to buy the stocks outright. The three call options have expirations ranging from 11 months up to almost 2 years, giving you plenty of time to hold on to these options and replicate a buy and hold position.

To show you how well the three ITM calls work as a proxy for the stock positions, we can look at the portfolio months later and track its progress. As of September 2006, about 5 months later, all three stocks had dropped in price, as indicated in Table 2.8, and the stock portfolio lost a total of $2,484 over that time period. In the same table, we see that the portfolio of three long-term calls lost a total of $2,430. The comparison shows that the long-term calls lost almost exactly as much as the long stock portfolio in dollar value per position, as well as total combined loss, which is due to the high Deltas of the long-term calls. The slight differences between the performances of the two portfolios is attributed to the fact that the long-term calls did not have Deltas of exactly 1.00, as well as possible bid/ask spreads in closing the options. However, the differences are extremely minor. This example shows how we were able to participate in the price movements of the three stocks and risk only $6,550 instead of $15,937 but still have almost a year of time on the earliest of the three expirations.

Using this advantage of deep-in-the-money LEAPS calls, we can not only risk less money in purchasing or tracking a group of stocks but also take advantage of the extra available cash and put it in a risk-free

TABLE 2.8 Update on LEAP/STOCK Portfolio Example of EBAY, SBUX, and MMM

LEAP v. Stock Portfolio

Stock Performance		Price as of 9/14/06	Change
EBAY	@ $34.11	$28.32	$ −5.79
SBUX	@ $38.79	$32.96	$ −5.83
MMM	@ $86.47	$73.25	$−13.22
			$−24.84
2,484.00 $ loss on	15,937.00	portfolio =	**−15.6%**

LEAP v. Stock Portfolio

Leap Performance		Price as of 9/14/06	Change
EBAY JAN08 $20 Call	@ $16.60	$11.10	$ −5.50
SBUX JAN07 $20 Call	@ $19.70	$13.40	$ −6.30
MMM JAN08 $60 Call	@ $29.20	$16.70	$−12.50
			$−24.30
$2,430.00 loss on	$6,550.00	portfolio =	**−37.1%**

investment and thus protect a large portion of our capital. Moreover, if we so choose, we can use the extra available cash and invest in more deep-in-the-money LEAPS calls and add more diversification to the portfolio. Instead of investing in three different stocks, we could possibly invest in six or more LEAPS calls and add more diversity to our portfolio. The only drawback to using LEAPS calls is that the option holder does not collect dividends, so we would not necessarily recommend this course of action for high-dividend stocks you wish to own for income purposes versus gains, but otherwise it is a great way to use options and high Deltas to your advantage.

IMPLIED VOLATILITY

Volatility is a measure of the speed at which a stock's price changes over time. High-volatility stocks are more likely to make large percentage moves up or down, and therefore options on such stocks have a higher likelihood of expiring in the money, perhaps deep in the money. Therefore, options on stocks with high volatility will tend to have higher relative option premiums than stocks with lower volatility. As a result, call and put buyers are

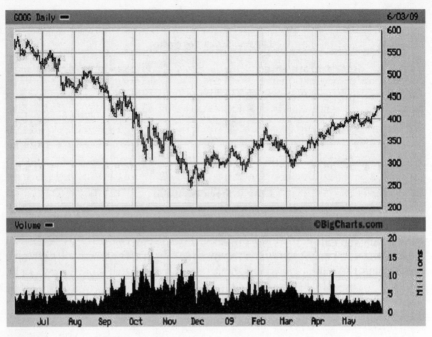

FIGURE 2.5 GOOG Price Chart

willing to pay higher premiums for higher volatility stocks, given the higher probability of large price fluctuations, and option sellers demand higher premiums for the increased risk of those large price moves. No other risk factor is as significant to option pricing as volatility, and it is also the most misunderstood by beginners. To make matters worse, most beginners do not even take volatility into account when entering into an option trade.

First, let us look at volatility in general before discussing the Greek measure of volatility. If we look at a stock like Google (GOOG) and visually scan its price chart in Figure 2.5, it is easy to see how GOOG is an example of a high-volatility stock. With $50 or greater price swings within a month, GOOG certainly has a high probability to make large price fluctuations and is a very volatile stock. On any given day, if you were to price at-the-money calls and puts on GOOG going out 1, 3, and 6 months in time, you can see how the premiums would have to be relatively more expensive to reflect the greater probability for larger price swings than for a stock that is much less volatile. Therefore, we need to pay close attention to the volatility of the underlying. Specifically, we need to study and track the underlying's implied volatility (IV).

Implied volatility is a great tool to not only measure one of the risk parameters of an option position but also help us choose more appropriate strategies, given the current implied volatility of the underlying we are analyzing. One key area that IV helps in is determining relative pricing, that is, whether an option is relatively cheap or expensive.

Assume that AMZN is trading at $55 a share. One analyst says that AMZN is relatively expensive based on its price to earnings (P/E) ratio, expected earnings growth, and/or recent price history. Another analyst says that AMZN is relatively cheap when compared with other stocks within the same industry and its potential for future earnings growth. Do you go long on AMZN because it is relatively cheap, or do you short it because it is relatively expensive? The most frustrating thing you can do as a trader is purchase an overpriced security. Therefore, you turn to various indicators to help you decide whether the stock in which you are interested is overpriced. The problem with determining whether a stock is cheap or expensive is that the decision is highly subjective.

Now assume that a 2-month AMZN $55 Call is trading for $4.50. Is that a relatively expensive option? You cannot look at P/E ratios, price history, or expected earnings growth to make such a determination. Fortunately, with options there is a way to determine whether a certain call or put is relatively expensive or cheap—implied volatility. The IV is the current volatility of the stock implied in its observed option price.

As noted previously, understanding the characteristics of volatility and how to use IV in trading situations will improve your understanding of the various option strategies and when to use them. Many of the strategies highlighted in this chapter are better utilized on stocks with relatively high or relatively low IV. Moreover, many of the adjustments covered in the subsequent chapters are dependent on understanding the IV of the underlying asset.

Using IV to determine whether an option is relatively expensive or relatively cheap will help prevent costly trading mistakes, such as overpaying for long options. Just as with stocks, we do not wish to buy a security that is extremely expensive. The more you pay for long options, the greater your risk and the more the stock will have to move to surpass the breakeven points. Therefore, understanding IV gives you an advantage in selecting stocks and option strategies.

To compute IV, let's assume you have the following information:

AMZN: $55
2-Month $55 Call: $5.50
Dividends: $0.00
Risk-free interest rate: 1.5%

The only information with respect to pricing that we are missing is the volatility of the stock. However, using the Black-Scholes formula, we can solve for the volatility input that would result in the model producing an option price of $5.50. We simply plug different volatility values (trial and error) into the formula until it produces the current option price; otherwise, we can use nonlinear estimation techniques. Once we arrive at a volatility value that will result in the actual current option price ($5.50 in this case), we then have solved for the volatility value implied by the current option price. The good news is that we do not have to undergo these complicated calculations every time we observe an option price in the market, as most brokers and option analysis software automatically calculate and simultaneously update current IV calculations for all options. We have a quick snapshot of the volatility the market is expecting or implying by the price.

Obviously, there will be times when the market overestimates or underestimates implied volatility, just like the market often overvalues or undervalues the price of a stock. Because volatility affects the price of an option, an overestimation of volatility will result in relatively overpriced options, and an underestimation of volatility will result in relatively underpriced options. We should warn the reader that accurately estimating current and future volatilities is quite a difficult and elusive venture and that the likelihood of being able to accurately make such predictions is quite small. However, as option traders, we can try to take advantage of such situations when we perceive that the premiums are relatively expensive or relatively cheap, in much the same way that stock traders try to purchase undervalued stocks and sell short overvalued stocks.

When we speak of options that are "cheap" or "expensive" based on IV, we speak in terms of relative pricing. We are trying to determine whether the option is relatively cheap or relatively expensive compared with where it has been priced in the past. Many traders who begin to incorporate the use of IV into their trading compare the IVs of different stocks. For example, they observe an IV of 30% for XYZ and an IV of 60% for ABC, and because XYZ has a lower IV, they consider XYZ options relatively cheaper than ABC options. We are not looking at absolute values of implied volatilities and comparing those numbers across different stocks. Each stock has its own volatility range. GE has a much lower implied volatility range than GOOG because GE has much smaller price fluctuations. Therefore, comparing the IV of the two will not produce any useful information, as we will be comparing apples and oranges.

We must compare the IV of a particular stock with its own historical IV range. Every stock has a historical range within which the IV of that stock moves. If the current IV derived from an option is at the high end of the range, then we can say that this option is relatively expensive compared with where similar options have been priced in the past. For example, assume that XYZ has an IV range over the past year of 20% to 60% and

TABLE 2.9 Volatility Effect

Volatility (%)	Theoretical XYZ $50 Call Price ($)
20	1.80
30	2.70
40	3.50
50	4.40
60	5.30

currently the IV of XYZ options is around 60%. Then, these options are expensive in relative terms.

To illustrate the effect of volatility on the price of an option, we use the Black-Scholes formula with all pricing factors remaining constant except volatility (see Table 2.9). Assume that XYZ is trading at $50 and we are comparing the 1-month $50 Call by simply changing the input for volatility in the Black-Scholes model. (XYZ has no dividends, and the risk-free rate is 1.5%.)

The difference between XYZ options with volatilities of 60% and 40% is significant. Even more striking is the difference in price between the $50 Call with volatilities of 60% and 20%. We would prefer to purchase a 1-month ATM $50 Call with an IV at the lower end of its historical range. Therefore, we can say that with an IV of 60% and a historical 1-year range of 20% to 60%, the current XYZ options are relatively expensive compared with where they have been priced in the past. If the current volatility is 20%, then this option would be relatively cheap.

There are two theories that allow us to use IV analysis as an advantage when trading. The first theory is that the range of a stock's IV over a 1- or 2-year period is mean reverting. There is a mean IV value for the relevant time period, and when IV gets too far above or below that mean value, it will revert back to the mean. Therefore, when IV is too high, it will move lower, and when IV is too low, it will move higher. Because changes in IV affect the price of an option, you could take advantage of this mean-reverting characteristic of IV for trading.

Assume that you expect XYZ to move higher, and at the same time you observe the IV of XYZ options to be relatively low. You could purchase long calls because you are bullish and because they are relatively cheap. Not only do you expect the stock to move higher but also you expect the IV to revert back higher toward its mean. Because the options are relatively cheap, you pay a lower premium and therefore have a lower breakeven point and lower risk. You have two ways to make money on this position. First, if the stock moves higher as expected, your long call will increase in value for a profit. Second, if the stock does not move at all but the IV does increase from its low values, then the value of the long call will increase as well. If the stock increases in price and IV increases as well, then you have the potential for an even bigger profit because you have two factors pushing the option price higher. In all such situations, you assume no significant time has passed. Thus, taking advantage of IV when purchasing the long call gives you an edge in your position.

If the IV of XYZ was at the upper end of its historical range and we blindly purchased long calls, we would be purchasing options that were relatively expensive. This would result in a higher premium, a higher breakeven point, and more risk. If the stock did not move higher as expected and IV came crashing down, we would lose money. Even if XYZ did move slightly higher but IV still came crashing down, then our long call would lose money even if the stock moved as expected. With IV dropping, the stock would have to make a bigger move upward to counteract the negative value of the decrease in IV. Purchasing options with relatively high IV creates a situation where IV can work against us even if the stock moves as expected. Nothing is more frustrating for option traders who ignore IV than watching the underlying stock move as expected while their position still loses money.

The second theory regarding the use of IV is the contrarian theory of investing. When an option has a relatively low IV, the market is forecasting a relatively quiet period in the price movement of the stock. A contrarian would go against the market view and bet that the stock will actually become very volatile and IV will increase. On the other hand, a relatively high IV implies that the market expects a stock to be very volatile. A contrarian would again go against the market perception and expect the stock to enter a quieter period and the IV to drop. Therefore, a contrarian would buy volatility low and sell volatility high.

We are not recommending that traders simply purchase options when IV is low and sell options when IV is high. Instead, we recommend that IV be taken into consideration before opening a position. Remember, in the SCORE trading formula under Choose, we stated that part of choosing an appropriate option strategy was taking IV into consideration. Some strategies are preferable when IV is high, and others are better when IV is low.

Using IV when trading can give you an advantage in selecting strategies. It is easy to use IV when it is at one extreme or the other. When IV is somewhere in the middle of its historical range, then the focus will be more on comparing the risk/reward profile to find the most appropriate strategy. However, IV can be a great initial screen to prevent buying or selling options when it is not the appropriate time, given the relative cost. There are more advanced uses of IV for trading, but it is sufficient for you to understand simply how IV can indicate whether options are relatively cheap or expensive and could dictate the type of strategy you use in a given situation.

The best way to use IV to determine relative pricing of options is to view a historical chart of a stock's IV and then analyze where the current value is with respect to its historical range. One site that provides very useful free historical IV data and charts is www.ivolatility.com. In Figure 2.6, we see a snapshot from GOOG's page at www.ivolatility.com which shows various data points regarding front-month volatility, including a historical IV chart. Notice that under implied volatility, we see current values, as well as values 1 week and 1 month ago to follow the trend in recent changes in implied volatility. Also included are the 52-week high and low values for implied volatility so we can see where the current values are relative to the high and low values over the past year. Finally, below that we see a chart showing historical IV over the past year, as well as the actual historical volatility.

The information in Figure 2.6 shows that GOOG currently has an IV of about 35%, with a 52-week high of about 94% in October 2008 and a 52-week low of about 28% in August 2008. GOOG's high point for IV came in October and November, which is expected, given the huge downward price spikes GOOG, and the market as a whole, experienced in the fall of 2008. With huge price swings, GOOG's options were being priced with relatively high premiums.

With a value of 35%, GOOG's IV is trading close to the yearly low (28%), which is also visually evident in the IV historical chart. Based on this information, we can say that GOOG's options are relatively cheap based on IV, given where they have traded in the past year. This means that when selecting option strategies, we should look for those that benefit from increasing volatilities and try to avoid strategies that will get hurt from increasing volatilities. In other words, we can use this information on IV to screen out some strategies that are not appropriate, given the current levels of IV. Therefore, it is a good practice to regularly check the current IV of the underlying stock you are considering trading options on and compare it against the trading range over the past year to make an informed decision on the relative price of those options.

This is where learning the Greek profile of each strategy covered later in this chapter becomes very important and shows how mastering the principles of the Greeks alone will make you a better trader and allow you to make more informed option trading decisions. Later in this chapter, we go into more detail in how to apply your knowledge of the Greeks to make better trading decisions. Remember that using IV in this way is simply to get a sense of relative pricing, not to make a prediction of where GOOG is going to go in the future. IV does not predict direction but is mainly useful in helping us make a relative determination of the stock's option pricing.

Price	Change (%)	52 wk High	52 wk Low	Stock volume ?	Avg. options volume ?	Avg. options open interest ?
389.49	↑ +4.80 (+1.25%)	594.90 05/05/2008	257.44 11/24/2008	3,376,388	32,840	289,880

HISTORICAL VOLATILITY ?

	Current	1 WK AGO	1 MO AGO	52 wk Hi/Date	52 wk Low/Date
10 days	31.07%	32.11%	39.09%	146.78% - 13-Oct	17.74% - 20-May
20 days	29.89%	32.81%	48.04%	118.11% - 21-Oct	23.52% - 03-Sep
30 days	32.91%	39.94%	50.01%	106.70% - 28-Oct	27.69% - 11-Jul

IMPLIED VOLATILITY ?

IV Index call ?	34.54%	37.59%	49.80%	95.54% - 30-Sep	28.03% - 15-Aug
IV Index put ?	36.40%	37.83%	49.00%	93.16% - 09-Oct	28.23% - 15-Aug
IV Index mean ?	35.47%	37.71%	49.40%	94.12% - 09-Oct	28.13% - 15-Aug

GOOG: DAILY 1 YEAR VOLATILITY CHART (3 months   6 months   1 year)

IV Index Call   IV Index Put   IV Index Call & Put   IV Index Mean

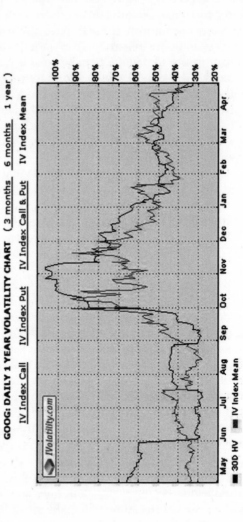

■ 30D HV   ■ IV Index Mean

FIGURE 2.6 GOOG Ivolatility.com Data: April 2008–April 2009

In addition to understanding the relationship between IV and relative option pricing, we need to discuss several general principles with respect to implied volatility. These general characteristics will help us understand IV better and give us more necessary information to make better option trading decisions. Before discussing these principles, we want to warn the reader that these principles are true in most situations, but as unpredictable as the market can be, IV can still sometimes have a mind of its own and move in a very unexpected way. Therefore, look at these principles as general guidelines, not absolute statements of fact.

The First General Principle of IV is that IV is a representation of uncertainty in the markets. When an underlying is expected to make a large price move but there is real uncertainty as to the direction or magnitude of the move, IV will increase and option premiums will increase. The uncertainty means that there is a greater likelihood of large price fluctuations, so the market will price options higher, and traders are willing to pay more for these options. Uncertainty is often seen with respect to a stock prior to a significant earnings announcement by a company, an announcement by the Food and Drug Administration (FDA) on drug trial results, or even before a critical Federal Open Market Committee announcement on interest rates. Understanding these tendencies will give you a better understanding of how option prices can suddenly change drastically, even if every other pricing factor remains constant. You will see how this knowledge of IV can avoid some serious trading mistakes when used in conjunction with some of the other IV principles discussed here.

The Second General Principle of IV is that IV tends to increase when markets fall. When stocks drop sharply, there is usually an increase in fear and panic in the markets, as people tend to be afraid of how far the market could fall and how fast. This increase in fear and panic leads to a lot of put buying to hedge their stock portfolios by large institutions and investors who remember all too well the financial ruin caused by the crash in October 1987, the tech sector collapse and post 9/11 markets in 2001, and the market turmoil in 2008. This increased demand for puts pushes prices higher, and since no one can tell how far the market might fall, the fear and panic hedging leads to extreme uncertainty in the market, affecting both puts and calls. Therefore, as the market begins to sell off, we tend to see IV rise for the most part, and it often continues to climb higher as the markets keep selling off, pushing option premiums higher.

The Third General Principle of IV is that IV tends to decrease when markets rise. This principle is sometimes confusing for traders because volatility measures price fluctuations whether they are up or down, and up moves can be as violent and fast as down moves. However, IV is a reflection of market behavior since it is directly related to option prices, and that is why we look at it to give us such useful insight into options. When the markets are rising, everyone is generally happy because the majority of investors are bullish and long. As the market moves up, people are not panicking or fearful or concerned that the market might run up too far. Even though investors are not certain as to how long the bull move will last, the fact that it is primarily expected means that uncertainty levels drop. Thus, lower levels of fear, panic, and uncertainty lead to lower IV and relatively lower option premiums, even though it might not make intuitive sense if the market is making huge price moves higher. Basically, the majority of investors are sitting back and letting their portfolios run higher, and IVs pull back on this general good feeling in the markets.

As noted before, sharp sell-offs bring out the put buyers en masse to hedge portfolios, and this buying surge pushes prices and IV higher. When markets surge higher, major institutions and investors are not necessarily looking to hedge their portfolios but tend to sell calls against their portfolio to bring in premium and increased income as their stocks rise. This selling pressure reduces relative option prices and IV.

The Fourth General Principle of IV is that IV tends to decrease or collapse once the uncertainty is removed, the long-awaited news is announced, or the panic in a market sell-off subsides and the market rallies strongly. All of these are examples of what is known as an "IV Crush," a term often used to describe a situation where an inflated IV dramatically collapses immediately after a news release. The first two principles describe situations where IV can not only move higher but also explode and get quite inflated, such as prior to an FDA announcement or a significant earnings report. Once the news is out—the FDA approves the drug or earnings are worse than expected—the uncertainty is now gone as to what the news would be and what effect it might have. The market might still not know exactly where the stock will move next and how far, but the real uncertainty of what the news would be is now gone, and there is no longer any need for the inflated IV.

Prior to the news, the uncertainty over the magnitude of the move in the stock means the option premiums and IV get inflated. After the news, the traders' reaction is known immediately, and the IV Crush usually happens very quickly. This is another situation where it is irrelevant if the stock postnews is making a huge price move, which would lead one to think intuitively that IV should stay high. However, IV is a forward-looking data point, and once the news is out, the forward-looking expectations are not as uncertain or potentially wild as they were prior to the news, when no one knew what to expect.

IV Crush is very significant when it comes to option pricing. Earlier, we looked at a hypothetical AMZN long call position with different IV positions from 20% to 60% and how much the option premium changed as the IV indications went up to 60%. Imagine how serious the IV Crush would be on

TABLE 2.10	General Principles of IV Summary Table
Principle	IV is a measure of uncertainty in the market over a stock or index's future moves.
Principle	IV tends to increase when markets fall.
Principle	IV tends to decrease when markets rise.
Principle	IV tends to decrease or collapse when the uncertainty is removed, such as after an earnings or FDA announcement.

your option premiums if you bought long options on AMZN when its IV was 60% and then it collapsed down to 30% or 40%. The premiums would lose a lot of value just on a pure collapse in IV, assuming all other factors were held constant. This principle, above all the others, is why we recommend always checking the IV data on the underlying stock you are considering to trade options on.

Table 2.10 summarizes the four basic principles of IV just discussed, and these principles provide a good overview of the nature of IV and its relation to market movements. The more familiar you are with these principles, the fewer trading mistakes you will make, and more important, you will have a greater understanding of how to pick appropriate strategies given the current IV conditions. These principles are better illustrated when we study the overall index of market implied volatility and compare it with moves in the overall market.

The VIX index is a good measure of overall market volatility. This index is derived from calculating the implied volatility of the front-month call and put options of the S&P 500 index, which often is used as a proxy for the market. So by looking at the IV of the current S&P 500 options, VIX attempts to track the current implied volatility of the overall market. If we compare movements in the VIX with movements in the SPX, we can see some of the general principles in action.

Figure 2.7 shows a 1-year chart of the VIX index from mid-2008 to mid-2009 on the bottom and the S&P 500 index over the same time period on the top, to make it easier to compare movements in the VIX and the S&P 500. In late 2008, the SPX had two large sell-offs in October and November, which you can see in the middle of the SPX chart. As the market sold off sharply, VIX spiked from the 20% to 30% range to a high of almost 90% and then recovered somewhat before spiking again back to 80%. As the market rallied after those two sharp sell-offs from a low of about 750 on the SPX back to almost 950, you can see how VIX also dropped back close to 40% before running back up over 50% as the market again began to sell off. In the last few months, as the market once again rallied strongly, VIX moved back from 50% down to about 30%. Looking at these two charts, we can see

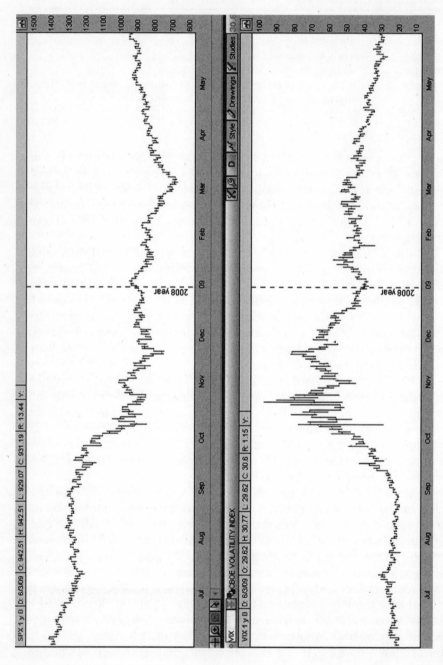

FIGURE 2.7 VIX and SPX Historical Charts

the general characteristics of volatility with respect to market crashes and rallies.

With this basic understanding of implied volatility and its unique characteristics, we can now look at the risk parameters used to measure sensitivity of option premiums to changes in volatility. We already discussed how changes in volatility can seriously affect the prices of options, so we must look at how to measure those changes. For illustrative purposes, the Greek parameter that indicates how much an option premium would change for a 1% change (i.e., 49% to 50%, 80% to 79%, etc.) in the value of implied volatility is called Vega.

One interesting characteristic of Vega is that it shares a lot of similarities with the relationship of time to expiration and option premiums. Basically, an option-pricing formula such as Black-Scholes is calculating a theoretical price for the option by relying on a probability of whether that specific option will be in the money by expiration. The more time you have to expiration, the more time you have for out-of-the-money and at-the-money options to be in the money. Likewise, a stock with a higher volatility will make larger price moves, and more out-of-the-money and at-the-money options have a higher probability of being in the money by expiration. Therefore, more time to expiration and greater volatility have similar effects on increasing option premiums. Some people even refer to volatility as "synthetic time," in that a volatility increase has an effect on option premiums (increases them) similar to extending the time to expiration.

Table 2.11 shows the Greek values for three different GOOG $400 Call options with the same strike but with different expiration months. The first main characteristic of Vega is that it is greater the further out in time you go. In other words, options with more time to expiration are more sensitive to changes in volatility than those with less time. This makes sense because an option with a lot of time to expiration has more chances to finish in the money, and if volatility increases, it has the ability to make greater price moves within that longer time frame. Therefore, as volatility increases, the option premium also increases, and options further out in time increase by a greater amount than shorter-term expiration options. As Table 2.11 shows, GOOG's September Vega is 0.94 versus the then current-month Vega of 0.31 for May. Thus, the long-term SEP $400 Call is more sensitive to changes in volatility than the MAY $400 Call.

KEY PRINCIPLE

Longer term options are more sensitive to changes in volatility and thus have higher Vegas than shorter term options.

TABLE 2.11 GOOG Call Options—Vegas/Three Different Months

Volatility Across Time

GOOG@$394

GOOG MAY $400 Call $9.60			GOOG JUNE $400 Call $19.10			GOOG SEPT $400 Call $38.00		
Theoretical Data			Theoretical Data			Theoretical Data		
Implied Vol.	38.5149	Delta	Implied Vol.	38.7464	Delta	Implied Vol.	39.4735	Delta
	0.44889			0.4992			0.5524	
Gamma	0.0133	Theta	Gamma	0.0077	Theta	Gamma	0.0042	Theta
	−0.4421			−0.2693			−0.1631	
Vega	**0.3055**	Rho	**Vega**	**0.5336**	Rho	**Vega**	**0.9414**	Rho
	0.0642			0.2046			0.6553	

Now let us look at the characteristics of Vega within the same expiration month across all strikes, as opposed to just looking at Vega across time. Table 2.12 shows an option chain for calls on GOOG in the current month to expiration. Vega within a strike month is greatest at the at-the-money options and scales down the deeper in-the-money and out-of-the-money options. The deeper in the money the options are, the more they are made up of pure intrinsic value with little or no time value premium, which is usually where volatility premiums are reflected. With little or no time value premium and pure intrinsic value, these options are less and less influenced by changes in volatility the deeper in the money they are. Therefore, Vega decreases steadily and approaches zero as options move deeper in the money.

The deeper out of the money the options are, the further away from the current underlying price the strikes are, and the smaller the amount of time premium those options have. As volatility increases, the far-out-of-the-money options might move a little, since higher volatility does mean bigger price fluctuations and greater potential for the underlying stock to reach some of those out-of-the-money options. However, initially the option premiums will not change too much, since there is already a large price difference built between the strike price and the current underlying price. Therefore, the deeper out of the money the options are, the less sensitive they will be to volatility and thus the smaller the Vega.

If Vega decreases as you move out of the money and in the money, then the opposite will hold as you move toward the at-the-money option. As Table 2.12 shows, Vega does increase as you move to the at-the-money option and peaks right at the at-the-money option, in much the same way that Gamma does. Therefore, the best balance with respect to Vega and price within the same expiration month can be found at the money.

Early Assignment

A common question asked by many option investors is how to determine when they are most likely to be assigned on their short options. Theoretically, you can be assigned at any time on your short options.

However, the odds are you will not get assigned as long as there is still time value left on your short options. Therefore, the time value premium is important to understand for any trader who uses short options.

To illustrate how you can use time value premiums to anticipate early assignment on short options, let's assume that with AMZN at $57, a 1-month $55 Call is trading at $4.25. The $55 Call has an intrinsic value of $2.00 and a time value of $2.25. Assume that you are bearish on AMZN and decide to sell the $55 Call and collect $4.25.

TABLE 2.12 GOOG Call Option Chain—Vega

Strike	Last	Bid	Ask	Delta	Gamma	Rho	Theta	Vega
GOOG $405							June 2009 (38 days to expiration)	
$ 360.00	$ 48.20	$ 45.70	$ 46.20	0.8585	0.0053	0.3112	-0.1380	0.2922
$ 370.00	$ 40.10	$ 37.70	$ 38.20	0.7922	0.0067	0.2923	-0.1724	0.3711
$ 380.00	$ 33.30	$ 30.40	$ 30.80	0.7154	0.0081	0.2672	-0.2053	0.4402
$ 390.00	$ 24.40	$ 24.00	$ 24.20	0.6268	0.0089	0.2375	-0.2241	0.4899
$ 400.00	$ 18.40	$ 18.20	$ 18.50	0.5348	0.0095	0.2048	-0.2389	0.5143
$ 410.00	$ 13.70	$ 13.50	$ 13.70	0.4445	0.0093	0.1713	-0.2318	0.5112
$ 420.00	$ 10.00	$ 9.50	$ 9.80	0.3543	0.0089	0.1390	-0.2221	0.4830
$ 430.00	$ 6.90	$ 6.70	$ 6.80	0.2804	0.0079	0.1094	-0.1965	0.4355
$ 440.00	$ 4.87	$ 4.40	$ 4.60	0.2081	0.0068	0.0837	-0.1693	0.3758
$ 450.00	$ 3.00	$ 2.85	$ 3.00	0.1568	0.0056	0.0621	-0.1395	0.3113

What would happen if you were assigned on your option the minute you sold the $55 Call with AMZN at $57? You would be short 100 shares of AMZN at $55. However, you collected $4.25 in premium when you sold the $55 Call, and therefore your effective sale price is $59.25. Because AMZN is at $57, you could purchase the stock at $57 to close out the short position for a profit of $2.25 ($59.25 − $57). Let's look at the trade from the point of view of a buyer who purchased the $55 Call for $4.25 with AMZN at $57. If the $55 Call is exercised immediately, 100 shares of AMZN will be purchased at $55. However, because the cost of the option is $4.25, the effective purchase price is really $59.25. Because AMZN is at $57 at the time of the exercise, the $55 Call buyer has a loss of $2.25 ($59.25 − $57). With a loss of $2.25, it would not be prudent for the long $55 Call holder to exercise the option because there is $2.25 of time value. As soon as the $55 Call is exercised, the time value is lost. Therefore, as long as there is a time premium, it is highly unlikely that a call will be exercised. Nobody likes to give away money for free.

Once the time value premium erodes or disappears, it is most likely that a long holder of that option will exercise it early, and you could be assigned on your short option. Because there is no time value premium, there is no difference between holding and exercising the option. For example, assume that the AMZN $55 Call is trading at $2.05 with AMZN at $57. If you own the $55 Call and exercise it, you will be giving up only $0.05 of time value premium, which is not enough of a premium to deter someone from exercising the option.

It is impossible to accurately predict whether a short option will be assigned early. However, the best early-warning indicator is if the time value premium shrinks to almost nothing. As a result of time decay, the time value premium will usually shrink the fastest in the final weeks before expiration. Therefore, if you have an ITM short option in the final weeks before expiration, watch the time value premium closely and if the premium is practically gone, then you are at a high risk of being assigned. If you wish to avoid assignment, close out the short position as soon as possible.

SYNTHETIC POSITIONS

There are three components of the investment strategies and adjustments discussed in this book: stocks, calls, and puts. Any strategy or position is made up of a combination of one or more of these components, either short or long. With these three components, we can establish a stock or option position or a combination of the two that covers any investment outlook or scenario, as demonstrated later in this and subsequent chapters.

However, there is a fundamental relationship among these three components that most traders may be unaware of. If you understand this relationship, you can exploit it to create trades that bring higher returns on your investment and provide better use of your capital. The unique relationship among these three components is that any one component can be replicated synthetically through a combination of the other two components. For example, a long stock position can be synthetically replicated through a combination of calls and puts, and long calls can be replicated through a combination of stocks and puts. The best way to illustrate this complementary relationship and the benefits of using synthetic positions is to analyze specific examples.

Synthetic Stock

Long Stock Assume that XYZ is trading at $80 and the 3-month XYZ $80 Call and Put are trading at $5.00 each. If you were bullish on XYZ, you might consider purchasing 100 shares of XYZ. However, you could also synthetically own 100 shares of stock by purchasing the $80 Call for $5.00 and simultaneously selling the $80 Put for $5.00, for a net debit of $0.00. To see how the option position is equivalent to the long stock position, we compare the profit and loss of both positions in Table 2.13.

Table 2.13 shows that the profit and the loss from the long call/short put position are exactly the same as those from the long stock position. The two options create a synthetic long stock position with the same risk/reward profile as the long stock. The synthetic stock position has one distinct advantage over the long stock position—smaller investment. To purchase 100 shares of XYZ, you would need $8,000 in capital, or $4,000 if purchased on margin.

The synthetic position is established with no capital outlay—the cost of the call is covered by selling the put at the same price. However, because

TABLE 2.13 Long Stock versus Synthetic Long Stock

XYZ at Expiration ($)	XYZ $80 Call P/L ($)	XYZ $80 Put P/L ($)	Combined Option P/L ($)	Long Stock P/L ($)
65	−5.00	−10.00	−15.00	−15.00
70	−5.00	−5.00	−10.00	−10.00
75	−5.00	+0.00	−5.00	−5.00
80	−5.00	+5.00	0.00	0.00
85	0.00	+5.00	+5.00	+5.00
90	+5.00	+5.00	+10.00	+10.00
95	+10.00	+5.00	+15.00	+15.00

the synthetic position has a naked put, there is a collateral margin requirement, which is the put premium plus 20% of the stock price minus/plus the amount the put is OTM/ITM. The collateral requirement would be 20% of $8,000, or $1,600, plus the $500 put premium, for a total initial collateral requirement of $2,100. (Because the option is ATM, there is no further collateral adjustment.) That amount is significantly less than the $8,000 required to purchase the stock outright, and even less than the $4,000 needed to purchase the stock on margin. Although the collateral requirement increases as the stock moves lower, the overall capital outlay is still less than that required for the purchase of the stock. Therefore, using the synthetic option position instead of purchasing the long stock requires a smaller capital outlay.

The reduction in the capital outlay gives you increased leverage in your position. Assume that XYZ climbs to $90 by expiration, where both positions would have a profit of $1,000. For the long stock position, the $1,000 profit is earned on a margin of $4,000 for a return of 25%. However, the synthetic position earns the $1,000 profit on a margin of $2,100 for a return of about 48%. Therefore, the reduction in capital outlay using a synthetic long stock position allows for greater returns on your investment over a long stock position from the same movement in the underlying security. This is the effect of leverage. Keep in mind, though, that leverage makes good results very good and bad results very bad.

Although combining the long call and the short put is equivalent to holding the long stock, the holder of the synthetic stock position does not collect dividends or have voting rights, whereas the stock owner does. However, the synthetic stock position has a capital outlay of $1,900 less than the stock cost (assuming the stock is purchased on margin; if no margin is used, then capital outlay is $5,900 less). The synthetic trader can earn interest on those funds and partially offset the loss of dividends or even invest the proceeds elsewhere.

Short Stock   If you reverse each component of the synthetic long stock position, you can synthetically create a short stock position. For example, instead of purchasing the call and shorting the put at the same strike price, you would short the call and purchase the long put. Using the same assumed prices for XYZ, you could short 100 shares of XYZ at $80 or purchase the XYZ $80 Put for $5.00 and short the XYZ $80 Call for $5.00 for a synthetic short stock position. If you compare the profit and the loss of the synthetic short stock position with those of the short stock in Table 2.14, you see that they are identical.

A synthetic short stock position has the same leverage benefits over a short stock position as the synthetic long stock position has over the long stock position. Because we are only using options and subject only

TABLE 2.14   Short Stock versus Synthetic Short Stock

XYZ at Expiration ($)	XYZ $80 Call P/L ($)	XYZ $80 Put P/L ($)	Combined Option P/L ($)	Short Stock P/L ($)
65	+5.00	+10.00	**+15.00**	**+15.00**
70	+5.00	+5.00	**+10.00**	**+10.00**
75	+5.00	+0.00	**+5.00**	**+5.00**
80	+5.00	−5.00	**0.00**	**0.00**
85	0.00	−5.00	**−5.00**	**−5.00**
90	−5.00	−5.00	**−10.00**	**−10.00**
95	−10.00	−5.00	**−15.00**	**−15.00**

Note: P/L, Profit or loss.

to the margin requirements of the short call as opposed to the short stock position, we have a lower margin requirement for the position. Therefore, whatever profit is realized on the position is derived from a smaller capital outlay. Another benefit of using the synthetic short position is that you do not have to pay out any dividends, which you would have to do if you shorted a dividend-paying stock.

Synthetic Call

Just as we created a synthetic long and short stock position using calls and puts, we can create a synthetic long call position using stocks and puts because each component can be synthetically created by a combination of the other two. Assume as before that XYZ is trading at $80 and the XYZ $80 Call and Put with the same expiration date are trading at $5.00 each. You could purchase a long ATM call on XYZ at a strike of $80 for $500 or create a synthetic call by purchasing 100 shares of XYZ for $8,000 ($4,000 if bought on margin) and simultaneously purchasing the XYZ $80 Put for $500 for a total cost of $8,500 ($4,500 if stock bought on margin).

What is the maximum loss on each position? For the long call, your maximum loss is limited to the initial debit paid of $500. No matter how far XYZ drops by expiration, you lose only $500. The synthetic long call position comprises 100 shares of XYZ at $80 and an $80 Put purchased for $500. If XYZ is anywhere below $80 by expiration, you can simply exercise the long put to sell the stock at $80 for no loss. However, you paid $500 for the long put, so your maximum loss for the synthetic long call is $500, no matter how far XYZ falls by expiration—same as for the long call.

If XYZ moves higher, your long call will have a profit as long as XYZ is above $85. Because you paid $5.00 for the call, XYZ will have to move $5.00 higher to recover the cost of the trade before a profit is made. Your synthetic long call has the same breakeven point. Because you paid $5.00 for the XYZ $80 Put, your long stock position needs a profit of $5.00 to offset the cost of the long put before the combined position makes a profit. Both the synthetic long call and the long call have the same breakeven point. Both positions will earn $1.00 for every $1.00 XYZ moves above $85. Therefore, the long stock/long put has the same risk/reward profile as the long call and can be used to create a synthetic long call.

Many conservative investors purchase stock and then add a protective put to their position to hedge their risk. What they fail to realize is that this position has the same exact risk/reward profile as a long call but at a significantly higher cost. If you compare the foregoing costs, you see the long XYZ $80 Call cost $500, whereas the synthetic long call cost $8,500 ($4,500 if stock bought on margin)—quite a difference in price. If you have no preference for holding the stock—that is, no dividends to collect—then understanding the synthetic positions will allow you to achieve the same risk/reward profile at a much lower cost—$500 versus $4,500. We discuss long stock/long put positions and their equivalents in greater detail in Chapter 3.

To create a synthetic short call, you reverse the synthetic long call position by shorting the stock and the put. For example, with XYZ at $80, you short 100 shares and sell the XYZ $80 Put for a credit of $5.00. The short XYZ $80 Put creates the obligation to purchase 100 shares of XYZ at $80 if XYZ is below $80 by expiration. Because you shorted XYZ at $80, the short put closes out the short stock position for no loss or gain. However, you do have a profit of $5.00 from shorting the $80 Put. Therefore, if XYZ is at $80 or below by expiration, the synthetic short call has a profit of $5.00. You realize the same profit if you only sold the XYZ $80 Call short for $5.00. If XYZ is below $80, the short call will expire worthless for a profit of $5.00.

Both the synthetic short call (short stock/short put) and the short call have the potential for unlimited risk on the upside. Both positions will lose money if XYZ moves above $85. In the synthetic short call, the short stock produces a loss of $5.00 at $85, which is offset by the $5.00 in premium collected from selling the short $80 Put. The short call also has a breakeven point of $85 because the $5.00 loss on the short call will be offset by the $5.00 in premium collected from selling the short call. Therefore, you can replicate a short call by shorting the stock and selling a put at the same strike price and expiration date.

The short stock portion of the synthetic short call will have a greater margin requirement than the short call alone. Therefore, you would have less margin requirements by simply shorting the call than by combining a short stock position with a short put. The only benefit the synthetic short call has over the short call is that you can reinvest the proceeds from the short stock sale because the synthetic short call will have greater proceeds than the $500 received from shorting the $80 Call. Both the short call and the synthetic short call are extremely risky positions, and we do not recommend either unless combined with other positions.

Synthetic Put

A long put can be synthetically created by shorting a stock and purchasing a call. Adding the long call to a short stock position limits your risk to the upside because you can exercise the long call to close out your short position before expiration, no matter how high the stock may climb. On the downside, your short stock position will produce a profit once you have recovered the costs of adding the long call. Consider the XYZ stock example; you could either purchase the XYZ $80 Put for $5.00 or short XYZ at $80 and purchase the XYZ $80 Call for $5.00. Both positions have the same maximum risk, maximum reward, and breakeven point.

Many investors who short stock add a protective call to limit their risk (see Chapter 4 for short stock/long call positions). With synthetic positions, you can achieve the same result by simply purchasing a put with the same strike price and expiration date. Because the long put has no margin requirements—you only have to pay initial debit for a long put—the position is cheaper to establish than shorting the stock and dealing with those margin requirements. You may prefer to use the synthetic short put position if you can reinvest the proceeds from the short stock.

To create a synthetic short put, you reverse the synthetic long put position by purchasing the stock and shorting the call. For example, with XYZ at $80, purchase 100 shares of XYZ and sell the XYZ $80 Call for $5.00 to create a synthetic short put that is equivalent to selling the XYZ $80 Put for $5.00. This synthetic short put position of long stock and short call is commonly known as a "covered call" position.

The synthetic short put is a perfect example of why understanding synthetics will give you a better understanding of options. There are investors who feel that selling naked puts is too risky. On the other hand, they feel that a conservative trading strategy would be to purchase stock and sell a covered call to bring in more income. However, purchasing a stock and selling a call against it has the same risk/reward profile as selling a naked put of the same strike price. The synthetic position is not less risky than naked puts, and investors sometimes make the mistake of thinking that a covered call is a lower risk investment than a naked put.

Covered calls require a significant capital outlay to purchase 100 shares of stock. In the XYZ example, you would need $8,000 to purchase 100 shares of XYZ ($4,000 if bought on margin) and would collect $500 from selling the XYZ $80 Call. On the other hand, selling the XYZ $80 Put naked would bring in $500 in premium and require a margin of $2,100 (20% of the stock price plus the put premium). Therefore, using the naked put over the covered call could produce a higher return on investment because the naked put has a lower margin (capital) outlay than the covered call position.

The six synthetic positions are summarized as follows (the call and put in each position have the same expiration date and strike price):

Synthetic long stock = Long call + short put
Synthetic short stock = Short call + long put
Synthetic long call = Long stock + long put
Synthetic short call = Short stock + short put
Synthetic long put = Long call + short stock
Synthetic short put = Short call + long stock

Synthetic positions illustrate the complementary relationship among stocks, calls, and puts. Although each line represents two positions that have the same risk/reward profile, they can differ in one important area— cost and margin. One side of the synthetic equation might be more advantageous than the other with respect to margin treatment and cost, and understanding synthetics will allow you to choose the more cost-efficient strategy for a better return on investment for the same risk/reward profile.

BASIC STRATEGIES

In this section and the one covering more advanced strategies, we highlight most of the option strategies with an overview of their risk/reward profile and breakeven points. We also give an overview of the position's Greek profile, which reviews the risk factors the strategy is exposed to. We focus only on the three most important risk factors, which are Delta, Theta (time decay), and Vega (volatility). Unless noted, we assume the examples to be that of an at-the-money position. For clarification, when we say a position is short time decay, we mean that the Greek risk factor Theta is negative and your position loses money as time passes, holding all other factors constant. When we refer to long Deltas, we mean that you have a directional bias either up or down, as in long calls or long puts, respectively, and we are not referring specifically to positive or negative Deltas.

Long Call

Overview: Bullish. The IV should be low to purchase relatively cheap options. Allow enough time to expiration for the stock to move and to reduce the effect of time decay (Figure 2.8).
Position: Long XYZ $50 Call.

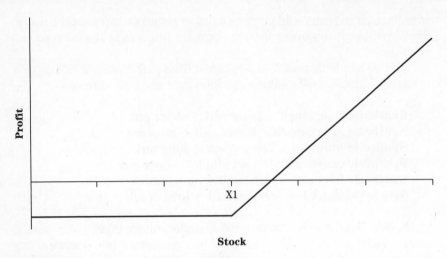

FIGURE 2.8 Long Call Risk/Reward Profile

Maximum risk: Limited to initial debit paid.
Maximum reward: Unlimited.
Breakeven point: Long call strike + debit paid.
Greek profile: Long calls are long Deltas generally with directional bias
   higher, short time decay, and long volatility.

Short Call

Overview: Expect the stock to move lower, sideways, or stay below
   the strike price and have the short call expire worthless to keep
   the entire premium collected from selling the call. The IV should
   be high in order to sell overpriced or relatively expensive calls. Use
   short time to expiration to take advantage of time decay and give
   the stock less time to move against you. Assignment obligates the
   seller to be short 100 shares of stock at the short call strike price.
   Margin is required (Figure 2.9).
Position: Short XYZ $50 Call.
Maximum risk: Unlimited.
Maximum reward: Limited to credit received.
Breakeven point: Short call strike + credit received.
Greek profile: Short calls are short Deltas generally with directional
   bias dependent on strike selection, long time decay, and short
   volatility.

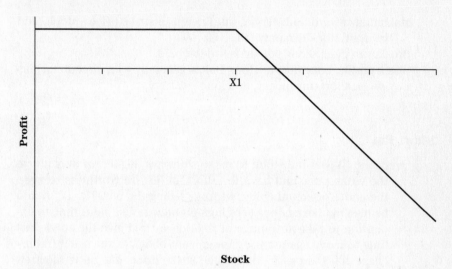

Profit

X1

Stock

FIGURE 2.9 Short Call Risk/Reward Profile

Long Put

Overview: Bearish. Expect the stock to move lower. The IV should be low to purchase relatively cheap options. Give the position enough time to expiration to be profitable and reduce the effect of time decay (Figure 2.10).

Position: Long XYZ $50 Put.

Maximum risk: Limited to initial debit paid.

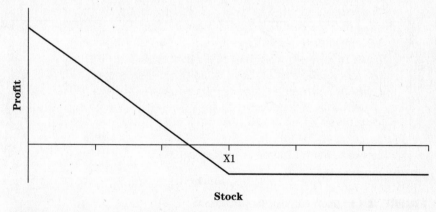

Profit

X1

Stock

FIGURE 2.10 Long Put Risk/Reward Profile

Maximum reward: Substantial but limited to strike price – debit paid because stock can only fall to $0.

Breakeven point: Long put strike – debit paid.

Greek profile: Long puts are long Deltas generally with directional bias lower, short time decay, and long volatility.

Short Put

Overview: Expect the stock to move sideways, higher, or stay above the strike price and have the short put expire worthless to keep the entire premium collected from selling the put. The IV should be high to take advantage of high premiums. Use short time to expiration to take advantage of time decay and give the stock less time to move against you. Assignment obligates the seller to purchase 100 shares of stock at the strike price. Margin is required (Figure 2.11).

Position: Short XYZ $50 Put.

Maximum risk: Substantial but limited to strike price – credit received because stock can only fall to $0.

Maximum reward: Limited to credit received.

Breakeven point: Short put strike – credit received.

Greek profile: Short puts are short Deltas generally with directional bias dependent on strike selection, long time decay, and short volatility.

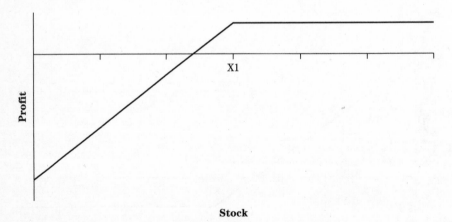

FIGURE 2.11 Short Put Risk/Reward Profile

BASIC SPREADS AND COMBINATIONS

Spreads are positions consisting of either all calls or all puts where you have both long and short options. Combinations, however, consist of calls and puts together.

Bull Call Spread

Overview: Bullish. Expect the stock to move higher. Purchase a call and sell another call at a higher strike price with the same expiration date for a net debit. The short call is covered by the long call, so no margin is required. Profit is limited in exchange for reduced risk because credit from the short call reduces the cost of the long call. Use a bull call spread over a long call when the cost of the long call is too high and the stock is expected to move somewhat higher (Figure 2.12).

Position: Long XYZ $50 Call + short XYZ $55 Call.

Maximum risk: Limited to initial debit paid.

Maximum reward: Limited to difference between the strikes minus initial debit paid.

Breakeven point: Long call strike + debit paid.

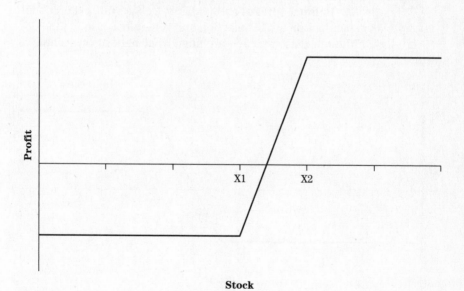

FIGURE 2.12 Bull Call Spread Risk/Reward Profile

Greek profile: Bull call spreads are net long Deltas with an upward bias and generally net short time decay. Although these spreads are somewhat neutral on volatility, they still have a long volatility bias, which is evident on large changes in volatility.

Bull Put Spread

Overview: Bullish. Sell a put and purchase another put at a lower strike price with the same expiration date for a net credit. Expect the stock to move higher or sideways so that the puts expire worthless and you keep the entire credit collected. A bull put spread is preferable over a short put because the spread has limited risk, as opposed to the significant risk of the short put. Use a short time to expiration to take advantage of time decay and give the stock less time to move against you. The margin requirement is the difference between strike prices, but credit received can be applied to the margin requirement (Figure 2.13).

Position: Short XYZ $50 Put + long XYZ $45 Put.

Maximum risk: Limited to difference between strikes minus credit received.

Maximum reward: Limited to credit received.

Breakeven point: Short put strike – credit received.

Greek profile: Bull put spreads are net short Deltas with a directional bias dependent on strike selection and generally net long time decay. Although these spreads are somewhat neutral on volatility,

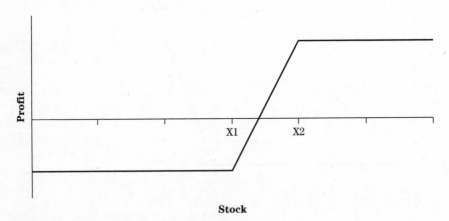

FIGURE 2.13 Bull Put Spread Risk/Reward Profile

they still have a short volatility bias, which is evident on large changes in volatility.

Bear Call Spread

Overview: Bearish. Sell a call and purchase another call at a higher strike price for a net credit. Expect the stock to move lower or sideways so that the calls expire worthless and you keep the entire credit collected. A bear call spread is preferable over a short call because the spread has limited risk, as opposed to the unlimited risk of the short call. Use a short time to expiration to take advantage of time decay, and give the stock less time to move against you. The margin requirement is the difference between the strike prices, but credit received can be applied to the margin requirement (Figure 2.14).

Position: Short XYZ $45 Call + long XYZ $50 Call.

Maximum risk: Limited to difference between strikes minus credit received.

Maximum reward: Limited to credit received.

Breakeven point: Short call strike + credit received.

Greek profile: Bear call spreads are net short Deltas with a directional bias dependent on strike selection and generally net long time decay. Although these spreads are somewhat neutral on volatility, they still have a short volatility bias, which is evident on large changes in volatility.

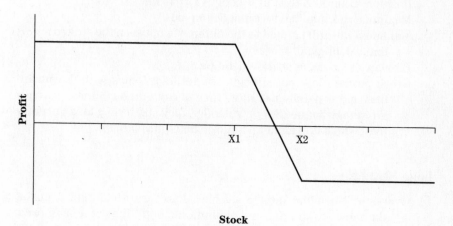

FIGURE 2.14 Bear Call Spread Risk/Reward Profile

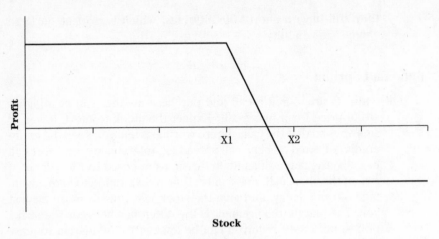

FIGURE 2.15 Bear Put Spread Risk/Reward Profile

Bear Put Spread

Overview: Bearish. Expect the stock to move lower. Purchase a put and sell another put at a lower strike price for a net debit. There is no margin requirement because the short put is covered by the long put. Use a bear put spread over a long put when puts are overpriced or the stock is only expected to move somewhat lower (Figure 2.15).

Position: Long XYZ $50 Put + short XYZ $45 Put.

Maximum risk: Limited to initial debit paid.

Maximum reward: Limited to the difference between the strikes minus initial debit paid.

Breakeven: Long put strike – debit paid.

Greek profile: Bear put spreads are net long Deltas with downward bias and generally net short time decay. Although these spreads are somewhat neutral on volatility, they still have a long volatility bias, which is evident on large changes in volatility.

Long Straddle

Overview: No initial directional bias. Purchase a call and a put at the same strike price and expiration month. Expect a large price breakout but not sure of direction. The position makes money if the stock moves up or down beyond the breakeven points by expiration. Want as much time as possible to expiration to give the

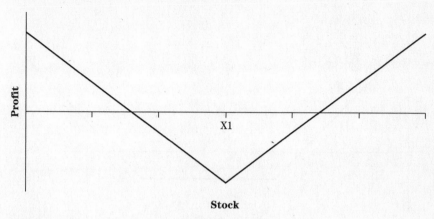

FIGURE 2.16 Long Straddle Risk/Reward Profile

stock time to make a large move in either direction and reduce effect of time decay on both options. Best to use before a specific event that will move the stock (earnings report, litigation result, etc.) or when the price is expected to break out from a consolidation pattern assuming IV is not relatively high (Figure 2.16).

Position: Long XYZ $50 Call + long XYZ $50 Put.

Maximum risk: Limited to combined debit paid.

Maximum reward: Unlimited on the upside; limited on the downside to strike – debit paid because stock can only fall to $0.

Breakeven points: Strike price +/– combined debit paid.

Greek profile: A long straddle, with a long call and a long put, is initially very close to Delta neutral, as the + call Delta and – put Delta mostly offset each other. However, as the underlying starts to move, the position will shift to a directional bias in either direction, depending on the underlying's move. The long straddle is also short Theta and long volatility.

Long Strangle

Overview: No initial directional bias. Purchase an OTM call and an OTM put. Lower cost than a long straddle but requires an even greater move in the stock in either direction to be profitable. Establish the position with as much time to expiration as possible to give the stock sufficient time to make the large required move for the position to be profitable and to reduce the effect of time decay on both options. As with straddles, it is best to use before a

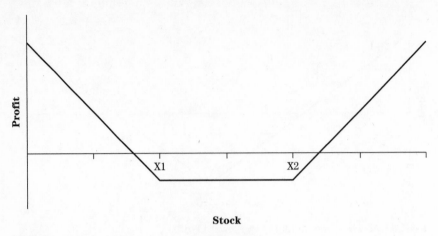

FIGURE 2.17   Long Strangle Risk/Reward Profile

specific event (earnings, Food and Drug Administration announce-
ment, etc.) or when the price is expected to break out from a consolidation pattern assuming IV is not relatively high (Figure 2.17).
Position: Long XYZ $55 Call + long XYZ $45 Put.
Maximum risk: Limited to combined debit paid.
Maximum reward: Unlimited on the upside; limited on the downside to
put strike – combined debit paid because stock can only fall to $0.
Breakeven points: (a) Long call strike + combined debit.
(b) Long put strike – combined debit.
Greek profile: A long strangle, with a long call and a long put, is initially very close to Delta neutral as the + call Delta and – put
Delta mostly offset each other. However, as the underlying starts
to move, the position will shift to a directional bias in either direction, depending on the underlying's move. The long strangle is also
short Theta and long volatility.

Short Straddle

Overview: Neutral strategy. Sell a call and a put at the same strike
price and expiration date. Expect the stock to move sideways until expiration and have options expire worthless or shrink in value.
Extremely risky position due to the presence of two naked options.
Use as short a time to expiration as possible to take advantage of
time decay on both short options and not give the stock time to
make a significant move away from the short strike. Margin is required as a result of naked options (Figure 2.18).

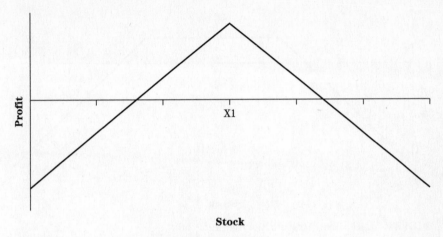

FIGURE 2.18 Short Straddle Risk/Reward Profile

Position: Short XYZ $50 Call + short XYZ $50 Put.

Maximum risk: Unlimited on the upside; limited on the downside to strike – combined credit received because stock can only fall to $0.

Maximum reward: Limited to combined credit received.

Breakeven points: Strike price +/– combined credit received.

Greek profile: A short straddle, with a short call and a short put, is initially very close to Delta neutral, as the – short call Delta and + short put Delta mostly offset each other. However, as the underlying starts to move, the position will shift to a directional bias in either direction, depending on the underlying's move. The short straddle is also long Theta and short volatility.

Short Strangle

Overview: Neutral strategy. Sell an OTM call and an OTM put. Expect the stock to move sideways and be between the short strikes at expiration. Extremely risky position due to the presence of two naked options. A wider profit zone than a short straddle due to the difference between the short strikes, but smaller credit received. Use as short time to expiration as possible to take advantage of the time decay of both OTM options and not give the stock time to move against you. Margin is required due to the presence of naked options, but slightly less than in the case of a short straddle (Figure 2.19).

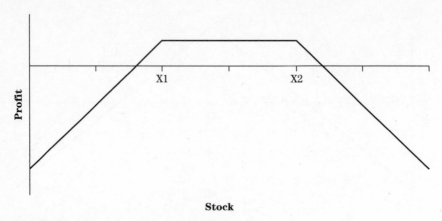

FIGURE 2.19   Short Strangle Risk/Reward Profile

Position: Short XYZ $55 Call + short XYZ $45 Put.

Maximum risk: Unlimited on the upside; limited on the downside to lower strike – credit received because stock can only fall to $0.

Maximum reward: Limited to total credit received.

Breakeven points: (a) Short call strike + credit received
(b) Short put strike – credit received.

Greek profile: A short strangle, with a short call and a short put, is initially very close to Delta neutral, as the – short call Delta and + short put Delta mostly offset each other. However, as the underlying starts to move, the position will shift to a directional bias in either direction, depending on the underlying's move. The short strangle is also long Theta and short volatility.

ADVANCED SPREADS

Call Ratio Spread

Overview: Expect the stock to move sideways or slightly higher. Purchase a call and sell more calls at a higher strike price in a ratio of 1:2 or 1:3. Combination of a bull call spread and naked calls. Recommend that the position be opened for a credit, which removes the potential for loss if the stock moves lower and calls expire worthless. A short time to expiration is preferred to take advantage of the time decay in short options and not give the stock time

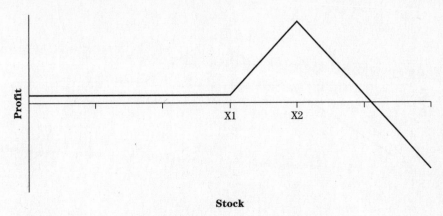

Profit

Stock

X1   X2

FIGURE 2.20 Call Ratio Spread Risk/Reward Profile (Net Credit)

to move very high in price and produce a loss. Margin is required due to the presence of extra naked calls (Figure 2.20).

Position: Long XYZ $50 Call + short two XYZ $55 Calls (1:2 ratio).

Maximum risk: Unlimited on the upside. Limited on the downside to initial debit paid or none if position is opened for credit.

Maximum reward: Short call strike – long call strike plus/minus credit received/debit paid.

Breakeven points: Initial credit (1): short strike + difference in strike prices + credit.

Initial debit (2): (a) short strike + difference in strike prices – debit; (b) long strike + debit.

Greek profile: Delta bias of call ratio spreads (CRS) can be negative, positive, or neutral, depending on location of the strikes relative to the underlying stock price and the distance between the long and short strikes. Moneyness and distance between strikes also affects whether the CRS is long or short Theta and volatility.

Put Ratio Spread

Overview: Expect the stock to move sideways or slightly lower. Purchase a put, and sell more puts at a lower strike price in a ratio of 1:2 or 1:3. Combination of a bear put spread and naked puts. Recommend that position be opened for a credit, which removes the potential for loss if the stock moves higher and puts expire worthless. A short time to expiration is preferred to take advantage of the time decay in short options and not give the stock time

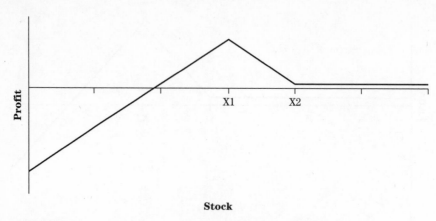

FIGURE 2.21   Put Ratio Spread Risk/Reward Profile (Net Credit)

to move very low in price and produce a loss. Margin is required
due to the presence of extra naked puts (Figure 2.21).

Position: Long XYZ $55 Put, short two XYZ $50 Puts (1:2 ratio). Maximum risk: Downside is substantial but limited to short strike –
difference between strikes –/+ credit received/debit paid. Upside
is limited to initial debit paid or no risk if position is opened for
credit.

Maximum reward: Long put strike – short put strike +/– credit re-
ceived/debit paid.

Breakeven Points: Initial credit (1): short strike – difference between
strikes – credit.

Initial debit (2): (a) short strike - difference between strikes + debit;
(b) long strike – debit.

Greek profile: Delta bias of put ratio spreads (PRS) can be negative,
positive, or neutral, depending on location of the strikes relative
to the underlying stock price and the distance between the long
and short strikes. Moneyness and distance between strikes also
affects whether the PRS is long or short Theta and volatility.

Call Ratio Backspread

Overview: Bullish strategy. Expect the stock to make a large move
higher. Purchase calls and sell fewer calls at a lower strike, usually in a ratio of 1:2 or 2:3. The lower strike short calls finance the
purchase of the greater number of long calls, and the position is
usually entered into for no cost or a net credit. The stock has to

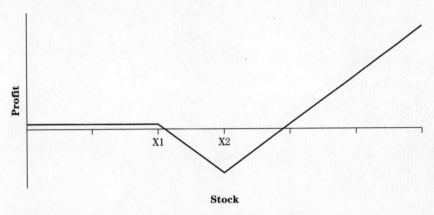

FIGURE 2.22 Call Ratio Backspread Risk/Reward Profile (Net Credit)

make a large enough move for the gain in the long calls to over-come the loss in the short calls because the maximum loss is at the long strike at expiration. Because the stock needs to make a large move higher for the backspread to make a profit, use as long a time to expiration as possible (Figure 2.22).

Position: Short XYZ $50 Call, long two XYZ $55 Calls (1:2).

Maximum risk: Long Strike–short strike minus/plus credit received/debit paid.

Maximum reward: Upside is unlimited. Downside is limited to initial credit received, if any.

Breakeven points: Initial debit (1): long strike + difference between strikes + debit

Initial credit (2): (a) short strike + credit.

(b) long strike + difference between strikes – credit.

Greek profile: Delta bias of call ratio backspreads (CRBS) can be negative, positive, or neutral, depending on location of the strikes relative to the underlying stock price and the distance between the long and short strikes. Moneyness and distance between strikes also affects whether the CRBS is long or short Theta and volatility.

Put Ratio Backspread

Overview: Bearish strategy. Expect the stock to make a large move lower. Purchase puts and sell fewer puts at a higher strike price, usually in a ratio of 1:2 or 2:3. The higher strike puts finance the purchase of the greater number of long puts, and the position is usually entered into for no cost or a net credit. The stock has to

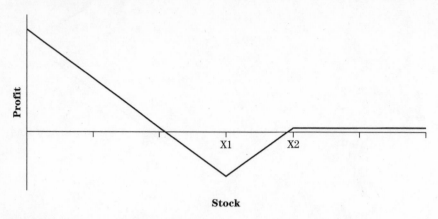

FIGURE 2.23   Put Ratio Backspread Risk/Reward Profile (Net Credit)

make a large enough move lower for the gain in the long puts to overcome the loss in the short puts because the maximum loss is at the long strike at expiration. Because the stock needs to make a large move lower for the backspread to make a profit, use as long a time to expiration as possible (Figure 2.23).

Position: Short XYZ $55 Put + long two XYZ $50 Puts (1:2).

Maximum risk: Short strike – long strike +/– debit paid/credit received.

Maximum reward: Downside is substantial but limited to long strike–difference between strikes –/+ debit/credit. Upside is limited to initial credit received if any.

Breakeven points: Initial debit (1): long strike–difference between strikes – debit.

Initial credit (2): (a) short strike – credit.

(b) long strike–difference between strikes + credit.

Greek profile: Delta bias of put ratio backspreads (PRBS) can be negative, positive, or neutral, depending on location of the strikes relative to the underlying stock price and the distance between the long and short strikes. Moneyness and distance between strikes also affects whether the PRBS is long or short Theta and volatility.

Long Butterflies

Overview: At-the-money long butterflies are generally nondirectional, looking for rangebound price action around the middle strikes. Directional bias can be created by choosing OTM/ITM strikes for

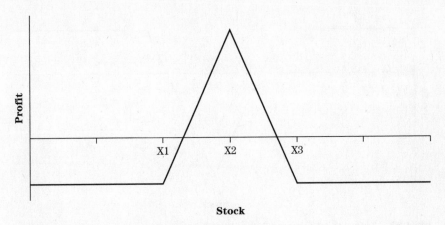

FIGURE 2.24 Long Butterfly Risk/Reward Profile

the body. Established using all calls or all puts and done for a net debit. For example, a long call butterfly is created by purchasing a call, selling two calls at a higher strike, and purchasing another call at an even higher strike, with the strike prices evenly spaced apart. The maximum reward occurs when the stock is right at short strikes at expiration. The number of options sold equals the number of options purchased (Figure 2.24).

Position: Long $45 Call/Put + short two $50 Calls/Puts + long $55 Call/Put.

Maximum risk: Limited to debit paid.

Maximum reward: Difference between long strike and short strike – debit paid.

Breakeven Points: (a) Lowest Strike + debit paid.
                        (b) Highest strike – debit paid.

Greek profile: An at-the-money butterfly is initially Delta neutral, but a Delta bias can be introduced by using, for example, OTM calls or OTM puts for the middle strikes. A long butterfly is generally long Theta and short volatility.

Short Butterflies

Overview: Initially nondirectional where you expect the stock to make a large move higher or lower but are not sure of direction. Established by using all calls or puts and done for a net credit. For example, a short call butterfly is created by selling a call, purchasing

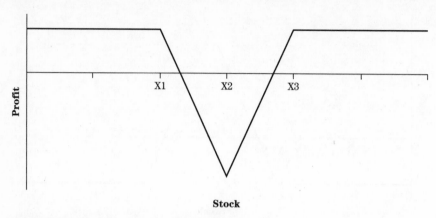

FIGURE 2.25 Short Butterfly Risk/Reward Profile

two calls at a higher strike price, and selling another call at an even higher strike, with the strike prices evenly apart. The number of long options equals the number of short options (Figure 2.25).

Position: Short $45 Call/Put + long two $50 Calls/Puts + short $55 Call/Put.

Maximum risk: Difference between long and short strikes – credit received.

Maximum reward: Limited to credit received.

Breakeven points: (a) Lowest strike + credit received.
                            (b) Highest strike – credit received.

Greek profile: An at-the-money short butterfly is initially Delta neutral, but a Delta bias can be introduced by using OTM calls or OTM puts for the middle strikes. A short butterfly is generally short Theta and long volatility.

Long Calendar Spreads

Overview: At-the-money long calendars are generally nondirectional, looking for rangebound price action, and may sometimes be used solely as a play on volatility skews. Directional bias can be created by choosing OTM strikes. Established by using all calls or all puts where you are short a front month call or put and long a back month call or put for a net debit using the same strike price. When using at-the-money strikes with a rangebound bias, you want the underlying to be as close as possible to the front month short strike price, so the option expires nearly worthless and the back month

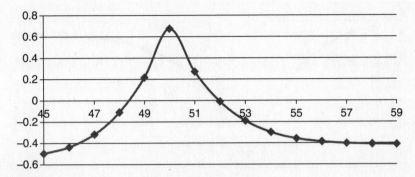

FIGURE 2.26 Long Calendar Risk/Reward Profile

still has significant time value premium. When using the long calendar as a volatility play, you want the higher skewed implied volatility of the front month to collapse faster than the implied volatility of the back month, so that the spread in premium between the two widens, or you want the equivalent volatility of both the short and the long to increase equally, since you are net long volatility (see Greek profile), and the position will gain in value (Figure 2.26).

Position: Short MAY XYZ $50 Call + long JUNE XYZ $50 Call.

Maximum risk: Limited to net debit paid.

Maximum reward: At MAY expiration, significant if the MAY option expires worthless.

Breakeven points: Breakeven points at the front month expiration are entirely dependent on the value of the long-term month implied volatilities, which affect the premium in the long-term month and are difficult to predict ahead of time.

Greek profile: At-the-money long calendars are initially Delta/Gamma neutral, long Vega, and long Theta. You can add Delta/Gamma bias by shifting the strike price above or below the current underlying.

Short Calendar Spreads

Overview: At-the-money short calendars are initially nondirectional, looking for a big move in either direction, and often are primarily a play on volatility. Established by using all calls or all puts where you are long a front month call or put and short a back month call or put, for a net credit using the same strike price. When using at-the-money strikes, the position will profit from either a large move

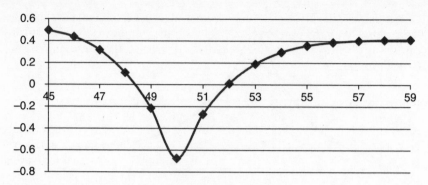

FIGURE 2.27 Short Calendar Risk/Reward Profile

in either direction or a roughly equal decrease in volatility for both options. Since you are long in the front month and short the back month option, your position requires margin, and has a potential for significant losses (Figure 2.27).

Position: Long MAY XYZ $50 Call + short JUNE XYZ $50 Call

Maximum risk: Significant if the long option expires worthless; the short longer term short option can have significant value, depending on IV at the long option month's expiration.

Maximum reward: Limited to net credit received.

Breakeven points: Breakeven points at the front month expiration are entirely dependent on the value of the long-term month implied volatilities, which affect the premium in the long-term month and are difficult to predict ahead of time.

Greek profile: At-the-money short calendars are initially Delta/Gamma neutral, short Vega, and short Theta. You can add Delta/Gamma bias by shifting the strike price above or below the current underlying.

THE GREEKS AND SPREAD TRADES

In addition to explaining the Greeks and the Greek profiles of the different strategies, we want to discuss in more detail how vertical spreads affect the net Greeks of your positions. Remember from the previous section that spreads refer to strategies like the bull call spread or the bear put spread. We feel that understanding the way spreads affect the Greeks might help you make decisions between similar strategies such as, for example, long calls and bull call spreads. Both are bullish strategies, but one may be more appropriate than the other in certain situations; comparing the risk/reward profiles is one way to help make the decisions, but so is comparing the net Greek profiles.

Delta/Gamma

As noted in our previous discussions on Delta and Gamma, these Greeks give us a good indication of the sensitivity of options to moves in the underlying price. This information is useful not only for looking at individual options but also for looking at spreads. A spread generally is an option position where you are both long and short the same number of calls or puts at different strike prices. Spreads may provide a lot of advantages over individual option positions, such as reduced costs and reduced risks, and if we look at the Delta/Gammas of spreads, we can also look at their sensitivities versus individual options.

Let us look at a typical 1-month-to-expiration bull call spread on IBM. With the stock trading at $100.50, the $100 Call is trading at $5.30, with a Delta of 0.55 and a Gamma of 0.03. The $110 Call in the same expiration month is trading at $1.45 with a Delta of 0.275 and a Gamma of 0.025. Assume that instead of purchasing the $100 Call, we decide to enter into a bull call spread that involves purchasing the $100 Call and selling the $110 Call to create the spread. Buying the $100 Call costs $5.30, but selling the $110 Call brings in a credit of $1.45, for a net debit of $3.85. In addition to a lower cost, the bull spread also has a limited maximum profit of the difference between the strikes minus the cost of the spread, which is in this case $6.15 ($10.00 spread minus $3.85 cost).

To calculate the net Delta of the spread, we follow the same math we used to derive the net debit or cost of the spread. We are long 0.55 Deltas through buying the $100 Call and short 0.275 Deltas by selling the $110 Call, for a net spread Delta of 0.275 and net spread Gamma of 0.005. Theoretically, if IBM increases in price by $1.00, based on the Deltas holding all other factors constant, the long $100 Call will move from $5.30 to $5.85, and the bull call spread will move from $3.85 to approximately $4.13.

Since you are both long and short options in the bull call spread, the net Delta reflects the reduced sensitivity to price movements of spreads versus single long options. This is one of the trade-offs between the reduced costs/risks of the spread versus the decreased price sensitivity. A common misperception from beginner option traders usually arises when they purchase their first spread trade such as a bull call spread. The stock will make a nice move higher, but the spread moves only a small amount, and the trader will wonder why. Holding all other factors constant, a smaller net Delta is the reason but not one that makes the spread a bad trade. As with single options, as the spread moves from out of the money to at the money, the net Gammas of the spread keep ticking higher and push the net Delta of the spread higher as well. So the reduced sensitivity simply means the spread might need more of a move in the underlying for the Deltas to be significant.

With any spread, you can easily calculate the net Deltas/Gammas to see the sensitivity of the position. As with individual options, understanding the sensitivity of your position to moves in the underlying will help you make better strike selections (i.e., in the money versus out of the money) or at least better understand how your position is affected by the strikes you select. Moreover, you will hopefully avoid unrealistic expectations, such as when beginners choose a set of strikes for a spread and are disappointed when the spread does not move as fast or as far as they had hoped. Checking the net Deltas will give you the accurate representation of your position's sensitivity so you are aware of what is most likely to happen to your spread with respect to the underlying and not what you hope will happen. Having an objective understanding of these points prior to entering an option position will not only help you understand how options work but also help you make better trading decisions.

Vega

Changes in implied volatility do have a significant effect on the price of options, but we might not always want to be susceptible to Vega risk when entering certain positions. Understanding Vega and how to use vertical spreads will allow us to somewhat hedge against change in volatility that could negatively affect our positions. A vertical spread is when you are long and short either calls or puts within the same expiration month but using different strikes. When you are both long and short calls, for example, you are also both long and short Vega, which will cancel each other out for the most part and hedge to some degree against changes in volatility.

Let us look at an example to see how a spread can neutralize Vega risk to some extent. Assume that RIMM currently has a relatively high IV and is trading at $90 with a 1-month $90 Call trading at $7.00 and a Vega of 0.12, and the $100 Call is trading at $3.00 with a Vega of 0.11. If you bought the $90 Call outright because you were bullish on RIMM, your position could suffer a loss if for some reason IV dropped significantly from its current levels. Your position Vega would be 0.12, which is the Vega of the $90 Call. Therefore, you are taking a directionally biased position but are subject to Vega risk.

If you still want the same directional bias (bullish) without the significant Vega risk, then you can enter into a bull call spread by purchasing the

$90 Call for $7.00 and selling the $100 Call for $3.00, for a net debit of $4.00. To calculate the Vega of the spread, we simply take the Vega of the $90 Call (0.12) and subtract the Vega of the short $100 Call (0.11) to get the net Vega of the spread, which in this case is 0.01. Entering into the spread reduces our Vega exposure from 0.12 down to 0.01, and the position is essentially hedged at the inception from volatility shocks. If volatility changes significantly, the spread premium will still change, but you are still somewhat hedged.

Other Greeks and Spreads

We discussed two general examples of how understanding the Greeks not only better explains how certain spreads work but also allows us to make a comparison between spreads and single options trades to truly find the most appropriate strategy given the current circumstances. Although we focused on Delta and Vega, the same analysis can be applied to the Greek Theta. The point is that if you understand the Greeks and the different strategies, you can truly make an informed decision about how different strategies will react under the same circumstances and how to take advantage of spreads to reduce the risks of certain Greek factors. Basically, the more information you have at your fingertips, the more intelligent trading decisions you can make. We explore a method in how to truly use the Greeks to make more intelligent decisions in the next section.

VALUABLE DERIVATIVE TRADERS PROGRAM

Mastering the individual tools of the trader, especially the Greeks, is an important step in obtaining a good detailed knowledge of what options are and how they work. However, the real secret to becoming a better trader is being able to effectively use all these tools together to make better trading decisions and avoid common mistakes, as well as the not-so-obvious ones. We have put together a basic systematic approach to help you successfully apply the tools discussed in this chapter and avoid the mistakes that cost traders money. We call this program the Valuable Derivative Traders Program based on the letters V, D, and T, which are useful in helping you remember the three main steps to this approach. The three letters represent the three main Greek symbols, Vega, Delta, and Theta, and outline the basic steps in our program to teach you the right way to apply the tools of the trader.

Step 1: VEGA and Implied Volatility (IV)

The first step in approaching a trading decision on an option trade is to analyze the implied volatility of the underlying. IV has such a significant effect on option pricing that we need to first have a general idea how the market is pricing the underlying's options relative to how it has been priced in the past and also look at the IV for clues or information. The first question to be asked is whether there is an unusual spike or skew in the IV that might indicate that a major earnings report, FDA announcement, or other such significant event is pending.

For example, assume that after looking at stock XYZ's option chains, you notice that the MAY options are trading at an average IV of 80% and the JUNE and next few expiration months are trading at an average IV of 50%. There is a noticeable skew between the MAY options and how they are being priced and the rest of the other months. This skew tells us that something significant is expected to happen with respect to stock XYZ prior to MAY expiration, and before going any further, you need to investigate what that could be.

The skew means the MAY options are relatively expensive versus the remaining months, and you might not want to rush in and buy relatively overpriced options. Assuming you ignored this information and bought May calls, you could face significant IV Crush once whatever event is expected occurs, and those calls could go from an IV of 80% down to 50% to be more in line with the other months, leading to a significant loss of premium solely with respect to Vega exposure. Even if you are right on direction and stock XYZ moves higher, you could still lose money on the collapse in volatility. Therefore, we take a quick glance at the first few expiration months (usually current month, next month, and the one after that) and make sure there is no extraordinary skew. The implied volatility will not be exactly the same across these first three expiration months, so we are only looking for significant spikes or skews.

In addition to looking for a skew in volatility, we also want to know where implied volatility is in the expiration month we are looking at (choosing time to expiration is discussed later) and how that compares with where IV has been over the past year. As mentioned earlier in the chapter, you can use www.ivolatility.com to see historical IV price charts and then compare where the current IV is relative to its yearly range. Is IV at the lower end of its annual range? Is it near the upper end of its range? Is it somewhere in the middle?

You must also take into account whether the market has undergone any significant changes in its historical ranges of IV based on a change in the market environment. For example, up until August 2007, the overall market had a period of relatively low volatility, with VIX trading in a range of 9% to 20% for several years. After the initial shockwaves of the housing financial crisis became known, VIX spiked up into the 30s and more and did not come back down to the pre August 2007 levels. So you need to make an independent assessment of whether there has been any change in the market environment or circumstances such that the current IV levels might be entering a new range going forward. Studying the IV of the underlying and assessing whether its options are relatively cheap, relatively expensive, or about average is the first key step.

Once you have made an implied volatility determination, you can better match your IV analysis with a more appropriate strategy. That is why it is important to read and understand the Greek profile of every strategy discussed earlier in this chapter. For example, if IV is relatively high, then we can assume that IV might be high because of significant pending news, uncertainty surrounding the underlying, large price swings lower that raise IV, or increased expectations of large price swings. Either way, we know that we might be susceptible to Vega risk and want to either hedge that risk or enter a trade that can take advantage of falling implied volatility.

Based on this analysis, we can choose to use vertical spreads, such as bull call or bear put spreads, to make a directional trade and hedge somewhat against Vega risk. If the front-month volatility is skewed significantly higher, we could use a long calendar spread that sells the relatively more expensive front-month volatility and hedges it by buying relatively cheaper back-month volatility. We could look into butterflies, which are short Vega and could profit if IV drops as expected. On the other hand, we might be more tempted to avoid positions with too much Vega exposure, such as long straddles and long strangles or long calls or long puts. If we enter such positions without looking into implied volatility, we could suffer losses purely from a collapse in IV, even if the underlying stock moves as expected.

If implied volatility is relatively low, then we want to look to strategies that give us Vega exposure, such as long calls, long puts, long straddles, or even ratio backspreads. This allows us to profit not only if the underlying moves as expected but also if volatility increases. Therefore, it does not matter if our trade is purely a directional one or one looking to exploit an extreme in volatility; we must take IV into account when selecting our strategies to make Vega work for us and not against us. If implied volatility is somewhere in the middle range and not at any specific extreme, then we really have no specific indication with respect to volatility, nor can we make any clear-cut volatility determination.

Therefore, the first step is to do a little research on the IV of the options you are considering and check out the historical IV range to make a determination of relative pricing. Once you have some direction from your analysis of IV, you can then match it up with your directional or nondirectional bias in the underlying and start narrowing down the option strategies to a specific few that are the most appropriate, given the current values of volatility. So this first step helps to weed out inappropriate strategies and, more important, guides us to strategies better suited to the levels of volatility.

Step 2: Delta and Strike Selection

Once we have analyzed volatility and made a determination of the appropriate option strategy, we then move on to Delta analysis, which involves sensitivity to moves in the underlying. Remember that with single calls or puts, we looked at Delta/Gamma to see the sensitivity of in-the-money, at-the-money, and out-of-the-money options in relation to the amount of premium in the option. We know that in-the-money options generally have higher sensitivities in exchange for higher relative costs and that out-of-the-money options are relatively cheaper but with much lower sensitivity to moves in the underlying. At-the-money options have the best balance between cost and sensitivity. The same is generally true for most option strategies, not just long calls or long puts.

One of the hardest parts of trading options with a directional bias is that we have to be correct on not only direction but also the magnitude of the move, depending on which strike we choose. For example, if we choose far-out-of-the-money strike calls, then not only does the stock have to move higher for the position to generate a profit but also it really has to make a significant move higher because of the reduced sensitivity of that far-out-of-the-money call. Therefore, at this stage of the program, we need to determine our directional bias and assess to what extent we expect the underlying to move.

For long calls and long puts, it becomes a direct trade-off between sensitivity and cost. Far-out-of-the-money calls are certainly cheaper but give up a lot of sensitivity, and this works well only if we expect a move large enough for the Gammas to kick in and push those Deltas higher. It is often a good idea to pay a little more for the option and move closer to at the money or even in the money to take advantage of the gearing or leverage that options provide. The same is true with vertical spreads, such as bull call and bear put spreads, which have smaller Delta/Gammas than outright options. One small exception is the rare situation where you feel very strongly that the underlying is about to make a very strong move in one direction and you can sacrifice some of the sensitivity for cheaper cost.

Whenever you want a directional bias, you can adjust any strategy by moving the strikes in the money or out of the money. This works well for taking a nondirectional strategy and adding some directional bias. For example, an at-the-money butterfly has a Delta/Gamma close to zero, as it is a neutral position and there is no sensitivity at its inception. Moreover, if the intent is nondirectional, such as in the previously mentioned butterfly or even the long calendar, you actually do not want any increased sensitivities, so choosing the at-the-money strike makes the most sense.

However, understanding Delta now gives you the ability to add price sensitivity to your positions to take full advantage of your knowledge. For example, the butterfly using an at-the-money strike for the body is Delta neutral and, as described in the strategy summaries, is also short volatility. Assume we want the short volatility aspects of the butterfly but want the position to actually have a positive Delta sensitivity such that it makes money if the underlying moves higher. We can no longer choose the at-the-money strikes because if the underlying starts to move higher away from the at-the-money strikes, then the butterfly will lose value. However, if we shift the butterfly higher, using out-of-the-money calls, for example, then the butterfly still can be short volatility, but it is no longer Delta neutral; it is now slightly Delta/Gamma positive. If the market moves higher and volatility drops, then the butterfly is short Vega and long Delta and will have two ways of increasing in value. Thus we can shift a position out of the money or in the money to add sensitivity to an otherwise neutral strategy.

Basically, we need to be aware of the net Delta/Gamma position of any strategy we enter into so that we know exactly in what way it should react to moves in the underlying. The sensitivity analysis tells us whether the underlying needs to make a little move, a large move, or a sideways move, and you can see if the position and strike selection matches your expectations. Of course, you have to have realistic expectations going into the position on where the underlying is likely to move or not move. But the key aspect of Step 2 is making sure the sensitivity of the position to moves in the underlying matches your bias and expectations so that you know you are choosing the most appropriate strikes or strategy.

Step 3: Theta and How Much Time to Expiration

Once you have analyzed implied volatility to better choose the most appropriate strategy (Step 1) and then compared different strikes to see which ones provide the net Delta/Gamma profile that best fits your outlook on the underlying (Step 2), then it is time to figure out what expiration months to choose for your strategy. Since options are decaying assets, it is not enough to be right on volatility and direction; you also need to be somewhat accurate on the timing of the expected move in the underlying. Your understanding of Theta and its characteristics will help you make the best decision you can.

When purchasing long options, you are susceptible to time decay in your options if the stock moves sideways. For each day the stock does not move in the right direction, your option loses value. This loss in value is smaller the further out you go in time. Therefore, the best way to minimize the effect of time value on your long option position is to use options with as much time to expiration as possible, based on your risk/reward requirements. When purchasing a long call or long put, for example, you want to have as much time as possible, not only for your option to move in the money but also to reduce the effects of time decay in case the underlying stock moves sideways for a period of time. As we saw, Theta is smaller the further out in time you go, so giving yourself more time to be right reduces the risks from Theta that exist in the short-term months.

Most traders do not understand this concept of time value or time decay because they think short term. When a stock is expected to move, many beginners fall into the habit of buying options with less than 30 days to expiration because they are the cheapest. The stock begins to move back and forth—that is, sideways—and traders wonder why the premium in their option begins to disappear so fast. That is why we really do not recommend purchasing options with short expiration periods, especially if they are out of the money. You have not only the stock potentially working against you but also time. Using long-term options will reduce the effect of time decay greatly and therefore allow you to wait patiently for the expected move in the underlying stock without watching your money decay.

Just as we use time decay in our favor with the purchase of long-term options, we can also use time decay in our favor when we have a position of short options. As we saw from our analysis of Theta, options decay fastest in the last 30 to 45 days prior to expiration. When we sell options, we want them to expire worthless or buy them back at a lower price for a profit. For example, if AMZN is at $55 and we are bearish on the stock, we could sell a naked $55 Call and hope to keep the entire premium collected if AMZN does not move above $55 and the $55 Call expires worthless (a very risky trade, which we do not recommend, but show for illustrative purposes).

Using the AMZN $55 Call example, assume we could sell either a 4-month $55 Call for $6.40 or a 1-month $55 Call for $3.15. At first glance, one would be more inclined to sell the 4-month call to collect a higher premium (more than double that of the 1-month call). However, there are two important reasons not to sell the long-term call. First, the more time to expiration, the more chances for the stock to move higher and produce a loss on our naked call. Therefore, we want to give the stock as little time as possible to move against us.

Second, the premium will suffer hardly any time decay in the first month or so because it is so far away from expiration and Theta is relatively small. Time decay works to your benefit on a short option because it decreases the premium of the option, thereby producing a profit for the short seller. You should not only take advantage of the underlying moving lower to make a profit on your short $55 Call but also take advantage of time decay. If you sell the 1-month $55 Call, you will take in less premium, but you have a better chance of making money quicker if AMZN moves sideways, lower, or slightly higher. Time decay will eat into the premium of the $55 Call, and the amount it swallows will get bigger and bigger as expiration approaches.

Theta is also relevant for more complex positions and spreads. If you are considering long straddles or long strangles, for example, based on your program analysis, then you have to be concerned with Theta as you are long both calls and puts. You certainly want to give your position time to make money and avoid buying these type of combinations using front months. Therefore, if your volatility analysis shows relatively low levels and you are looking to be Delta neutral, then Step 3 should guide you to avoid front expiration months with high rates of decay. Of course, as with all the other risk factors, there is a balance between benefit and cost. You do not have to use the farthest expiration months possible. The analysis is just guiding you to avoid using front-month options for these positions on account of the high Theta exposure.

If you know the Greek profile of the various advanced spreads and combinations, then figuring out whether your focus should be on the front or later months when choosing an expiration is much easier. For example, an at-the-money long butterfly is short Vega and long Theta, and therefore, it will profit if volatility drops, time passes, and the underlying stays in a tight trading range. If you choose a 4-month expiration, then you will not get any significant Theta, and you actually give the underlying more time to move away from your butterfly short strikes. A butterfly is great option strategy, but you will negate any benefits of the strategy if you ignore its Greeks and do not use them to your advantage. In this example, the Theta profile will convince you to choose a much shorter time to expiration to put Theta to work for you.

Putting the Program to Work

The Valuable Derivative Trader Program is set up to make you think methodically about entering into an option position while taking into account all significant risk factors. The order of Vega, Delta, and Theta is done on purpose, as we feel that this is the best order to consider the risk factors in working through your analysis. Working through each step will eliminate mistakes and focus you toward the most appropriate strategy, strike, and expiration month for your assumptions or expectations and put the risk factors to work for you. Understanding the Greek profile for each strategy makes it easier to know which strategies work best in which situations and will get your mind working the right way.

INTRODUCTION TO TRADE ADJUSTMENTS

This chapter is intended to provide you with a good detailed knowledge of all the tools required to truly understand what options are, how they work, and how to use them with a risk manager's mind-set. We went into great detail on the Greeks as risk management tools and also to really demonstrate how different factors affect the pricing of options and how we can use this information to improve our trading decisions and avoid some common mistakes. With these tools, application of the SCORE overall trade approach from Chapter 1, and the Valuable Derivative Traders Program in this chapter, you have the groundwork needed to trade options effectively and devise an efficient trading approach.

The remaining chapters of this book are meant to focus on what you can do as possible trade adjustments once you have entered the trade, with the assumption that all of the key risk management analysis and preparation have gone into the trade already, using the approach described here. However, once in the trade, your role as a risk manager does not end, and the flexibility and versatility of options that exist prior to entering the trade can also help you once you are in the trade and the underlying either moves as expected or a set of changed circumstances arises. *The Option Trader Handbook* is meant to give you an overview of the numerous trade adjustments that can be made to various option positions in different situations so that you can learn them and plan ahead on what adjustments, if any, you would make to your original position to adapt to changed circumstances, lock in profits, or partially hedge your position. Before moving on to the next chapters, we want to discuss some general principles and guidelines with respect to adjustments to make sure the learning process in the tools of the trader carry over to the rest of the book.

We want to explain our approach to adjustments in general. There are two general categories of adjustments when it comes to options. The first is using the Greeks on a portfolio basis to adjust specific risk factors such as Delta or Vega. With a good analytical software program, you can look at the instant net Greeks of your entire portfolio and determine what exposure your portfolio has to different risk factors. Once you identify your net exposure in any individual risk factor, you can then use another security, such as index options or futures, to counter or negate that Greek for the moment.

For example, if your portfolio of various option and stock positions has a net positive Delta value, then your entire portfolio has a risk exposure to a falling market that would hurt your overall portfolio. You could either close some of your long Delta positions to bring the net portfolio Delta back closer to zero to reduce some of the directional bias, or you could short index futures or buy index puts to add some negative Deltas to achieve the same results. However, we do not advocate this approach for the retail trader for several reasons.

One reason is that the portfolio Greek measurement is an instantaneous snapshot of the net risk exposure, and the underlying stocks or option positions in your portfolio are changing constantly. That means that the portfolio net Greek values will be changing constantly as well, and what might seem like a risk exposure one day may be negated the next day with a significant move in the overall market or in some of the underlying stocks in your portfolio. Therefore, we recommend that the investor should perform individual risk management on each position and understand the position Greeks to be able to address specific risks on each position rather than look at the portfolio as a whole.

A macro portfolio view has too many factors to track at once and will change much too frequently to give useful information to the average retail investor. A market maker or large institution that has a huge number of positions and must manage significant portfolio risks on a daily basis certainly can utilize net portfolio Greek exposures to hedge and balance their large book of positions, especially market makers who try to flatten their risks on a daily basis to profit from the bid/ask spreads. The large institutions need to use portfolio Greeks because of the enormous size and number of their positions, but the average retail trader will not be able to take advantage of the macro Greek data in the same way.

We advocate that the average retail trader should avoid thinking in macro Greek terms and focus more on being aware of the net Greek exposure of each position since your total positions will be much smaller than those of a major institution and easier to assess. You should use the individual position risk exposure information and assess your risks in a qualitative way. For example, assume you have about 10 different option positions and 7 of the 10 positions are positive Vega positions. This means that these positions are basically long volatility, are positively affected by increasing volatility, and will get hurt if volatility falls across the board. Therefore, the qualitative assessment is that your net risk exposure is long volatility, and you should analyze whether this is in agreement with your assessment of overall market volatility and either reduce some of your long volatility exposure by closing some positions or perhaps adding some positions in general that might profit from falling volatility.

In our view, this kind of assessment is a much better skill set to develop in analyzing option positions for the retail trader with a more manageable book of positions, versus looking at a net Greek portfolio number as large institutions do, which does not give you any qualitative information you need to understand your true risk exposure. It forces your mind to use all the tools of the trader together and make qualitative assessments that will help you become a better trader and truly think like a risk manager.

A second reason that we do not advocate looking at net portfolio Greek values and adjustments for the retail trader is that since the portfolio Greek values are instantaneous calculations, they will change frequently, minute by minute, as the markets move. If you were trying to hedge your risk exposure, you might spend all day trading and adding options or stock positions simply to balance out your portfolio Greeks—and spend a lot of money in transaction costs to do so. You will lose focus on the actual risks and rewards of your individual positions and spend more time hedging either on an hourly or daily basis, as the Greeks constantly change.

Large institutions or market makers with huge option portfolios to hedge can certainly take advantage of lower transaction and operating costs to hedge these risks since their exposure is large and they are trying to lock in portfolio profits. The average retail trader, even with today's discounted brokerage commission rates, will swallow up all of the profits by trying to hedge constantly. You are better off making qualitative assessments that might require fewer and far less frequent portfolio adjustments (e.g., perhaps simply closing one long Delta position) and lower transaction costs than trying to balance your risks on a macro basis. For these reasons, we do not discuss portfolio Greek adjustments in the following chapters.

We also will not discuss position-specific Greek adjustments in this book. We feel that the Greeks make you understand the risk exposure of the position when you first enter it, and as the underlying moves, your understanding of the Greeks means you already know what is likely to happen with the position moving forward. Your concern at that point is the maximum risk/reward of the position, and it is the gain or loss you are trying to lock in, hedge against, or limit. The Greeks are merely the explanation of why the position is moving the way it is.

For example, if you enter a long call position that is long Delta, the stock can either move higher or lower, and we know that based on the initial Delta values and our understanding of the Delta/Gamma relationship, how the position should react, keeping all other factors constant. Once the position is underway, the biggest concern for the retail trader is managing the risk/reward relationship that the trader had going into the trade. We always say you need to know how much you can lose and how much you can make for every trade you enter into, and that must be monitored constantly as long as you are in the position. Changes in the Delta exposure are directly reflected in the profit and loss profile of the position as the underlying moves. In other words, as the underlying moves higher, the Deltas increase, and profit increases as well, holding all other factors constant.

The adjustments discussed in this book are focused on whether we are locking in a profit, hedging our gains, limiting our losses, or adjusting the bias of the position based on changed circumstances. We are managing the risk/reward profile, and all the adjustments are presented in this way, since the ultimate goal is to make money and limit losses. Even if we were to look at the adjustments from the perspective of the position Greeks, the end result would be the same, which is focused on adjusting the profit profile or the risks. However, we feel that focusing on the specific Greeks for an adjustment to a single position would lose sight of the overall picture of the position and your risk and trade management plans. In this case, qualitative assessments on your specific strategy and expectations of how the underlying is going to move, mixed in with quantitative analysis of the actual profit and loss profile, will lead to a successful risk management type of analysis and better adjustment decisions.

In addition to explaining our rationale for focusing our adjustments on the actual profits and losses at expiration and comparing the original to the adjusted position, we also need to make one clear point to the reader that might get overlooked, given the numerous adjustments discussed in the following chapters. Adjustments are a tool, like many of the tools discussed in this chapter. Learning the different adjustments that are possible gives you a much deeper understanding of how options work and the relationship between different strategies, since adjustments are merely methods to transform positions from one strategy into another.

However, many adjustments are appropriate only in certain situations, and many times, closing a position is the superior trade choice over adjusting a position. The key to studying trade adjustments is not just in knowing what adjustments to use in which situations but also in knowing when to adjust and when to either let the position stand on its own or close it outright. Throughout this book, we caution the reader to understand this important point: Just because you can adjust a position does not mean you should. The same risk/reward analysis you performed before entering a position is also required before adjusting a position to determine whether an adjustment is advisable and, if so, which adjustment. Most of the determination over whether to adjust comes down to your own expectation of where the underlying is going to be at expiration and if you expect the circumstances underlying the original trade to change. This is not an exact science but a skill you develop over time as you experience different trading situations.

The best approach when it comes to trade adjustments is to compare the risk/reward profiles of the original trade versus the profiles of the position after the potential adjustment and then make the independent determination of whether the proposed adjustment adds to or subtracts from your position, improves it or makes it worse, reduces or increases your risks, limits or improves your profit potential, and better matches your changed assumptions regarding the underlying. Going through detailed analysis for an adjustment as though you were entering a new position will prevent you from making mistakes or overadjusting and will sometimes lead you to the conclusion that the best adjustment is either doing nothing or closing the trade. As long as you are making a rational decision, taking into account all the risk/reward factors, you will profit from it.

CHAPTER 3

Long Stock

INTRODUCTION

The most common form of investment is to buy a stock and hold it for the long haul. Say you are bullish on EBAY, for example, and buy 100 shares of stock. For each $1 increase in the price of the stock, you make $1 on each share. The maximum reward is unlimited because EBAY can keep moving higher, whereas the maximum loss is theoretically limited to the price of the stock because EBAY can go no lower than $0. Figure 3.1 represents the risk/reward profile of purchasing EBAY at $100.

Because options are derivatives whose value is based on the movement of the underlying stock, options can be used in conjunction with a long stock position to lock in a profit, hedge or limit a potential loss, or create an additional profit or leverage. This chapter covers the various adjustments that can be made to a long stock position using calls and puts and various combinations of the two. The goal, as always, is proper risk management. Whatever adjustment you make, always keep in mind what the adjusted risk/reward profile is and how it meshes with your expectations of the movement of the underlying stock. No one adjustment is better than another; each adjustment is suited for certain situations. The key is to not make an adjustment simply for the sake of trading. Each possible adjustment serves an investment purpose and you should understand the purpose of each adjustment to make the right investment decision.

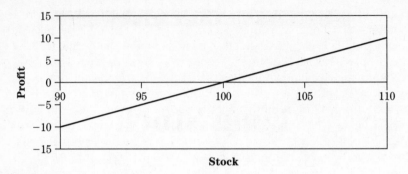

FIGURE 3.1   Long Stock

PROTECTIVE PUT

You can take out an insurance policy at the same time you initiate a long stock position by purchasing puts to protect against any downward movement in the stock until expiration. Because a put gives the holder the right to sell 100 shares of stock at a given strike price, the put hedges against any decline in the price of the stock below that strike. As with any insurance policy, the two main ingredients are the premium and the deductible. The premium is the cost of the insurance, and the deductible is the amount of loss you will bear before the protection of the insurance policy kicks in. With puts, the premium is the cost of the put, and the deductible depends on which strike price you select in relation to the price of the stock.

Let's assume you purchased 100 shares of EBAY at $100. In order to hedge against a drop in the price of EBAY, you could purchase a protective put in conjunction with the purchase of EBAY. Which strike price you choose will depend on the premium and deductible of the insurance policy that is needed. Assume that EBAY has options traded at the following prices with 3 months to expiration. Although you are long in EBAY, you are concerned about short-term weakness in the market and an upcoming earnings announcement and wish to acquire insurance against a drop in the price of the stock:

EBAY @ 100

EBAY 95 Put	$2.30
EBAY 100 Put	$4.60
EBAY 105 Put	$8.20

If you wish to hedge EBAY at $100, you can purchase one $100 Put for $4.60. This put will give you the right to sell EBAY at $100 at any time up until expiration and therefore hedge against a drop in EBAY price. The premium or cost of this insurance policy is the price paid for the put, $4.60. The deductible is the maximum loss incurred under the hedge. If EBAY is at $100 at expiration, the put will expire worthless for a maximum loss of $4.60. At any price below $100, the maximum loss on the position is $4.60. For example, if EBAY is at $97, you could exercise the put to sell the stock at $100 and break even on the stock position. However, you will lose the premium paid for the put, for a loss of $4.60. Therefore the deductible on this insurance policy is also $4.60 because that is the most you can lose. To illustrate the potential profit and loss of EBAY with the protective put, the following gives the results for the combined position at different prices at expiration (P/L indicates profit or loss):

EBAY	Stock P/L ($)	Put P/L ($)	Position P/L ($)
90	−10.00	+5.40	−4.60
95	−5.00	+0.40	−4.60
100	0.00	−4.60	−4.60
105	+5.00	−4.60	+0.40
110	+10.00	−4.60	+5.40

The breakeven point for this combined position is $104.60. At that price, the gain on EBAY of $4.60 offsets the loss on the put of $4.60. Adding the protective put raises the breakeven point due to the premium paid for the insurance. The breakeven point is equal to stock price + put premium. By adding the protective put, you have given up some of the upside profit in exchange for limiting your loss on the downside. Compare the risk/reward graphs of the protective put at $100 combined with stock versus the outright purchase of EBAY in Figure 3.2.

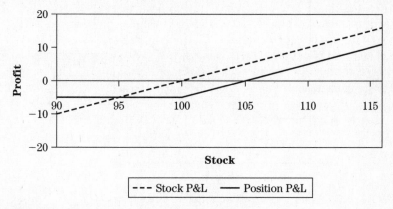

FIGURE 3.2 EBAY Long Stock and Protective Put

As with any insurance policy, there is a trade-off between the deductible and the premium. The deductible decreases if you increase the premium paid. You can increase the premium paid for the EBAY insurance, and thus decrease the deductible, by using an in-the-money protective put to hedge the long stock position. Using the option quotes just given, you can purchase the EBAY $105 Put for $8.20. Although the premium paid is higher, the maximum loss is now $3.20. For example, if EBAY is at $95 at expiration, the $5.00 loss on the stock is offset by the $1.80 gain on the put for a net loss of $3.20. If EBAY is at $105 at expiration, the $8.20 loss on the put is offset by the $5.00 gain on the stock for a net loss of $3.20. Therefore, although you pay a higher premium for an ITM put versus an ATM put ($8.20 vs. $4.60), the deductible, or maximum loss, is lower ($3.20 vs. $4.60).

If you select an OTM put, the premium paid is lower, but then the deductible is much higher. By purchasing the EBAY $95 Put for $2.30, you limit your maximum loss to $7.30. The protection of the put does not begin until EBAY moves below $95. Figure 3.3 compares the different risk/reward profiles on the combined EBAY stock and protective put using the different strike prices.

The strike price you choose depends on your level of risk tolerance, how much protection you wish to have, and your ability to pay. If you feel that there is a potential for a price shock in EBAY in the short term, then you might want the best insurance available, that is, the one with the lowest deductible. Therefore, you would choose the ITM put to hedge your position. If you feel the likelihood of a drop in price is low but still want some protection, then you might opt for the OTM put. As Figure 3.3

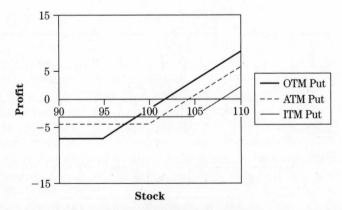

FIGURE 3.3 Protective Puts Using Different Strike Prices

indicates, changing the strike price not only changes the maximum loss of the position, it also adjusts the breakeven point. The lower the premium, the lower is the breakeven point. Therefore, the choice of which strike price to use when purchasing a put depends on whether you expect a large or small movement in the stock price and how much protection you need.

Stock Moves Higher

A protective put can also be applied to a long stock position after the stock has moved higher. If after a stock moves higher you have a concern of possible reversal in price but still wish to own the stock, the protective put can guarantee a minimum profit while hedging against any downside movement. More importantly, the protective put allows you to participate in any further upside movement in the stock for additional profits.

Assume the same EBAY stock was purchased at $100 and has risen to $110 with the following put prices:

EBAY @ $110

EBAY 105 Put	$2.30
EBAY 110 Put	$4.60
EBAY 115 Put	$8.20
EBAY 120 Put	$12.20

To hedge the possible drop in price of EBAY, you can adjust the position by adding the EBAY $110 Put for $4.60. The $110 Put guarantees that you can sell EBAY at $110 until expiration, no matter how far the stock price drops. The guaranteed profit is the difference between the strike price and the purchase price ($110 − $100 = $10.00) minus the premium paid for the put ($10.00 − $4.60 = $5.40). By adding the put to the long stock position, you have locked in a minimum profit of $5.40 until expiration, with the potential for greater profit should EBAY keep rising. By using an ATM put, you continue to earn more profit as the stock rises above the strike price. The adjustment has turned a risky trade of owning 100 shares of EBAY into a risk-free trade until expiration of the put. Figure 3.4 compares the long position in EBAY with the risk/reward profile once you add the protective put at $110.

You can increase the guaranteed profit by selecting a higher strike price. If you use the EBAY $120 Put at $12.20, the guaranteed minimum profit is calculated as $120 − $100 − $12.20 = $7.80. The trade-off for selecting a higher strike is that the stock would have to make a larger move upward before the overall profit increases above the guaranteed minimum.

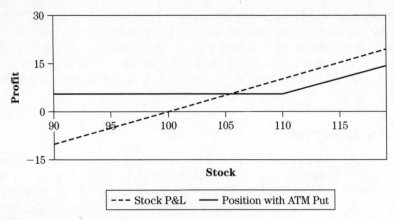

FIGURE 3.4   Long EBAY versus ATM Protective Put

For example, using the $120 strike price, we see that the position will not make more than $7.80 until the stock rises above $120, as indicated in the following (P/L indicates profit or loss):

EBAY	Stock P/L ($)	Put P/L ($)	Position P/L ($)
95	−5.00	+12.80	+7.80
100	0.00	+7.80	+7.80
105	+5.00	+2.80	+7.80
110	+10.00	−2.20	+7.80
115	+15.00	−7.20	+7.80
120	+20.00	−12.20	+7.80
125	+25.00	−12.20	+12.80

The position does not make more than the minimum profit unless the stock moves above the strike price. Therefore the trade-off of using a higher strike for increased minimum profit is that we need a bigger move in the underlying stock to make more than the minimum profit. This is a bearish hedge because it allows for a greater profit on the downside and is used when the stock is not expected to move much higher.

If you want to lock in a profit but feel that it is very likely that EBAY will move much higher than $110, then the selection of the strike for the protective put is very important. With an at-the-money put, you can still participate on the upside of the stock movement, although the minimum profit is lower. By increasing the strike price, you get a larger minimum profit, but then you need a larger move in the stock price to earn more than the locked-in profit.

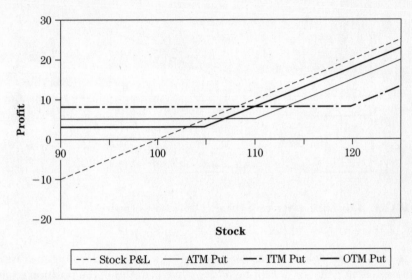

FIGURE 3.5 Protective Puts Using Different Strikes

If you choose an out-of-the-money strike price, then the guaranteed profit is lower. However, the position is already worth more than the minimum profit because the stock is above the strike price. If you select the EBAY $105 Put, the guaranteed minimum profit is $105 − $100 − $2.30 = $2.70. However, at $110 the total position has a profit of $7.70 ($10 profit in stock − $2.30 premium of put) versus a profit of $5.40 if you used the ATM $110 Put. This is a more bullish hedge because it allows for greater profit on the upside while still locking in a risk-free profit. Figure 3.5 compares the risk/reward profile of your adjusted EBAY position using the ITM, ATM, and OTM protective puts.

Stock Moves Lower

It is a straightforward adjustment to add a protective put to a stock position that has increased in value. What happens if the stock drops in price? If the stock is dropping and you feel it will continue to fall, then by all means cut your losses and sell the stock. However, if the stock has dropped but you still feel that it can rebound and you are investing for the long term, then you might be inclined to hold on to the stock. If the potential for the stock to keep falling still exists and has you worried, then you can add a protective put to limit your loss on the stock, should it continue to fall. If the stock rebounds, you can still participate on the upside, but if the stock continues to drop, your put will hedge your loss. It might seem strange to

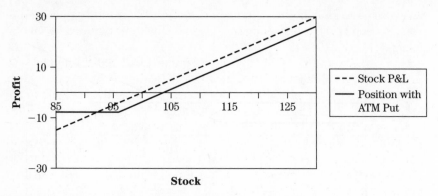

FIGURE 3.6 Adding Protective Put after EBAY Moves Lower

use options to lock in a loss as opposed to a profit, but sometimes risk management calls for accepting a loss while preventing the position from losing any more money as you give it a chance to rebound.

Assume you bought EBAY at $100 but it has now dropped to $95. If your feeling is that the drop in price is temporary and it will rebound, but you still have fears that it could drop further, then a protective put will allow you to continue to hold on to the stock while limiting further losses (Figure 3.6). If you purchased a 2-month EBAY $95 Put at $3.00, then no matter how far the stock continues to fall in the next 2 months, the protective put would limit your loss to $8.00 after exercising the put ($5.00 loss on stock + $3.00 premium of put).

If EBAY rallies higher, then you can still participate on the upside. The only downside to adding the put is that the addition of the insurance has raised your breakeven point from $100 to $103 due to the premium of the $95 Put. This is the trade-off with purchasing insurance. The benefit is that for 2 months you can relax and hope EBAY will recover without worrying about losing more of your money. If EBAY drops, you are hedged, and if it reverses and moves higher, you still participate on the unlimited profit potential. You have effectively capped your loss at 8% ($8.00 loss on $100 stock), and that is good risk management.

You can adjust the capped loss amount simply by adjusting the strike price. The foregoing example used an ATM put. If you move the strike to a deep ITM put, such as a 2-month EBAY $100 Put at $7.50, the premium is higher, but you reduce your locked-in loss to 7.5% ($7.50 premium to sell stock at original price of $100). Of course, this increased benefit of a lower limited loss does not come without a downside. The downside is that you have also raised your breakeven point to $107.50 and therefore need an even bigger rally in EBAY to recoup your cost of insurance. Therefore, using a deep ITM put is not advised, given the better risk/reward profile of using ATM puts.

Selecting a slightly OTM put is another method of hedging and locking in a maximum loss should EBAY continue to fall further. If you selected a 2-month EBAY $90 Put trading at $1.75, then you locked in a higher maximum loss of $11.75 ($10.00 loss on stock plus $1.75 premium). Your maximum loss cap is higher than the $8.00 from using the ATM puts. On the plus side, you have not increased your breakeven point by that much over your original purchase price ($101.75). Therefore, if you are not inclined to add too much to your breakeven point and are willing to accept a slightly larger loss, then the use of OTM puts is recommended (Figure 3.7).

However, in balancing maximum loss versus breakeven point, you want to take into account your underlying assumptions on the future movement of EBAY. If you are still very bullish on EBAY but just wish to be cautious, then you are expecting the stock to make a nice reversal and move higher during the life of the put. You would not like to add too much to your breakeven point because you want to participate in the upward movement of EBAY. In that case, an OTM protective put may be the best choice. Using an OTM put still gives a loss hedge but increases your breakeven point only slightly. If your fears of a continued drop in EBAY price are quite strong but you are not yet ready to part with the stock because a rally is still possible, then using ATM puts will lock in a lower loss. Your fears may lead you to want to limit your loss as much as possible yet still make some money if EBAY rallies.

It may seem odd to purchase a put and then wish the stock to move higher, but remember that your main investment, where you are looking to

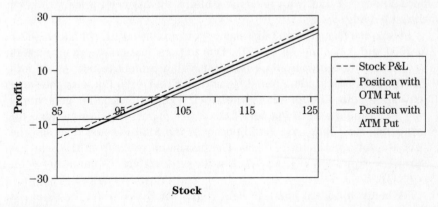

FIGURE 3.7 ATM versus OTM Protective Puts after EBAY Moves Lower

profit from, is the 100 shares of EBAY and not the put. The put is simply a hedge addition to your primary position, and when making trade adjustments, you should never lose sight of your primary investment objective. You may have to accept a loss on the put in exchange for protection, but then again, that is what insurance is for.

Bear Put Spread

In the real world, if you want to purchase insurance for your car or home and premiums are very high, you have no choice but to pay if you want protection and peace of mind. The beauty of using options to provide insurance is that there is a way to reduce the cost of insurance if option premiums for a particular stock are relatively expensive. In addition to purchasing a long put to hedge your stock position, you can also sell a put at a lower strike price with the same expiration date to bring in some premium to reduce your cost of the long put.

The sale of the lower strike put turns the protective put into a bear put spread. The maximum profit potential of a bear put spread is the difference between the strike prices minus the debit paid for the position. For example, if you bought an EBAY $110 Put for $4.00 and sold an EBAY $105 Put for $1.00, the net debit for the position would be $3.00, and the maximum profit on the spread at expiration would be $2.00 ($5.00 difference in strikes minus $3.00 debit).

In exchange for the lower cost of insurance, the bear put spread does not completely hedge the stock position or provide a capped maximum loss. Instead, the bear put spread simply reduces the loss that occurs when the stock drops. Therefore, it is a partial hedge. However, with the different choices of combinations of strike prices, you can create different levels of partial hedges to suit your needs and match the assumed price swings of the underlying stock.

Using the former example, assume you purchased 100 shares of EBAY at $100 and it has moved to $110. Due to your fears of a price reversal, you wish to hedge your stock position with a protective put. A 2-month EBAY $110 Put is trading for $4.60, and an EBAY $105 Put with the same expiration is trading for $2.00. The stock position can be hedged simply by purchasing the $110 Put for $4.60. If this price seems a little high for protection for EBAY, you could purchase the $110 Put and then sell the $105 Put for a net debit of $2.60. The maximum profit from the bear put spread at expiration is $2.40 ($5.00 strike price difference minus net debit of $2.60).

When you bought just a protective put for EBAY when the stock hit $110, you locked in a guaranteed minimum profit. However, with bear put spreads, there is no guaranteed minimum profit, just a partial hedge against the stock dropping in price. For example, if EBAY were to plummet to $95, the stock would show a $5 loss, whereas the bear put spread would have a profit of $2.40, for a total loss of only $2.60. Therefore, the bear put spread takes some of the sting out of the loss, but you still have a loss. The breakeven point for the combined position is $97.60. At that price, the loss in the stock of $2.40 would equal the profit in the bear put spread. This can be used as a target price to close out the entire position. Because EBAY was at $110, the breakeven and target price of $97.60 gives plenty of room for the stock to fall and still not show a loss. Compare the use of the protective put alone versus the use of the bear put spread in Figure 3.8.

Thus, the bear put spread reduces the amount of the loss in the position but does not prevent a loss entirely. The lack of a locked-in minimum gain is counterbalanced by the fact that the bear put spread reduced your insurance cost by almost 50%, from $4.60 to $2.60. The bear put spread is a good alternative to the lone protective put when you find the options to be relatively expensive or the extent of the expected drop in price in the stock is not further than the breakeven point created by the use of the bear put spread. In the foregoing example, if you feared EBAY could drop to below $95, then the protective put would offer much better protection than the bear put spread with a breakeven above $95.

As with any investment decision, the choice comes down to a comparison of what the risk/reward adjustment using either the protective put or the bear put spread makes to your primary stock investment and which profile better suits your assumptions of what the underlying stock might do.

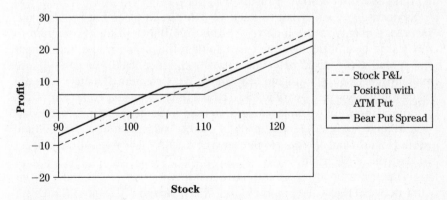

FIGURE 3.8 Comparison of Protective Put versus Bear Put Spread

Rolling from a Protective Put into a Bear Put Spread

Even if you choose to hedge a long stock position with a protective put, you can still roll the hedge into a bear put spread. By rolling into a bear put spread, you can reduce the cost of your insurance policy and even make some money without removing your hedge. This is illustrated using our earlier example on adding a protective put to EBAY after it moves from $100 to $110. Remember that after EBAY hit $110, you decided to purchase a 2-month $110 Put for $4.60. With the EBAY $105 Put trading at $2.00 and the fear of EBAY dipping back to $100 or lower, you decide against the use of the bear put spread because that will limit the hedge from the long put. Even though the $100 Put is trading at $1.50, you are still hesitant to use a bear put spread because you fear that EBAY may drop below $100 and want the best protection available, even if it costs more. This only comes from the protective put, which allows you to lock in a minimum profit.

If after a few weeks EBAY does indeed fall to $101, then your $110 Put has locked in a minimum profit of $5.40 ($1.00 stock profit plus minimum $4.40 profit on EBAY $110 Put, although it may be more, given the time value premium left on the put.).

Some traders might sell the put to take the cost of the insurance and profit from that trade off the table and then allow EBAY to run higher for more profits. The $4.40 profit made from the protective put in effect lowers your breakeven point on EBAY and gives you more room for downward movement before a loss occurs. Any adjustment that reduces your breakeven point is always a good thing. However, once you take your insurance policy away, you are no longer hedged, and this is not good risk management. With options you can recoup the cost of the insurance, make a profit, and still retain your insurance policy.

Because you still want to keep your hedge in place but recoup your insurance cost, you can look to sell the $105 Put to bring in premium to cover your cost of the insurance and convert the protective put into a bear put spread. If the EBAY $105 Put is now trading for $5.25, you can sell it to roll into a bear put spread and bring in $5.25 in premium. Because you paid $4.60 for the long put, by rolling into a bear put spread and collecting $5.25, you have recovered your costs and created a risk-free spread. Moreover, you brought in an additional $0.65 in credit that is guaranteed additional profit from the put spread. No matter where EBAY is at expiration, you get to keep the $0.65 credit.

Thus, your bear put spread has a maximum profit of $5.65, the difference between the strike prices ($110 − $105) plus the $0.65 credit. If EBAY is at $100 at expiration, you still make $5.65, a good 2-month return for a stock that went from $100 to $110 back to $100. With a debit bear put

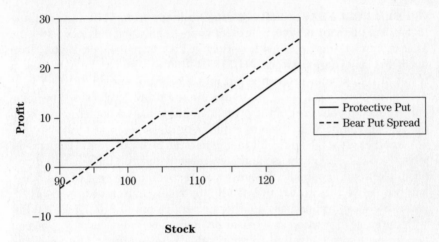

FIGURE 3.9 Comparison of Protective Put versus Rolling into Bear Put Spread

spread, any profit on EBAY above $110 is reduced by the cost of the spread. However, by rolling into the bear put spread for a credit, you increase the profit of EBAY above $110 by the amount of the credit received.

By rolling into the bear put spread, you have established a breakeven point for the position because you are no longer completely hedged by a protective put (Figure 3.9). The breakeven point on EBAY from rolling into a bear put spread is $94.35 because at that price the loss in the stock is completely hedged by the profit from the bear put spread. This gives the position a large cushion from $101 for you to still get out of the trade with a profit if the stock continues to drop.

You might wonder why you should roll from a protective put position, with a guaranteed minimum profit locked in, to a bear put spread, which actually can produce a loss if the stock drops far enough. The answer is based on your expectations. The protective put alone is a better downside hedge, but the cost of the hedge eats into EBAY profits on the upside, should the stock move higher. If you feel that EBAY has bottomed out after a price drop, you can roll into a bear put spread to recover your cost of insurance and then participate fully on the upward movement of the stock. Yet you still have some downside protection. Remember that rolling into the bear put spread does not remove the hedge entirely but does create a lower breakeven point on the stock, giving you some room to absorb more downward movement. If the stock hits the new breakeven point at expiration, you simply close the position for no loss.

Basically, your option adjustments will allow you to ride EBAY from $100 to $110 to $94.35 and not lose any of your trading capital. Of course you hoped that EBAY would not drop so much from $110 and continue higher, but you took actions to protect yourself in case it did not cooperate. That is how you use options for effective risk management. If you close out EBAY anywhere between $94.35 and $100, you still make a profit as a result of rolling your protective put into a bear put spread. If EBAY is at $110 or above at expiration, you make the full profit on the stock because you recovered your cost of the protective put and, as a bonus, get to keep the $0.65 credit because the puts expire worthless.

Another great advantage of rolling into the bear put spread for a credit is that you can still purchase another protective put on the position if you need additional insurance. Because you recovered the cost of your original protective put with EBAY at $101 by rolling into a bear put spread, you can choose to purchase another protective put at $100. If a $100 Put with the same expiration as the bear put spread is trading at $3.75, you can purchase the protective put to now hedge EBAY entirely. Moreover, because you collected a credit of $0.65, the actual cost of the new protective put is $3.10.

With the bear put spread, the position has a breakeven point of $94.35. If you add another protective put, the position has no breakeven point because you have guaranteed a profit. If EBAY is at $100 at expiration, you lose no money on the stock position, make $5.00 on the bear put spread (remember the credit is now applied to the cost of the new protective put), and lose $3.10 on the protective put, which expires worthless, for a net profit of $1.90. As EBAY drops below $100, the profit remains constant at $1.90. If EBAY is at $90, the loss on the stock is $10.00, the profit on the bear put spread is $5.00, and the profit on the protective put is $6.90, for a net profit of $1.90. Anywhere above $100, the profit on EBAY is unlimited. Thus, by rolling the protective put into a bear put spread for a credit, you have the ability to purchase another protective put at a reduced price.

The choice of whether to roll from a protective put into a bear put spread is based on your expectations. If you purchase a protective put and still have fears of a large drop in the price of EBAY, then you are better off keeping your protective put to lock in a minimum gain, as opposed to rolling into a bear put spread. However, if you roll into a protective bear put spread for a credit and still want to hedge your position, you can use the net credit to purchase a lower strike protective put at a reduced cost and lock in a profit.

Rolling from a Bear Put Spread into a Protective Put

Just as you can roll from a protective put into a bear put spread, you can roll out of a bear put spread into a protective put. Assume as before that after EBAY rose from $100 to $110, you purchased the $110/$105 bear put spread for a net debit of $2.60. If EBAY then makes a large jump to $115, the premiums of the puts will go down in price. If the price jump is temporary and you expect EBAY to reverse in price, then you could simply sell the stock for a profit and either close out the put spread to recover some of the value remaining or let it run to make money in case EBAY reverses and moves lower. The profit on the stock will more than cover the initial cost of the bear put spread.

If you are hesitant to part with the EBAY stock but still have concerns that EBAY is in for a major price correction, then you could simply do nothing because you have the bear put spread in place as a hedge. However, if you are feeling uneasy, you might be more inclined to lock in a guaranteed minimum profit so that you could wait out any downward price pressure and ride out the storm. Because the protective put offers a guaranteed minimum profit, the best adjustment to the position would be to buy back the short $105 Put to convert the bear put spread into a protective put. As indicated earlier, the $105 Put was sold for $2.00. Assume that with EBAY at $115, the $105 Put has shrunk to $1.00 in value.

If you repurchased the put for $1.00, then you would be long the $110 Put at a cost basis of $3.60 (net debit of bear put spread of $2.60 plus the $1.00 to repurchase the short $105 Put). Another way to look at the new cost basis is to say that you paid $4.60 for the $110 Put but made a profit of $1.00 on the short $105 Put for a net cost of $3.60. Therefore, by rolling the bear put spread into a protective put after a price surge in EBAY, you reduced the overall cost of the protective put from $4.60 to $3.60.

The original bear put hedge costs $2.60, and you increased the cost of your insurance by $1.00 by purchasing back the short put. However, the benefit that is derived from the $1.00 extra cost is the guarantee of a minimum profit of $6.40 from the $110 Put until expiration no matter where EBAY moves. This adjustment is easier to make when the stock rises after the bear put spread is established. When the stock rises, the short put will decrease in value, making it easier to repurchase the put. If the stock drops after adding the protective spread, then it will cost more money to repurchase the short put. If the increased cost of repurchasing the short put still guarantees a minimum gain that is acceptable, then rolling the bear put spread back into a protective put is still viable if complete protection is desired.

If EBAY fell from $110 back to $105 and you desired to roll out of the bear put spread, then you would need to buy back the short $105 Put. If the $105 Put climbed from $2.00 to $3.50, then you would need to spend $1.50 to close out the short put. This would raise the effective cost of the $110 Put from $2.60 (net debit for the spread) to $4.10. That is still cheaper than the original cost of the protective put of $4.60. Therefore, you can roll from a bear put spread into a protective put and still end up paying less than the original cost of implementing the protective put.

Because a bear put spread only limits the potential loss and does not provide a guaranteed profit, it makes sense to roll the spread into a protective put when you feel that the potential drop in price in EBAY warrants the additional protection. If your assumption is that EBAY is going to drop far in price and keep falling, then closing the entire position is the best choice. If you still have some expectation that the stock will rise, then it makes sense to hold on to the stock, but risk management calls for providing the best hedge available. If the potential short-term drop in the price of the stock appears to be large, then rolling into a protective put for a locked-in gain is the best option.

A put locks in a price at which we can sell stock. Therefore, the put is the easiest adjustment to make to a long stock position in order to hedge against any downward price movement. The important thing to remember is that you should have some expectation that the stock will move higher at some point. Applying a protective put or bear put spread to a long stock position allows you to still participate in the upside movement of the stock yet control and limit your risk to the downside. Otherwise, the best decision is simply to sell the stock and cut your losses.

CALL REPLACEMENT

Assume you purchase 100 shares of EBAY at $100 and it moves to $110. Your emotions build because you have made a great trade with a nice return. You expect EBAY to continue moving higher but begin to have doubts. Should you sell the stock now and take your profit? What if EBAY continues to rise? After all, you bought the stock because you expected EBAY to move higher. However, despite establishing an exit strategy, you begin to wonder whether $110 is the top. What if you hold on and the stock drops back to $100 and you watch your profit disappear? What if, after you sell EBAY, the stock continues to move to new highs and you see how much money you could have made? The emotional side of trading can drive you crazy. The good news is that options can provide the appropriate therapy to answer all those fears—call replacement therapy.

Call replacement therapy is simply selling the stock to take your profit now and replacing the stock position with an equivalent call position, using some of the profit to pay for the call. Selling the stock allows you to take your profit so that if the stock drops in price, you already have taken your money off the table. By purchasing the call, you can still make more money on the stock if it continues to rise. Therefore, call replacement therapy locks in a minimum profit and still allows you to participate in the upward movement of the stock. This sets all those fears aside because you have money in your hands if the stock drops and you still make more money if the stock rises. This is a perfect therapy for an investment anxiety attack.

Stock Moves Higher

Going back to the EBAY stock that you purchased at $100 and that has moved up to $110, assume a 3-month EBAY $110 Call is trading for $4.00. The stock has produced a nice gain but due to uncertainty in the market, you are not sure whether EBAY can continue higher or will reverse and drop, resulting in the loss of your profits. Under call replacement, you sell the EBAY stock and realize the $10.00 profit. You can then use $4.00 of the profit to purchase the $110 Call. The remaining $6.00 of profit is in your pocket and if EBAY drops in price, you have already realized a gain. If EBAY continues to rise, the $110 Call will increase in value, resulting in greater profits. If EBAY moves lower or sideways and the $110 Call expires worthless, you have already locked in the $6.00 gain so the overall position is still profitable. Therefore, after replacing the stock with the call, you can remove all emotion from the trade and let it run its course (Figure 3.10).

Another benefit of using the call replacement therapy is that after selling EBAY, the proceeds from the stock sale, minus the premium paid for the call, can now be used in other investments. You can continue your bullish position in EBAY while using your money elsewhere. Even if you find no other suitable investment, you can place the proceeds in a money

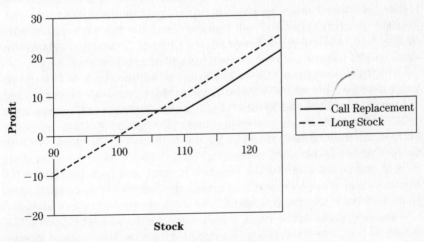

FIGURE 3.10 Call Replacement versus Long Stock

market account or use them to purchase treasuries for the life of the replacement call so that your capital can earn interest and provide additional income. If you combine the proceeds of the sale of EBAY invested in interest-earning securities with the long call, you have created a synthetic EBAY stock position that pays a dividend. The interest earned on the sales proceeds provides the "dividend," and the replacement call allows you to participate in the upward movement of the stock.

When using a replacement call, it is best to choose an at-the-money strike price. In-the-money calls are more expensive, and the cost will use up more of the realized profit to replace the stock with calls.

Out-of-the-money calls are cheaper, but the stock has to make a larger move for the call to become profitable and add to the overall realized profit. If you expect the stock to make a significant move higher, then out-of-the-money calls can be profitable. Therefore, at-the-money calls offer the best balance of cost and upward profit potential. If a stock is trading between strikes when the choice is made to replace it with calls, then choosing the next higher out-of-the-money strike is better than choosing the in-the-money calls.

Stock Moves Lower

If EBAY drops in price after the initial purchase, you can still use the call replacement strategy in the same way you can use the protective put to lock in a maximum loss, and still give the stock time to recover. Remember that under the protective put, when EBAY fell from $100 to $94, you bought a protective put at $95 to lock in a minimum loss should EBAY continue to fall. The put still allowed you to profit if EBAY reversed itself and moved higher, and your breakeven point was increased by the value of the put. Because protective put and call replacement have the same risk/reward profile (long stock + put = long call; see Chapter 2), you can achieve the same results using a call replacement instead of a protective put.

If EBAY drops from $100 to $94, you can sell the stock at $94 and replace it with a 2-month $95 Call for $3.00. At this point, your maximum loss is locked in at $9.00 ($6.00 loss on stock plus $3.00 for call premium). If EBAY keeps on dropping, you cannot lose more than $9.00. Of course, once you sell the stock at $94, you locked in the $6.00 loss on the stock. With the protective put, if the stock moves higher, it reduces the loss on the stock until it moves back above the breakeven point and then becomes profitable. Using call replacement, you accept the loss on the stock and expect to make it back with the call, should the stock reverse and move higher.

The advantage of the replacement call over the protective put in this situation (i.e., when the stock has dropped) is that your locked-in maximum loss can actually be reduced slightly if you invest the remaining proceeds from the sale of EBAY in T-bills or money market securities. The interest earned on that investment could reduce the amount of the loss slightly, and your principal is more or less protected. You could look for better returns by reinvesting the sales proceeds in bonds or fixed-income funds, but you would take on some risk as well. This is one advantage of using the replacement call over the protective put—the reuse of the capital originally invested in the stock while still having the potential for profits should the stock move back higher.

Call Replacement versus Protective Put

The strategy characteristics of the call replacement therapy when a stock has moved higher are locking in a minimum profit while still participating in the upward movement of the stock. These characteristics are the same for the protective put adjustment explained earlier. If the risk/reward characteristics are the same, then when would you choose the protective put over the call replacement or vice versa, because both strategies are excellent ways to adjust stock positions?

The main difference between the two strategies is that one involves stock ownership whereas the other uses calls as a substitute for stock ownership. Therefore, the best strategy depends on whether it is better for the investor to hold the stock or the calls. Stock ownership gives the holder certain rights and benefits that option holders do not get, such as dividends and voting rights. Also, the issue of long-term and short-term capital gain/loss taxes could play a role in what adjustment strategy to follow because the call replacement strategy requires selling the stock and incurring a capital gain/loss, a taxable event (assuming the investor is not trading in a tax-free account, such as an IRA).

If the stock has fallen, the same considerations apply for whether to choose the protective put or the replacement call as a good risk management adjustment. Both hedge the position by locking in a maximum loss so that you could possibly wait and see whether the stock reverses without risking your entire position. Therefore, the decision comes down to whether you desire to continue to hold onto the stock for the benefits that come with stock ownership or to commit the funds tied up in the stock to other investments.

SELL COVERED CALLS

Selling a call against a stock that you already own creates a covered call position. By selling the call, you collect a premium and are obligated to sell the stock at the strike price if you are assigned on the short call. The maximum profit from selling a call against a stock position is the difference between the strike price and the purchase price of the stock plus the premium collected. For example, if you purchase EBAY at $98 and sell a $100 Call for $3.00, the maximum profit is $5.00, which is realized if EBAY is at $100 or above at expiration. If EBAY is at $101, then the stock will be called away at $100 for a $2.00 profit on the stock, plus the $3.00 premium collected from selling the call. The downside to this strategy is that the position will only make a maximum of $5, no matter how high EBAY climbs by expiration, because selling the $100 Call creates an obligation to sell EBAY at $100 (Figure 3.11).

If you wish to sell your long stock position at a specific price, you can pay for the right to sell at that price with the use of a put. However, if you are willing to part with the stock at a specific price and can get paid for that willingness, then selling a call is an appropriate trade adjustment to make. You accept the obligation to sell the stock at the short call's strike price if the option is in the money at expiration, and you receive the premium from selling the call. The added benefit is that if the stock is not in the money at expiration, you still get to keep the premium as added income and still hold your stock position. You can use these characteristics of selling calls against a long stock position to increase your returns, and even provide a slight hedge to your position. The only downside—and this is by no means a minor consideration—is that the short call does not prevent losses from occurring, should the stock begin to take a dive. The premium collected cushions that loss somewhat for a slight drop in the price of the stock. However, if the stock really tanks, that cushion is similar to using a pillow

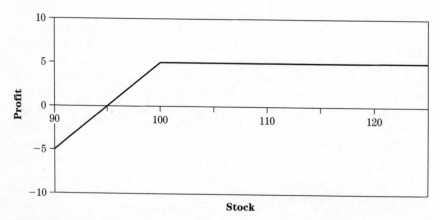

FIGURE 3.11 Covered Call

to brace the fall of a piano. This is a risk that all covered call sellers should be aware of.

Stock Moves Higher

You purchased 100 shares of EBAY at $100 and it has moved to $110. You do not expect the stock to move much higher, or you expect it to move sideways for a period of time, and are willing to sell the stock at $110 and pocket a nice 10% return. Your first option, naturally, is to just sell the stock at $110 and pocket your return. However, if you wanted to squeeze a little more profit by selling the stock at $110, then selling a call against your position will obligate you to sell the stock at $110 and collect a premium for doing so.

Assume a 1-month EBAY $110 Call is trading for $2.50. You can sell the $110 Call and collect $2.50. If EBAY is above $110 at expiration, your stock will be called away at $110, the price at which you would be willing to sell the stock. If EBAY is above $110, you will make $12.50, the $10.00 gain from the sale plus the $2.50 premium collected from selling the call. The downside is that your gain on the upside is capped at $12.50 no matter how high EBAY climbs before expiration because selling the call places the obligation on you to deliver EBAY at $110, no matter what. That is why before selling the call, you have to be content with selling EBAY at the strike price and not expect the stock to move much higher, that is, trade sideways. If you expect EBAY to keep moving much higher, then it would be better to simply hold the stock rather than sell the call.

If you sold EBAY at $110, you would realize a profit of $10.00 and a return of 10%. By selling the call at $110 and collecting $2.50 in premium, you can realize a profit of $12.50, a 25% increase over the profit realized without selling calls! This profit boost is received in exchange for giving up all further profit should EBAY move above $110. However, if you are content to sell EBAY at $110, then you should accept the potential of lost profits if EBAY jumps to $115 by expiration. Figure 3.12 compares the profit profiles of EBAY stock versus selling the call and creating a covered call position.

As Figure 3.12 indicates, the covered call position has a better profit profile until EBAY hits $112.50. Above this price the profit in the covered call position is capped, whereas the long stock continues to earn more profit. This comparison point is easily calculated—simply add the option premium collected to the strike price. The covered call position will always outperform the long stock up until this point. If EBAY is at $105 at expiration, both positions will realize $5.00 on the stock but the covered call writer will also receive the $2.50 premium on the $110 Call, which will expire worthless.

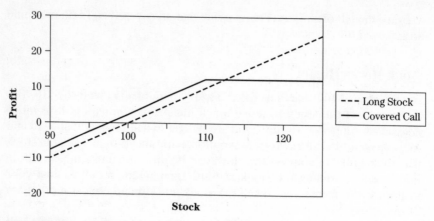

FIGURE 3.12   EBAY Long Stock versus Covered Call

Even if EBAY is below $100 by expiration, the loss on the stock under the covered call position will be reduced by the amount of the premium received, resulting in a slight hedge against downward movement in the stock. Under the covered call, the breakeven point of EBAY is lowered from $100 to $97.50 by the amount of the premium collected. Selling a call not only increases your potential profit from selling the stock, but also provides partial downside price protection. Therefore, in deciding whether to sell a covered call, you need to determine the likelihood of the stock moving above the comparison point. The more unlikely it is for the stock to move above that point, the better it may be to sell the call.

If the stock drops in price by expiration, you are presented with an interesting choice. The short call expires worthless, and you keep the premium of $2.50. Selling the call brought in additional income to your stock position. At this point, you could either sell the stock or sell another call for the next month. If EBAY drops to $107 by expiration, you can either sell the stock and make $9.50 ($7.00 on EBAY gain plus $2.50 Call premium) or sell another call at $110 for the next month.

If the next-month EBAY $110 Call is trading at $2.75, you can sell that call and add another $2.75 in income to your EBAY position. Should EBAY trade above $110 by expiration and you are assigned and forced to sell your stock at $110, you would make $15.25 ($10.00 stock gain plus $5.25 in total call premiums collected). Another way to look at it is that you sold EBAY at $110 and collected $2.50 of income in the first month and $2.75 of income in the second month. If EBAY stays below the strike price at expiration, you can keep selling a call each month to bring in more income and increase your returns on a stock that is, in effect, trading sideways. Eventually, if you are called out of your stock, your return is much bigger than if you simply sold the stock at $110.

The other added benefit of being able to continually sell calls against your long stock position is that the added income continues to reduce your breakeven point. After the first month, you reduced your breakeven point from $100 to $97.50. Selling another call in the second month further reduces your breakeven point to $94.75. At this price, the loss in the stock is offset by the short call premiums collected. Just remember that selling a call does not provide a complete hedge against a downward movement in the stock, only a partial hedge.

It goes without saying that one should not sell calls against a stock that you are not willing to part with. If the stock moves higher and you wish to hold on to receive the benefits of stock ownership (i.e., dividends) or avoid short-term capital gains, then selling calls is not appropriate because they result in the obligation to sell the stock. If the stock moves above the strike price, the only way to remove the obligation before assignment is to spend money to purchase back the short call. However, if you have no desire to sell the stock, then avoid selling covered calls.

Strike Selection

Selecting the appropriate strike for selling covered calls after the stock has moved higher is a straightforward task. The selection of the strike price is based on two criteria—a target sales price and the likelihood of the stock moving above the "comparison point." The strike price selected should be a price at which you are willing to sell the stock. If the stock has made a significant move upward, then at-the-money strike prices are the best choice. At-the-money calls still have significant premiums, depending on the time to expiration (discussed in what follows), and the strike price should be an attractive exit point if the stock has made a nice move upward. In the EBAY example, you chose the ATM call with a strike price of $110 because $110 was a great exit point, given that you paid $100 for the stock.

The other consideration with at-the-money calls is the comparison point. If you feel that the stock could still move well above the comparison point, then selling an at-the-money call might cap your profit on a stock with more room to grow. If you felt that the likelihood of EBAY moving above $112.50 was very high, then selling the $110 Call for $2.50 could severely limit your potential profits. Imagine how frustrating it would be to watch EBAY move well above $112.50 as expected and know that you sold a call at $110 and are not participating in any way in that upward movement.

If you expect EBAY to continue to move higher above the comparison point, you should look at out-of-the-money calls. The premium collected is

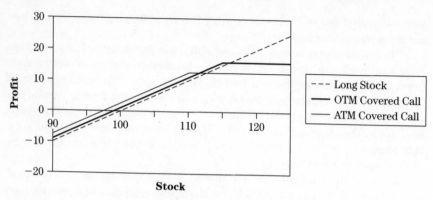

FIGURE 3.13 OTM Covered Call versus ATM Covered Call

less, but you have more room to participate in the upward movement of the stock. At the same time, the partial downward hedge is reduced because less premium is collected. This is the old-fashioned trade-off of risk/reward in covered calls—higher profit potential means less downside hedge, and more downside hedge means lower profit potential on the upside. Because the premium is less and less the more out-of-the-money you go, it is best to only sell calls within one strike price of the at-the-money calls. If a stock is between strikes, then sell the call at the next strike above the stock price.

Looking back at EBAY at $110, assume you sold the 1-month $115 out-of-the-money call for $0.95. The premium collected is lower, but now the comparison point is higher at $115.95 ($115 strike price plus $0.95 premium). Therefore, the covered call position will outperform the long stock up until EBAY hits $115.95. If you feel that with EBAY at $110, it has a good chance of moving higher toward $115, then selling the out-of-the-money call is preferable to selling the $110 Call. As Figure 3.13 indicates, there is a trade-off between potential profit and loss between the two choices, and the right one depends on your expectations of EBAY price movement. The more likely it is that EBAY will continue to rise in price, the better it may be to sell the out-of-the-money option versus the at-the-money option.

In the Money Calls

The foregoing discussion raises the question of whether you should ever consider selling an ITM call against a stock position. Remember that when a call is ITM, the strike price is below the stock price. If you sold an ITM call, you would be obligated to sell the stock below the current market price. In general, you would never want to be forced to sell a stock at a price below the current market. Of course, when selling an ITM call, you do receive a premium that covers the difference between the stock price and the strike price (i.e., the intrinsic value of the ITM call), and in addition there would be some time value premium, depending on how much time there was until expiration. For example, with EBAY at $110, a 1-month $105 Call could be trading at $6.00. Therefore, if you sold the $105 Call and you were assigned, the actual selling price would be $111 ($105 for the stock plus the $6.00 premium). The deeper ITM the call, the smaller is the time value premium and the closer to the current market price is the actual selling price.

Why sell an in-the-money call, then, if the difference between selling it at the current market price and selling the call is very small? Assume you bought EBAY at $100 and it has risen to $110. You have some fears that EBAY will reverse its price movement but you do not wish to sell the stock just yet. Perhaps you need to hold the stock for 2 more months to avoid short-term capital gains. There may be various other reasons why you choose not to sell the stock at this particular time. What is important is that you do not want to give back the unrealized profit if EBAY moves lower.

Because selling the stock is not what you want to do right now, the easiest adjustment would appear to be to add a protective put to hedge the position and lock in a sale price of the stock. However, adding a protective put requires an outlay of capital and reduces your unrealized profit by the amount of the premium. Assume you do not want to spend more money or that your stock position is considerable and it would require a significant capital outlay to buy protective puts. With the flexibility of options you still have a choice. You can sell ITM calls to lock in your unrealized gain and defer sale of the stock. Let's see how this would work with your EBAY stock position.

With EBAY at $110, a 2-month EBAY $100 Call is trading at $11.50. The premium consists of $10.00 intrinsic value and $1.50 of time value. If EBAY is at $100 or above at expiration, your covered call will be assigned, and you will sell your stock at an effective price of $111.50 ($100 strike price plus $11.50 premium). You guarantee a minimum profit even if EBAY drops back to your original purchase price. Moreover, you still guarantee a profit if EBAY falls below $100, until your breakeven point, which is now $88.50. At $88.50, the loss in the stock position is offset by the profit in the short call premium. Figure 3.14 compares the profit/loss profile of EBAY to selling the $100 Call.

Therefore, selling the deep ITM call can guarantee a minimum profit, assuming the stock is above the strike price at expiration, and significantly lower your breakeven point and allow for profit even if the stock drops below your original purchase price. You defer the sale of the stock until you are assigned on the short call. Because the option is deep ITM, the chances

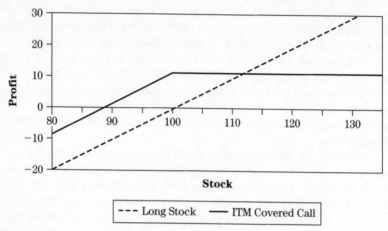

FIGURE 3.14 Long Stock versus ITM Covered Call

of being assigned early are much higher, and you may not be able to entirely control when the stock will be sold. This is the risk of selling deep ITM calls. However, if you are assigned early, you still realize a profit from your position, and converting an unrealized profit to a realized profit is always a good thing. The obvious trade-off is that you no longer participate in the upside movement of EBAY because you are obligated to sell the stock at the short strike price.

It may seem odd to use deep ITM calls to defer sale of the stock when deep ITM calls have the greatest risk of early assignment. This is one of the disadvantages of using deep ITM calls, and therefore, once the covered call is sold, you must watch the time value premium closely to see if early assignment is possible. However, there is a way to guard against early assignment. Because the time value premium shrinks fastest in the last 30 to 45 days of the life of an option, you can sell a covered call with an expiration 1 or 2 months past your holding period. This will ensure that before your minimum target date is reached, there will still be enough time value on the deep ITM calls you sold to make early assignment less likely. Once the target date is reached, time value will begin to shrink more rapidly, and as long as the option is still ITM, early assignment will be much more likely and acceptable because the minimum target date has passed.

One important advantage of selling the deep ITM call versus purchasing the protective put, beyond the fact that the put requires you to spend more money, whereas selling the covered call brings in premium, is that there are no additional margin requirements. Therefore, the premium collected is available for use in another investment. Remember that in the call replacement strategy, one of the benefits was taking your realized profit and original capital outlay off the table by selling the stock and being able to commit those funds to other investments. Selling deep ITM calls provides a similar benefit in that it allows you to take your unrealized gain from the stock's rise in price out now, plus a time value premium from selling the call, without selling the stock.

Although you do not get the present use of the initial capital outlay, you do get the present use of the unrealized profit. A dollar today is always worth more than a dollar in the future, and it may be worth more to have access to that profit now rather than later. In other words, you do not sell the stock yet, but get the use of the unrealized profit. You can take the $11.50 Call premium, which represents your profit, and invest it in other option trades or, if the number of calls sold is significant, simply park the cash in T-bills or a money market account and earn profit on your profit without having to sell the stock. Thus, selling deep ITM calls can provide significant benefits, despite the fact that it prevents you from participating in the continued upward price movement of EBAY.

Time to Expiration

Selecting the time to expiration for a covered call is important with respect to the time value premium associated with the calls. Naturally, the greater the time to expiration, the greater is the time value premium on the options. However, because you cannot control when a call will be assigned and the long stock will be sold under the covered call, selling longer term calls also defers the realization of profits until a later date. Moreover, selling calls with a longer time to expiration gives the stock more time to move higher and deeper ITM. No matter how high the stock moves, your profit is capped by the covered calls. In other words, although the premium is higher selling longer term covered calls, the stock could also explode and triple in value in that time period and you would be prevented from participating in such a large price move upward.

Let us examine these factors in selecting time to expiration by revisiting the EBAY example. You purchased 100 shares of EBAY at $100 and it has risen to $110. If you are looking to sell ATM calls, assume the following option prices:

EBAY @ $110

1-month EBAY $110 Call	$2.50
2-month EBAY $110 Call	$3.25
4-month EBAY $110 Call	$6.75

The 4-month call looks the most attractive to sell for a covered call because it has the highest premium. The benefit of using the 4-month call is that you can collect a large premium and increase your profit from selling EBAY at $110 by more than half (addition of the $6.75 premium). You also get a larger partial downside hedge if EBAY should move significantly lower, due to the larger premium collected. The downside is that with more time to expiration, EBAY has more time and a greater chance to make a significant move higher or lower. With so much time to expiration, EBAY could potentially drop sharply in price and create a losing position. With more time, there are more opportunities for price shocks that could tumble EBAY quickly and hurt the position. With less time to expiration, there is less time for the position to move against you.

A significant move higher would not really affect your guaranteed profit from your position, but because your profit is limited to $16.75 (stock profit of $10 plus $6.75 Call premium), it would be inefficient to tie up your capital for 4 months to give EBAY the time to run to $130. In other words, why give EBAY so much time to move significantly higher if you are going to limit your profit unless you feel confident that EBAY will not be much higher than $117 at expiration? The other downside to using long-term options is that you would have to wait so long for the option to expire and thus realize your profit. Even if EBAY stays sideways at $110, you would most likely have to wait the full 4 months before realizing your maximum profit potential.

Scaling-Out Strategy

For large stock positions, you may not want to sell the entire position at once using covered calls. You could sell a few calls each month to scale out of the entire position a few hundred shares at a time. Each month you could continue selling calls until the entire position is called away, bringing in more and more premium income. Also, if you keep selling calls at a higher strike price, then you are also participating in the upward movement of the stock and making a larger profit, something you cannot do if you write covered calls for the entire stock position in 1 month.

Assume that you hold 1,200 shares of EBAY at $100 and 1-month EBAY $105 Calls are listed at $2.75. To initiate a scaling-out strategy, sell four EBAY $100 Calls to cover 400 of the 1,200 total shares. If, at expiration, EBAY is at $106, then 400 shares will be called away at $105 for a profit of $7.75 per share ($5.00 stock profit plus $2.75 Call premium collected). The remaining 800 shares still participate fully in the upward movement of the stock and have an unrealized profit of $6.00 per share.

If the next-month $110 Calls are trading for $2.50, you can then sell another four $110 Calls covering 400 of the remaining 800 shares. If EBAY is at $112 at expiration, the 400 shares will be called away at $110 for a profit of $12.50 ($10.00 stock profit plus $2.50 Call premium collected). With 400 shares remaining, you could then sell the next-month's $115 Call for $2.50. If EBAY is above $115 at expiration, then the final 400 shares would be sold for a profit of $17.50 ($15.00 stock profit plus $2.50 Call premium collected).

Assuming that EBAY was at $116 at expiration of the last set of covered calls, let's compare the profits from scaling out of EBAY by selling 400 shares of EBAY at expiration in each month and scaling out of them over the 3 months using covered calls. With respect to the stock, 400 shares would have been sold the first month at $106 ($2,400 profit), another 400 shares would have been sold the second month at $112 ($4,800 profit), and the final 400 shares would have been sold at $116 ($6,400 profit) for a total profit of $13,600. Under the scaling-out strategy, the profit on the first 400 shares is $3,100 ($7.75 profit × 100 × 4 contracts). The profit for the second 400 shares is $5,000 and the profit for the final set of 400 shares is $7,000. The total profit on the scaling-out strategy is $15,100, 11% better than simply scaling out by selling stock each month. Therefore, you can boost your overall returns when scaling out by using covered calls.

At first glance, the additional profit from using covered calls to scale out does not seem to be significant. Some might argue that it would have been better to just hold all 1,200 shares and sell all of them at a high price for greater profit. However, you made the assumption that EBAY would move above the strike price each month. Let's assume that after the first month EBAY was at $104 at expiration. You would keep the $2.75 premium collected from selling the $105 Calls and still have your 1,200 shares. Therefore, you could sell another four calls at $105 for the next month. Assume that the $105 Calls, which are at-the-money, are trading for $4.00. You could sell another four calls and bring in another $4.00 in premium to go with the $2.75 you already collected. If EBAY is above $105 at expiration, then those 400 shares will be called away at $105 with an effective sales price of $111.75 ($105 strike price plus $6.75 in total call premiums collected).

If EBAY happens to hover around $105 by expiration, then you can roll your short calls out another month and collect more premium. By scaling out you can continue to sell calls because the entire stock position is not called away at once as it would be if you sold 12 calls at once. If EBAY is moving higher at a slow pace or trading sideways, you can keep selling partial covered calls each month and collect more premium. If the options expire worthless, then you still have the full amount of stock and additional income from selling calls. If the stock ever is above the strike price at expiration, then you are only called out of 400 shares of stock and still have 800 shares left to run higher or sell more covered calls. If you can extend the scaling-out strategy over several months, the additional profits from scaling out using selling covered calls could be quite substantial. Of course, stocks do not always go up and if EBAY starts moving lower, the premiums collected could also help offset some of the loss to the downside until EBAY recovers or you are called away from all 1,200 shares.

COLLARS

As an adjustment to a long stock position we discussed adding a protective put to hedge our position by limiting our risk completely and still allow us to participate in upward movements in the stock. We also discussed selling covered calls, which brings in additional income, boosting our overall return, but at the expense of capping our maximum profit. If we combined the two positions, we would most likely get a strategy that hedges our downside risk completely and allows us a limited profit on the upside. This is exactly what a collar does.

A collar is a combination of a covered call and protective put. Both the call and the put are usually one strike OTM. In many cases the premium received from selling the call pays for the purchase of the put, resulting in a no-cost or small debit/credit collar. Because the covered call is out of the money, you can still participate on the upward movement of the stock up until the strike price. As for downside protection, the protective put, being OTM, provides a hedge only if the stock moves below the strike price of the put. Therefore, there is room for profit on the upside, although it is limited, and there is room for loss on the downside, although it is also limited. Collars are sometimes referred to as "set and forget" strategies because the risk and reward are predefined up until expiration, so you do not need to follow the position on a daily basis.

Opening Position—Regular Collar

Collars are a great adjustment to make to an initial stock investment for conservative investors. The put limits the total loss on the position no matter how far the stock falls, and the covered call establishes a predetermined exit strategy no matter how high the stock rises. This is the no-brainer version of risk management and a perfect example of how options make risk management when trading stock so much easier.

Assume you purchased 100 shares of EBAY at $100 and a 2-month $105 Call is trading at $3.00 and a 2-month $95 Put is trading at $2.75. To establish the collar, sell the $105 Call and simultaneously purchase the $95 Put for a net credit of $0.25. The maximum profit for this collar is $5.25, which is obtained if EBAY is trading at $105 or above at expiration ($5.00 profit from assigned stock plus $0.25 credit). The maximum loss on the collar is

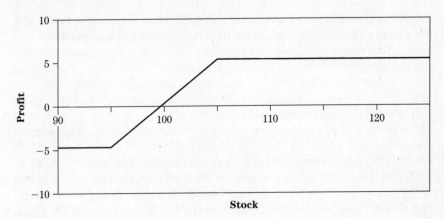

FIGURE 3.15 EBAY Regular Collar

$4.75, which is reached if EBAY is at $95 or below at expiration ($5.00 loss on stock from exercising put minus $0.25 credit). Figure 3.15 shows the risk/reward profile of the EBAY collar.

The collar provides a predetermined exit point on the upside of $105 and a predetermined stop-loss price of $95 on the downside. Between these two points, you accept the loss or gain from the movement of the stock. The collar creates perfect risk management parameters and removes some of the thinking from the trade. You can simply let EBAY run over the next 2 months without worrying about at what price to sell on the upside or when to cut your losses on the downside. The price for this security, of course, is that you do not participate in any upward movement of the stock above the covered call strike price and you are liable for the loss in the stock below the strike price of the put. This is a small price to pay for the benefit of conservative risk management.

In most cases, collars can be put on for a credit or at no cost. These are the best types of collars because it costs nothing for the added protection. If the stock pays a dividend during the life of the collar and it was put on for an initial credit, then the maximum profit of the collar is increased and the maximum risk is reduced by the amount of the credit and dividends received. Therefore, one possible strategy is to place credit collars on dividend-paying stocks that you expect to move higher. If the stock is between the strike prices at expiration of the collar, then you could sell the stock for any unrealized profit or roll into another collar, hopefully for another credit or at no additional cost.

If 2 months seems to be too short a time period for placing the collar, then longer options can be used as well. Collars can even be placed using LEAPS. It is important to remember that although your loss is capped when using a collar, so is your potential profit. Therefore, if you use LEAPS to create a collar, you have to be willing to forgo any profits above the short strike price and, more importantly, wait until close to expiration before your stock will be called away to realize your profits. Waiting for the stock to be called away is not such a detriment to the position if you select dividend-paying stocks. Thus, while waiting for the stock to be called away if it has moved higher, you can still earn a return by collecting the dividends until close to expiration of the LEAPS, when assignment is more likely.

It is important to remember that no matter what time frame you use to establish the collar, it is a covered position with respect to the short call as long as you still own the stock. If you exercise the put at any time, remember to close out the short call, even if it is only trading at $0.05. If you exercise the put and leave the short call, you will have a naked position, which could lead to unlimited losses if the stock should quickly reverse itself and move above the short call strike price. Also, the short call could have high margin requirements, which do not exist with the collar because the call is covered. Therefore, remember that when closing out the position when the stock has not been called away, do not leave the short call uncovered.

A collar does not necessarily have to be opened using OTM calls and puts. If you want to reduce the downside risk somewhat, then you can purchase an ATM put and sell an OTM call and create an upward-biased collar. Because the ATM put will cost more than the OTM put, the premium collected from selling the OTM call will not cover the cost of the put, and therefore the collar will most likely be put on for a net debit, albeit a small one.

If EBAY is at $100 and a 2-month $105 Call is trading for $2.50 and a 2-month $100 Put is trading for $3.75, you could establish an upward-bias collar with 100 shares of EBAY by selling the OTM $105 Call and purchasing the ATM $100 Put for a net debit of $1.25. Because you purchased an ATM protective put, your maximum risk is limited to $1.25, no matter how far EBAY drops until expiration. At the same time, your maximum profit is $3.75, which is the difference between the $105 Call and the purchase price of EBAY minus the net debit paid.

If you compare the risk/reward profile of the upward bias collar in Figure 3.16 to the regular EBAY collar, you can see that the upward-bias collar has a much smaller maximum risk in exchange for a smaller maximum reward. Still, the maximum reward is higher ($3.75) than the maximum risk ($1.25), and that is a good risk/reward ratio. The upward-bias collar is a good conservative strategy when you fear a possible downward movement in the stock.

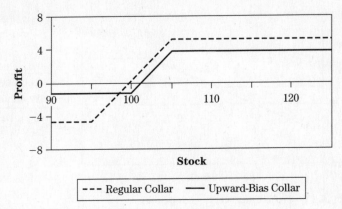

FIGURE 3.16 Regular Collar versus Upward-Bias Collar

Stock Moves Higher—Profit Collar

Although a collar is a great low-risk strategy adjustment to apply when purchasing stock, it can also be a great low-risk follow-up adjustment if the stock has moved higher. Because a collar consists of a protective put and a covered call, applying a collar to a stock that has risen in price is a way to lock in a profit and still participate in some of the upward movement of the stock up until the short strike. This is called a profit collar. Also, if the collar is placed for a credit, then the collar can add to the potential profit.

Assume that after you purchase EBAY at $100, it moves higher to $110 and a 3-month $115 Call is trading for $5.50 and a 3-month $105 Put is trading for $5.00. A profit collar can be added to the position by selling the $115 Call for $5.50 and purchasing the $105 Put for $5.00 for a net credit of $0.50. The new risk/reward profile of the adjusted stock position created by adding the profit collar is shown in Figure 3.17. The guaranteed minimum profit is $5.50, which is achieved if EBAY falls back below $105 by expiration. At $105, the put can be exercised for a $5.00 profit in the stock position, which is added to the $0.50 credit received from the profit collar.

The maximum profit occurs when EBAY moves above the short strike of $115. At that price, EBAY is called away at $115 for a profit of $15.00, which is added to the credit of $0.50 received from the profit collar, for a total maximum profit of $15.50. Therefore, adding the profit collar to the EBAY stock position has guaranteed a profit from $5.50 to $15.50, depending on where EBAY is at expiration, and you were able to guarantee this profit at no additional cost. In fact, you actually received a credit of $0.50 for initiating the profit collar.

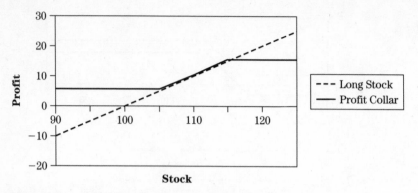

FIGURE 3.17   Profit Collar versus Long Stock

In other words, you received compensation for locking in a profit. If you just added the protective put alone, you would have been required to pay for the put with additional capital. By adding the covered call to the protective put to create the collar, you can achieve similar results without additional cost. Even if the profit collar is put on for a small debit, you still guarantee a range of profit on the position. Assume that the forgoing profit collar was put on for a net debit of $0.50 as opposed to a net credit. The minimum guaranteed profit would be $4.50 ($5 Put profit minus $0.50 debit), and the maximum profit would be $14.50 ($15 covered call strike profit minus $0.50 debit).

Although it would be optimal to establish a profit collar for a net credit to increase your guaranteed profit, creating a profit collar with a net debit still achieves the goal of guaranteeing a profit and converting a risky long stock position into a no-risk trade until expiration of the collar. Remember that the position has no risk until expiration of the options. If both the covered call and protective put expire worthless, that is, EBAY is between the strikes at expiration, then the hedge is removed and the risk of owning EBAY returns. Therefore, at expiration, you need to decide whether to initiate another profit collar, make a different option adjustment, or simply close out the position and collect the profits.

If you want to establish a higher minimum guaranteed profit, then you can add an upward-bias profit collar to the EBAY position at $110. You still sell the $115 Call for $5.50, but instead of using an OTM put, you can purchase the 3-month $110 Put for $7.50, establishing the upward-biased profit collar for a net debit of $2.00. The new minimum guaranteed profit is $8.00, which is achieved by exercising the $110 Put for a profit of $10.00, minus the $2.00 net debit for purchasing the profit collar. The maximum profit is $13.00 ($15.00 profit from covered call minus $2.00 net debit).

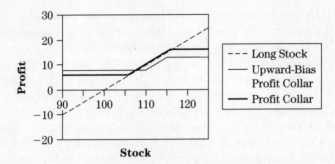

FIGURE 3.18 Profit Collar versus Upward-Bias Profit Collar

The upward-bias profit collar has a higher minimum profit because the protective put is at a higher strike. In exchange for this higher minimum profit, you give up some upside profit potential as compared to the simple profit collar. Figure 3.18 compares the profit collar with the upward-bias profit collar.

The strike prices to be selected for a profit collar once the stock has moved higher are up to you. Depending on the level of minimum guaranteed profit required or maximum profit desired, the strikes can be adjusted to suit your needs. Although the most common collars use either OTM puts and calls one strike away from the stock price or an ATM put and an OTM call, the strike prices can be moved further away to create different risk/reward profiles.

We will not consider the adjustment of adding a collar to a stock that has moved lower, because a collar has limited upside profit potential. If a collar was placed on a stock that moved lower, then the collar might be locking in a loss with no added benefit. This is not good risk management. For example, if EBAY fell to $95 and you created a collar using the $100 Call and the $90 Put, then you would only break even if EBAY moved above its original price of $100 because you would be called out of the stock at $100. Even if the collar is put on for a credit, it usually is not a good idea to lock in a loss when there are other option strategies available.

RATIO WRITE

A ratio write is a slight variation of the covered call strategy. Ratio writes are created by being long stock and then writing more calls than the number of shares you own. The name of the strategy is derived from the fact that you are writing calls in a ratio to each 100 shares of stock owned.

For example, you would purchase 100 shares of stock and write two calls against the position. In effect it is a combination of a covered call and a naked call. Writing the calls brings in premium just as in a covered call strategy, but because you are writing more calls than you have shares of stock, you have the potential for loss on the upside if the stock moves too far above the short strike. However, the extra premium collected from selling the calls hedges against some of the loss on the upside and downside. Therefore, a ratio write is a good strategy or adjustment to make if you expect the stock to trade in a fixed range until expiration of the short options. Naturally you would choose short-term options to take advantage of time decay and not give the stock too much time to possibly trade outside of the profit zone of the strategy. The trading range is established by the breakeven points created by the ratio write. From the following examples, you will see how to derive the breakeven points and use ratio writes to enhance the return on a stock holding and even provide a partial hedge to downward movement in the stock price.

The most common ratio write is a 1:2 ratio, that is, buy 100 shares of stock and then sell two calls. Because there is a naked call, the position does have a margin requirement, which may be in addition to any existing requirements if the long stock was bought on margin. You can sell three and four calls per 100 shares, but then the margin requirement will be much larger and the potential losses if the stock makes a large move upward could be substantial. Because your goal is effective risk management, you only want to handle risk that is manageable and therefore we recommend a ratio of 1:2 or perhaps 1:3.

Opening Position

Assume you purchased 100 shares of EBAY at $100 and wanted to create a ratio write using the following 1-month EBAY call prices:

EBAY @ $100

EBAY $ 95 Call	$7.50
EBAY $100 Call	$4.00
EBAY $105 Call	$2.25
EBAY $110 Call	$1.00

To create an ATM ratio write using a 1:2 ratio, sell two EBAY $100 Calls for $4.00 against your 100 shares of EBAY and collect $8.00 in premium. To understand the risk/reward profile and breakeven points of this strategy, let's look at different potential profit and loss outcomes at different stock prices at expiration. If EBAY is $100 at expiration, both calls expire worthless, and the total profit is $8.00 from the premium collected

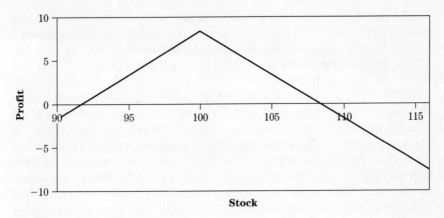

FIGURE 3.19 ATM Ratio Write

from the short calls. At $105, there is a $5.00 profit on the stock and the calls are worth $5.00 each for a total of $10.00. Because you received $8.00 from selling the calls, there would be a $2.00 loss to close the short calls. Thus, at $105, the total profit is $3.00 ($5.00 stock profit minus $2.00 loss on calls). At $95, the calls would expire worthless for a profit of $8.00, and the stock would have a loss of $5.00 for a net profit of $3.00.

The breakeven point on the upside is $108. At $108, the stock will be called away at $100 for no loss or gain on the stock, and the remaining short call will be worth $8.00. Because you originally received $8.00 in premium, you could buy back the short call at $8.00 and have no loss or gain on the short call. Thus, the total position would have a net profit of $0. The breakeven point on the downside would be $92. At $92, the $8.00 profit on the short calls (both calls would expire worthless) would offset the $8.00 loss on the stock for a net profit of $0.

If you look at the risk/reward profile in Figure 3.19 of the EBAY ratio write using the ATM calls, you can see that there is a wide profit zone between $92 and $108, with the maximum profit realized if EBAY is at $100 at expiration. The picture of the risk/reward profile makes it evident that because you purchased EBAY at $100, you expect EBAY to trade sideways until expiration of the short calls. You would prefer EBAY to stay right at $100, but even if it moves a little up or down, you still make a profit. If EBAY moves too far up or down, then the position has unlimited loss potential. Therefore, selection of the ratio write as an opening position has to be based on the assumption that the stock will move sideways.

You can achieve the same neutral stance on EBAY if you split the strike prices of the calls to be sold for the ratio write, that is, sell one call above the stock price and one call below the stock price. If you purchased 100 shares of EBAY at $100, then, based on the previous option prices, you would sell the EBAY $95 Call for $7.50 and the EBAY $105 Call for $2.25 for a total credit of $9.75. As with the foregoing example, let's look at different prices of EBAY at expiration to see what the potential profit and loss from this position would be.

If EBAY is at $100 at expiration, the $105 Call will expire worthless but the $95 Call will be assigned for a $5.00 loss on the stock. This $5.00 loss is offset by the $9.75 premium collected from selling the calls for a net profit of $4.75. The same net profit is achieved if EBAY is at $105 at expiration. At $105, the stock will be called away at $95, whereas the $105 Call will expire worthless for a net profit of $4.75. Both calls would expire worthless if EBAY is at $95 at expiration and the $5.00 loss in the stock is offset by the $9.75 in premiums collected from the short calls for a net profit of $4.75. The effect of splitting the strikes is that the profit is the same if EBAY is at or between the strike prices at expiration.

As EBAY moves above or below the strike of the short calls, the profit begins to decrease until a loss is realized if EBAY moves far enough up or down. The downside breakeven point is calculated by subtracting the premium collected from the stock price. Therefore, we subtract $9.75 from $100 to get a downside breakeven point of $90.25. At $90.25, the loss on the stock is $9.75, which is offset by the $9.75 profit of the short calls, which expire worthless. The upside breakeven point is calculated the same way by adding the premium collected to the stock price, which is $109.75. At that price, EBAY is called away at $95 for a $5.00 loss, and the short $105 Call is worth ($4.75) for a total loss of $9.75, which is offset by the $9.75 in premium collected.

Figure 3.20 shows the risk/reward profile of the variable strike ratio write compared to the ATM ratio write. As with the ATM ratio write, the variable strike ratio write has the largest profit if EBAY trades sideways until expiration. However, the maximum profit range is much wider for the variable strike write than it is for the ATM ratio write, and the breakeven points are also wider apart. The maximum profit zone is flatter for the variable strike ratio write, but you give up some maximum profit in exchange for a wider profit zone. Both strategies require EBAY to stay in a sideways trading pattern until expiration, but the variable strike write has more of a cushion for up and down movement than the ATM write. Therefore, in choosing between the two, you have to compare the breakeven points and the maximum profits and determine which strategy best fits your needs.

The foregoing ratio write examples involved an ATM ratio write and a variable strike ratio write using ITM and OTM calls. You could use any combination of strike prices as long as you are aware of the risk/reward profile and are comfortable with the breakeven points and profit zone.

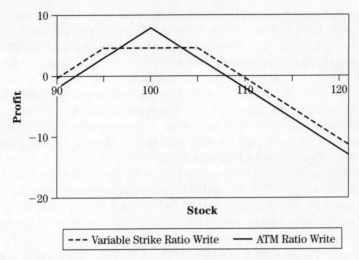

FIGURE 3.20 ATM Ratio Write versus Variable Strike Ratio Write

Stock Moves Higher—Regular Ratio Write

Earlier in the chapter we discussed selling a call as an adjustment to a long stock position that has moved higher. If we sell an extra naked call or two in addition to the covered call, then we have converted the long stock position into a ratio write. The difference between the covered call adjustment and the ratio write adjustment is that by selling more calls than the number of shares of stock, we take in more premium and have a wider profit zone. The downside is that the additional naked calls create a potential for significant losses if the stock continues to move higher. As with covered calls, you can adjust the risk/reward profile of the ratio write adjustment by adjusting the strike price selected or the number of calls sold. Because you expect the stock to move sideways and want to take advantage of time decay, you should create ratio writes using short-term options.

Assume you purchased 100 shares of EBAY at $100 and it has moved higher to $110. If you feel that the stock will move sideways for a specific period of time, then you can sell calls against the EBAY position. Using the following 1-month option quotes, you can look at different ratio write adjustments to the EBAY position:

EBAY @ $110

EBAY $105 Call	$7.00
EBAY $110 Call	$3.00
EBAY $115 Call	$1.00

The simplest ratio write adjustment to make to the EBAY position that has moved from $100 to $110 is to use ATM calls, especially since you expect the stock to move sideways. If you sell two EBAY $110 Calls at $3.00, you bring in $6.00 in premium and have one covered call and one naked call. If the stock is above $110 at expiration, it will be called away at $110 by one of the calls. The profit or loss on the other call depends on how high above the strike price the stock moves by expiration. Of course, if the stock moves back below $110, both calls expire worthless and you keep the entire premium. Let's look more closely at the potential profit/loss profile from the ATM ratio write adjustment.

If the stock is at $110 at expiration, both calls will expire worthless for a profit of $6.00. This is in addition to the $10.00 profit from the EBAY stock position. Therefore, at expiration the total profit is $16.00. By selling the two calls against your long stock position when you expect the stock to move sideways, you have increased your overall profit by 60%. The maximum profit in a call ratio write occurs when the stock is at the short strike at expiration. Therefore, when selling ATM calls, it cannot be stressed enough that you should expect the stock to hover right at the short strike price by expiration.

If the stock is above $110 at expiration, then your maximum profit is reduced by the short call dollar for dollar for each point the stock moves above $110. For example, if EBAY is at $111 at expiration, then your stock is called away at $110 for a $10.00 profit plus the $3.00 from selling the covered call for a total profit of $13.00. The naked call is worth $1.00 at expiration, and because you received $3.00 for selling the call, the net profit is $2.00. Thus at $111 the total net profit on the position is $15.00. As Figure 3.21 indicates, the maximum profit decreases in a straight line as the stock moves above $110 at expiration.

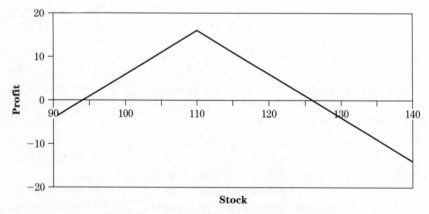

FIGURE 3.21 Adjusted Ratio Write after Stock Moves Higher

Because you have a naked call, good risk management dictates that you determine your upside breakeven point, which is $126. At $126.00 your stock will be called away at $110 for total profit of $13.00 ($10.00 gain on stock plus $3.00 premium of short call). Your other short call will be worth $16.00 for a net loss of $13.00 (short call value of $16.00 minus $3.00 premium collected). Therefore the $13.00 loss on the short call is offset by the $13.00 gain on the covered call portion of the ratio write for a total net profit of $0.00. In general, the upside breakeven point for a long stock position that has moved higher and is adjusted by an ATM ratio write is calculated by adding the gain if the stock is sold at the strike price to the breakeven point of the combined short calls.

The downside breakeven point is calculated by simply determining the point where the loss on the stock from moving lower is offset by the gain on the short calls that will expire worthless. If the stock moves lower, both of the $110 Calls expire worthless for a profit of $6.00. This would completely offset a $6.00 loss on EBAY if it moves down to $94 (remember you bought EBAY at $100).

If you look again at the risk/reward profile of your adjusted EBAY position in Figure 3.21, you see the breakeven points of $94 and $126. The picture shows how the maximum profit is obtained if EBAY stays close to $110 by expiration. However, if EBAY does make a small move above or below $110, you still have a nice profit. The wide upside-down triangle profit zone of the ratio write lets you squeeze more profits out of a stock that you expect to not move anywhere in the near future. Although you cut off some profit on the upside, you get some additional downside protection and even increased profits when EBAY is above your original purchase price. For example, if EBAY is at $105 at expiration, instead of a profit of only $5.00 on a long EBAY position, your adjusted ratio write has a profit of $11.00 ($5.00 from EBAY and $6.00 from short calls).

One obvious question is what happens if you sell three $110 Calls instead of two to bring in more premium—$9.00 for selling three $110 Calls versus $6.00 for selling two $110 Calls? The maximum profit is much higher if EBAY is at $110 at expiration ($19.00 vs. $16.00). The additional premium will lower your downside breakeven point, but it will also lower your upside breakeven point. The downside breakeven point is $91 ($9.00 loss on EBAY offset by $9.00 gain on expired short calls) and the upside breakeven point is now $119.50. Thus, selling additional calls creates a bearish bias in the ratio write adjustment because the upside breakeven point for selling three calls is lower than for selling two calls. The bearish bias of adding an additional naked call is evident in the comparison of the 1:2 ratio write and 1:3 ratio write in Figure 3.22.

If you were to sell four or maybe five calls as part of the ratio write adjustment, the upside breakeven point would move too close to the current price of the stock. Even though your assumption is that the stock will move

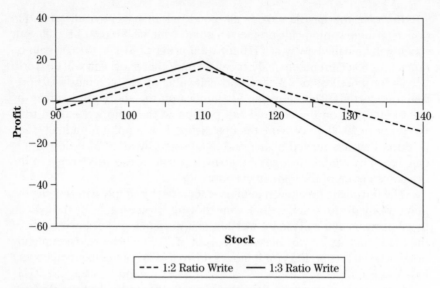

FIGURE 3.22   1:2 Ratio Write versus 1:3 Ratio Write

sideways until expiration, you still want some profit if EBAY happened to move higher. Therefore, adding more than two or three calls would create a position with too much upside risk. However, choosing between two and three calls depends on whether you want more downside protection.

You can create a different bias in your ratio write adjustment simply by selecting a different strike price. Previously you used ATM calls because you expected the stock to move sideways. If you feel that the stock will move sideways but also expect that any possible movement in the stock could be more on the upside, you can create an upward bias by selling two $115 Calls at $1.00 each. The total premium collected—$2.00—is lower than if you used ATM calls, but the risk/reward profile is shifted higher to allow for greater profits if EBAY moves higher.

The maximum profit is $17.00, which occurs if EBAY is at $115 at expiration. The downside breakeven point is $98 because the $2.00 loss in the stock is offset by the $2.00 profit from the short calls expiring worthless. The upside breakeven point is $132. At $132, EBAY is called away at $115 for a $16.00 profit ($15.00 profit on EBAY plus $1.00 premium collected from short call). The remaining short call is worth a negative $17.00, and once the $1.00 premium collected is subtracted, the net loss is $16.00, which offsets the profit in the stock. Comparing the risk/reward profile of using the ATM calls in Figure 3.21 versus the $115 Calls in Figure 3.23, you can see how using the $115 Calls has a slight bias to the upside. Therefore,

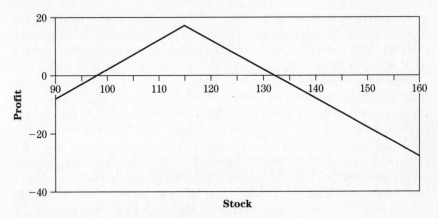

FIGURE 3.23　Adjusted Ratio Write Using OTM Calls

if you expect EBAY to move sideways or slightly higher, you can use OTM calls to create the ratio write.

Just with the ATM calls, you can also sell three of the EBAY $115 Calls instead of two to change the risk/reward profile. By selling three EBAY $115 Calls, you bring in $3.00 in premium. Your new downside breakeven point is $97, and the upside breakeven point is $124. Because the OTM calls have small time value premiums 1 month out, adding the third call to the ratio write does not increase the overall profit by much, but it does reduce the upside breakeven point by $8.00 from $132 to $124. Therefore, the increase in profit is usually not worth the decrease in the upside breakeven point when using short-term OTM options as a ratio write adjustment. The tendency would be to then go further out in time to sell OTM options for a ratio write adjustment, but more time adds more risk to the position. The more time to expiration, the more time there is for the stock to move away from the short strike price.

Another choice for strike selection in establishing the ratio write adjustment is to use ITM strikes, such as the $105 Calls. With EBAY at $110, you could sell two EBAY $105 Calls at $7.00 each for a total of $14.00. By selling ITM calls, you are already cutting short the profit potential on the upside if EBAY moves higher. If EBAY stays above $105 at expiration, the total profit on the stock is $19.00 ($5.00 from sale of the stock plus the $14.00 premium collected). The other naked call is already in the money, and therefore you have to be aware of the upside breakeven point. The upside breakeven point is $124, which gives you some protection on the upside because EBAY has enough room to move before a loss occurs. Of course, the expectation of adjusting the stock position with a ratio write is that the stock will move sideways. Because the maximum profit is obtained when the stock is at the short strike of $105 at expiration—which in this case is $19 ($5.00 stock profit plus $14.00 profit from short calls)—using ITM calls with a strike of $105 implies a slight downward bias because the stock is currently at $110.

The downward bias is more evident when the downside breakeven point is calculated. By selling two $105 Calls for a total of $14.00, you lower the downside breakeven point to $86.00 because the $14.00 loss on the stock is offset by the $14.00 gain from the short calls. Figure 3.24 compares the adjustment of adding a ratio write with two short calls by using the ITM, ATM, and OTM strikes. As Figure 3.24 indicates, the difference between selecting the ITM, ATM, and OTM strikes depends on your bias in how the stock will move by expiration. Although all three anticipate sideways movement, you can select different strikes to adjust that assumption up or down slightly. For example, if you expect EBAY to enter a sideways trading pattern with a possible move lower, you would choose the ITM strikes.

As with the ATM and ITM ratio write, you can adjust the slightly downward bias in the ITM ratio write by selling three EBAY $105 Calls instead of two. By selling three EBAY $105 Calls at $7.00 each, you bring in $21.00 of premium. Your new downside breakeven point is $79 because the $21.00 loss on the stock will be offset by the $21.00 profit from selling the three calls. As expected, the new upside breakeven point is moved lower from $124 to $118. The maximum profit, achieved if EBAY is at $105 at expiration, is now $26.00 ($5.00 profit from stock plus $21.00 profit from sale of short calls). Thus, selling the third call increases your maximum profit

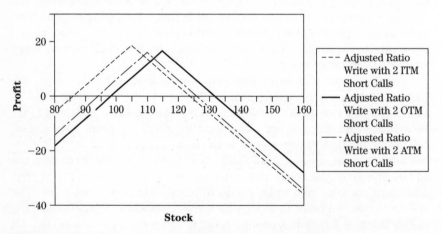

FIGURE 3.24   OTM, ATM, and ITM Ratio Write Adjustments

and lowers your downside breakeven point in exchange for also lowering your upside breakeven point. Therefore, the already downward bias created in using the ITM ratio write adjustment is increased by selling the third call.

In making the ratio write adjustment, you can see that despite your assumption of sideways movement in EBAY, your choice of strike (ITM, ATM, and OTM), as well as the choice between selling two or three calls, gives you various ways to create an upward or downward bias in the position, as well as adjust the breakeven points. Therefore, the ratio write gives you plenty of flexibility in adjusting your stock position. Another important factor to consider when establishing the ratio write adjustment is the amount of unrealized profit in the stock. The higher the stock has moved from your original purchase price, the wider is the profit zone created by adding the ratio write. For example, in your EBAY position you had $10.00 of unrealized gain from $100 to $110. Recalculate the risk/reward profiles with the assumption that you had purchased EBAY at $105 instead of $100 and you will find that the "profit triangle" is narrower.

Therefore, before deciding to adjust a stock position with a ratio write, in addition to strike and number of calls sold, you should take into consideration how far the stock has moved from the original purchase price. If the stock has not moved very much, then the position is very similar to the initial ratio write strategy discussed earlier. The real advantage of the ratio write adjustment after a stock has moved higher is using the unrealized gain in the stock to augment the gain and reduce the risk of having naked calls in the position. The higher the unrealized return in the underlying stock, the greater is the increase in potential profit and the greater is the decrease in the potential risk. That is using options to achieve the best advantage and, as always, is a sign of good risk management.

Stock Moves Higher—Variable Strike Ratio Write

We discussed the use of ITM, ATM, and OTM strike prices where you sell calls all with the same strike price. However, you can further refine your ratio write adjustment by selling calls at different strike prices. Let's see what happens to the position if you split the strike prices apart. As before, assume you bought EBAY at $100, it has climbed to $110, and 1-month EBAY options are trading at the following prices:

EBAY @ $110

EBAY $105 Call	$7.00
EBAY $110 Call	$3.00
EBAY $115 Call	$1.00

Instead of selling two ATM $110 Calls, you can split the strike prices and sell one ITM and one OTM call. Therefore, you would sell the $105 Call for $7.00 and sell the $115 Call for $1.00 for a total credit of $8.00. You examined the risk/reward profile of the variable strike ratio write earlier as an opening position with the purchase of long stock. Let's examine the risk/reward profile of a variable strike ratio write added to a stock position with an unrealized gain by looking at the overall profit and loss at different stock prices at expiration.

If EBAY is at $105 at expiration, the stock has a profit of $5.00. Both short calls expire worthless for a profit of $8.00. Therefore, at $105 the entire position has a profit of $13.00. If the stock is between $105 and $115 at expiration, the profit will still be $13.00 because the stock will be called away at $105 as a result of the short call and the $115 Call will expire worthless. Therefore, the $8.00 premium collected is added to the $5.00 profit from the sale of the stock. This is one very important difference between the variable strike ratio write and the regular ratio write. With the regular ratio write, the maximum profit is reached when the stock is at the short strike at expiration, whereas with the variable strike ratio write, the maximum profit is reached if the stock is anywhere between the short strikes at expiration. Although the maximum profit is lower with the variable strike ratio write, it exists over a wider range, and therefore there is a higher probability of achieving this maximum profit.

As the stock moves above $115 or below $105—that is, outside of the maximum profit range—the profit is reduced dollar for dollar, either as a result of the decreasing stock price on the downside or the short $115 Call on the upside. The downside breakeven point is $92 because the $8.00 loss on the stock price is offset by the $8.00 in premium collected. The upside breakeven point is $128, which is the point where the gain from having the stock called away at $105 plus the option premium is offset by the loss in the $115 short call. As the risk/reward profile in Figure 3.25 indicates, the variable strike ratio write using one strike below and above the current stock price creates a wide, flat maximum profit zone with a wide overall profit area. This is a good adjustment to make when you feel the stock will move sideways until expiration but you still fear some volatility in the stock or that it will bounce in a tight trading range. The variable strike ratio write lets you profit from the stock staying within a specific trading range as opposed to having to finish at a specific price at expiration.

The choice between the regular ratio write adjustment and the variable strike ratio write adjustment depends on your comfort level. Because the ratio write has a higher overall maximum profit when the stock is right at the short strike of the calls, it depends on how confident you are on the sideways movement of the stock. If EBAY is expected to be dead in

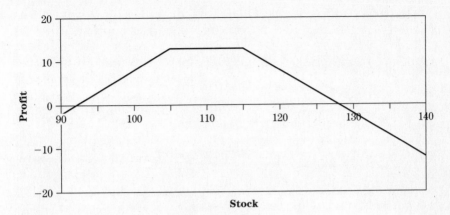

FIGURE 3.25 Variable Strike Ratio Write

the water, then the regular ratio write has potential for higher returns. If, however, the assumption is that EBAY could still float a little higher or pull back a bit before expiration, the variable strike ratio write gives a wider range of stock prices to collect the maximum profit. It comes down to a trade-off between risk and reward, which you must make by comparing the two potential adjustments and determining which one gives the best return for the supposed move of EBAY.

The basic variable strike ratio write adjustment is to sell an ITM and an OTM call around the current price of the stock. This creates a wide profit zone and gives room for the stock to drift higher or lower and still achieve the maximum profit. However, you can still put a slight bias into the variable strike ratio write by selecting different strikes. For example, if you want a slightly bearish bias, you can use an ITM and an ATM option for the ratio write. Using your EBAY stock and the 1-month option quotes, you could sell the $105 Call for $7.00 and also sell the $110 Call for $3.00 for a total credit of $10.00. Let's examine the potential profit and loss at different stock prices at expiration.

If EBAY is between $105 and $110 at expiration, the maximum profit is $15.00 ($5.00 from EBAY being called away at $105 plus $10.00 in premium collected from the calls). Because selling the ATM call is worth more than the OTM call, your maximum profit is higher in this adjustment than the previous adjustment using the ITM and OTM calls. Your downside breakeven point is now $90 because the $10.00 loss in the stock will be offset by the $10.00 gain in the short calls. The upside breakeven point is $125, where the gain on EBAY being called away at $105 will be offset by the loss on the $110 Call.

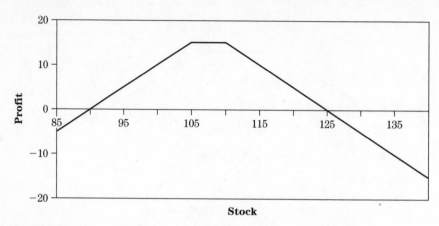

FIGURE 3.26   Variable Strike Ratio Write Using ITM and ATM Calls

As Figure 3.26 indicates, moving the strikes together creates a narrower maximum profit zone than if you used the ITM and OTM strikes. However, the beneficial trade-off is that the maximum profit zone is higher. Also, the use of the ITM and ATM strikes creates a slight bias to the downside for the maximum profit zone. Therefore, the use of the ITM/ATM variable strike ratio write is more appropriate than the use of the ITM/OTM variable strike ratio write when the stock is expected to move sideways but possibly move slightly lower than the current price by expiration. As the variable strike ratio write adjustment demonstrates, you have many ways to tailor the adjustment to your expectation of where the stock might be by expiration with a wide margin for profit in case you are slightly off on your predictions.

Your variable strike ratio write adjustment can also have a slightly upward bias if you sell an ATM call and an OTM call. With EBAY moving to $110, you can sell the $110 Call for $3.00 and sell the $115 Call for $1.00 for a total credit of $4.00. The maximum profit, which occurs if the stock is between the short strikes at expiration, is $14.00 ($10.00 stock profit plus $4.00 in short call premiums). Because you used the $110 and $115 strikes with the stock at $110, the maximum profit zone has a slight upward bias; that is, the stock has to stay sideways or move higher to achieve the maximum profit. The downside breakeven point is $96.00 (purchase price minus short premium collected), where the $4.00 loss on the stock is offset by the $4.00 collected from selling the two calls. The upside breakeven point is $129, where the $14.00 gain on the sale of the stock at $110 with the call premiums is offset by the $14.00 loss on the $115 short call. The risk/reward

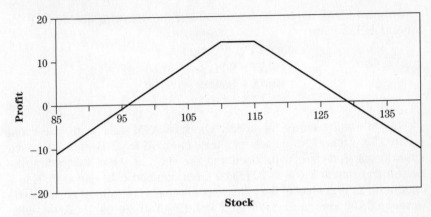

FIGURE 3.27 Upward-Bias Variable Ratio Write

graph in Figure 3.27 shows the upward bias in the ATM/OTM variable strike ratio write.

The variable strike ratio write is best used as an adjustment on a stock that has moved higher when the stock is expected to move sideways until expiration. If you have a slight bias regarding where the stock might drift or perhaps a slight fear that the stock will move slightly lower by expiration, then you can choose different combinations of the ITM, ATM, and OTM strike prices. The breakeven points are always an important consideration because the variable strike ratio write adjustment does not lock in a risk-free profit, nor does it allow unlimited profit if the stock moves significantly higher. Good risk management dictates that you be aware of the breakeven points and use them in determining which variable strike ratio write adjustment is appropriate to increase the returns of your original long stock position.

Stock Moves Lower—Ratio Write/Variable Strike Ratio Write

If you purchase EBAY and it moves lower, it is possible to adjust the losing stock position with a ratio write to help salvage a losing cause. However, remember that a ratio write only provides a slight hedge against a downward movement in the stock price. Because you are starting from a losing position, the ratio write will not prevent further losses if the stock keeps falling. If the stock moves higher, you may be cut out of earning any profits on the position because you are possibly selling calls with strike prices below the original purchase price. Let's run through a few examples to illustrate this point.

Assume EBAY fell to $95 from $100 and the following quotes exist for 1-month EBAY calls:

EBAY @ $95.00

EBAY $ 90 Call	$7.50
EBAY $ 95 Call	$4.00
EBAY $100 Call	$2.25

If you want to adjust the position with an ATM ratio write, you could sell two $95 Calls at $4.00 each for a total credit of $8.00. Because the maximum profit in a ratio write occurs at the short strike at expiration, the maximum profit at $95 is $3.00 ($8.00 profit on short calls minus $5.00 loss on stock). At first glance, the adjustment seems to be helpful because you turned a $5.00 loss into a $3.00 gain with EBAY at $95.00. However, what happens if EBAY falls to $90? The $10.00 loss on the stock is offset by the $8.00 gain on the short calls for a net loss of $2.00. Again, the ratio write adjustment seems to work because it reduced a potential $10.00 loss to a $2.00 loss. After all, the goal of using options is to reduce your risk, and therefore on the downside your potential losses are reduced by $8.00, should EBAY keep falling.

Let's look at what happens if EBAY moves higher. If EBAY moves back to $100 by expiration, the stock will be called away at $95 for a stock loss of $5.00. The remaining short call will be worth $5.00 for a profit of $3.00 ($8.00 collected premium). Therefore, if the stock moves back to $100, the total net loss on your EBAY position is $2.00. If EBAY moves to $105, you still have a $5.00 loss on EBAY, which will be called away by one of the short calls. The remaining short call will be worth $10.00. After subtracting the $8.00 in premium collected from selling the two calls, the loss is $2.00. Thus the net loss on the position if EBAY moves to $105 is $7.00. Figure 3.28 shows the profit and loss from making the ATM ratio write adjustment when EBAY drops to $95.

As Figure 3.28 indicates, the downside breakeven point of the ratio write adjustment is $92, at which point the $8.00 loss on the stock is offset by the $8.00 gain on the short calls. The upside breakeven point is $98.00, where the $5.00 loss on the stock (after being called away by one short $95 Call) is offset by the $5.00 gain on the remaining short option (the short call is repurchased for $3.00 for a net gain of $5.00.) The breakeven points are very narrow in the ratio write adjustment on a stock that has moved lower, and this is because you are in effect locking in a loss on the stock by selling calls with strike prices below your purchase price. Although a profit is realized if EBAY stays between $92 and $98, this is too narrow a profit zone, given that the stock is trading at $95 and has the potential to easily move outside this range by expiration. With very little room for error, an ATM ratio write adjustment on a losing stock position is not recommended.

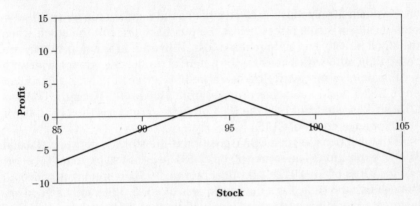

FIGURE 3.28   Ratio Write Adjustment after Stock Moves Lower

Using ITM options for the ratio write further locks in a loss in your stock position because you are using strike prices much further below your initial purchase price. For example, selling two $90 Calls brings in more premium than the ATM calls but then you are guaranteeing a $10.00 loss on your stock position, which will only be offset by the premiums from the short calls in a narrow trading range. The OTM $100 Calls provide a similar limited profit opportunity because the premium collected is smaller. If the stock continues to move lower, your loss increases, and if EBAY moves back above $100, you are prevented from participating in any upside due to the short calls.

In short, using a ratio write as an adjustment on a stock position that has moved lower puts a clamp on your ability to earn significant profits from your position. The stock is already down, and the ratio write adjustment can actually make your position worse. The only time the ratio write adjustment would truly work and produce a nice profit is if the stock was right at the short strikes at expiration. Predicting such an event is quite difficult, and it is not good risk management to put all your profitable eggs in one basket, that is, expecting the stock to be at one specific price at expiration. Therefore ratio writes of any kind are not recommended on a stock position that has moved lower unless the stock has only dropped slightly. For example, it is still possible to create an effective ratio write adjustment on EBAY if it only fell to $98. Exactly how far down is too far for a ratio write adjustment? You, the investor, will have to conduct the analysis using the current option prices to determine whether such an adjustment meets your risk/reward criteria, given your assumptions of what EBAY will move to in the near future.

What about a variable strike ratio write adjustment? Variable strike ratio write adjustments are inferior adjustments to make to a stock that has declined in value for the same reasons the regular ratio write is bad—selling calls at strike prices below the purchase price of the stock when the stock already has an unrealized loss. However, in some ways they are better than ratio writes because the potential profit zone is much wider. To see this point more clearly, let's use a variable strike ratio write adjustment on an EBAY position that has dropped from $100 to $95. Using the ITM and OTM strikes, you would sell the $90 Call for $7.50 and sell the $100 Call for $2.25 for a net credit of $9.75.

What happens to your EBAY position if the stock is between $90 and $100 at expiration? The stock will be called away at $90 by your ITM short call for a loss of $10.00. This is offset by your $9.75 in premiums collected from selling the calls, for a maximum loss of $0.25. It is rarely a good adjustment to lock in a guaranteed loss in a stock position with no chance of making a profit. Not only did you lock in a loss of $0.25, but you could lose substantially more money if the stock makes a significant move higher or lower before expiration. On one hand, you could say that the adjustment took a $5.00 unrealized loss and converted it into a locked-in $0.25 loss, a great reduction in risk. However, this reduction in risk comes with no added benefit, that is, the potential for positive returns. No matter what EBAY does, you still lose money, and therefore the variable strike ratio write is an inferior adjustment to make to a stock that has declined in value. In this chapter, there are much better alternatives for adjusting a losing stock position.

As with any trading rule, there is always the possibility for exceptions. If a stock has declined slightly, then you may still be interested in adding the ratio write or variable strike ratio write as an adjustment to your stock position. All that matters is that you understand the risk/reward profile of the proposed adjustment and determine whether it matches your expectations of the future movement of the stock. More importantly, you should beware of locking in losses with potential for greater losses and no ability at all to make money if the stock reverses and moves higher. If you follow these general rules, then there may be limited situations where you find the ratio writes to be an acceptable stock adjustment when the stock has moved lower in price from the initial purchase price.

SHORT STRADDLE/SHORT STRANGLE

Opening Position—Short Straddle

Why would you use such a risky option strategy as a short straddle to adjust your long stock position? A short straddle can be a great adjustment to a stock position based on your assumptions of the future movement of the stock and investment strategy. Because a short straddle has a short call and a short put, you create the obligation to sell stock at the call strike and purchase stock at the put strike. When the short straddle is added to a long stock position, the short call becomes a covered call because it is paired with the long stock. Therefore, the stock will be called away at the short call strike if the option is ITM at expiration. The short put creates the obligation to purchase an additional 100 shares of stock at the strike price. The effective purchase price of this additional purchase is lowered by the double premium collected from selling the put and the call.

To see why these two aspects make adding a short straddle to a stock position a good adjustment, consider the following scenario: You purchased 100 shares of EBAY at $100. Because you follow the SCORE trading formula, you have established some trade management and exit strategies. If in 2 months EBAY is above $110, you would gladly sell the stock and take a nice 10% return. On the other hand, if EBAY ever dipped back to $90 in the next 2 months, you would definitely pick up another 100 shares because you like EBAY at that price and the future prospects for the stock. These are assumptions you have made, given your analysis of the stock. As long as you are confident in your assumptions, you can use a short straddle adjustment to lock them in.

Assume the following 2-month quotes exist for EBAY options:

EBAY @ $100	Call	Put
EBAY $ 95	$8.50	$2.50
EBAY $100	$5.00	$5.00
EBAY $105	$2.50	$8.75

With EBAY at $100, you can add a short straddle to your position by selling the EBAY $100 Call for $5.00 and the EBAY $100 Put for $5.00 for a total credit of $10.00. To understand what the short straddle adjustment does to your stock position, let's look at what happens at expiration. If EBAY is anywhere above $100 at expiration, the stock will be called away at $100 by the short call. The short put will expire worthless. You keep the $10.00 in premium collected from selling both the call and the put as profit and add that to the $100 sale price. Thus, you are "selling" your EBAY stock at an effective price of $110 for a profit of $10.00. Remember that your initial exit strategy was to sell at $110 for a 10% return. What if EBAY is below $100 at expiration? Because you have a short put at $100, you will be obligated to purchase an additional 100 shares of EBAY at $100. However, because you collected $10.00 in premium from selling the straddle, your effective purchase price is $90.

Selling the short straddle therefore obligates you to sell your existing shares of EBAY at $110 or purchase another 100 shares of EBAY at $90.

This matches your previous assumptions that you would be willing to sell your stock at $110 or pick up another 100 shares if EBAY dipped back to $90. The only downside is that you are obligated to do either of these actions if EBAY is above or below $100 at expiration because you have short options. Therefore, before selling the short straddle, you must truly be willing to sell your stock or purchase more shares. Of course, you may remove the obligation simply by closing out the short options at any time before expiration if the options can be repurchased for a profit.

Now that you realize that you have a purchase or sell obligation at specific prices if EBAY is above or below $100 at expiration, you need to look at the profit profile of the long stock/short straddle position to determine your exact profit or loss depending on where EBAY is at expiration and, because you always are thinking of risk management, what your breakeven points are. The best way to do this is to look at the position in detail above and below $100 at expiration.

We already stated that no matter how far EBAY is above $100 at expiration, it will be called away by the short strike at $100 for a profit of $10.00 when the premiums collected are included. Because this is true whether EBAY is at $101 or $1,001 at expiration, you know that on the upside, the position will always make $10.00. Thus, there is no potential for loss on the upside (not counting lost potential profits if EBAY moves above $110) and no upside breakeven point. Selling a straddle against a long stock position locks in a guaranteed return as long as EBAY is above the short call strike price at expiration. This should come as no surprise because the short call side of the short straddle creates a covered call with your EBAY stock. Your potential profit is just higher because you are adding the premium from the short put to the premium collected from selling the short call.

The same $10.00 profit is realized if EBAY is right at $100 at expiration. At $100, both the short call and the short put expire worthless, and you keep the $10.00 premium as profit. Therefore, at or above $100 at expiration, the short straddle/long stock position has a guaranteed profit of $10.00. For any short straddle/long stock position, your guaranteed profit on the upside is simply the strike price plus the total premiums collected minus the purchase price of the stock.

The profit/loss profile on the EBAY short straddle/long stock position is slightly different if EBAY is below $100 at expiration. Remember that your short put at $100 will obligate you to purchase 100 shares of EBAY at $100 no matter how far EBAY has dropped. Therefore your profit or loss is highly dependent on where EBAY is at expiration. Assume EBAY is at $95 at expiration. With respect to your EBAY position, you have a loss of $5.00. You are also now the owner of another 100 shares of EBAY with a basis of $90. Because your effective purchase price for those 100 shares is $90, you have a profit of $5.00 with the current market price at $95. The $5.00 loss on your original EBAY position is offset by the $5.00 gain on your new shares of EBAY for a net profit/loss of $0.00. Therefore, your downside breakeven point is $95. Do not overlook that $95 remains your breakeven point as long as you hold the 200 shares of stock, because you purchased 100 shares at $100 and 100 shares at $90 for a combined cost basis of $95. Therefore, if you maintain the 200 shares after assignment of the short put, you need to be aware of your new breakeven points and risk/reward characteristics.

What if EBAY is at $90 at expiration? You will have a $10.00 loss on your 100 shares of EBAY and be even on your new set of shares purchased at an effective price of $90 for a net loss of $10.00. If you use different examples of EBAY below $100 at expiration, you will see that the potential loss on the downside can grow quite quickly. As EBAY moves below $90, you not only have a loss on your EBAY stock position, but you also incur a loss on the additional 100 shares of EBAY you are obligated to purchase with an effective price of $90.

The risk/reward profile in Figure 3.29 gives a good visual picture of the risk and reward of adding a short straddle to your long stock position. Although you have a nice flat guaranteed profit on the upside, you do have the potential for huge losses on the downside, not to mention the additional capital outlay of purchasing an additional 100 shares of EBAY if you are assigned on the short put.

As Figure 3.29 indicates, the combined position has a better risk/reward profile than being long EBAY when the stock is between $90 and $110, although a loss still occurs below $95. Even though you entered

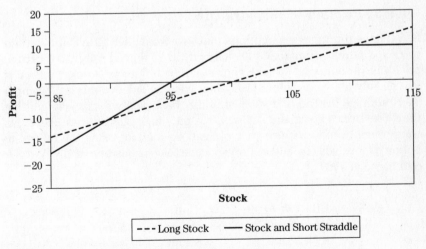

FIGURE 3.29 Stock Combined with Short Straddle versus Long Stock

into this short straddle adjustment with the idea that you would be willing to sell EBAY at $110 and/or be willing to pick up another 100 shares at $90 if you could, you should still be aware of what circumstances make the short straddle the best adjustment. If you feel that EBAY could move well above $110 by expiration, then the short straddle would just be cutting you out of huge potential profits and therefore would not be the best adjustment. At the same time, if you feel EBAY could dip down to $90 and continue to fall, then you would not be so willing to pick up another 100 shares of EBAY.

The risk/reward profile of the short straddle/long stock combination looks similar to the covered call profile. Because you have a long stock position and a short call, that portion of the short straddle/long stock combination does create a covered call. Remember that in Chapter 2, when we discussed synthetic positions, we demonstrated that a covered call position has the same risk/reward profile as a short put position. Therefore, the covered call portion of the short straddle adjustment is equivalent to a short put. The other short put in the short straddle is added to the synthetic short put and makes the position synthetically equivalent to two naked puts.

Adding the short straddle to the long stock position is therefore the same as a double naked put position or two covered calls. That is why the risk/reward profile has the same shape as a covered call position. However, because it is really equivalent to a double covered call position, the potential profit is higher. In exchange for the higher potential profit, the position will lose money faster if the stock drops in price, due to the presence of the short put in the naked straddle.

Opening Position—Short Strangle

If you have the same assumptions that you would sell EBAY at a certain price and purchase another 100 shares if EBAY dipped lower to a certain price but do not want to lose your stock or buy more stock if EBAY is just slightly above or below $100, then you can achieve this goal using a short strangle instead of a short straddle. Basically, you are just splitting the strike prices apart and selling OTM puts and calls so that EBAY has some room to move before your obligations kick in. Using the following option quotes, you can add a short strangle to your position of EBAY stock purchased at $100:

EBAY @ $100	Call	Put
EBAY $ 95	$8.50	$2.50
EBAY $100	$5.00	$5.00
EBAY $105	$2.50	$8.75

The short strangle is added by selling the $105 Call for $2.50 and the $95 Put for $2.50 for a net credit of $5.00. This net credit is smaller than the credit received for selling the short straddle because the options you are using are OTM as opposed to the ATM options used for the straddle. To understand the profit profile of the position, let's look at what happens when EBAY is at different prices at expiration.

If EBAY is between $95 and $105, both the short call and the short put will expire worthless. However, whether a profit occurs depends on the premium collected. In this example, you collected $5.00 in premium. If EBAY is between $100 and $105, then the profit is the $5.00 in premium collected plus any gain in the stock. If EBAY is between $100 and $95, the profit/loss is the $5.00 in premium collected minus any loss in the stock. If EBAY is above $105 at expiration, then your stock will be called away at $105 for a $5.00 gain plus the $5.00 in premiums collected for a total profit of $10.00. This profit of $10.00 is achieved no matter how far above $105 EBAY is at expiration, and just like the short straddle/long stock combination, there is no upside breakeven point.

What happens if EBAY is below $95 at expiration? Just as with the short straddle, you will not only have a loss on your initial stock position, but you will also be obligated to purchase an additional 100 shares of EBAY at an effective price of $90 ($95 strike price minus $5.00 in premiums collected from short call and short put). Your downside breakeven point is $95, where the $5.00 in premiums collected offsets the $5.00 loss in your EBAY stock position. Figure 3.30 gives the complete profit and loss picture.

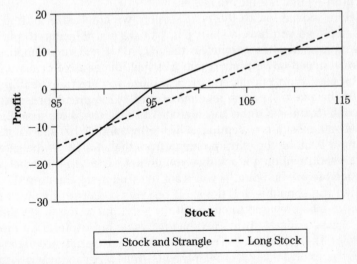

FIGURE 3.30 Long Stock Combined with Short Strangle

The risk/reward profile for the short strangle/long stock combination in Figure 3.30 is slightly different from the short straddle/long stock combination profile in Figure 3.29, especially between $95 and $105, where the profit is lower. Because you are selling OTM options in the short strangle, the premium collected is going to be lower, and therefore the combined position will have a lower maximum profit than if the short straddle is used. Then why use the short strangle instead of the short straddle?

The short strangle has one benefit over the short straddle that makes it more desirable in certain situations. Because the strike prices are split apart, EBAY can be between $95 and $105 at expiration and the stock will not get called away nor will you be required to purchase an additional 100 shares. Using OTM strikes allows EBAY some room to move before your short options are assigned. This is the main distinction between the short straddle and the short strangle, and if you do not truly want any obligations from only a slight movement in the stock price, then the short strangle adjustment is preferred.

These examples indicate that adding the short straddle or the short strangle to a long stock position as an opening combination does have a slightly upward bias. In other words, the maximum profit is obtained when the stock moves higher. Because the profile of the combination looks similar to that of a covered call but with slightly higher risk, a covered call or ratio write might be a better initial combination. Compare the foregoing risk/reward profiles to those of the initial risk/reward profiles of the covered call and ratio write positions. As we will demonstrate shortly, the better use of short straddles and short strangles is as an adjustment to a stock position that has moved higher.

Before moving on to the next section, we emphasize an important point. Although you have a short put, you are not obligated to purchase another 100 shares of stock unless the put is ITM and, more importantly, you are assigned on your short put. Although the odds of being assigned early on your short put depend on how close you are to expiration, how far ITM the put is, and the amount of time value premium is left, it is still a risk that needs to be considered. You may use short straddles and short strangles with no intention of acquiring another 100 shares of stock but simply wanting the extra premium from the addition of the short put with the short call on a stock that you do not expect to move below the downside breakeven point. If you want to avoid assignment on the short put, then you should watch the short put very closely if the stock drops in price and be prepared to close out the short put as the time value premium begins to shrink away (review time value in Chapter 2 for more on this topic). Therefore, you can avoid the additional use of funds to purchase the 100 shares of stock, which simply adds even more capital at risk to your position.

Stock Moves Higher—Short Straddle

If your stock has moved higher, what benefit does the adjustment bring of adding a short straddle or a short strangle to the position? First and foremost, you are bringing in a credit from the sale of the call and the put. This premium increases your profit potential and hedges some of your loss on the downside. The short call portion of the straddle or strangle gives you a predetermined exit point because your stock will be called away if the short call is ITM. Your short put brings in extra premium and allows you to add another 100 shares to your position at a below-market price as long as the stock has not fallen too far by expiration. These benefits are of course outweighed by the large risks if the stock drops too far below the short put strike. If that happens, your entire position results in a loss and could require additional outlay to purchase another 100 shares of stock. Let's examine how a short straddle/strangle adjustment can be used properly to leverage your returns and even provide a slight downside hedge.

Assume you purchased EBAY at $100 and it has moved higher to $110. You expect EBAY to move sideways somewhat over the next month or so and would not mind selling the stock if it moved above $115. On the other hand, you also would want a small hedge on your profits if EBAY drops slightly and may even consider purchasing another 100 shares on a price dip. With these assumptions in mind, you notice the following quotes for 1-month EBAY options and consider selling a straddle against your stock position:

EBAY @ $110	Call	Put
EBAY $105	$7.50	$2.00
EBAY $110	$4.50	$4.50
EBAY $115	$2.50	$7.25

With EBAY at $110, you would adjust your long stock position with the short straddle by selling the $110 Call and $110 Put for $4.50 each for a total credit of $9.00. Because you already have a $10.00 unrealized gain in your position, let's see how the addition of the short straddle affects your risk/reward profile.

If EBAY were exactly at $110 at expiration, both the short call and the short put would expire worthless for a profit of $9.00. Added to your $10.00 gain in the stock, you would have a total profit of $19.00 with EBAY at $110. This is your maximum profit, which is always at the short strike of the straddle. If EBAY is anywhere above $110 at expiration, you will still have a total profit of $19.00 because your stock will be called away at $110 by your short call ($10.00 profit on stock sale plus $9.00 in premiums collected). Therefore, your effective sales price if EBAY is called away is

$119.00. This is important to calculate because if EBAY is expected to rise well beyond your effective sale price, then you might reconsider selling the straddle, which will cut off potential profits. Of course, this is an assumption you have to make, given your analysis of the underlying stock. That is why you tend to use short-term options when selling straddles so that the probability of the stock moving well above your effective sale price is lower.

More importantly, you must consider what will happen if EBAY is below $110 at expiration, because you have a short put at $110. If EBAY is below $110, you will be obligated by your short put to buy 100 shares of EBAY at $110. However, because you collected $9.00 in premiums (the call will expire worthless), your effective purchase price of the additional shares of EBAY is $101. Therefore, above $101 you could have a profit on your original shares of EBAY as well as on the additional 100 shares you would be obligated to buy. Your profit could also be calculated on the repurchase of the short put to remove the possibility of assignment if EBAY is below $110 but above $101 (for calculating profit and loss you will just assume you are assigned on the short put even though the same profit and loss are calculated as if you bought back the short put at expiration because it will have no time value).

For example, if EBAY is at $108, you will have an $8.00 profit on your original shares of EBAY. You will also have a $7.00 profit on your additional shares of EBAY with a cost basis of $101 for a total profit of $15.00. Using the same method, you can see that you would have a total profit of $9.00 if EBAY was at $105 at expiration. At $101, you would have no profit or loss on your additional 100 shares of EBAY but still have a profit of $1.00 on your original position. The breakeven point is $100.50 because the $0.50 profit on your original position would be offset by the $0.50 loss from your additional shares of EBAY purchased at $101. Figure 3.31 graphically represents the profit and loss of adding the short straddle to your EBAY position, which has moved from $100 to $110.

As mentioned earlier, the risk/reward profile looks similar to a covered call profile with a limited reward and much greater risk on the downside. Your reward is increased by selling the short put to increase your premium received along with selling the short call. However, as Figure 3.31 indicates, selling the short put means you lose on two positions as the stock moves lower. Your breakeven point is $100.50, which is slightly higher than your original purchase price, so this position not only has risk, but it has slightly more risk than without the short straddle adjustment.

What you gain from adding the short straddle to your position is that between $101 and $119, your adjusted position has a higher reward than your stock position without the adjustment. If you refer back to

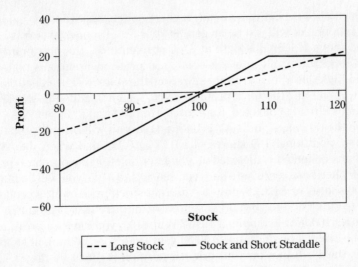

FIGURE 3.31   Stock Combined with Short Straddle after Stock Moves Higher

Figure 3.31, which compares the adjusted position to EBAY stock without the adjustment, you can see the higher profit between $101 and $119. It is no coincidence that this range is $9.00 above and below your current price of $110 for EBAY (which is also the strike price) because the premiums add to your profit on the upside and downside to the extent of the amount collected from selling the straddle. Therefore, when considering selling the straddle as an adjustment, you need to take the premiums into considera-tion to understand the range you would want the stock to trade within. If your assumptions are that EBAY will trade within this range, then the short straddle is a good adjustment to increase your returns.

   In the previous example, EBAY was trading right at a strike price so it was easy to add the ATM short straddle to your position. What if EBAY is between strikes? If EBAY is within $1 of a strike, then you still can focus on the ATM strike. If EBAY, for example, is at $107, you need to decide whether you use the $105 strike or the $110 strike for your short straddle. Whichever one you choose will involve a short option already ITM, be it the short call at $105 or the short put at $110. The decision will come down to comparing the risk/reward profiles to determine which one best fits your assumptions and risk/reward characteristics.

   First, let's analyze the use of the $105 short straddle with EBAY trad-ing at $107. Let's assume that the option prices for the $105 straddle with EBAY at $107 are such that a $105 straddle can be sold for $8.50. The call is already ITM in this straddle, so you should be aware of early assignment.

However, because EBAY is already higher in price than what you paid for it, early assignment will just mean getting your profit sooner, which is always a good thing. If EBAY is right at $105 at expiration, the maximum profit is $13.50 ($5.00 profit in stock plus $8.50 profit in premiums collected). Should EBAY be above $105 at expiration, the stock will be called away by the short call at $105 for a profit of $5.00, which is added to the $8.50 in premiums already collected, for a total profit of $13.50.

On the downside, if EBAY is below $105, you will be obligated to purchase an additional 100 shares of EBAY at $105, and when the $8.50 in premiums collected is factored in, you have an effective purchase price of $96.50. Therefore, anywhere between $96.50 and $105, you will be purchasing 100 shares of EBAY below the current stock price, which produces a profit to either add to your original position or offset any loss on EBAY if it is below $100. For example, if EBAY is at $100, you have no profit or loss on your original position but a $3.50 gain from your additional shares. At $98.25, the $1.75 loss on your original position is offset by the $1.75 gain from your newly acquired shares at $96.50. Therefore, $98.25 is your downside breakeven point.

Let's compare the use of the $105 short straddle as an adjustment to the $110 short straddle to see which one is a better adjustment to your EBAY position at $107. If you sold the $110 straddle, you would bring in $9.00 in premium. In the $110 straddle, your short put is ITM, so you need to be aware of early assignment, which will obligate you to purchase an additional 100 shares of EBAY at $110. Because you collected $9.00 in premiums, your actual effective purchase price of these additional shares is really $101.

If EBAY is at $110 at expiration, both options will expire worthless and you will have a $10.00 gain on the stock, which, combined with the $9.00 in premiums collected, equates to a total profit of $19.00. If EBAY is anywhere above $110 at expiration, the profit will still be $19.00 because the stock will be called away at $110. If EBAY is anywhere below $110, as noted earlier, you will be obligated to purchase another 100 shares at an effective price of $101. Therefore, between $101 and $110, your combined position will have an additional profit derived from the additional 100 shares of stock. For example, if EBAY is at $105, you not only have a $5.00 profit from your original position, but another $4.00 in profit from your additional shares purchased at $101 for a total profit of $9.00. Below $100, the loss on your additional shares is added to the loss on your original shares, which increases your risk to the downside. Your breakeven point on the downside is $100.50, where the $0.50 gain on your original shares offsets the $0.50 loss on your additional shares purchased at $101.

Now that you understand the different characteristics of using a straddle above and below the current price of the stock, let's compare the

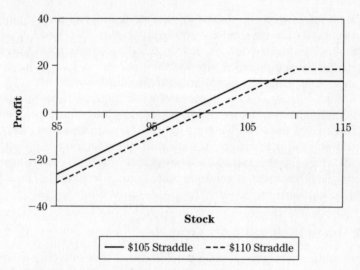

FIGURE 3.32 $105 Straddle versus $110 Straddle

two to visually understand the risk/reward profiles. Figure 3.32 graphs the risk/reward profile of using the $105 short straddle and the $110 short straddle with EBAY at $107. The $105 short straddle is already ITM on the call side and therefore does not allow for as much profit potential on the upside as the $110 short straddle. Because the strike price on the short put for the $105 straddle is also below the current price, the stock has some room to move before the short put is in the money. This results in the lower breakeven point on the downside. Therefore, the $105 short straddle gives you a lower reward but reduces your risk by giving you a lower breakeven point and, therefore, has a downward bias.

The $110 short straddle allows for more upside room because the short call is OTM and the stock can move slightly higher before it will be called away. Even though in our example the $110 short straddle brought in $0.50 more credit than the $105 short straddle, this difference is minor when compared to the effect of the different strike prices. The $110 short put is already ITM because it is above the current price of EBAY, and therefore the breakeven point is higher than the $105 short straddle. The OTM straddle (from the perspective of the short call) has an upward bias. Therefore, if a stock is between strike prices and you wish to add a short straddle, the choice of the strike above or below the stock price will depend on what bias you have about the possible movement of the stock.

When using the short straddle, the underlying assumption does not have to be that you are willing to purchase another 100 shares at a lower price if the short put is ITM. Selling the put may simply be a way of bringing in more premium with the short call on a stock that has gone up in price but is expected to move sideways or slightly higher. In general, if you expect the stock to move sideways, then you sell options to collect premium and hope for the options to expire worthless or shrink enough in value to result in a profit. Thus, the intention with the short straddle is to close out the position sometime before expiration when the time value premium of the ITM option has shrunk to a point where early assignment is a possibility. In that case, if the stock has truly moved sideways, then you can pocket any profit on closing the short straddle and still maintain your position in the stock. Once the short straddle is closed, you are free to make any additional option adjustment to generate more income from selling options, to hedge the position, or to leverage for greater profits on the upside.

Stock Moves Higher—Short Strangle

You can add a short strangle on a stock that has moved higher to achieve the same goals of selling the stock at a predetermined price or possibly picking up another 100 shares at a below-market price. The short strangle could also be used when your long stock position is expected to trade sideways over a short period of time to bring in some income to your position in addition to your unrealized gain. Using the short strangle has one distinct advantage over using the short straddle. Because you tend to use the ATM strike for the short straddle, you will have an obligation to either sell your stock or purchase an additional 100 shares if the stock moves even slightly higher or lower, causing one of your short options to be ITM. You could always close out the short straddle as expiration approaches and the time values begin to disappear, but not only will you have to monitor the position much more closely, early assignment on one of the short options is always a risk. If you want simply to bring in some income to your stock position as it enters into a sideways pattern, then you have to be vigilant and ready to close out the short straddle to lock in some or all of that income and avoid assignment.

The short strangle has the advantage of giving you room to breathe. Because the short strangle consists of an OTM call and put, the stock has some room to move up or down before any of the options move ITM. In other words, you may never have to be assigned on any of your short options if the stock stays between the two strike prices used in your short strangle. This "cushion" gives you the breathing room you need to allow the stock to fluctuate slightly and still have a good possibility of keeping the entire premium collected. Even if the stock does make a move up or down, the premium still gives you a nice wide profit zone just as with the short straddle. This beneficial cushion that you receive does not come for free. The cost is less premium collected than the short straddle because you are using OTM options. With this distinction in mind, let's look at how you can use the short strangle to adjust your stock position that has moved higher.

Assume you purchase EBAY at $100 and it has moved to $110. The observed 1-month option prices that you can use to make the short strangle adjustment are listed as follows. Because EBAY is at $110, you will sell the $105 Put and the $115 Call to add the short strangle to the position. Selling these two options brings in a premium of $4.50:

EBAY @ $110	Call	Put
EBAY $105	$7.50	$2.00
EBAY $110	$4.50	$4.50
EBAY $115	$2.50	$7.25

If EBAY is above $115 at expiration, then the short put will expire worthless and your stock will be called away by the short call at $115 for a $15.00 gain. Because you collected $4.50 in premiums, the effective selling price of your stock when called away is $119.50 for a total profit of $19.50. This is the maximum profit because no matter how high EBAY climbs, you can only make $19.50 on the sale of the stock due to the short call. If EBAY is between the $105 and $115 strike prices at expiration, both the short put and the short call will expire worthless, and you keep the $4.50 in premium collected. The profit realized between $105 and $115 is simply the price of the stock at expiration minus the cost basis of $100 plus the $4.50 in premiums. For example, if EBAY is at $111, the profit is $111 minus $100 ($11.00) plus the $4.50 for a total profit of $15.50. Basically, your profit between $105 and $115 is increased by the profit from selling the short strangle.

If EBAY is below $105, you will be obligated to purchase another 100 shares of stock at $105. Because you collected $4.50 in premiums, your effective purchase price of the additional shares of EBAY is $100.50. Between $100.50 and $105, the profit in your original position will be increased by the profit realized in your additional 100 shares of stock. For example, if EBAY is at $103.50 at expiration, your profit of $3.50 on the original stock is added to the profit of $3.00 on the additional shares for a total profit of $6.50. Your downside breakeven point is $100.25 because the $0.25 gain on your original 100 shares will be offset by the $0.25 loss on the additional 100 shares purchased at $100.50. Below $100, you will have a combined loss on both EBAY positions.

Figure 3.33 indicates that the return on the combined position is better than that of just the EBAY stock alone if EBAY is between $100.25 and $119.50 at expiration. This example again illustrates why doing profit and loss calculations before entering a trade adjustment is important. If you did the calculations prior to adding the short strangle and determined that the increased profit zone between $100.25 and $119.50 covered the range

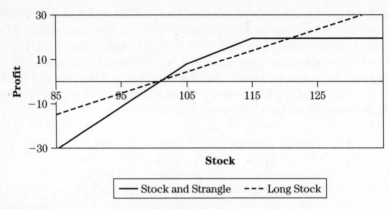

FIGURE 3.33 Long Stock versus Short Strangle Combination

of where you expected EBAY to fall at expiration, then you would be very inclined to add the short strangle as an adjustment to your long stock position in order to increase your returns. With EBAY at $110, the short strangle gives you a wide range for enhanced profits so that if EBAY does not stay sideways but indeed moves in one direction, you can absorb some of that movement and still have a higher return than if you did not adjust your position.

The use of the short strangle over the short straddle has another advantage—when the stock falls between strike prices. If EBAY is at $112, the decision to add a short straddle to the position raises the question as to whether to sell the $110 straddle or the $115 straddle. The issue can be avoided by simply using the short strangle and using the strike prices around the current price. Assume you purchased EBAY at $100 and it has moved to $112 and you observe the following 1-month EBAY option quotes:

EBAY @ $112	Call	Put
EBAY $110	$4.50	$2.50
EBAY $115	$2.25	$5.00

To add the short strangle to your long stock position, sell the $115 Call for $2.25 and sell the $110 Put for $2.50 for a total credit of $4.75. If EBAY is above $115 at expiration, then your stock will be called away at $115 due to the short call, for a profit of $19.75 ($15.00 profit on sale of stock plus $4.75 in premiums collected). If EBAY is between $110 and $115, then both the short put and the short call will expire worthless, and you will add the $4.75 in premiums collected to your profit in the stock position. For example, if

EBAY is still at $112 at expiration, you will add the $4.75 to your $12.00 profit in the stock for a total profit of $16.75.

If EBAY is below $110 at expiration, then you will be obligated to purchase an additional 100 shares of EBAY at an effective price of $105.25 ($110 strike price minus $4.75 in premiums collected). As EBAY moves below $105.25, the loss in the additional shares begins to offset the profit in the original shares of EBAY above $100; below $100, both sets of shares produce a loss. The downside breakeven point is $102.625, where the gain from your long stock position is offset by the loss from the additional 100 shares of EBAY purchased.

Figure 3.34 indicates that the adjusted stock position by the use of the short strangle achieves a better return over the long stock alone if EBAY is between $105 and $119.75. Again, it is important to know these points because you only want to make an adjustment by adding the short strangle if the adjustment has the potential to increase your returns on the long stock position. If you expect EBAY to move sideways and stay between the two comparison points in which the adjustment outperforms the straight stock position, then the short strangle is a good adjustment. Remember that if you are not committed to acquire another 100 shares of EBAY stock if it is below $105 at or before expiration, then you need to close out the short put whenever early assignment seems imminent. Early assignment can occur theoretically at any time but is most likely to occur when the short put is deep ITM and all time value has disappeared from the short put premium.

In the previous example, with EBAY at $112, we used the $110 and $115 strikes to add the short strangle. As stated before, option trading is

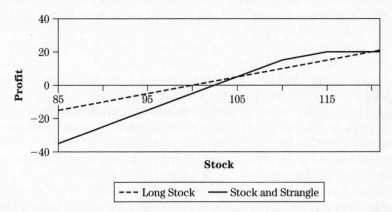

FIGURE 3.34 Long Stock Combined with Short Strangle after Stock Moves Higher

limited only by your imagination. A short strangle involves OTM strikes, and you are free to choose whichever strikes you feel comfortable with. In the previous example, you could have used the $105 and $115 strikes with EBAY at $112. You could have also used the $110 and $120 strikes. Changing the strikes adjusts the risk/reward profile, and therefore you can choose whichever strike prices produce a risk/reward profile, you are comfortable with. Remember, though, that if you move the strike prices further away, you will collect less premium. Wider strikes produce a wider zone without any fear of assignment on short options but also reduce the maximum reward because you take in less premium. As always, there is a trade-off that you have to make to determine the adjustment that best suits your assumptions and comfort level.

Stock Moves Lower—Short Straddle/Stock Repair

When a stock moves lower, any adjustment you make is usually to either prevent any further losses while hoping for a turnaround or create limited loss/potential profit from a losing situation. Very few option adjustments can accomplish both, but there are limited situations where the addition of a short straddle can work almost perfectly to achieve both goals when added to a stock position that has a slight loss. Therefore, a short straddle is an adjustment worth considering.

Remember that a short straddle consists of a short call and a short put. If you sell an ATM short straddle on a stock with a small loss, then you are selling a short call with a strike price below your purchase price. Does this not lock in a loss in your stock position without preventing further loss as the stock continues to drop? Normally this is true, and under covered calls, we discussed that selling an ITM call on a stock that has fallen in price at a strike that is below your purchase price is simply locking in a loss, no matter how far the stock recovers.

The difference with the short straddle is that you are also selling a short put and therefore bringing in more premium than if you simply sold a short call. The combined premium collected from the call and the put should produce a profit if the stock does move higher. If not, then you should avoid using the adjustment. How will you decide whether the premium collected is enough to create a profit if the stock moves back higher? The easiest method for making this determination is simply to see whether the premium collected plus the strike price of the short straddle is greater than your original purchase price. If not, then selling the straddle will lock in a guaranteed loss no matter what the stock does, even if it moves much higher. For example, if the stock you purchased at $100 drops to $85, then selling a short straddle at a strike price of $85 for $6.00 will not create a profitable trade, no matter how high the stock recovers. We analyze this in a moment, but first we discuss the short put portion of the short straddle adjustment.

The short put obligates you to purchase additional shares if the stock continues to move lower. As a good risk manager, you should be wary about adding an obligation to purchase more stock to a current position that has already fallen—in other words, why add more passengers to the sinking ship? This is a valid concern, which must be answered satisfactorily before adding a short straddle as an adjustment to a stock position that has fallen in price. Basically you are not looking to add to your fallen position. You are simply looking to take in additional premium to add to your short call to provide a better hedge against your current losing position and create the potential for increased profit, should the stock recover somewhat. You really are not looking to get assigned on your short put position, and therefore you should be ready to close out a short put that has moved too far ITM and is in danger of being assigned early.

With that in mind, you should not be adding a short straddle to a fallen stock position if your assumption is that the stock could continue to fall. The better risk management decision may involve a different type of option adjustment or even closing out the losing position before your loss increases. Therefore, before adding a short straddle, you should feel somewhat confident that the drop is temporary and that the stock will either move sideways or higher. However, even if you are wrong, then, as shown in the following example, the short straddle will still provide a significant hedge should the stock fall further by expiration.

With this framework in mind, we use an example to illustrate how a short straddle can reform a losing stock position into something profitable. Assume you purchased 100 shares of EBAY at $100 and it has dropped to $95. You still like the stock but are concerned about this recent slide in price. You still expect the stock to move higher but also fear it might move in a sideways pattern for a period of time. You also have some small fear that EBAY could continue to drop in price, but you feel that there is enough support such that the probability that EBAY will drop very much further is small. This analysis describes a situation where the short straddle may be a good adjustment to make. Let's also assume that a 1-month EBAY $95 straddle can be sold for $8.00.

If you sell the EBAY $95 straddle for $8.00, you will be obligated to sell your EBAY stock position at $95 as a result of your short call. As discussed earlier, why would you create an obligation to sell a stock at a strike price lower than what you paid for the stock? Well, you received $8.00 in premium for selling the straddle, so if you are assigned on your short call, your actual selling price is really $103 ($95 strike plus $8.00 in premium). Remember that to determine whether selling the short straddle is a good adjustment, you need to determine whether it allows for a profit. In this example, creating an effective selling price of $103 produces a $3.00 profit if your short call is assigned, and therefore, initially, your short straddle seems to be a good adjustment.

If EBAY is above $95 at expiration, then you will have your stock called away at $95 for a profit of $3.00. This $3.00 profit is quite welcome if EBAY is between $95 and $100. Without the adjustment, you would have a loss on your position. However, by adding the short straddle, you can still produce a profit even if EBAY does not get back to your original purchase price. Your adjustment has turned a losing position into a profitable and much improved one if EBAY is between $95 and $103 at expiration. If EBAY moves above $103 by expiration, you cannot participate in this upside movement because you have a short call at $95. This is the negative side of your straddle adjustment, but obviously if you felt that EBAY could rebound above $103 in 1 month, then you would not have considered using the short straddle. If EBAY happens to move above $103 unexpectedly, naturally you would be upset at not participating in this price upswing, but your adjustment still gives you a profit, and there is no such thing as a bad profit.

If you have a $3.00 profit on your assigned call at the $95 strike, then obviously the breakeven point on your EBAY stock is no longer $100. Selling the short straddle and collecting the premium lowers your breakeven point. Your new breakeven point needs to take into consideration the fact that you have a short put, which will be ITM if EBAY moves further below $95. For example, if EBAY is at $93.50 at expiration, the short call will expire worthless, and the short put will have a value of $1.50 ($95 strike minus $93.50 price at expiration). If you buy back the short put on expiration day to remove your obligation of assignment, then you will have a profit of $6.50 on your short straddle ($8.00 premiums collected minus $1.50 to purchase back short put). This $6.50 profit on the short straddle will be offset by the $6.50 loss on EBAY at $93.50. Therefore, your new breakeven point is now $93.50—or $6.50 lower than your original purchase price.

Your addition of the short straddle to the EBAY position, which has fallen from $100 to $95, has allowed you to achieve a profit even if EBAY stays below $100, and has also lowered your breakeven point to below $94. So far the adjustment has achieved the purpose of reducing your risk (i.e., lowering the breakeven point) and producing a potential profit from a losing position. What sort of hedge does the short straddle provide on further losses? Well, if EBAY falls below $93.50, your breakeven point, then the $8.00 in premiums collected will reduce the amount of loss, although it will not prevent a loss altogether. For example, if EBAY is at $90 at expiration, your $10.00 loss on your stock position will be offset somewhat by your short straddle. The short straddle will have an expiration day value of

$5.00. If you were to close it out, you would realize a profit of $3.00 ($8.00 in premiums collected minus $5.00 to close out the straddle). This $3.00 profit will reduce your otherwise $10.00 loss to $7.00. Although you still have a loss on your position, the short straddle adjustment has reduced the loss somewhat.

This loss reduction characteristic does not protect you if you begin to lose money on the short straddle; that is, the stock moves lower. Because you collected $8.00 for selling the $95 straddle, you will increase your losses on your stock position when the short straddle falls below its breakeven point. The short straddle breakeven point on the downside is simply the strike price of the short straddle minus the premium collected ($95.00 − $8.00 = $87.00). At $87, the short straddle will break even and therefore will no longer offset the loss of the stock position. Below $87, the short straddle will experience a loss, and this loss is added to your already losing position in the stock. Therefore, before adding the short straddle, you should be aware of the downside point at which the short straddle adjustment stops hedging your loss and actually begins to add to it. At that point, you should get out of not only the stock position, but the short straddle as well.

As Figure 3.35 indicates, the short straddle adjustment improves the profit profile of your long stock position if EBAY is between $87 and $103 at expiration. With EBAY at $95 when you added the short straddle, you can see that your adjustment contemplates EBAY moving either sideways or only slightly higher or lower. This adjustment is not appropriate for a stock you expect to have a large price swing higher or lower because the short put will add to your losses on the downside and your short call will

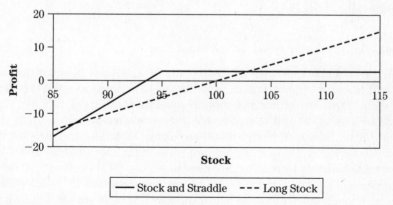

FIGURE 3.35 Long Stock Combined with Short Straddle after Stock Moves Lower

cut you off at some point of potential profit on the upside. Therefore, you need to calculate the range where the adjusted position outperforms the unadjusted position before deciding whether the short straddle is an appropriate adjustment.

Just to emphasize how a short straddle can be a bad adjustment if the stock falls too far, assume that EBAY has fallen to $90 from $100 and the $90 straddle can be sold for $8.00. If you sell the $90 short straddle, then your stock will be called away at $90 if the $90 short call is ITM at expiration. Because you collected $8.00 in premium, your effective selling price of the stock is really $98.00 for a $2.00 loss. At first glance, it may seem desirable to turn a potential $5.00 or $10.00 loss on your EBAY position into only a $2.00 loss, but it is never desirable to lock in a loss if there is any chance at all for a profit. If EBAY rallies above $100, then you will still have a $2.00 loss. You may consider selling further out straddles to bring in more premium and therefore avoid creating a guaranteed losing position. Although more time allows for more premium, it also gives the stock more time to make a significant move higher or lower, which could be detrimental to your adjusted position. If you want more time to allow the stock to recover, then other adjustments, which do not include selling options short, may be better.

A short straddle, therefore, could be an excellent adjustment to a stock position that has moved slightly lower by bringing in a premium to offset somewhat further losses and actually produce a profit even if EBAY does not move back above the original purchase price. Short straddles should not be added to any losing stock position that guarantees a locked-in loss. More importantly, the short straddle will not prevent significant losses if the stock continues to fall further. If you feel that a further drop in price is very likely, then avoid the short straddle adjustment on a stock that has already moved lower.

Stock Moves Lower—Short Strangle

The use of a short strangle as an adjustment to a stock position that has moved lower is appropriate in only limited situations. As with the short straddle, use the short strangle only if you expect the stock to move sideways or higher, yet still want a hedge if the stock happens to move somewhat lower. However, because you are using OTM calls and puts for the short strangle, the amount of premium collected is lower and therefore the downside hedge is lower. On the other hand, the OTM options also mean that you will not be assigned on your short options unless the stock makes a large enough move above or below the short strangle strikes.

As with short straddles, short strangle adjustments only work if the stock has fallen slightly and no guaranteed loss is locked in. Assume your

EBAY stock has fallen from $100 to $95 and a 1-month short strangle using the $90 Put and $100 Call strikes can be sold for $4.00. If EBAY is between $90 and $100 at expiration, then both short options expire worthless and you keep the $4.00 in premiums collected. Because you purchased EBAY originally at $100, you still have a loss on your stock position, but this is offset partially by the $4.00 collected from the short strangle. For example, if EBAY is still at $95 at expiration, then your $5.00 loss in the stock is reduced to $1.00 by the $4.00 short strangle premiums. If EBAY is at $96 at expiration, then the $4.00 loss on your stock position is offset by the $4.00 in premiums collected. Therefore, selling the short strangle has reduced your breakeven point to $96 from $100. If EBAY only moves $1.00 higher by expiration, you have no loss.

Because $96 is your new breakeven point, your adjusted position can therefore produce a profit if EBAY moves higher, even above $100. If EBAY is above $100, your stock will be called away at $100. Because you collected $4.00 in premium, your effective sales price is $104. If EBAY is between $96 and $100, you have a profit and still have your stock, and you can sell the stock to lock in that profit, add another adjustment, or simply let the stock continue to run. Between $96 and $90, you have a loss on your stock position, which is only partially offset by the premiums collected from the short strangle. For example, if EBAY is at $91, your $9.00 loss on EBAY is reduced by $4.00 to $5.00. Between $86 and $90, your loss is still partially hedged. Below $86, your short strangle begins to lose money because it will cost more than $4.00 to close out the short put. This loss is added to your stock loss. Therefore, below $86 your adjusted position performs worse than your unadjusted position.

As Figure 3.36 indicates, the adjusted position performs better than the EBAY stock alone between $86 and $104. More importantly, the position results in a profit between $96 and $100, where the unadjusted stock would result in a loss. This range is narrower than your short straddle out-performance range because the premium collected from selling the strangle is less than that received from selling the straddle. The reason for selecting the short strangle over the short straddle is that the wide strikes of the short strangle allow you to collect premium if the stock moves sideways until expiration and still not have any obligation to sell your stock or purchase more shares. If the stock stays between the strike prices, then your short options expire worthless, and you can still roll into another adjustment to bring in more premium.

Just as with the short straddle, the short strangle adjustment should not be used if the stock has fallen by a significant amount. For example, if EBAY falls to $90, using an $85/$95 strangle will most likely lock in guaranteed loss because the $95 strike price of your short call is below the purchase price. Because the premium taken in is much smaller than that

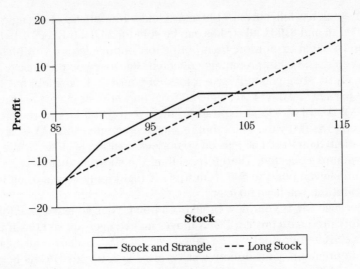

FIGURE 3.36   Long Stock Combined with Short Strangle after Stock Moves Lower

of the short straddle, the effective selling price will be below your original purchase price of $100. Therefore, as with the short straddle, a short strangle adjustment should only be added to a stock position that has fallen slightly and is expected to move sideways or slightly higher.

The short straddle and short strangle involve the sale of options, and therefore you should take the implied volatility of those options into consideration. To bring in the most premium, you want to sell options that are relatively expensive. To determine whether an option is relatively expensive, you use implied volatility as an indicator (see Chapter 2). When selling a straddle or strangle, you want to make sure that the implied volatility of the options you wish to sell is not relatively low. If the implied volatility is relatively low, then you will be taking in a very small premium. The lower the premium, the less potential profit and the less downside hedge you get. Also, if you sell options with low implied volatility, your position could suffer if implied volatility suddenly increases, even if the stock does not move at all. When that happens, the short options increase in price, which makes it more expensive to buy them back if you need to close out the position.

Therefore, you not only must consider where you expect your stock position to move to once you add your short straddle or strangle adjustment, but also understand the implied volatility of the options you wish to sell. If the implied volatility is relatively low, then you will be less inclined to create an adjustment that involves selling premium because the implied volatility indicates that the underlying stock's options are relatively cheap.

CALL RATIO SPREAD

A call ratio spread involves the purchase of calls at one strike price and the sale of more calls at a higher strike price in a ratio of either 1:2 or 1:3. For example, if we purchase one XYZ call at the $40 strike, we then sell two $45 strike calls to create a 1:2 ratio spread. This position is not different from the ratio write strategy discussed earlier except that we replace the long stock position with a long call. Another way to visualize a 1:2 ratio spread is that it is simply the combination of a bull call spread and one or two naked calls.

Short calls are neutral-to-bearish strategies, so it seems odd to combine that strategy with a bullish strategy—a bull call spread. However, a bull call spread is often used when we expect the stock to move slightly higher, because the maximum profit is not unlimited like that of a long call position. Therefore, the call ratio spread is suitable for a stock that is expected to move higher, but not too much higher.

Since we are selling more calls than we are long, the position is usually entered into for a credit, even, or for a slight debit. The premium from the short calls helps to pay for our long call. However, since we have naked calls, our position is hurt by a significant rise in the price of the underlying stock. The optimum for the ratio spread strategy is for the short calls to expire worthless, which will occur if the stock is at the short strike at expiration. Therefore, when selecting the short strike to sell calls against our long call, we would want a strike price that is not likely to be deep ITM at expiration.

First, let us become familiar with how the call ratio spread works on its own before we analyze it as an adjustment to a long stock position. Assume EBAY is trading at $100, a $100 Call is trading at $4.00, and the $105 Call of the same expiration month is trading at $2.20. If you expect EBAY to move higher by expiration, but not necessarily above $105, then you can create a call ratio spread using the $100 and $105 Calls. To create a 1:2 Call ratio spread, buy one $100 Call at $4.00 and sell two $105 Calls at $2.20 each ($4.40 total) for a net credit of $0.40.

If EBAY falls below $100 by expiration, then your calls will expire worthless and you keep the $0.40 credit. Because you put on the call ratio spread for a credit, you can be wrong about the direction of the stock and still make some money on the trade. Between $100 and $105, your short calls will expire worthless and your profit is the value of the $100 Call plus the credit you received. If EBAY is at $103 at expiration, your profit is $3.40. A great characteristic of the call ratio spread is that it cost you nothing to purchase the $100 Call because selling the two $105 Calls finances the transaction. Therefore, if there is any value in the $100 Call at expiration (EBAY is above $100), you have a potential profit.

What happens to your call ratio spread if EBAY is right at $105? At $105, your two short calls will expire worthless, and your $100 Call will be worth $5.00. No matter how high EBAY climbs above $105, your long call and one of the short calls combine to form a bull call spread whose maximum value is the difference between the strike prices. Therefore, your ratio call spread will have a maximum value of $5.00, which is achieved when EBAY is at $105 at expiration. Your total profit is more than $5.00, however, because you entered into the trade for a net credit of $0.40.

Your position also has a short $105 Call. As EBAY moves above $105, the short call begins to reduce your profit dollar for dollar until the breakeven point is hit. In this position, the breakeven point is $110.40. At $110.40, your short call at $105 will be worth $5.40, which will be offset by the $5.40 gain from the bull call spread portion of the ratio spread. Calculating the breakeven point is simply a matter of taking the difference between the strike prices of the spread plus/minus any credit/debit in creating the position and adding that figure to the short strike price.

Figure 3.37 shows that the call ratio spread has a profit if EBAY is below $110.40 at expiration. Even if EBAY moves lower, you still have a profit on the spread because you established your position for a net credit. The

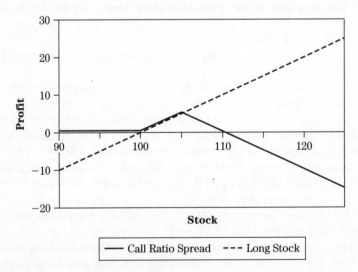

FIGURE 3.37 1:2 Call Ratio Spread

call ratio spread allows you to invest in a slight upward movement in the stock at no cost and not have to worry if you pick the wrong direction. Your maximum profit is right at the short strike at expiration and therefore you would like to pick a short strike that represents where the stock most likely will end up but with the knowledge that you do not have to be exactly right. This gives you some wiggle room and takes away the stress if EBAY should happen to fall, even if it drops to $0.

The call ratio spread is sometimes referred to as a neutral strategy. The spread is profitable if the stock stays sideways or moves only slightly higher. The strategy has an added bonus, however, because it makes money even if the stock drops. Compare the risk/reward profile of the call ratio spread to that of the short straddle in the previous section. Both strategies make the maximum profit if the stock moves sideways and is at the short strike at expiration. The short straddle, however, can have huge losses if the stock moves too far up or down. The short straddle profit chart is an upside-down triangle, and the call ratio spread looks like an upside-down triangle except that one end has a limited profit. The call ratio spread only can result in large potential losses if the stock moves too far up, but is "protected" from any loss on the downside, assuming you receive a net credit for opening the position.

With respect to risk management, you have a naked call in the call ratio spread and therefore you need to be vigilant if EBAY should make a strong move to the upside. You need to be ready to close out the trade if it appears EBAY is going to move above your breakeven point. A good risk management rule is to consider closing out the position as soon as the stock moves as high as the short strike price, assuming, as in this example, the short strike is OTM.

These examples highlight the ATM call ratio spread with the long call being ATM and the short calls being OTM. With respect to strike selection, remember that the maximum profit occurs when the stock is at the short strike price at expiration, so you would use the short strike selection as a target price. In the EBAY example, you expected EBAY to move toward $105 but not too much higher and therefore created a $100/$105 Call ratio spread. If you expected EBAY to move toward $110, you could have created a $100/$110 ratio spread. However, because the $110 Calls are so far OTM, the premium received for selling the calls will reduce the cost of the long $100 Call, but the position will be put on for a net debit, not a credit. If the position is put on for a net debit, then you do have additional risk if the stock ends up moving lower instead of higher. Many investors may be willing to accept that risk in exchange for lowering the cost of the long call because they expect EBAY to be between $100 and $110 at expiration. This is still a viable strategy, and you should be aware of the additional risks when establishing a call ratio spread for a net debit. More importantly, this example highlights the cost of selecting different strikes, which is an important consideration when adding a call ratio spread to a long stock position.

A discussion of the different strikes to be used in different situations for call ratio spreads by themselves is beyond the scope of this book. Our goal is to cover much of that information with respect to the use of a call ratio spread as an adjustment to a long stock position. The examples we cover focus on adding call ratio spreads to stock positions that have moved higher or lower for either a credit or even cost. You never really want to add a call ratio spread to a stock position at a net debit because that simply adds risk to your position, which you want to avoid. By adding the spread at a net credit, you get to make the adjustment for free and even add to your potential profits. As the following examples illustrate, a call ratio spread can be a powerful profit lever when added to a stock position. We will also show how call ratio spreads can fix a losing stock position and create a profit where one did not exist before.

Opening Position

The addition of a call ratio spread to an initial stock position acts as a profit lever to an overall position. In other words, you apply an ATM call ratio spread at the same time you purchase the stock. Assume you purchase 100 shares of EBAY at $100 with the expectation that the stock will move to $110, where you would want to exit for a nice $10.00 return. It would be nicer if you could earn that $10.00 return even if EBAY does not move all the way to $110. This can be accomplished simply by adding a call ratio spread at the same time as your initial stock investment, which will act as a lever to increase your profits even if EBAY is not at $110 by the time your options expire.

Assume that when you are purchasing your long stock position you observe 2-month $100 Calls trading at $5.00 and 2-month $105 Calls trading at $2.75. When you purchase 100 shares of EBAY at $100, you can add a 1:2 Call ratio spread by purchasing the $100 Call and selling two $105 Calls for a net credit of $0.50. It costs you nothing to add the call ratio spread to your position. In fact, you receive a credit of $0.50 to add the spread. More importantly, adding the spread does not increase your risk on your long stock position. On the contrary, the $0.50 credit actually reduces your breakeven point from $100 to $99.50. So far, the addition of the ratio spread provides some benefits to your stock position at no additional cost.

The ratio spread consists of one long call and two short calls. One of the short calls is covered by the long call and forms a bull call spread. The other short call, normally naked in a ratio call spread, is covered by the 100 shares of stock and forms a covered call position. Adding the call ratio spread results in a bull call spread combined with a covered call. There-fore, not only does the call ratio spread not add any downside risk to your position, it also does not add any upside risk because you do not have any naked calls.

Let's see how the ratio spread acts as a profit lever to your stock po-sition. If EBAY is at $105 at expiration, both of the short $105 Calls will expire worthless. Your long $100 Call will be worth $5.00, and you will also have a $5.00 profit in your stock position. Therefore, your profit is $10.00 with EBAY moving from $100 to $105. You add your initial credit of $0.50 for a total profit of $10.50. Without the call ratio spread adjustment, your profit would only be $5.00, but with the addition of the spread levers, your profit goes up to $10.50 due to the presence of the long call. This is a per-fect example of how options can sometimes increase your returns without adding any additional risk.

The addition of the long call makes your long stock position act as if you owned 200 shares of stock, and therefore you earn $2 for every $1 of gain in EBAY. Your long call gives you another way of profiting from the increase in EBAY, and therefore your profit is double on the way up, up to a point. That point is $105. Because you are long a $100 Call and short one $105 Call, the maximum profit from this combination, a bull call spread, is $5.00 no matter how far above $105 EBAY moves. Your other short call at $105 will cause you to have your stock called away from you at $105 no matter how high EBAY moves, for a maximum profit of $5.00. Remember that the call ratio spread has its maximum profit when the stock is at the short strike at expiration. When combined, the long stock/call ratio spread also has its maximum profit at the short strike, but also at any price above the strike price because the bull call spread and covered call components of your position will have a maximum profit of $10.50 no matter how high EBAY moves. In other words, if EBAY is at $120, you will still only earn a maximum profit of $10.50 on your combined long stock/call ratio spread position.

As Figure 3.38 indicates, the addition of the call ratio spread increases your potential profit on your long stock position at no extra cost, within a certain range. You earn twice as much on your position between $100 and $105 and still outperform the unadjusted position until $110.50. Above $110.50, the long stock position will continue to earn profits, whereas your adjusted position is capped at $110.50. If your expectation is that EBAY will not move much higher than $110, then adding the call ratio spread allows you to achieve the same return even if EBAY only moves to $105. This is the leverage you obtain from adding the spread to your position. You get this leverage at no additional cost, and even receive a credit for doing so. If EBAY is still at $100 or slightly below at expiration, then your calls will expire worthless and you keep the $0.50 credit and still own the stock.

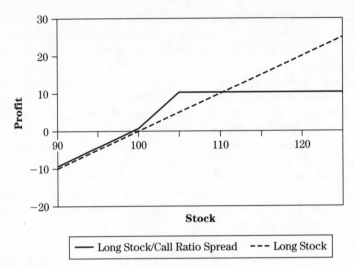

FIGURE 3.38 Long Stock Combined with 1:2 Call Ratio Spread

You can increase your maximum profit potential with the call ratio spread adjustment simply by selling three short calls instead of two. If you buy the $100 Call for $5.00 and sell three $105 Calls at $2.75, you create a 1:3 Call ratio spread for a net credit of $3.25. If EBAY is below $100 at expiration, then all calls expire worthless and you keep the $3.25 credit. Between $100 and $105, your position is the equivalent of owning 200 shares, and your profit is increased by the addition of the credit you received. For example, if EBAY is at $104 at expiration, you earn $8.00 on your long stock and long call plus the $3.25 credit for a total profit of $11.25. The maximum profit on the position, achieved when EBAY is at $105, is $13.25 ($10.00 combined profit on stock and long call plus $3.25 credit).

As EBAY moves above $105, your $13.25 maximum profit is reduced by $1.00 for each $1.00 EBAY is above $105 due to the presence of the third short call. Your upside breakeven point is now $118.25 because your short $105 Call will be worth $13.25, which will offset your profit of $13.25 on the remaining bull call spread and covered call portion of the call ratio spread. The fact that you bring in more premium from selling an additional call also produces the benefit of lowering your breakeven point from $100 to $96.75. Therefore, if EBAY does slide a little by expiration, you can still avoid a loss on your position.

Adding the 1:3 Call ratio spread to your long stock position creates an even greater lever to your potential profits, again at no additional cost (Figure 3.39). You do, however, add some additional risk in that if EBAY moves above $118.25, your position will start losing money as a result of

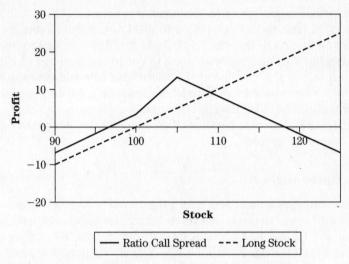

FIGURE 3.39 Long Stock Combined with 1:3 Call Ratio Spread

the third naked call. However, because you are purchasing EBAY at $100, you have plenty of room for EBAY to move higher before a loss does occur. Until that point, the adjusted position still outperforms the unadjusted long stock position. More importantly, if EBAY drops below $100, your large credit reduces the loss on your stock position and therefore provides a partial hedge. Therefore, the call ratio spread adjustment does not add any additional downside risk to your position but actually reduces it slightly.

You may ask why you would ever choose the 1:2 ratio spread to combine with the long stock position when the 1:3 ratio spread provides so many additional benefits for potential profits. The one important distinction between the two is that the 1:3 ratio spread adjustment does have the potential for loss should EBAY move too high, whereas the 1:2 has no upside breakeven point. A conservative investor who does not wish to have any risk to the upside would be more inclined to choose the 1:2 ratio spread over the 1:3 ratio spread. The beauty of options is that you are free to make your own choice based on your own criteria.

As an addition to an opening position in a long stock, a call ratio spread can provide a nice boost to your potential returns. The best part about this profit boost is that it comes at no additional cost. This can only be achieved if you purchase the call ratio spread for a credit or even. We do not recommend adding a ratio spread for a net debit unless the debit is extremely small or you are willing to accept the additional risk the debit spread adds to the position. As always, you must make your own evaluation before making any adjustment.

The most straightforward adjustment to your initial stock position is to use the ATM ratio spread or as close to ATM as possible. There are many different permutations that can be created using different strike prices, and the possibilities are endless. We leave it to you to experiment with different strike prices, but always remember that the goal is to add the ratio spread for a credit when possible. We also advise entering a spread with a ratio no greater than 1:3 because having more naked calls leads to higher margin requirements and greater potential losses should the stock move too far above your short strike.

Stock Moves Higher

The call ratio spread also acts as a profit lever for a stock position that has moved higher. Because you already have an unrealized gain in your position, the 1:2 and 1:3 Call ratio spread adjustments add to your overall return and even provide a partial hedge against any downward movement in the stock if you can establish the ratio spread for a net credit. Moreover, because your stock already has an unrealized gain, you have a little more flexibility in which strike prices you use to create your spread adjustment. Let's see how the call ratio spread can improve the performance of your trade by examining a few examples.

Assume you purchased EBAY at $100 and it has moved up to $110. You observe 2-month $110 Calls trading at $5.00 and 2-month $115 Calls trading at $2.75. If you expect EBAY to keep moving higher toward $120 but are not sure how much further the stock will move, you can ensure increased profits from even a small continued move higher by adding a call ratio spread adjustment. To add a 1:2 ratio spread adjustment, purchase one $110 Call for $5.00 and sell two $115 Calls for $2.75 for a net credit of $0.50.

Remember that at $110, you already have an unrealized gain of $10.00 in your position. If EBAY is at $110 at expiration, you still have your $10.00 gain, but you can add the $0.50 credit you collected for establishing the call ratio spread. You keep the $0.50 credit no matter where EBAY is below $110 at expiration. Therefore, you immediately reduce your breakeven point from $100, your original purchase price, to $99.50. The true benefit of your adjustment is felt if EBAY is between $110 and $115 at expiration. Because you are long a $110 Call, your position will act as if you are long 200 shares of EBAY, and therefore your return will be double for price increases in that range. For example, if EBAY is at $113 at expiration, you have a $13.00 gain on your stock and a $3.50 gain from the $110 Call (your short $115 Calls will expire worthless) for a total profit of $16.50.

At $115, you will have a total profit of $20.50 ($15.00 stock gain plus $5.50 gain from call ratio spread). The call ratio adjustment lets your position have a profit equivalent to what you would have earned if the stock had moved to $120.50 even though the stock is only at $115 at expiration. This is the profit boost provided by the call ratio spread.

If EBAY is above $115, your profit is limited to $20.50 no matter how high EBAY climbs. Remember that your ratio spread consists of a long call and two short calls at a higher strike. One $115 short call is covered by your long $110 Call, and above $115, this spread has a maximum profit of $5.00. You can add the credit you received for establishing the position for a total profit of $5.50. Your other short call at $115 is covered by your long stock position. If EBAY is above $115, then your stock will be called away at $115 for a $15.00 profit. Adding this to your $5.50 profit on the bull call spread portion of your ratio adjustment gives a total profit of $20.50.

Figure 3.40 compares the call ratio spread adjusted position to an unadjusted position in EBAY and gives a clear picture of how the addition of the call ratio spread boosts the performance of your position. Your adjusted position outperforms the unadjusted position until EBAY moves above $120.50. The adjusted position also outperforms the unadjusted position on the downside because the $0.50 credit, albeit small, reduces your total loss.

If you wish to provide an even bigger boost to the foregoing stock position, you can establish a 1:3 Call ratio spread instead of the 1:2 ratio spread by selling a third $115 Call. With EBAY at $110, you establish the adjustment by purchasing the $110 Call for $5.00 and sell three EBAY $115 Calls at $2.75 each for a net credit of $3.25. The first thing you notice is that the

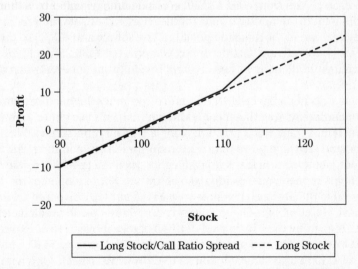

FIGURE 3.40 Long Stock/1:2 Call Ratio Spread after Stock Moves Higher

$3.25 credit you receive lowers your breakeven point from $100 to $96.75, and thus reduces your risk slightly. If EBAY is between $100 and $110, all of the calls will expire worthless and the profit in your stock position is increased by the amount of the credit you received from establishing the call ratio spread. For example, if EBAY is at $105 at expiration, you have a $5.00 profit in the stock, which is added to your credit received of $3.25 for a total profit of $8.25.

Between $110 and $115, your profit in EBAY is increased by your long $110 Call as well as the $3.25 credit you collected. For example, if EBAY is at $113 at expiration, you have a profit of $19.25, which includes $13.00 profit from your EBAY stock, $3.00 profit from your $110 Call, and $3.25 from your net credit received. The call ratio adjustment boosts your $13.00 profit in the stock to a $19.25 overall profit. The maximum profit occurs when EBAY is at the short strike at expiration. When EBAY is at $115 at expiration, the position has a total profit of $23.25 ($15.00 stock profit + $5.00 Call profit + $3.25 net credit). Your adjustment lets you earn a higher profit from a smaller upward move in the stock (i.e., you can earn a profit of $23.25 even though the stock has moved only $15.00 higher), and this is the leverage boost that you get from the 1:3 spread.

If EBAY is above $115 at expiration, your maximum profit begins to be reduced by the existence of your third naked call at $115. Two of your naked $115 Calls are covered by the long stock and the long $110 Call, so your third naked call will begin to reduce your profit $1 for each $1 that EBAY moves above $115. For example, if EBAY is at $120, your position has a profit of $18.25, which is the maximum profit of $23.25 minus the ($5.00) value of your third short $115 Call. The upside breakeven point is therefore the point where the negative value of the short call offsets the $23.25 profit already realized in the adjusted position. You simply add $23.25 to the $115 strike price to get your upside breakeven price of $138.25. As Figure 3.41 confirms, your adjustment has created a wide profit zone between $96.75 and $138.25.

If you do not expect EBAY to move too much higher from its price at $110 and are willing to accept additional risk and margin requirements, you can adjust your stock position using a 1:4 Call ratio spread. We do not recommend anything more than a 1:3 ratio spread as an initial position adjustment, but if the stock has moved higher, then the unrealized gain in the stock helps reduce your upside risk somewhat. For example, in the 1:3 ratio spread in the previous example with EBAY at $110, the potential loss on the short $115 Call is reduced somewhat, and the upside breakeven point pushed higher, by the $15.00 gain in EBAY if it is above $115 at expiration.

To create a 1:4 ratio spread adjustment with EBAY at $110, purchase one $110 Call at $5.00 and sell four $115 Calls at $2.75 each for a net credit

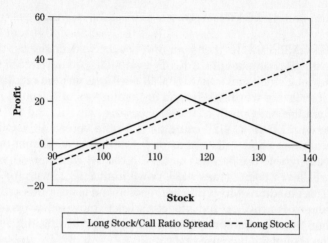

FIGURE 3.41 Long Stock/Ratio Call Spread Adjustment with Long $110 Call and Three Short $115 Calls

of $6.00. The $6.00 credit reduces your breakeven point from $100 to $94 (Figure 3.42). Your maximum profit, which occurs when EBAY is at the $115 short strike at expiration, is $26.00 ($15.00 stock profit plus $5.00 profit in the $110 Call plus $6.00 credit collected). As with your 1:2 and 1:3 ratio spread adjustments, your profit in EBAY between $100 and $115 is increased by the $6.00 credit collected from establishing

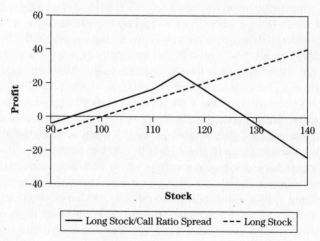

FIGURE 3.42 Long Stock/Ratio Call Spread Adjustment with Long $110 Call and Four Short $115 Calls

the spread and, if EBAY is between $110 and $115, increased by your $110 Call.

If EBAY is above $115, then your profit begins to decrease as your short calls move ITM. For example, if EBAY is at $120, you have a $36.00 profit from your long stock and long $110 Call position, plus the credit, and the four short calls are worth $5.00 each for a total loss of $20.00. Combined, the position has a net profit of $16.00. Compare this with the $18.25 profit you have with EBAY at $120 using the 1:3 ratio spread adjustment. The addition of more short calls begins to cut into your maximum profit and lowers your upside breakeven point. With the 1:4 ratio spread your new upside breakeven point is now $128, down from $138.25 with the 1:3 ratio spread. This illustrates why we do not recommend using ratios above 1:3 as an adjustment. However, if you expect a stock to move sideways or slightly lower, then the 1:4 ratio spread can be an appropriate adjustment as long as you can accept the increased risk.

If you compare the risk/reward profiles of the 1:2, 1:3, and 1:4 ratio adjustments, you can see that as you add short calls, the position begins to have a more bearish bias. These ratio spread adjustments can be used even if you expect the stock to move higher, but any bias you have to the upside must be taken into account when selecting between the ratio spread adjustments. If you expect sideways movement but fear a drop in price, then adding more calls helps to hedge that downside risk somewhat. However, additional calls increase your margin requirement and also create a potential loss if EBAY moves too far up in price. In that case, you should use the upside breakeven point as a target for closing out the position to avoid turning a winning position into a loss.

When using the 1:3 and 1:4 ratio spread adjustments for a stock that has increased in price, you also need to take into account the amount of the unrealized gain in the stock. In the foregoing examples with EBAY, remember that we included the unrealized gain in the stock when calculating the total profit. The bigger the unrealized gain, the bigger is the potential profit of the combined position. This factor is more important when considering the additional naked calls. You can afford to sell some naked calls because the unrealized gain in your stock gives you a buffer to absorb the loss on the naked calls up to the upside breakeven point.

Any adjustment made to a stock position that has increased in price using a call ratio spread should always be done using the ratios discussed here. The long calls should match the number of shares you own, and the short calls should follow the selected ratio. For example, if you own 200 shares of EBAY, then use ratios of 2:4, 2:6, and 2:8, although, as noted, we do not recommend exceeding the 1:3 ratio unless you are willing to accept the additional risk and do not expect the stock to run that much higher. As always, it is up to you to determine the breakeven points and maximum risk and reward before entering into any adjustment to determine whether that adjustment is appropriate.

Stock Moves Lower—Stock Repair Strategy

When your stock position moves lower, there is no profit for a ratio spread adjustment to boost or act as a profit lever. Moreover, the call ratio spread involves short calls, which if sold at a strike price below your original purchase price, could lock in a loss. Therefore, at first glance it may seem that a call ratio spread might not be the best adjustment to a stock position that has decreased in value. However, the benefits derived from adding a call ratio spread to a stock position from the beginning or after the stock has increased in value can also be used to salvage a losing position, or better yet, repair a position. A call ratio spread can be added to a losing stock position to "repair" a loss by allowing you to break even or generate a profit even though your stock has not moved back to the original purchase price.

Assume you purchased 100 shares of EBAY at $100 and it has fallen to $87 for a $13.00 loss. At this point you could close out your position and accept the $13.00 loss. Many people who expect the stock to recover would simply purchase another 100 shares at $87 to lower the breakeven point to $93.50 and therefore recover their costs even if EBAY does not get all the way to $100. You could achieve the same results using call ratio spreads, and the best part is, you could do it at no cost. What if you feel that EBAY could recover somewhat, but not necessarily back to $100? Perhaps you feel that EBAY could recover to $95 or so.

With EBAY at $87, let's assume that an $85 Call is trading for $5.25 and a $95 Call is trading at $2.75, both with 2 months to expiration. If you feel that EBAY might move back toward $95 but not necessarily back to $100 in the next 2 months, you can repair your stock position using a call ratio spread. To do so, purchase one $85 Call at $5.25 and sell two $95 Calls at $2.75 each for a net credit of $0.25. Use a 1:2 ratio spread because you are repairing 100 shares of stock so your two short calls are covered by the long call and the long shares. When using a repair strategy, you never want any naked calls because this will only add risk and greater loss potential to an already losing position.

By selling two $95 Calls and purchasing the $85 Call, you brought in a credit of $0.25. Thus, this position costs you nothing to establish and because there are no naked calls, you have no margin requirements. Therefore, adding this adjustment in no way puts you in a worse position than the unrealized $13.00 loss you have. It improves your position slightly because the $0.25 credit is yours to keep, but this is negligible.

What happens if EBAY recovers back to $95 by expiration as you had hoped? On your stock position, you have a loss of $5.00, and your two $95

Calls would expire worthless. However, your long $85 Call would be worth $10.00. The net profit on the position would be $5.25 (let's not forget the initial credit). Therefore, you make a profit of $5.25 on a stock that has fallen from $100 to $95. Not many long stock investments can produce a profit of $5.25 by falling $5.00 in price, but they can with the right option adjustment.

Because you have a profit on your EBAY position when it is at $95, your breakeven point is no longer $100. Your new breakeven point is where the loss in the stock is completely offset by the profit in your long $85 Call. This occurs at $92.375, where the $7.625 loss in the stock is offset by the $7.625 value of your $85 Call. If you purchased another 100 shares of EBAY at $87 to lower your breakeven point to $93.50, you would have to spend a large amount of money to purchase these additional shares. By adding the call ratio spread adjustment, you lowered your breakeven point to $92.375 and it did not cost you anything—in fact, you received $0.25 for doing so!

If EBAY moves above $95, what happens to your position? You have one long call at $85 and a short call at $95, which creates a bull call spread. The maximum profit on this spread is $10.00, which is simply the difference between the strike prices. Your other short call at $95 is covered by your long EBAY shares. If EBAY is above $95, your stock will be called away at $95 for a $5.00 loss no matter how high EBAY runs. Therefore, the addition of the stock repair ratio spread to your EBAY position has a maximum reward of $5.25 when EBAY is above $95 at expiration.

Below $92.375, your new breakeven point, the combined position begins to lose money, but, as Figure 3.43 indicates, the loss is still lower than

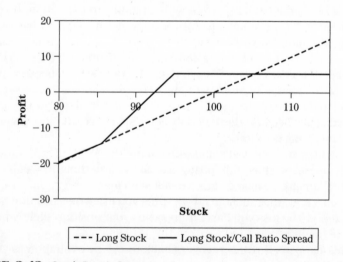

FIGURE 3.43 Stock Repair Strategy

on the unadjusted position until EBAY hits $85. Below $85, your long $85 Call expires worthless and no longer offsets any of the loss in your long stock. The only offset to your position is the $0.25 credit you received for establishing the position, which is quite small. Below $85, the position acts almost as if no adjustment were made at all. Therefore, remember that the stock repair strategy can lower your breakeven point and reduce your loss somewhat if the stock does move back higher, but provides no downside hedge if the stock continues to drop in price. The stock repair strategy is only to be used if the stock is expected to move back higher because the only downside hedge provided comes from the small credit received from establishing the position.

When selecting strike prices for the stock repair ratio spread, use the short strike as your target where you expect the stock to move back to. In the EBAY example, we used the $95 strike price for the short strike because of the assumption that EBAY would not move back to the original purchase price of $100 but toward $95. The maximum benefit of the stock repair spread occurs when the stock falls at the upper end of the spread at expiration. Therefore, the selection of the strike prices should be based on the expected range of where the stock will be at expiration. The long strike is usually near the current stock price since we want to generate income from the long call to offset the current loss in the stock. With EBAY at $87, we chose the $85 Call as the lower strike of the stock repair spread. The selection of the time remaining to expiration is simply a factor of when we expect the stock to make its move higher.

The most important aspect to remember when adding the stock repair ratio spread is to open the position for a net credit or even. The beauty of the adjustment is that you can lower your breakeven point at no cost, or even for a net credit. If the position can only be opened for a net debit, then we recommend the net debit be extremely small because the debit paid adds some risk to the position and reduces the potential profit on the upside.

CALL CALENDAR SPREAD

Earlier in the chapter, we discussed the use of a covered call as an adjustment to a stock position, which brings in extra income and calls away the stock if it moves above the short strike price. We also discussed the call replacement strategy, which involves selling our stock to lock in our profit and then replacing our stock position with a long call so that we could still earn a profit if the stock continues to run higher. There is a way we can combine the benefits of both strategies together using call calendar spreads.

A calendar spread is a unique type of spread that looks for volatility skews between short-term and long-term options of the same underlying stock with the same strike price. A skew occurs when the implied volatility of options on the same underlying stock has different values such that one series of options is skewed higher in its IV than the other options. When the short-term option's implied volatility is much higher than the implied volatility of the long-term options of the same strike, we have a volatility skew. We also can say that the short-term options are relatively expensive and the long-term options are relatively cheap when compared to each other. We try to exploit volatility skews by selling the relatively expensive option and purchasing the relatively cheap option.

A call calendar spread involves selling a short-term call and purchasing a long-term call, both at the same strike price. For example, you would sell a 1-month EBAY $100 Call and purchase a 4-month EBAY $100 Call. Although both calls have the same strike price, the longer term call will have more time value than the shorter term call. Therefore, entering the spread will involve purchasing a higher premium call than the one sold, and it will be created for a net debit. Basically you reduce the cost of the long-term call by selling the short-term call against it.

How can you use the calendar spread to replicate the two foregoing strategies? Let us look at the two different parts of the spread. First, you are selling a short-term option and purchasing a long-term option as a combination with your long stock position. If the stock moves above the strike price of your short call at expiration, then your stock will be called away at the strike price. This is similar to a covered call. Because you no longer have your long stock or the short call, what is left is your long-term long call, which still has time left to make money if the stock continues to rise. The long call acts as your replacement call.

The covered call portion of the calendar spread adjustment only produces a profit if you sell OTM calls. You need room for the stock to grow to create a profit when it is called away by the short call. Unlike a true covered call, your calendar spread is entered into for a net debit. And, you are not collecting premium as income. The premium you collect from selling the short call reduces the cost of your long call. Therefore, adding the calendar spread to your long stock position is a way of legging into a call replacement strategy. Let's examine how the call calendar spread adjustment permits you to leg into a call replacement strategy as an initial adjustment and after the stock has moved higher.

In our examples, we use 1-month and 3-month options to create our call calendar spreads for illustrative purposes. There are no hard-and-fast rules as to which expiration months to select. For the short term, we recommend 1-month options because we do not want to give the stock too much time to move above the short strike and therefore miss out on those profits. We also want time decay on our side to shrink away the time value in our short call.

For the longer term option, we recommend at least 3 months because for long options we do want enough time for the stock to move deep ITM. The reason for a minimum of 3 months is that we want time between our long option and 1-month short option so that if the short option expires worthless, we have another month available to possibly sell another short call and collect more premium. The more time to expiration we can use for the long-term call, the larger is the net debit of the calendar spread. It is up to you to balance out the amount of time desired for the long call portion of your adjustment (which will hopefully become the replacement call) with the debit you are willing to pay. We recommend that you select calendar spreads with a maximum net debit range of $2.00/$2.50. If the debit is larger, then it may eat too much into the potential profits from the stock position.

Opening Position

You can set up a predetermined exit strategy from a long stock position and a call replacement when you purchase your long stock by adding a call calendar spread. Assume you purchase 100 shares of EBAY at $100. At the same time, a 1-month EBAY $110 Call is trading at $1.00 and a 3-month EBAY $110 Call is trading at $3.00. You feel that EBAY could run to $110 in the next month or so and perhaps higher. As with all investments, it is always a good idea to have a predetermined exit and adjustment strategy. With EBAY, you could develop a plan to get out of your long stock position at $110 to lock in a nice profit and replace your position with a long call to continue to make money if EBAY continues to rise in price. You can lock in that plan with your calendar spread adjustment.

After purchasing the 100 shares of EBAY at $100, you can add the call calendar spread by selling the 1-month EBAY $110 Call for $1.00 and purchasing the 3-month EBAY $110 Call for $3.00 for a net debit of $2.00. The call calendar spread adjustment is created at a net debit, and therefore you are adding some risk to your position. We recommend adding this spread only if you feel strongly that EBAY will move close to or above your spread strike price. Because there are numerous scenarios that could occur by expiration of the short- and long-term calls, let's walk through the different potential situations to see how the adjustment affects your position.

If EBAY is above $100 but below $110 at expiration of the 1-month option, your short $110 Call will expire worthless, and you should not have any loss in your position because you will have a gain in your stock position and the long $110 Call will still have some time value left. If EBAY is at $100, then you have no loss or gain on the stock position. Your long $110 Call will still have significant time value with 2 months left to expiration.

What do you do now? EBAY is above $100 but below $110, and your short call has now expired. The easiest thing to do is nothing. Your stock has moved somewhat higher and you still have 2 months to expiration on your long call. As EBAY moves higher, your long call may increase in value and produce increased profits. If by expiration of the long $110 Call the stock is still below $110, then the overall position will still have a profit from the long stock position as long as it is above $102 (to cover your initial spread debit). If EBAY is above $110, then the value of the long call increases your overall return. In this scenario, you have a long stock position combined with a long call, and your calendar spread reduced the cost of adding the call.

Another option is to sell the next front month option at the same strike price ($110). If you sell the next 1-month-to-expiration $110 Call, then you collect additional premium, which further reduces the cost of your long-term call, perhaps turning it into a free trade. For example, if EBAY was at $105 at expiration of your short call, you could sell the next month's $110 Call for an assumed price of $2.50. Your initial debit for the calendar spread was $2.00, and selling the additional $110 Call has now turned your debit spread into a credit spread of $0.50. This credit will now be added to whatever profit you make from your combined position.

If EBAY moves above $110, your long stock will be called away for a profit of $10.50 ($10.00 stock profit plus $0.50 credit), and you still have your long call left for 1 more month for additional profit should EBAY continues to move higher. If EBAY stays under $110, then your new short call expires worthless, and you still have a profit in your long stock position. Moreover, you still have your long call with 1 month of time value.

Basically, the call calendar spread gives you the flexibility to make follow-up adjustments. However, if the stock does indeed rise above your short strike price, the stock will be called away for a nice profit, and you still have your long call. By adding this adjustment, you can establish an exit price and enter into the call replacement strategy adjustment ahead of time.

Stock Moves Higher

You can add a call calendar spread to a stock position that has moved higher and achieve the same goal of setting a specific exit price and creating your follow-up call replacement at the same time. Assume you purchased EBAY at $100 and it has moved to $110. If you feel EBAY has more room to move higher and are willing to lock in your profits at $115, then you can use the $115 strike to add the call calendar spread. Assume a 1-month $115 Call is trading at $1.75 and a 3-month $115 Call is trading at $3.75. You can add a call calendar spread to your position by selling the short-term $115 Call and purchasing the long-term $115 Call for a net debit of $2.00.

If EBAY stays between $100 and $115 by expiration of the short-term option, then you still have an unrealized profit in EBAY, and your short call will expire worthless. You still have your long call, which will have a time value premium. At that point, you could close out your stock position for a profit and let your long call continue until expiration without any risk. You already locked in a profit in the long stock, so you could therefore simply let the long call run, which gives you a chance for more profit should EBAY move higher. You could also close out the long call and add to your profits at the same time you close out your long stock position. The choice comes down to whether you feel EBAY has the potential to move above $115 by expiration of the long call.

Whether you decide to sell your stock or not, you can still choose to sell the next month's $115 strike call to bring in more premium and further reduce the cost of your long call. The best scenario occurs if the premium collected from selling the current month and previous month's calls is greater than the net debit paid for the calendar spread. If that is the case, then the calendar spread adjustment will end up costing you nothing and, better yet, bring in an actual credit. As long as there is time between the long call and the short call and your short call is expiring worthless, you can keep rolling your short call forward to bring in more premium each month. Remember that this portion of the spread is the same as the covered call adjustment and under that strategy you keep selling covered calls for extra income until either the stock is called away from you when the short calls are in the money or you close out the entire position.

What if EBAY moves above $115? As long as you still have your original short $115 Call, you will have your stock called away at $115 for a profit of $15.00. This profit, however, is reduced by your net debit paid for the calendar spread—or $2.00—for a net profit of $13.00. Your final profit, however, is not $13.00. At that point, you still have a long $115 Call, which is also in the money. If you decide to sell that call, then your profit will be higher than $13.00. Because you cannot estimate the actual value of that call in the future, it is difficult to estimate what would be the price of that call unless it was at expiration. However, if there are still 2 months left to expiration, then the ITM long-term $115 Call will have intrinsic value and significant time value for a nice profit boost.

Adding the OTM call calendar spread helps you to take some of the indecisiveness out of your trading. The adjustment gives you an exit point

($115) and provides you with a replacement long call so that once you have gotten out, you still have the luxury of participating in any EBAY rise until expiration of the long call. If EBAY never gets above $115, you could hopefully keep rolling your short call to take in more premium to pay for your long call. This way, if EBAY stays below $115 the entire life of the spread, you still have your profit in the stock position and a possible credit in your spread adjustment. If EBAY starts to head south, then you need to act fast to lock in your profit in EBAY, even with the net debit paid for the adjustment.

Remember that this adjustment does not hedge your unrealized EBAY profit in any way. If EBAY drops in price, you could lose your unrealized profit as well as the net debit paid for your spread. Therefore, before adding this adjustment, you need to be sure about your expectation that the stock will move higher. If you have any serious doubts about EBAY moving higher, then another hedge type of adjustment would be better.

Instead of using the OTM strikes for your calendar spread, you could also look into using ATM. In our EBAY example, with EBAY moving to $110 from $100, you could create a call calendar spread using the $110 strike price. Let's look at the ATM calendar spread to determine the differences and benefits from using ATM versus OTM strikes. You will not consider ITM strike prices for your call calendar spread adjustment because you do not want to sell short calls at a strike price below the current price of the stock, which will reduce your potential profit. This strategy can work when you sell covered calls and take in premium, but because your calendar spread is established for a net debit, selling ITM calls reduces your profit by having your stock called away at a lower price than the market price without any option premium to compensate for it.

Assume with EBAY at $110 after moving higher from $100, you observe the following 1-month and 3-month option quotes:

Strike Price	1-Month	3-Month
$110	$5.00	$7.50

You can add an ATM call calendar spread to your long stock position by selling the 1-month $110 Call for $5.00 and purchasing the 3-month $110 Call for $7.50 for a net debit of $2.50. Let's examine what this adjustment accomplishes to better understand why we would make such an adjustment. If EBAY is at $110 or above, your stock will be called away for a profit of $10.00, minus your debit paid for the spread ($2.50), for an interim profit of $7.50. We say interim because although the stock is gone, you still have your long call left and your final profit will depend on when you sell the long call.

With EBAY above $110, your long call will have intrinsic value plus time value premium. If you choose to close out the long call at the same time you have your stock called away, then your profit will actually be higher than $7.50. If you feel that EBAY will continue to move higher, then you can simply let your long call run until expiration. The cost of the long call is already absorbed by the proceeds from the sale of the stock. Therefore, this call is "free" and you can wait until expiration to give EBAY as much time as possible to continue moving higher. Your potential final profit is therefore unlimited.

Because you locked in a profit of $7.50 when your stock was called away, you will never make less money on your position. If EBAY tanks after you sell your stock, then even though the long call expires worthless, you still have taken your money off the table and pocketed your $7.50. Remember that this is the "therapy" you receive from using the call replacement strategy, which is built into the call calendar spread adjustment.

If EBAY is right at $110 at expiration of the short option, then your short call will expire worthless. You still have your $10.00 unrealized profit in the stock plus the value of your long call. At that time, you could take your total profit by selling the stock and long call together. You also could simply sell your stock position to lock in a profit and keep your long call in place to participate in any continued upward movement in EBAY price. Another option is that you could sell another short-term $110 Call to bring in more premium, which will reduce the cost of the spread adjustment, perhaps turn it into a credit spread, and allow you to keep your position in place for another month.

The same follow-up choices exist if EBAY is below $110 at expiration of the short-term option. The short $110 Call will expire worthless, and as long as EBAY is above $100, you will have an unrealized profit in your stock as well as remaining time value in your long $110 Call. At this point, you need to reassess your EBAY position to determine the best course of action. You could simply sell the long stock position and the long call and collect your profit and close out the entire position. This is always the wisest choice when you become uncertain of where EBAY will move next or if you expect it to continue dropping in price and you do not want to give back any profits you have made. When you sell the stock, you could also choose to leave the long call in place to make a profit should EBAY move back above $110. You also could choose to leave your stock and long call in place if you expect EBAY to rebound and continue moving higher and perhaps sell the next front-month $110 Call to bring in more premium.

Adding a call calendar spread to your long stock position is a great adjustment to make when you want to lay out your exit strategy in advance. The spread serves two purposes. It includes a covered call, which gives you your exit plan if the short call is in the money at expiration, and already establishes your call replacement adjustment. If the stock moves higher in price, then you will have your stock called away for a profit and continue to make money from your long call if the stock keeps moving higher. If not, you already took your money off the table and are looking for the next trade, and therefore you no longer are worried about a loss.

CHAPTER 4

Short Stock

INTRODUCTION

When investors are bearish on a stock, they will most likely short the stock to profit on any decline in the price of the security. When you short a stock, you are borrowing someone else's stock and selling it in the market with the hope that it will drop in price so that you can repurchase it in the open market and replace the stock you borrowed. For example, if you are bearish on IBM at $90, then you can sell IBM short. If it drops to $86, then you can repurchase the stock at $86 and make a $4.00 profit. Figure 4.1 shows the risk/reward profile of your hypothetical short IBM position.

As Figure 4.1 indicates, you make $1.00 for every $1.00 IBM drops in price. Also notice that you lose $1.00 for every $1.00 rise in IBM price. Stocks can theoretically rise in price forever. Therefore, your short stock position has the potential for unlimited losses. Shorting stocks is not only very risky, but also requires margin. Because the potential losses can be huge, your broker will want to make sure that you have the cash to repurchase IBM at a higher price if it climbs rapidly, so you can return the borrowed stock.

The typical margin requirement for a short stock position is 50% of the proceeds of the short sale. If you sell 100 shares of IBM short at $90, you will be required to deposit $4,500 in cash or securities into your account or have such an amount available to meet the margin requirement. You will also be responsible for maintenance margin, which could require more money placed into the account, especially if the stock moves higher. You should always check with your broker to understand the exact margin

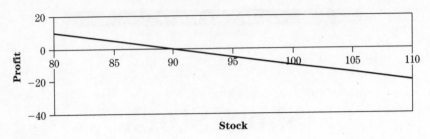

FIGURE 4.1 IBM Short Stock

requirements for short sales. Although we will not provide detailed discussions about margin and the effect of margin on the overall position, you
should always remember that shorting stock does create a margin obligation and therefore could affect your entire account if the margin and maintenance requirements become sufficiently large.

You should also be aware that when you short a stock, you are responsible for paying out any dividends due while holding your position.
The dividend payout does reduce the potential return if the stock drops in
price or increases the loss if the stock rises. In most cases, the dividend
to be paid out while holding a short stock is extremely small and has little effect on the potential return. Thus, for the purpose of the adjustments
discussed in this chapter, we assume no dividends are paid on the short
stock and therefore do not take dividends into account when discussing
the risk/reward profiles.

Just as we have seen with a long stock position in the previous chapter, you can use option adjustments to your short stock position to lock in
a profit, hedge against or limit potential losses, or even increase or boost
your potential profits. This chapter focuses on various option adjustments
that can be made to a short stock position. All of the long stock option adjustments discussed in the previous chapter can be applied to a short stock
position simply by reversing the type of options used (i.e., puts instead of
calls). Because a short stock has increased risks and margin requirements
not found with long stock positions, we do not cover every strategy covered in the long stock chapter. Instead, we focus on the more useful adjustments or the ones we recommend to apply to short stock positions.
You are free to experiment with some of the other long stock adjustments
on short stock as long as you always practice good risk management and
do not add unnecessary risk to an already risky position.

When you are long stock, you could realistically hold onto your stock
position indefinitely. However, with short stock certain restrictions limit
your holding period. If a stock begins to move against you—that is, it moves
higher—your broker will require additional margin from you and perhaps

force you to close out your position to prevent any further losses. You cannot prevent your broker from forcing you to close out your losing position, especially if the loss becomes quite large and the broker wants to avoid having to step in and cover the loss for you.

Another factor to consider is that even if your position is not at a loss, you borrowed someone else's stock to sell short. Therefore, if the broker is required to return the stock to its original account, you may be forced to close out your short sooner than expected. Anticipating when you will be forced to close out your short is not easy, but the main consideration is that you do not have unlimited time. Therefore, all short stock trades should be entered into for short time periods, and any adjustments made using options should use short-term expiration dates.

PROTECTIVE CALL—INSURANCE

If you sell a stock short, you can take out an insurance policy to protect your position against unlimited losses on the upside. This is similar to the protective put adjustment one makes to a long stock position where the long put gives one the right to sell one's stock at a specific price and insure against any drop in the price of the stock. Because you need to purchase stock to close out your short position, you can use calls the same way you would use puts for insurance. The call gives you the right to purchase stock and therefore allows you to close out your short position. As with any insurance policy, you have a premium (cost of the insurance policy) and a deductible (amount of loss absorbed by the policyholder before the insurance kicks in). These two factors are dependent on which strike price you choose for your protective call.

Opening Position—Protective Call

You can choose to add your insurance policy at the same time you short your stock so that you can take away the potential for unlimited risk. Because the biggest drawback to shorting stock is the unlimited risk, you can use options to reduce this risk significantly. You simply sell short the stock you are bearish on and immediately purchase a long call. If the stock runs higher unexpectedly, you can exercise your long call at any time to close out your short position for a limited loss, which you have predetermined with the selection of the strike price of the long call. Therefore, let's examine the use of different strike prices in adding a protective call to an initial short stock position.

Assume that IBM is trading at $90 and you are bearish on the stock, or expect a short-term drop in price. At the same time you observe the following 1-month IBM call option prices:

IBM @ $90

$85 Call	$6.00
$90 Call	$2.50
$95 Call	$1.00

Assume that you are expecting IBM to drop in price over the next 30 days or so and want to short IBM to make money on the drop in stock price. At the same time you would like some insurance in case you are wrong about IBM and it actually rises in price. Because you are considering a protective call, you will look at 1-month options because that time period correlates with how long you expect to hold your short. You are free to determine your own holding period and the term of the insurance. The next step is determining which strike price to select for your protective call adjustment—ITM, ATM, or OTM. We will look at all three and analyze the risk/reward benefits.

The easiest strike price to select is always the ATM strike. You are shorting IBM at $90 and therefore expect IBM to move lower than $90. Because you lose money if IBM moves above $90, you want to protect your position above $90. Therefore, the best choice for your protective call is the ATM call. If you short 100 shares of IBM at $90, then you would simultaneously purchase the $90 Call for $2.50. The $2.50 premium paid for the call is the premium you pay for your insurance policy.

If IBM moves above $90, then your short position will produce a loss. To close out your position and use your protective call insurance policy, you can exercise the call to purchase IBM at $90 and thus produce no loss on the short stock position. You sold IBM short at $90, and you are repurchasing it at $90. However, by exercising your long call, you do lose the initial debit paid of $2.50. Therefore, if IBM is anywhere above $90, you do have a loss of $2.50. This $2.50 is your maximum loss no matter how far IBM moves above $90 by expiration because you could always exercise the call to close out your position. Using good risk management, you have established a maximum loss on your short position through the use of the protective call. The $2.50 loss is the deductible on your insurance policy.

What if IBM does act as you predicted and drops in price? If IBM is below $90 at expiration of the long call, then it will expire worthless and you lose the $2.50 in premium paid. Your position will have a loss until the gain in the short stock position offsets the $2.50 loss in the long call. This breakeven point is at $87.50. To determine the breakeven point, you simply subtract the premium paid for the protective call from the short sale price.

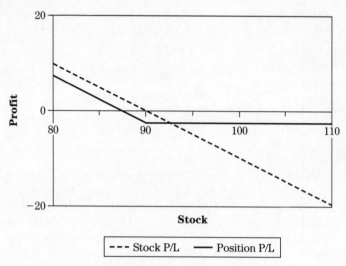

FIGURE 4.2   Short Stock with Protective ATM Call

Below $87.50, your position will begin to show a profit. For example, if IBM drops to $85, you will have a $5.00 profit on your short stock minus the $2.50 loss on your long call for a total profit of $2.50.

As Figure 4.2 demonstrates, the addition of the protective call allows you to short IBM with limited risk. In exchange for this benefit, you do need IBM to move lower in price far enough to compensate for the cost of your insurance policy. IBM needs to move at least $2.50 for you to realize a profit on your adjusted position. Therefore, before adding the ATM protective call, you need to assess whether IBM has the potential to drop in price far enough to make the position worthwhile.

If you want to raise your breakeven point and are willing to take on more risk, then you could use the OTM $95 protective call (Figure 4.3). An OTM call is cheaper than an ATM call, and therefore your premium for the insurance policy is less. However, by using the $95 Call, you absorb more of the loss before your protective call insurance policy kicks in. Assume you shorted 100 shares of IBM at $90 and purchased the protective $95 Call at $1.00. If IBM is at $95 at expiration of the long call, you have a $5.00 loss on your short stock position. In addition, you have a $1.00 loss on your $95 Call, which expires worthless, for a total loss of $6.00. No matter how far above $95 IBM moves by expiration, you will still only have a $6.00 loss because you can exercise your call to purchase IBM at $95 and close your position.

If IBM is right at $90 at expiration, then you have no gain or loss on your short stock, but you do have a $1.00 loss on your protective call, which

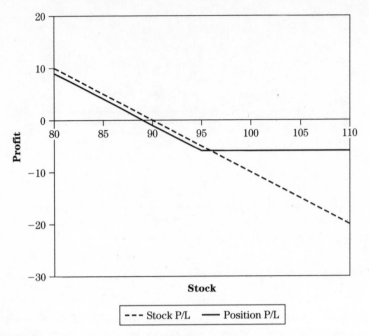

FIGURE 4.3 Short Stock with Protective OTM Call

expires worthless. As IBM moves below $90, you have a profit on your short stock. Your downside breakeven point using OTM calls is simply the short sale price minus the cost of the protective call. Subtracting the $1.00 cost of the $95 protective call from $90, your short sale price, you get a breakeven point of $89. At $89, the $1.00 profit in the short stock position offsets the $1.00 loss in your OTM protective call.

The use of the OTM protective call at $95 has raised your breakeven point from $87.50 with the ATM protective call to $89.00. It also has raised your maximum loss from $2.50 to $6.00. With options, there is always a trade-off between risk and reward. If you are certain of IBM's drop in price and wish to have the highest breakeven possible and if you are willing to accept the higher risk, then OTM protective calls are the better choice. If you are more concerned with a rise in the price of the underlying stock and wish to have tight risk control, then choose the ATM strike price.

What if you want the lowest maximum risk possible and you are willing to accept a much lower breakeven point, that is, you will need IBM to have a significant drop in price for your position to be profitable? If you expect IBM to drop sharply in price but want the least maximum risk, then you can use the ITM protective call (Figure 4.4). Assume you short IBM at

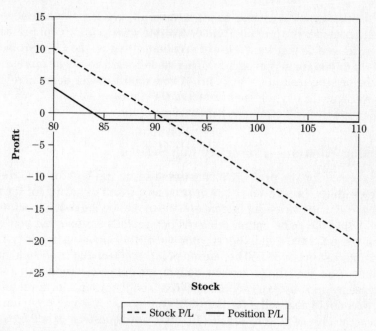

FIGURE 4.4   Short Stock with Protective ITM Call

$90 and purchase the $85 protective call for $6.00. If IBM is above $90 at expiration of the long call, then you can exercise your long $85 Call to close out your short. You sold IBM at $90 and would be closing it out at $85 for a $5.00 profit. However, you lose the $6.00 premium you paid for the protective call, and therefore your position would have a net loss of $1.00. Thus, your maximum loss on your short stock/protective call position using the ITM call is only $1.00.

A maximum loss of $1.00 is a very low risk on a short stock position. Of course, reduced risk comes at a cost, and your cost in this position is a much lower breakeven point. In other words, you will need IBM to drop further in price before you make a profit. Because you purchased the $85 Call for $6.00, your breakeven point, calculated by subtracting the protective call premium from the short sale price, is $84 ($90 minus $6.00). At $84, the $6.00 gain on your short position in IBM will offset the $6.00 loss from your long call. By choosing the ITM call you are making a trade-off between the maximum loss and the breakeven point. Because the ITM pushes the breakeven point lower, you should only choose the ITM protective call when you expect a potentially large drop in the price of the stock.

The choice of strike price for adding the protective call to your initial short stock position is based on your risk tolerance and the extent to which you feel the stock will drop in price. As with any insurance policy, you need to consider the premium and deductible when adding your protective call insurance. If you want a lower premium—that is, the OTM protective call—then you should expect a higher deductible (you bear more of the loss before the insurance kicks in). If you want a lower deductible, then you will have to pay a higher premium (ITM protective call). Usually the ATM protective call offers the best balance of the two.

Opening Position—Protective Call Spread

If the prices for the protective calls seem to be too high or you are not happy with the breakeven points created as a result of paying for the protective call, you can use additional options to reduce the cost of your insurance. Using the same option prices as before, let's assume that you want to use the ATM $90 Call to hedge your short stock position but do not like the $2.50 cost or the $87.50 breakeven point. You feel that IBM could move higher so you want the protection, but you are only concerned with a slight increase in price by expiration. Instead of simply purchasing a protective call, you could also sell a further OTM call to take in some premium and reduce the cost of your insurance. In other words, instead of adding a protective call, you would add a protective bull call spread.

Using the same example as before, assume you wish to short IBM at $90 and you observe the following 1-month IBM call option prices:

IBM @ $90

$85 Call	$6.00
$90 Call	$2.50
$95 Call	$1.00

If you feel that the $2.50 premium for the $90 protective call is too high, you can reduce the cost of this insurance by purchasing the $90 Call and simultaneously selling the $95 Call for a net debit of $1.50. The hedge provided to your position by the addition of the call spread comes from the potential profit the call spread will have if IBM moves above $90. The maximum profit in the $90/$95 Call spread is the difference between the strikes minus the initial debit. Because the strikes are $5.00 apart and your initial debit is $1.50, the maximum profit in the spread is $3.50.

One main difference between using the call spread versus the protective call is that to close your combined position with the call spread if IBM is above $90, you do not exercise your long call. Because you have a call spread, exercising your long call will leave you still with a naked call. Instead, you repurchase the stock in the market to close out the short and close out the call spread and use whatever profit you have in the call spread to offset any loss in the short stock.

Let's compare the profit and loss in the protective call spread versus simply using the protective call. If IBM is at $90 at expiration, then you will have no net loss or gain on your short stock position. Your call spread will expire worthless, and you will have a loss of $1.50, which is the total loss for the position. If IBM is at $95 at expiration, you have a $5.00 loss on your short stock position. At the same time, you have a $3.50 profit in your protective call spread. If you close out all positions simultaneously, then you will have a net loss of $1.50 instead of $5.00 on an unprotected short position. Actually, you will have a $1.50 loss if IBM is anywhere between $90 and $95 at expiration. Using the protective call spread gives you a limited loss over a range of stock prices.

What if IBM rose to $100 at expiration? You would have a $10.00 loss on your short stock position and still have your $3.50 profit on your protective call spread for a total net loss of $6.50. Basically, the profit of the protective call spread reduces your potential loss by $3.50 as IBM moves above $95. Although you still have the potential for unlimited loss, you have partially hedged that loss. If you used just a protective call, you would have limited loss but also would have paid more for the insurance. Because the protective call spread has a limited loss between $90 and $95 ($1.50), you can use the upper strike of the call spread as your exit target. If IBM moves higher, you can predetermine that you will get out of the position if IBM hits $95 and therefore have a limited loss of $1.50. Even if IBM gets above $95 and you do not close out the position right away, you still have less of a loss than if you left the position unprotected.

The call spread as insurance does not limit your loss in entirely the same way as the protective call does. The call spread merely reduces the potential loss because the spread itself has a limited profit. However, the spread does give you an increased benefit should IBM move lower as expected. Because your initial debit is lower, your downside breakeven point is now $88.50, as opposed to $87.50 with just using the $90 protective call. Using the spread helps you to raise your breakeven point. Because you do have some protection against a rise in IBM's price, the protective call spread gives you partial insurance at a lower cost. If you are confident that any rise in IBM's price will be slight or not much greater than $95, then add the protective call spread as insurance over the protective call so that your position can make money sooner, that is, at a higher breakeven point.

Figure 4.5 compares the use of the $90/$95 protective call spread versus the $90 protective call versus simply shorting IBM without any insurance. As Figure 4.5 indicates, the call spread provides more of a benefit on the profit side in exchange for potentially higher risk on the loss side. When

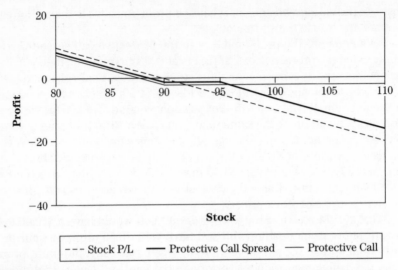

FIGURE 4.5 Short Stock with Protective ATM Call/Protective Call Spread

deciding between using a protective call versus a protective call spread, you need to take into consideration your level of risk tolerance and the degree to which IBM could move against you and produce a loss. The potential for a larger move against you would necessitate using insurance with the most protection—the protective call. If the possibility of IBM moving higher seems small, then using the protective call spread may be more advisable to reduce the cost of insurance.

Short Stock + Protective Call = Long Put

One of the synthetic positions covered in Chapter 2 was how a short stock/long call combination has the same risk/reward profile as a long put at the same strike price. For example, assume IBM is at $90, and the $90 strike call and put expiring in 1 month are both trading at $2.50. If you are bearish on IBM, you could short IBM at $90 and add the $90 protective call for $2.50. You could also simply purchase the long $90 Put, which also costs $2.50.

If you compare the profit and loss on both positions, as in Table 4.1, you will find that they are exactly the same. The question is why would you short IBM and buy a protective call when you can achieve the same risk/reward profile from purchasing a put? Why would you incur the margin requirements of shorting stock and restrict funds in your account to satisfy that margin requirement? Moreover, why short stock and deal with the

TABLE 4.1 Long Put versus Short Stock/Protective Call

Stock Price ($)	Short P/L ($)	$90 Call P/L ($)	Short Stock/Protective Call P/L ($)	Long $90 Put ($)
105	−15.00	12.50	−2.50	−2.50
100	−10.00	7.50	−2.50	−2.50
95	−5.00	2.50	−2.50	−2.50
90	0.00	−2.50	−2.50	−2.50
85	5.00	−2.50	2.50	2.50
80	10.00	−2.50	7.50	7.50
75	15.00	−2.50	12.50	12.50

responsibility of paying out any dividends or having your position closed prematurely by your broker if the borrowed stock has to be returned? Finally, although the actual profit and/or loss is equivalent, the return on investment is vastly different. With short stock, you are required to put up 50% of the short sale price as collateral. The realized profit or return is made on that 50% collateral requirement because that money is put aside and cannot be touched until the short is closed. The return on the long put is based on the purchase price of the put ($2.50). Comparing the costs, you can see that your short will "cost" you $4,500 in margin plus $250 for the protective call, whereas the long put will cost only $250.

If IBM drops to $85, you earn $2.50 on both positions, but in the case of your short stock, you earn $2.50 on a collateral requirement of $45.00 (50% of $90) plus $2.50 for the protective call, for a return of 5.3%. With your long put, you also earn $2.50, but that profit is based on the cost of the put of $2.50 for a return of 100%. Therefore, the long put requires significantly less capital and produces higher returns.

Based on this comparison, it would not make sense to ever enter into a short stock/protective call initial position when you can select the long put at the same strike. Realistically, the call and the put of the same strike are never exactly the same price, as in our example, but the difference between the two premiums is usually small, and the cost is still much lower than the combined cost of the short stock/protective call.

We include the discussion of the short stock/protective call as an initial position because some investors feel comfortable shorting stock and therefore will still choose the short stock/protective call combination as a way to reduce the risk of shorting stock. In Chapter 3 on long stock, we discussed synthetics as well, with respect to long stock/protective put versus a long call, and discussed how some investors prefer the benefits that come with stock ownership (dividends, voting rights, etc.) over using the long call. However, a short stock holder does not have such benefits, so we are inclined to recommend that as an initial position, a long put is preferred over a short stock/protective call combination.

Stock Moves Lower—Protective Call

You can add a protective call insurance policy to a short stock position that has already moved lower in price in order to guarantee a minimum profit. Nothing is more frustrating than watching a short stock drop in price to produce a profit and then have it reverse and move back higher, not only wiping out your profit but sometimes producing a loss. When traders short a stock and it moves lower, they sometimes place a trailing stop behind the stock price so that if it reverses and moves higher, the stock will be purchased at the stop price and the position is closed for a profit. You can achieve the same result using options and guarantee a trailing stop without worrying about the stock gapping higher for a large loss.

Assume you shorted IBM at $90 and it has dropped to $83. At the same time you observe the following 1-month IBM call prices:

IBM @ $83

$80 Call	$4.00
$85 Call	$1.50
$90 Call	$0.50

With IBM at $83, you have a $7.00 unrealized profit. If you feel that IBM can continue to move lower, then you would want to hold on to your short position to increase your return. However, there is always a chance that IBM could move higher and wipe out your profits. With option adjustments, you can still hold onto your short position for the potential to make more money while locking in a profit. Specifically, you can use a protective call to lock in a guaranteed minimum profit while still allowing IBM to fall further for increased returns.

Because you have an unrealized profit, the best strike to choose for your protective call adjustment is the ATM strike price because you want to lock in your current profit as best as possible. With IBM at $83, the nearest strike price is the $85 Call. To adjust your short stock position, purchase the $85 Call for $1.50. Let's examine the effect of this adjustment on your short stock position.

If IBM moves back above $85 by expiration, you can exercise your long call to purchase IBM at $85 and close out your short for a $5.00 profit (remember you shorted IBM at $90). Your profit is reduced by the $1.50 debit paid for the $85 Call for a net profit of $3.50. No matter where IBM moves above $85, you can always exercise your long call up until expiration to realize a guaranteed $3.50 profit. Therefore, there no longer is a

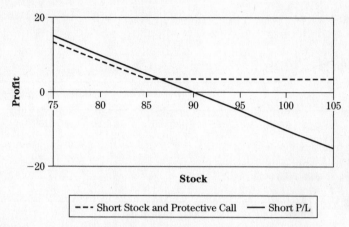

FIGURE 4.6 Short Stock and Protective OTM Call versus Short Stock

breakeven point because you have a risk-free trade. Your protective call still allows IBM to move lower and add to your potential profit. However, this profit is reduced by the cost of your protective call. For example, if IBM is at $80 at expiration, you will have a $10.00 profit in your short stock but you will also have a $1.50 loss in your protective call for a net profit of $8.50.

As Figure 4.6 indicates, your protective call adjustment has turned your risky short stock position into a risk-free trade with a guaranteed minimum profit. More importantly, you can sit back and wait until expiration of the short call and give IBM a chance to move lower for increased profit without worrying about your position. Your insurance "cost" for locking in this profit is the reduction of future profits by the cost of your protective call. However, because you are using a short-term OTM protective call, the option is relatively cheap.

If you want to lock in a higher minimum profit, then you should be willing to pay a little more for your protective call insurance. Instead of using the OTM call, you could purchase the ITM $80 Call for $4.00. Because your strike price is $80, you can exercise your protective call and purchase IBM at $80 to close out your short position for a $10.00 profit. However, because you paid $4.00 for the protective call, your net profit is actually $6.00. If IBM is at $80 or above, you therefore guarantee a minimum profit of $6.00. Compare this to the lower guaranteed profit of $3.50 from using the OTM $85 protective call. This higher guaranteed profit does come at a cost. As IBM moves lower, your overall profit is reduced by the $4.00 paid for the protective call. For example, if IBM is at $77 at expiration, you will have a $13.00 profit on your short position, which will be reduced by the $4.00 cost of your protective call for a net profit of $9.00.

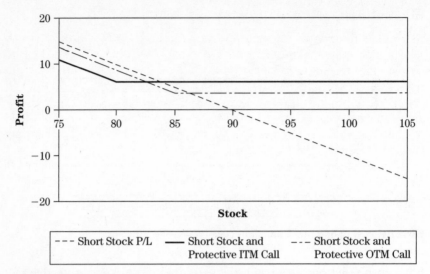

FIGURE 4.7 Short Stock and ITM Call versus Short Stock and OTM Call

Figure 4.7 demonstrates the difference between using the ITM and OTM protective calls versus your unadjusted short position. Your ITM protective call has a higher guaranteed profit but reduces your overall profit on the downside due to the increased cost of the ITM call. The OTM call is cheaper and allows greater profit if IBM drops in price but has a lower guaranteed profit. The choice of which strike price to use for the protective call depends on what you are willing to spend on insurance and how much profit you are willing to give up in exchange for security.

In this example, we do not recommend using the deep OTM $90 protective call despite its cheaper cost because it cannot guarantee any minimum profit. If you purchase the $90 protective call and IBM climbs back above $90, then you could exercise the protective call to purchase IBM at $90 for no loss or gain on your short position. However, because your protective call costs you $0.50, you will have locked in a loss of $0.50. This small potential loss may seem appealing to you if you are willing to risk $0.50 on a short position for the possibility of earning a large return. The low cost of your protective call will not eat into your profits by any significant amount if IBM stays below $90 or moves even lower.

However, for just a little more premium, you could purchase the $85 protective call and lock in a guaranteed profit with only a small decrease in your overall profits should IBM stay below $85. Therefore, we recommend that you do not go further than one strike above the current stock price.

Stock Moves Lower—Protective Call Spread

As we saw in our protective call adjustments, the cost of the protective call eats into our potential profits. Some investors are willing to accept the cost of insurance in exchange for the peace of mind that comes from locking in a guaranteed profit. Other investors, however, may feel that the potential for IBM to pull back after they short the stock is small, and they would rather have a lower cost insurance and are willing to accept some risk. Those looking for lower cost insurance can use a protective call spread instead of a simple protective call.

Using the previous example, where you shorted IBM at $90 and it dropped in price to $83, you can examine the use of protective call spreads based on the following 1-month option prices:

IBM @ $83

$80 Call	$4.00
$85 Call	$1.50
$90 Call	$0.50

With IBM at $83, you want to hedge against a rise in IBM's price that would reduce your potential profit and perhaps result in a loss. If you do not want to pay the premium for a protective call, you can add an OTM protective call spread by purchasing the $85 Call for $1.50 and selling the $90 Call for $0.50 for a net debit of $1.00. The maximum profit on the call spread is $4.00, which you derive from subtracting the cost of the spread from the difference between the strike prices. Table 4.2 shows the effect of the protective call spread on your short position at expiration of the short call.

As Table 4.2 demonstrates, the profit from your protective call spread partially reduces your potential loss if IBM moves back above $90. Even if IBM jumps back up to $95 by expiration, you still only have a loss of

TABLE 4.2 Short Stock and Protective Call Spread

Stock Price ($)	Short P/L ($)	$85–$90 Spread ($)	Combined P/L ($)
105	−15.00	4.00	−11.00
100	−10.00	4.00	−6.00
95	−5.00	4.00	−1.00
90	0.00	4.00	4.00
85	5.00	−1.00	4.00
80	10.00	−1.00	9.00
75	15.00	−1.00	14.00

$1.00 on your combined position. Because you have the possibility of a loss should IBM move high enough in price, you will have an upside breakeven point. Your new upside breakeven point using the protective call spread is $94. At $94, the $4.00 loss on the short stock position will be offset by the $4.00 gain from the $85/$90 protective call spread. Although the protective call spread does not prevent a loss entirely, it does serve to reduce your risk somewhat by raising your breakeven point from $90 to $94, giving you a larger cushion in case the position moves against you before you actually suffer a loss.

Between $85 and $90, the strike prices of your protective spread, you actually lock in a profit of $4.00. Below $85, your profit on your short position is reduced by the cost of your protective call spread, which is a lower cost than if you only bought a protective call. This is the benefit of using the protective call spread over the protective call alone—lower cost. Figure 4.8 shows the difference between using the OTM protective call and the OTM protective call spread. As always, it is up to you to determine your own risk/reward trade-off when selecting the appropriate adjustment to make to the short stock position.

You could also decide to use the ITM protective call spread as opposed to the OTM protective call spread demonstrated in the foregoing example. With IBM at $83, you could add the ITM protective call spread by purchasing the $80 Call for $4.00 and selling the $85 Call for $1.50 for a net debit of $2.50. The maximum profit on the protective call spread alone is $2.50, which is simply the difference between the strikes minus the debit paid.

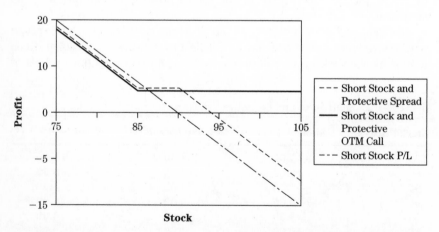

FIGURE 4.8 Short Stock and Protective OTM Call Spread versus Short Stock and Protective OTM Call

TABLE 4.3 Short Stock and Protective $80/$85 Call Spread

Stock Price ($)	Short P/L ($)	$80–$85 Spread ($)	Combined P/L ($)
105	−15.00	2.50	−12.50
100	−10.00	2.50	−7.50
95	−5.00	2.50	−2.50
90	0.00	2.50	2.50
85	5.00	2.50	7.50
80	10.00	−2.50	7.50
75	15.00	−2.50	12.50

Table 4.3 examines the profit and loss on your combined short stock ITM protective call spread position.

Your new upside breakeven point is raised from $90 to $92.50 by adding the ITM protective call spread. If you compare the profit and loss in Table 4.3 to Table 4.2 associated with the OTM protective call spread, you can see that the ITM protective call spread does not really provide much of an improved risk/reward profile over the OTM protective call spread. The easiest measure of this comparison is the upside breakeven point. The ITM spread raises your breakeven point from $90 to $92.50, whereas the OTM spread raises your breakeven point from $90 to $94 (Figure 4.9). In this example, you would choose the OTM protective call spread over the ITM protective call spread. Every adjustment requires analysis to determine the best choice, and it is difficult to develop simple and fast rules.

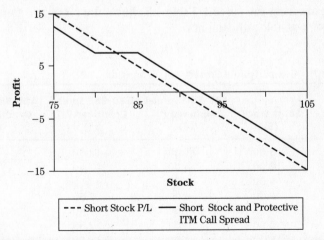

FIGURE 4.9 Short Stock and Protective ITM Call Spread versus Short Stock

TABLE 4.4 Short Stock and Protective $80/$90 Call Spread

Stock Price ($)	Short P/L ($)	$80–$90 Spread ($)	Combined P/L ($)
105	−15.00	6.50	**−8.50**
100	−10.00	6.50	**−3.50**
95	−5.00	6.50	**1.50**
90	0.00	6.50	**6.50**
85	5.00	1.50	**6.50**
80	10.00	−3.50	**6.50**
75	15.00	−3.50	**11.50**

Does this mean that the ITM protective call spread in the current example is not useful? Option adjustments give you flexibility in your trading, and therefore you must also be flexible. If the $80/$85 protective spread is not an effective adjustment to your short stock position, then you could consider the $80/$90 protective call spread. You create the $80/$90 spread by purchasing the $80 Call at $4.00 and selling the $90 Call at $0.50 for a net debit of $3.50. The maximum profit on the $80/$90 protective spread is $6.50, which is the $10.00 difference between the strikes minus the debit of $3.50. The best way to see whether this spread is a viable adjustment to your short position is to review the potential profit and loss, reproduced in Table 4.4.

Your new upside breakeven point using the $80/$90 protective call spread is $96.50, compared to $92.50 for the ITM protective spread and $94 for the OTM protective spread. The wider ITM protective call spread gives you a larger hedge against a rise in the price of IBM because of the higher profit from the spread. Table 4.5 shows the profit and loss profiles of all three possible adjustments.

TABLE 4.5 Comparison of Protective Call Spreads

Stock Price ($)	Short Stock ($)	$85–$90 Spread Combined P/L ($)	$80–$85 Spread Combined P/L ($)	$80–$90 Spread Combined P/L ($)
105	−15.00	−11.00	−12.50	−8.50
100	−10.00	−6.00	−7.50	−3.50
95	−5.00	−1.00	−2.50	1.50
90	0.00	4.00	2.50	6.50
85	5.00	4.00	7.50	6.50
80	10.00	9.00	7.50	6.50
75	15.00	14.00	12.50	11.50

One thing that is obvious is that your adjusted positions all have a lower loss than the unadjusted short position when IBM moves above $90, your original short price. This is the hedge your protective call spread adjustments provide. Although you still can have a loss on your short stock, the protective spreads have raised your breakeven points and allowed you to produce a profit even if IBM climbs all the way back to $90. The criteria for selecting one spread over the others for adjusting your short stock position come down to personal preference. Of course, it all depends on the option prices and the time to expiration you choose, and therefore you need to test the different spreads to see which risk/reward profile best matches your objectives and risk tolerance.

Rolling between Protective Calls and Protective Call Spreads

When you analyze all the necessary factors and choose an appropriate adjustment to your short stock position, you still are not locked into your choice depending on how IBM behaves. In other words, if you choose a protective call as an adjustment to your short stock position, you can still roll that protective call into a protective call spread. Rolling from a protective call into a protective call spread can reduce the cost of your insurance policy and even make you some money without removing your hedge.

Assume as before that you shorted IBM at $90 and it has moved lower to $83 for an unrealized profit of $7.00. At that time, you purchased an OTM $85 Call for $1.50 to lock in a minimum profit of $3.50. Assume that IBM has a reversal in price and moves back up to $89. If you feel that IBM will continue to move higher above $90, then you can simply exercise your long $85 Call at any time to collect your guaranteed profit of $3.50. However, what if you felt that the run-up in price was just a temporary move and IBM was going to move lower?

You could simply do nothing because you will still make money if IBM moves lower, yet still have your protective call hedge in place just in case you are wrong. However, if you can maintain your hedge somewhat and pay for your insurance, then you should consider it. Assume that with IBM back at $89, the $90 call with the same expiration as your long $85 Call is trading for $2.00. You can roll your protective call into a protective call spread simply by selling the $90 Call and bringing in $2.00 in premium. What is the effect on your position?

Originally you purchased a protective $85 Call for $1.50, and now you have sold a $90 Call for $2.00. The premium collected from selling the $90 Call not only pays for your protective call, but has brought in a credit of $0.50. You also now have an $85/$90 Call spread. The maximum profit on this call spread is the difference between the two strikes minus the debit paid (or plus the credit). You have a $5.00 difference between the strike prices but you received $0.50 for creating this spread, as opposed to a debit. Therefore, the maximum profit on this spread is $5.50. Because your call spread is at no cost, you have a profit on the spread if IBM is anywhere above $85 at expiration. Let's see what rolling into the spread does for your overall profit. Remember that you keep that $0.50 credit no matter what, and therefore the overall profit or loss is increased or decreased by that amount.

If IBM is back at $90 at expiration, then you will have no loss or gain on your short stock position but a $5.50 profit on your protective call spread. With your $85 protective call purchased for $1.50, you would have had a profit of only $3.50 if IBM was at $90 at expiration. Because your protective call spread does not lock in a guaranteed minimum profit, you now have an upside breakeven point. Your new breakeven point is now $95.50, where the $5.50 loss in the short stock is offset by the gain in the protective call spread.

The true benefit of rolling into a protective call spread for a credit is that now if IBM does move back lower, you do not need to recover any cost of insurance or have your profit reduced by that cost. For example, if you use the $85 protective call for $1.50, then if IBM drops further in price, your profit is reduced by that $1.50 cost of your insurance. Because the protective spread brought in $0.50 in credit, your overall profit is actually increased. For example, if IBM moves back lower to $84 by expiration, then you have a $6.00 profit in your short position plus the $0.50 credit received from rolling into the protective spread. Figure 4.10 compares the rolled into protective call spread combination versus the protective call combination.

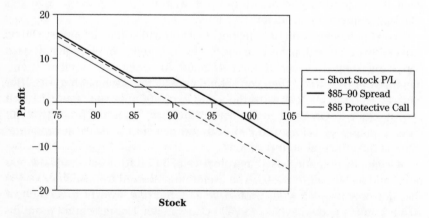

FIGURE 4.10 Rolling into Protective Call Spread

Because your upside breakeven point is now $95.50, you can use that price as your exit price should IBM continue to move higher. Although you are not completely hedged as you were with your protective call, you still have a nice cushion to absorb a rise in the price of IBM before you have a loss. More importantly, you now have the ability for increased profits if IBM does reverse and move lower. Remaining flexible is important when trading options, and just because you have made one adjustment to your short stock position (i.e., protective call) does not mean you will not have an opportunity to improve your position with another small adjustment (protective call spread). We recommend rolling into the protective call spread only when it can be done for a net credit, or at worst, even. This way you get the maximum profit from the spread to hedge against any potential losses and to remove the cost of your insurance.

Stock Moves Higher

When your short stock moves higher, you not only have an unrealized loss in your position, you also have the risk of getting a margin call from your broker or being forced to close out your short sooner than you would like. Normally, good risk management would call for closing out the short at a certain point before your loss gets away from you. However, sometimes when you short a stock it might experience a temporary rise in price before moving as expected. You might not want to close out your position yet because you expect the stock to reverse and move back lower for a profit.

Because there is always a chance of being wrong, and practicing good risk management means always considering what would happen if you were wrong, you could consider a protective call to make sure you do not lose more than a predetermined amount on your short. For example, assume you shorted IBM at $90 and it has jumped to $93. If you feel the price jump is temporary, you may wish to put a hedge in place while you wait to see whether IBM will move lower without opening yourself up to unlimited risk.

Assume that with IBM at $93, the 1-month $90 Call is trading for $4.00 and the $95 Call is trading for $1.00. You can add some insurance to your position by either adding the $90 or the $95 Call. If you add the $90 Call for $4.00, your maximum loss on your short position will be $4.00 because you can exercise the call at any time and repurchase IBM for $90 to close out your short. Although you will have no gain or loss on the short position, you will lose $4.00 on your exercised $90 Call. No matter how high IBM moves above $90, your $90 Call will limit your loss to $4.00. Your breakeven point will no longer be $90 because you paid for your additional insurance. The new breakeven point is now $86, where the $4.00 gain in your short stock will be offset by your $4.00 loss in your $90 Call. This is your trade-off for adding insurance and reducing your risk—you will then need IBM to make a larger move in order to realize a profit.

If you want a lower cost of insurance and are willing to accept a higher maximum loss, then you could purchase the OTM $95 Call for $1.00. Your maximum loss on your short stock with the $95 Call is $6.00. If IBM moves above $95, you could always exercise your $95 Call and close out your short with a $5.00 loss. Adding the $1.00 premium paid for the insurance, you have a total loss of $6.00. In exchange for this higher loss, you do have a higher breakeven point. IBM will only have to move to $89 before you would break even on your position because the $1.00 gain on the short stock will be offset by the $1.00 loss on your insurance $90 Call.

Figure 4.11 gives the risk/reward picture of using the $90 or the $95 Call to adjust your losing short stock position. Remember that you already have an unrealized loss in your short stock position, and your adjustment is about making sure you do not lose more than a predetermined amount while taking a chance that IBM will move back lower. It is simply adding a safety net. The choice between the strike prices depends on how much loss you are willing to absorb, that is, the deductible on your insurance policy. If you feel the potential for a move in IBM lower is high, then you might not want to spend too much on your insurance because that cost will eat into your profits. On the other hand, if you do not like taking large losses on your short position, you may be inclined to spend more on your insurance to have a lower deductible. The difference in maximum loss between the

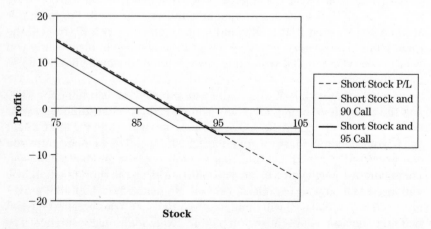

FIGURE 4.11   Short Stock that Moved Higher and Long Call

two choices is really only $2.00, so it may just come down to a comparison of the breakeven points.

When you short stock as a bearish position, you open yourself up to potentially unlimited liability. Proper risk management requires you to control your risk, especially on short or naked positions. Protective calls and protective call spreads are viable tools you can use to hedge your risk or remove it entirely. Although adding a protective call or protective call spread requires an initial debit, it is simply the price for insurance that helps you control your risk. When it comes to selecting strike prices, in deciding whether to establish the adjustment at the opening of the short position or after it has moved lower or higher, or when to roll from a protective call into a protective call spread, you must remember to let the risk/reward profiles be your guides. You just need to determine what reward you require and how much risk you are willing to take.

PUT REPLACEMENT

Imagine you shorted IBM at $90 and it suddenly drops to $85. You have a nice unrealized profit of $5.00 and you are faced with a difficult decision. Do you close out the position now and take your money off the table? What if you feel that IBM will most likely continue to fall and you would prefer to hold on to your short for more time? However, you are nervous that IBM could reverse itself and move back higher, wiping out your profit and perhaps producing a loss. On top of everything, you are not sure whether you want to hold on to the margin requirement that is necessary if you decide to keep your short position open to make more money on IBM. All of these can lead to considerable anxiety, and when you are stressed, you are more prone to making the wrong decision based on the information available.

Options give you the cure to your investment anxiety with respect to your short stock position through put replacement therapy. Put replacement involves closing your short position to take your profit off the table and replacing your position with a long put. First, by closing your short position you lock in a profit by putting the money in your pocket. Second, by using some of your profit to purchase a replacement put, you still can participate on the downward movement of IBM, making more money from your put. Finally, if IBM does indeed reverse itself and move higher, you already have your profit in your pocket, and therefore you can rest easy. Using a replacement put not only takes the stress out of your short position, but frees up your margin requirement so that you can invest in other positions.

Stock Moves Lower

Assume you shorted IBM at $90 and it has dropped in price to $85. You feel that IBM could drop further in price but you are also afraid of the chance that IBM could move back higher, wipe out your profit, and perhaps produce a loss. Investor paralysis usually sets in under these circumstances because you always feel that as soon as you close the position, IBM will drop further in price, and if you hold the short in place, IBM will move back above $90. You can avoid this investor paralysis by using put replacement therapy.

With IBM now at $85, assume that you observe the following 2-month put prices for IBM:

IBM @ $85

$80 Put	$0.75
$85 Put	$2.25
$90 Put	$6.00

You are considering 2-month puts because once you replace your short position, you would like some time for IBM to possibly move lower. You are no longer in your short position and therefore can use more time to expiration for your long put. With IBM at $85, the best replacement candidate is the ATM $85 Put, which will allow you to continue to profit as IBM falls below $85 (Figure 4.12). Therefore, you will cover your short at $85 for a

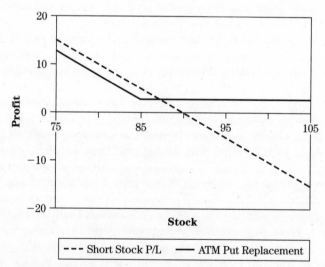

FIGURE 4.12 ATM Put Replacement Therapy

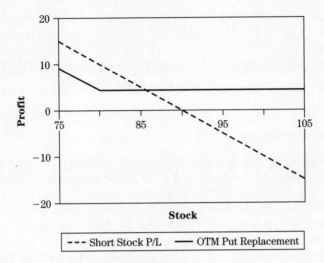

FIGURE 4.13 OTM Put Replacement Therapy

$5.00 profit and use $2.25 of that profit to purchase the $85 Put. After deducting the cost of the put, you have locked in a minimum profit of $2.75. No matter what happens to your long put, you have locked in your profit.

If IBM drops further in price, you will add to your locked-in profit due to the presence of your put. For example, if IBM is at $80 at expiration, then your $85 Put will be worth $5.00 and your total profit on your IBM position will be $7.75. Even if IBM moves back higher and your put expires worthless, you still have your $2.75 profit pocketed and your short margin cleared up for other investments.

If you want to lock in a higher minimum profit, you can replace your short stock with the OTM $80 Put for $0.75 (Figure 4.13). You will lock in a minimum profit of $4.25 ($5.00 short profit minus $0.75 cost of $80 Put). Although you have a higher locked-in profit, your OTM put will not increase in value unless IBM moves below $80. If IBM stays above $80, the put will expire worthless but you will still have your locked-in profit of $4.25. You should only consider using the OTM put if you feel that IBM can drop much further in price, that is, below $80. If you do not feel that IBM will drop below $80, then you do not get any benefit from replacing your short stock with the $80 Put.

What if you want to use the ITM Put to replace your short stock position? If you close your short stock position at $85 for a $5.00 profit and then purchase the ITM $90 Put to replace your short position, you will spend $6.00, which is greater than your profit. Therefore, you could potentially be locking in a loss of $1.00 if IBM moves back higher, as opposed to locking in a profit. ITM puts are more expensive and take away too much of your profit, even if the cost of the put is actually less than your minimum profit. Therefore, if you choose to take some option therapy and replace your short position with a put, we do not recommend using the ITM puts or any put more than one strike price away from the price of the stock when you choose to close out your short.

Stock Moves Higher

When your short position moves higher and produces an unrealized loss, you can use the put replacement therapy in the same way you use protective calls to prevent any further loss in your position while giving you the chance to make a profit if your stock does reverse and move back lower. Assume that IBM has moved from $90 to $94 after you shorted the stock at $90. You also observe a 2-month $95 Put trading at $2.50. If you feel that IBM's rise was only temporary and the stock will move back lower but you are not willing to keep yourself open to unlimited risk, then you can close out your short position and replace it with a put to prevent any further loss and actually give the position a chance to make a profit should IBM move lower. The other benefit of replacing your short stock with a long put is that by closing out your short position, you free up your margined assets for other investments.

Let's assume you feel that IBM could move back lower and you want some time to be right. Therefore, you close out your short and replace it with the long 2-month $95 Put for $2.50. You already have a $4.00 loss in your position and you have added $2.50 to your risk, the purchase price of the put. If IBM moves above $95 by expiration, then your maximum loss on the combined position is $6.50 ($4.00 short stock loss plus $2.50 for the $95 Put). If IBM does move back below $90, then your long $95 Put could become profitable and turn your total position into a winning trade. Because you spent an additional $2.50 on the replacement put, your breakeven point on the trade is no longer $90. IBM would have to move back to $88.50 for the position to break even. At $88.50, the long $95 Put would be worth a minimum of $6.50, depending on the length of time to expiration, which would offset the maximum loss on the combined position.

At first glance, it may not seem worth it to add risk to a losing position and lower your breakeven point at the same time. Basically, if a position moves against you, you may feel that the upward movement in the price of the stock is temporary and it will reverse and move lower as you expected when you shorted the stock. However, to wait for that to happen, you may have to leave open the possibility for unlimited losses in case you are wrong and the stock keeps moving higher. Replacing the short stock with the long put removes the risk of holding the short and still allows you

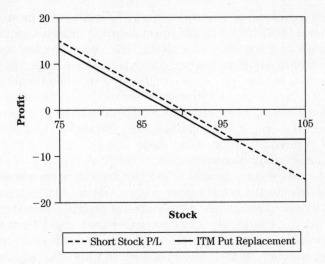

FIGURE 4.14 ITM Put Replacement Therapy after Stock Moves Higher

to make a profit if the stock drops in price. As Figure 4.14 shows, your put replacement on a losing short position is simply a way to continue to hold your short position in theory without the margin requirements or potential for increased loss.

If you wish to spend less money on your put replacement, you can use an OTM put. However, lowering your cost for the replacement put results in costing you in the breakeven point. Assume that a 2-month $90 Put is trading for $1.00. You can cover your short stock position at $94 for a $4.00 loss and replace it with the $90 Put for $1.00. Your maximum loss on this combination is $5.00 ($4.00 short stock loss plus cost of $90 Put). Your breakeven point is now lowered from $90 to $85. With IBM at $94, you would need IBM to make a large decline in price to $85 and below before you realize any profit. Therefore, OTM options are cheaper but require a much bigger movement in the stock for the position to become profitable, and we do not recommend using OTM replacement puts on a losing short stock position.

Put Replacement versus Protective Call

Put replacement allows you to lock in a profit by closing your short position and still participate in any further downward movement in the price of the stock due to the presence of your long put. The protective call also allows you to lock in a minimum profit and still participate in the further downward movement of your short stock. The risk/reward profile of each adjustment is similar. When would you choose one strategy over the other?

Although both strategies have similar risk/reward profiles, the two positions have different characteristics, and the choice between the two depends on your needs. The one main difference between the put replacement and the protective call strategy is that the put replacement strategy results in the closing of the short position, whereas the short position remains open in the protective call adjustment. Because a short position has a margin requirement, it may come down to the decision of whether you prefer to keep the short position open.

Some investors may be able to use the proceeds from a short sale in other investments and possibly earn a higher return, but that is not very common. Other investors may have sufficient margin where they do not need to rush to close any short as long as they are hedged. Most investors would gladly replace their short for a replacement put in order to free up their margin and invest their money elsewhere while still participating in their bearish position on the stock as a result of the long put. The decision between the two depends on whether the puts or calls are relatively inexpensive and whether you are willing to hold on to your short position.

COVERED PUTS

The sale of a put obligates the seller to purchase stock at the put strike price. If you sell a put against a short stock position, then the put will obligate you to close out your short stock at the strike price if the put is ITM at expiration. Selling the put creates a covered short position and you collect the premium. The profit in such a position is simply the difference between the strike price and the price at which you shorted the stock, plus the premium received from selling the put.

For example, let's assume you short 100 shares of IBM at $93, and a 1-month $90 Put for IBM is trading at $1.00. If you sell the $90 Put, you collect $1.00 in premium and have the obligation to purchase 100 shares of IBM at $90 if IBM is below $90 at expiration. If IBM is below $90 at expiration, then your short position will be closed out at $90. Your profit on the covered put is $3.00, which is the difference between the short sale price and the strike price of your short put. You also collected the $1.00 premium from selling the short put, which you get to keep. Therefore, your total profit is $4.00 no matter where IBM is below $90 at expiration because your short put obligates you to repurchase IBM at $90. If IBM is above $90, you still keep your $1.00 premium, which is added to your profit or loss depending on whether IBM is above or below $93 at expiration.

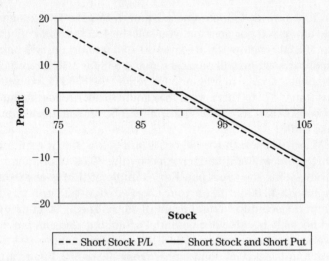

FIGURE 4.15 Short Stock and Short Put

As Figure 4.15 indicates, the covered put strategy has a limited reward/unlimited risk pattern. For example, after collecting the premium, your new upside breakeven point is $94 instead of $93. By selling the put, you establish a predetermined exit price while receiving payment for such an exit strategy. Your position will be closed if the stock moves below your strike price and you keep the credit from selling the put.

The most glaring aspect of the foregoing risk/reward profile is that selling covered puts only hedges your risk slightly. Therefore, we must really stress that the covered put adjustments do not reduce your short stock risk beyond the premium you receive. The premium collected does raise your breakeven point slightly but does little to reduce your risk if the stock surges higher. This point cannot be stressed enough when considering covered puts on a short stock position.

Stock Moves Lower

Assume you shorted IBM at $90 and it has dropped to $85. You expect IBM to move slightly lower or sideways for the next 30 days or so, but do not expect the stock to move back higher. At this point, you could either close your short stock and collect your $5.00 gain, or you could try to earn a little more profit on your short stock by selling a put and turning your short stock position into a covered put. Your short put will obligate you to close out your short position if the option is ITM at expiration, and you get to keep the premium collected for selling the put as additional income.

With IBM now at $85, assume a 1-month $85 Put is trading for $2.00. To create a covered put position, you sell the $85 Put and collect $2.00 in premium. If IBM is below $85 at expiration, your short put will be assigned, and your short position will be closed out at $85 for a $5.00 profit. Because you also collected $2.00 in premium for selling the $85 Put, your total profit in the position is $7.00. This is your maximum profit because no matter how far IBM drops below $85, your short put will be assigned, and you will still only make $7.00.

If IBM moves back above $85 but is still below $90 by expiration, then your short profit will still be increased by the $2.00 in premium you collected from selling the short put. For example, if IBM is at $88 at expiration, you have a $2.00 profit on your short stock in addition to your $2.00 in premium collected for a total profit of $4.00. The $2.00 in premium you collected not only boosts your potential profit, but also can provide a partial hedge against any losses should IBM move back above $90. The $2.00 will move your breakeven point higher from $90 to $92. Figure 4.16 shows how the short put improves the return on your position unless IBM drops below $83. Below $85, your covered put has a capped profit, whereas the short stock unadjusted is free to earn increased returns. Therefore, your choice to add a covered put depends on whether you feel IBM could move much lower than $83.

When adding the covered put, you take the guesswork out of exiting your position if IBM continues to move lower. Because you have a short put

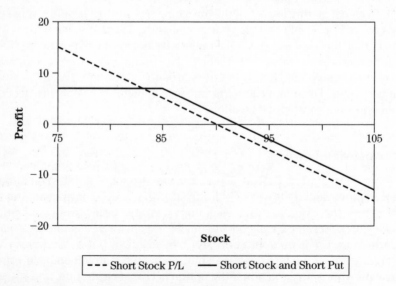

FIGURE 4.16 Short Stock and a Covered Put

at $85, you will be forced to close out your short at $85 if the stock moves lower. You have predetermined your exit price and collected a premium for doing so. The covered put is a nice way to establish your exit price and let it occur automatically. Of course, you must not forget that the covered put does cap your potential profit on the downside at $7.00. Therefore, you should only choose this adjustment when you are comfortable with the maximum profit and do not feel that the stock will move much lower than your predetermined exit price.

What if IBM does move back higher above $85 at expiration? As indicated previously, if IBM is still below $90, you still have a profit in your short position, which is added to the premium you collected from selling the put. At that time, you could either close out the entire position or, if you feel that IBM will continue to move sideways or lower, sell another short put in the next month to bring in more premium. The increased premium not only raises your potential maximum profit, it also raises your breakeven point and gives you a bigger cushion in case IBM keeps moving higher to get out of the position without a loss.

Assume that at expiration, IBM has moved back higher to $88 and a 1-month $85 Put is trading for $1.00 and a 1-month $90 Put is trading at $3.00. Your previous $85 Put has expired worthless, and you still have your short position. Because you feel that IBM will move sideways or continue slightly lower, you can sell another put to bring in more premium and again establish a predetermined exit price. Which put should you sell? Depending on whether you sell the ITM or the OTM put, you will get different results, and it is up to you to determine which results are in line with your expectations of where IBM will move.

Let's assume you sold the ITM $90 Put for $3.00. If IBM is below $90 at expiration, you will be obligated to close out your short at $90 for no profit or loss. However, you collected $3.00 from selling the $90 Put, plus the $2.00 you collected the previous month from selling the $85 Put, for a total of $5.00. Therefore, with IBM at $90 or below, you will have a maximum profit of $5.00. If IBM moves above $90, your additional premium collected will help provide a partial hedge against any loss. Your breakeven was raised from $90 to $92 from the sale of your previous $85 Put and is now raised another $3.00 to $95 with the sale of the current $90 Put. The benefit of selling the ITM put is that if IBM stays sideways, you know you will be forced out of your short stock position because your option is already ITM. If you are satisfied with a $5.00 return on your short position, you can choose the ITM put.

If you feel that IBM could move lower, then you would be inclined to sell the next-month OTM $85 Put to give the stock room to move lower before you are called out of your short position. You could sell the $85 Put and collect $1.00 in premium to be added to your already collected premium of $2.00. If IBM did move below $85 by expiration, then your short stock will be closed out at $85 for a $5.00 profit. This profit is added to your $3.00 in premiums already collected, for a total profit of $8.00. This is the maximum profit you can earn no matter how far IBM moves below $85. The $1.00 in premium collected also raises your already higher breakeven from $92 to $93.

If the puts you sell against your short stock position expire OTM, you can keep rolling your short puts to the next expiration month and collect more premium. You can keep collecting premium until your short stock position is covered through assignment on one of your short puts, or you close the position if the stock moves higher and you want to prevent any further losses. Each put you sell raises your breakeven point and increases your potential profit. For good risk management, you should consider closing out the position if the stock ever hits your breakeven point.

In the IBM example, we discussed the use of an ATM $85 Put with IBM at $85 after you shorted the stock at $90. If you use ITM puts, you collect more premium, but your maximum profit is lower. Assume a 1-month ITM $90 Put is trading for $6.00 with IBM at $85. If you sell the $90 Put, you bring in $6.00 in premium. At expiration, if IBM is below $90, your short will be closed at $90 for no loss or gain and you keep the $6.00 in premium. No matter how far below $90 IBM is at expiration, you only make $6.00 maximum profit. Compare this with the higher $7.00 maximum profit you realize if you sell the ATM $85 Put as in the previous example (Figure 4.17).

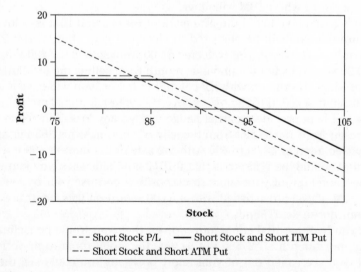

FIGURE 4.17 ITM Covered Put versus ATM Covered Put

Although the ATM covered put has a higher maximum profit than the ITM covered put, notice how the ITM covered put has moved your breakeven point from $90 to $96. You sacrifice some of your return in exchange for a larger cushion on the upside before your position results in a loss. If you are satisfied with the return you can achieve on the ITM covered put and have some fears of IBM moving back higher, then the ITM covered put gives you the best hedge.

One benefit of selling the ITM covered put is that if IBM moves higher, you can take the profit on your short put, which has served as a temporary hedge, and still keep your short stock position in place to sell another put and bring in more premium. For example, if IBM moves back to $88 by expiration, your short $90 Put will be worth $2.00 for a profit of $4.00 (remember you sold the put for $6.00). With IBM at $88, you also have a profit of $2.00 in your short stock position. As Figure 4.17 indicated, if you closed your short put and short stock together with IBM at $88, you would have a $6.00 profit. However, if you feel that IBM will reverse and continue to move back lower, you can close the ITM covered put and, while keeping your short stock position open, sell the next month's ITM $90 Put or even the OTM $85 Put to bring in even more premium. Because you already have a $4.00 profit on your first short put, you have raised your breakeven point from $90 to $94. Selling another short put will raise that breakeven point even higher and increase your potential profit when you eventually close out your short stock position.

Your final choice for a covered put adjustment after your IBM short position has moved from $90 to $85 is to consider the OTM $80 Put (Figure 4.18). Assume the 1-month $80 Put is trading for $0.75. Selling the OTM put brings in the least amount of premium and therefore provides the smallest hedge against a rise in the price of IBM. However, the OTM put allows the greatest maximum profit. If IBM is below $80 at expiration, your short put will be assigned and you will close out your short position for a profit of $10.00. When you add the $0.75 in premium you collected, your total profit is $10.75.

However, as the risk/reward profile in Figure 4.18 demonstrates, IBM would have to move below $80 before you could achieve that maximum profit. Also, because you are selling a short-term OTM option, the premium collected is small, and therefore the profit boost you receive to your short position is also small. Notice that the OTM covered put position performs only slightly better than the unadjusted position until IBM hits $80. Below $80 your profit is capped on your adjusted position at $10.75. Therefore, you should only choose the OTM put if you feel that IBM will continue to move lower but not quite below $80.

If IBM is above $80 at expiration, then your short $80 Put will expire worthless, and you are presented with some interesting choices. You

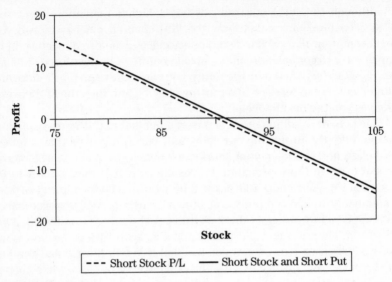

FIGURE 4.18   Short Stock and Covered Put

can close out your short stock position at that time for a profit (assuming IBM has stayed below your new breakeven point of $90.75), or you can choose to simply let your short put expire worthless and sell another covered put to bring in more premium. Which strike price you choose depends on where IBM is at the expiration of your short OTM put. You would go through the same analysis as before to determine whether your next short put should be the ITM, the ATM, or the OTM put.

SHORT COLLARS

One of the adjustments to a short stock position discussed in this chapter was purchasing protective calls as a means of insurance. The protective call can be used at the opening of your short position to limit your risk to a specific amount and establish an exit strategy in case the position moves against you. Another short stock adjustment discussed in this chapter is the covered put. Under the covered put adjustment, you would sell a short put to bring in premium and if the stock moves above the strike price of your short put, your short stock position would be closed and you would make a profit. The covered put establishes a predetermined profit level and exit strategy if your short stock moves down by a certain amount.

If you can combine the two adjustments, you can create a short stock position that has limited risk and limited profit. These are the characteristics of a short collar. A short collar consists of a covered put and a protective call that are usually OTM. If your short stock moves higher, your long call will limit any losses to the upside, and if your short stock drops in price, your short stock will be covered by your short put for a profit. The short collar gives you the predetermined exit points whether the stock goes up or down and demonstrates how options can make your trading easier.

Another way to look at a short collar is that you wish to purchase a protective call to limit your risk but do not like paying the premium for that insurance. Therefore, you choose to sell a put, which is covered by your short stock, in order to finance the purchase of your protective call. Hopefully the proceeds from selling the put will cover the cost of your protective call so that you can establish the hedge for no cost, or perhaps even at a small credit. If you do take in a credit, then this credit is applied to your overall profit and allows you to get paid for limiting your risk. Where else but with options can you get paid for limiting your risk?

Opening Position—Regular Collar

You can add a short collar at the same time you short your stock to create a "worry-free" short position. Remember that "worry-free" does not mean risk-free. The short collar does not prevent risk altogether; it simply manages it for you so you will not have to. It helps to take a lot of the worry out of shorting stocks. Assume you are shorting IBM at $90 and at the same time you observe a 1-month $95 Call trading for $1.00 and a 1-month $85 Put trading for $1.25. To create the regular short collar, you purchase the OTM $95 Call for $1.00 and sell the OTM $85 Put for $1.25 for a net credit of $0.25 (Figure 4.19).

Your $95 Call will allow you to purchase 100 shares of IBM and close out your short at $95 if your call is ITM at expiration. This will result in a loss on your short position of $5.00. However, because you collected $0.25 as a net credit for establishing the short collar, the maximum loss possible on your short is $4.75. No matter how far IBM moves above $95 by expiration, your loss will be capped at $4.75.

If IBM drops in price below $85 by expiration, your short put will be assigned and force you to close out your short at $85 for a profit of $5.00. You still have your $0.25 credit collected from establishing the short collar so your total profit will actually be $5.25. Therefore, no matter how far IBM drops in price below $85, your maximum profit on your short position will be $5.25. Between $95 and $85, however, you absorb whatever loss or profit is realized in your short stock position.

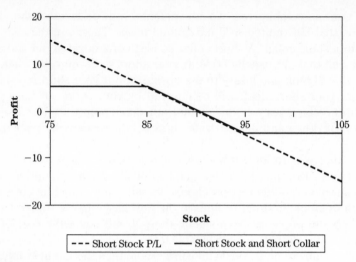

FIGURE 4.19   Short Collar and Short Stock

The collar serves to limit your maximum profit to $5.25 and, more importantly, reduce your maximum risk to $4.75. Good risk management calls for planning exit strategies for when the position moves in your favor or moves against you. The short collar allows you to set these exit points as you enter the trade and remove the possibility of straying from your plan. You get a bonus if you can establish the short collar for a net credit. The net credit increases your potential profit and reduces your maximum loss, as evidenced by the $0.25 credit you received in the foregoing example. Another benefit of establishing a short collar for a net credit is that you can use the net credit to satisfy any requirement to pay out dividends payable by the short stock. When you short stock, you are obligated to pay out any dividends paid while you hold the short, and the net credit received can offset this obligation.

If you are not satisfied with the risk/reward makeup of the short collar, you can adjust the parameters simply by adjusting the strike prices of the OTM call and put you use to construct the collar. For example, if you do not like the maximum risk in your short collar, you could lower the strike of your call so that your maximum loss is capped at a lower amount. Because you used an OTM in your standard short collar, you could lower the strike and select the ATM strike price for your long call. Assume that as before you short IBM at $90 and a 1-month $85 Put is trading at $1.25 and an ATM $90 Call is trading at $2.25. If you do not want a maximum loss of $4.75, as with the standard short collar, you could reduce your maximum risk by creating a short collar with a downward bias in the strikes.

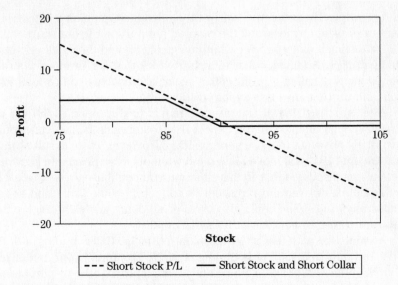

FIGURE 4.20   Short Stock and Short Collar

To create the downward-bias short collar, you short IBM at $90 and purchase the ATM $90 Call for $2.25 and sell the OTM $85 Put at $1.25 for a net debit of $1.00. Because your call is ATM, it will cost more to purchase than the OTM call and therefore result in establishing this type of collar for a net debit. However, the extra cost of the downward-bias short collar results in a lower maximum risk. If IBM moves above $90 by expiration, you can exercise your $90 Call and close out your short position for no loss or gain. You do have a loss of $1.00 on your short collar, which is the debit you paid to establish the position. Therefore, no matter how far IBM moves above $90 by expiration, your loss is limited to $1.00 (Figure 4.20).

In exchange for your limited loss, you do give up some of your profit on the downside. If IBM drops below $85, your short $85 Put will get assigned and close out your short for a $5.00 profit. Because you paid a net debit of $1.00 to establish the short collar, your actual total profit is $4.00. Therefore, your maximum profit on the downward-bias short collar is $4.00, and your maximum risk is $1.00. Compare this with the maximum risk and reward on the regular short collar example in Figure 4.19.

Stock Moves Lower—Profit Collar

You can use a short collar as a follow-up adjustment to a short stock position that has moved lower to lock in a profit or remove all risk from your short position. The protective call portion of your short collar will lock in a profit or prevent any loss, and the covered put portion of your short collar will establish an exit point for additional profit should the stock continue falling in price. Adding a collar to a short stock that has dropped in price creates what is called a profit collar because it enables you to lock in a profit and prevent any loss in your position.

After shorting IBM at $90, assume that it has dropped to $87 for an unrealized gain of $3.00. If you expect IBM to continue falling, you would most likely not want to close your position. However, there is still always that fear that IBM will move higher and wipe out your profits. In previous sections we discussed that in this situation you could use protective calls, covered puts, or even put replacement to lock in some profit and hedge against any losses. You could also use a profit collar and establish the position at no cost, or perhaps with a small credit.

Assume that with IBM at $87 a 1-month IBM $90 Call is trading at $1.00 and a 1-month IBM $85 Put is trading at $1.25. To protect your unrealized profit in your short position, you could create a profit collar by purchasing the IBM $90 Call for $1.00 and selling the IBM $85 Put for $1.25 for a net credit of $0.25. If IBM stays between $85 and $90 by expiration, then the options will expire worthless. Your profit will then be the unrealized profit in your short position plus the credit of $0.25. For example, if IBM is at $88 at expiration, your overall profit is $2.25—the $2.00 from your short stock position plus the $0.25 credit.

If IBM moves above $90 any time before expiration, you could exercise the $90 Call to close out the short at $90 for no profit or loss. However, you do have a profit on the overall position of $0.25 from the credit received. Therefore, adding the profit collar to your short position that has moved lower has guaranteed that you will not lose any money on the trade. The profit collar effectively removes the risk from the trade.

In exchange for adjusting your short stock into a risk-free trade, you do give up some of your additional profit on the downside. Because you have a short $85 Put, if IBM is below $85 by expiration, your short will be automatically covered at $85 for a $5.00 profit. Once you add the credit received for establishing the profit collar, you have a total profit of $5.25. No matter how far IBM drops in price by expiration, you have a maximum profit of $5.25.

As Figure 4.21 indicates, the profit collar removes the risk on your short position and establishes a predetermined exit point if IBM moves below $85. The best feature of the profit collar is that you adjusted your short stock position to a risk-free position at no cost. In fact, you received a credit for this benefit. Of course, you do give up additional profit on the downside if IBM moves below $85, but this is a small price to pay for removing the risk from your short stock position.

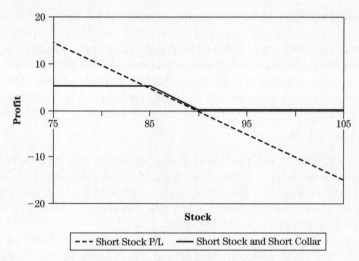

FIGURE 4.21 Profit Collar after Short Stock Moves Lower

Whenever you consider a profit collar on a short stock position that has moved lower, you should consider strike prices that lock in a guaranteed profit, or at least prevent any loss. In the foregoing example, you used the $90 strike price for your long call to close out your short stock position on the upside because $90 is the price at which you shorted IBM.

Collars are good adjustments to make to a short stock position at the opening of your short or after the short stock has moved lower. We do not recommend using a collar on a short stock position that has moved higher. Because a collar's profit is limited by the existence of a short put, adding a collar to a short stock that has moved higher may actually lock in a guaranteed loss. For example, if IBM moved higher to $93 after we shorted the stock at $90 and we added a collar using the $90 Put and the $95 Call, we would guarantee a loss or, at best, make no money on the trade. If IBM does reverse itself and move lower, our $90 Put will force us to close out our position at $90 and make no money. We do not give the position any chance of moving back below $90 to produce a profit. If we truly felt that IBM could move back below $90, then we would use a different adjustment, one that would allow us to profit if IBM moved lower but reduce or limit our risk on the upside. Therefore, we do not recommend collars on a short stock position that has moved higher.

PUT RATIO WRITE

The put ratio write is similar to the covered put strategy discussed earlier in this chapter. As with the covered put strategy, you are selling puts against your short position. However, in the put ratio write, you sell more puts than you are short stock, usually in a ratio of 1:2 or 1:3. For example, you would short 100 shares of IBM and sell two or three puts against your short position. Basically it is a combination of a covered put position and extra naked puts. The additional naked puts bring in additional premium over a covered put adjustment, but they also add risk to your short position.

Opening Position

When we discussed ratio writes as an adjustment to a long stock position in the previous chapter, we said that they are a good adjustment when we expect the stock to move sideways. The additional premium collected from selling extra options against our stock position creates a wide profit zone around the purchase price of the stock. If we expected a stock to move sideways and the implied volatility of the ATM options was high, we could purchase the stock and sell calls against the position to take advantage of the high implied volatility and the expected sideways movement of the stock. Similar strategies can be used with short stock and puts.

Assume that IBM is at $90 and 1-month IBM $90 Puts are trading at $2.00. If we expect IBM to move sideways in the next month, we can short IBM at $90 and sell more than one put against our short position to create a put ratio write. If we wanted to create a 1:2 ratio write, we would short IBM at $90 and sell two $90 Puts at $2.00 each for a total credit of $4.00. Our maximum profit when selling short options is always achieved when the stock is right at the short strike at expiration. If IBM is right at $90 at expiration, our short puts will expire worthless for a profit of $4.00. Because we have no loss or gain on our short stock position, the overall profit is $4.00.

As IBM moves above $90 by expiration, our potential profit will be reduced by $1.00 for every $1.00 IBM moves above $90. For example, if IBM is at $91 at expiration, our puts expire worthless for a profit of $4.00, but we have a $1.00 loss in our short position, for a total profit of $3.00. Our upside breakeven point will therefore be $94 because at that price the loss in our short stock position will offset the $4.00 profit received from selling the short puts.

If IBM moves below $90 by expiration, our short stock position will be covered at $90 by one of our $90 Puts for no gain or loss. The overall profit or loss in our position will therefore depend on the remaining short put and how far IBM is below $90. For example, if IBM drops to $86 by expiration, our short stock position will be closed at $90 using one of the puts and the remaining put will have a value of $4.00. The value of the remaining short put will be offset by the $4.00 credit received from selling the two $90 Puts for an overall profit of $0.00. Therefore, our downside breakeven point is

$86. For every $1.00 that IBM moves below $86, our position will lose $1.00 from the short put.

As Figure 4.22 indicates, the IBM put ratio write has a profit if IBM stays close to $90 by expiration. The premium we collected provides a cushion if IBM moves slightly higher. The advantage of adding the put ratio write is that when we short IBM at $90, we have a partial hedge against any upward movement in the price of the stock. Because our breakeven point is now $94, we have reduced our risk slightly by making the adjustment. The downside is that we have cut off our potential profit if IBM moves lower and even reduced it somewhat. For example, if IBM is at $87 at expiration, our total profit on the put ratio write position will be $1.00, as indicated in Figure 4.22, compared to a $3.00 profit in the unadjusted short position.

The potential return on the put ratio write is directly affected by the implied volatility of the puts we sell. Let's assume that the implied volatility in the IBM puts is significantly higher than that in the IBM $90 Puts we used in the foregoing example and that these higher implied volatility 1-month IBM $90 Puts are trading for $3.00 each as opposed to $2.00 each. If we create a put ratio spread using these higher implied volatility puts, then we would short IBM at $90 and sell two IBM $90 Puts at $3.00 each for a credit of $6.00. One immediate effect is that our upside breakeven point is raised from $94 in the previous ratio write example to $96 using the higher implied volatility puts. Therefore, selling relatively more expensive puts gives a greater hedge against upward movement in the price of the stock.

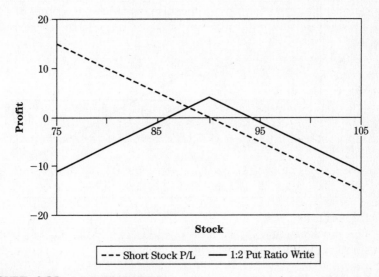

FIGURE 4.22 1:2 Put Ratio Write

The higher implied volatility puts also lower the downside breakeven point from $86 to $84.

Figure 4.23 compares the risk/reward profile of the two put ratio writes created using options with comparatively low and high implied volatility. The exact implied volatility calculations are not relevant because in our assumption we are simply demonstrating the effect of using puts with a higher implied volatility relative to puts with a lower implied volatility. Because we have not changed the strike price or time to expiration, the only difference between the two sets of puts is our assumption of implied volatility. As the figure indicates, you achieve a wider profit zone when you sell relatively more expensive puts. That is why in Chapter 2 we discussed the importance of implied volatility as a tool in trading options.

Although with respect to long stock ratio writes we did cover ratios above 1:2 (i.e., 1:3 and 1:4) in the previous chapter, we do not recommend using such higher ratios as an initial adjustment to a short stock position. Adding more naked puts will raise the breakeven on the upside but it will also raise the breakeven point on the downside. For example, using the IBM $90 Puts trading at $2.00, we could create a 1:3 put ratio write by shorting IBM at $90 and selling three IBM $90 Puts at $2.00 each for a credit of $6.00. Our new upside breakeven point will be $96 as a result of the $6.00 in premium collected from the short puts (compare this with an upside breakeven point of $94 in our 1:2 put ratio write). Our downside breakeven

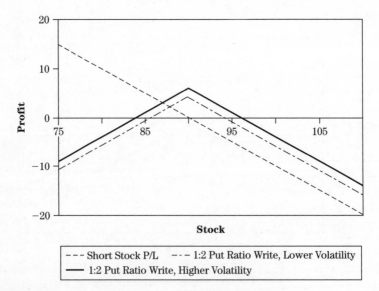

FIGURE 4.23   Effect of Implied Volatility on Put Ratio Writes

point, however, will also move higher from $86 in our 1:2 put ratio write to $87 in our 1:3 put ratio write.

If you want to choose a 1:3 or 1:4 put ratio write, which will result in having a lot of room on the upside for profit when shorting the stock, then you should not be considering such a bearish strategy. If your adjustment on a short stock position makes most of its profit on the upside, then your initial position should be a bullish one. Knowing the risk/preward profile of your adjustment beforehand will help you avoid making the wrong trade.

Stock Moves Lower—Regular Ratio Write

An excellent use of put ratio writes is when a short stock has moved lower for an unrealized profit and we expect the stock to move sideways for the next 30 days or so. If we expect the stock to move sideways, we can simply close out the short position and take our profit. We could also use the put ratio write to make some additional income off the sideways movement and even provide a slight hedge in case the stock does move higher.

Assume you shorted IBM at $90 and it has dropped to $85 for an unrealized gain of $5.00. If the analysis of IBM indicates that it is entering a sideways trading pattern for the next month or so, you can consider using the put ratio write adjustment to add a few dollars of profit to your already profitable position. After IBM has dropped to $85, assume that 1-month IBM $85 Puts are trading at $2.00. To add a 1:2 put ratio write adjustment to your short stock position, sell two IBM $85 Puts at $2.00 each for a credit of $4.00.

If IBM is right at $85 at expiration, then not only do you have a $5.00 profit in your short stock position, but you also collected $4.00 in premium from selling the puts for a total profit of $9.00. If IBM does move sideways until expiration, your put ratio write adjustment boosts your short stock profit from $5.00 to $9.00—an increase of 80%!

Should IBM move lower than $85 by expiration, then your short will be closed by one of the short puts at $85 for a $5.00 profit. The overall profit on the position will depend on how far below $85 IBM moves by expiration because you have a naked put as part of your put ratio write. If IBM is at $82 at expiration, your short stock will be closed for a profit of $5.00 and your remaining naked $85 Put will be worth $3.00. Because you collected $4.00 in premium when you established the adjustment, you can close out the short put at a gain of $1.00 for a total profit on our combined position of $6.00.

As IBM moves below $85 by expiration, the short put will cut into your profits until you hit the downside breakeven point. Your downside breakeven point for this combined position is $76. At $76, your short stock will be closed at $85 for a profit of $5.00. Your remaining short $85 Put will be worth $9.00, which results in a $5.00 loss when offset by the $4.00 in premium you collected when you added the put ratio write. The $5.00 loss on the naked $85 Put offsets the $5.00 gain on your short stock for a total net profit of $0.00.

By adding the put ratio write and collecting $4.00 in premium, you have effectively raised your upside breakeven point from $90, your original short price, to $94. At $94, the $4.00 loss on your short position will be offset by the $4.00 in premium collected from establishing the adjustment. Thus, the put ratio write adjustment reduces the risk in your short stock position by giving additional upside room for IBM to move before you would suffer a loss.

Figure 4.24 shows how the put ratio write builds a "profit house" over your unadjusted short stock position. In other words, the additional $4.00 in premium collected from selling the two $85 Puts raises the profit potential on your position if IBM does move sideways until expiration. On the upside, the adjusted position outperforms the unadjusted position. The best part is that even if IBM moves back to your original short price of $90 by expiration, you still make a $4.00 profit from the short puts. On the downside, the adjusted position only outperforms the short above $82. Therefore, the ATM put ratio write is recommended when we expect the short stock to move sideways or slightly higher.

You still have a cushion to the downside if IBM does drift lower, and you have a profit all the way down to $76. In general, your short stock

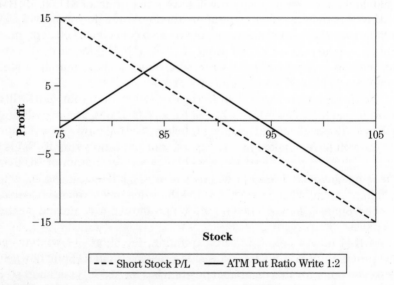

FIGURE 4.24 Put Ratio Write after Stock Moved Lower

position will still have a profit if IBM is anywhere between $76 and $94 at expiration. Therefore, putting aside whether the adjusted position outperforms the unadjusted position, the ATM put ratio write does give an extremely wide profit zone in case IBM does not move sideways as expected. However, because the adjusted position is biased to the upside, you should remember this bias when deciding to add the ATM put ratio write to your short stock position. Make sure your analysis of where IBM will move until expiration matches the profile of the adjustment you select.

Because options are flexible, we should remain flexible as well when making adjustments. Remember that you are not constrained by the profile of the ATM put ratio write. You can move the bias of the adjustment simply by selecting a different strike price to establish the put ratio write. If you feel that IBM will move sideways or slightly lower, then you will want to bias your adjustment to the downside. You can do this by simply selecting the OTM strike instead of the ATM strike for your put ratio write. Assume with IBM at $85 after shorting the stock at $90, the OTM 1-month $80 Puts are trading at $0.75. You can establish an OTM put ratio write by selling two $80 Puts for $0.75 each for a credit of $1.50.

Because the two $80 Puts are OTM, IBM could still move another $5.00 lower from $85 by expiration and the puts will expire worthless. However, the premium collected will add to your overall return. For example, if IBM is at $80 at expiration, then you will have a $10.00 profit in your short stock position. Your $80 Puts will expire worthless for an additional profit of $1.50, and your overall position will have a net profit of $11.50. If IBM is above $80 by expiration, your overall profit in the short stock position will be increased by the $1.50 credit received from selling the short puts. Therefore, using the OTM puts will allow IBM to continue to move lower and still permit the OTM put ratio write to outperform your unadjusted short position.

On the downside, your breakeven point is $68.50. At $68.50, your short position will be covered at $80.00 for a profit of $11.50, and the remaining short $80 Put will be worth $11.50 for an overall profit of $0.00.

On the upside, the additional $1.50 in premium collected from selling the two $80 Puts will raise your upside breakeven point from $90 to $91.50. Figure 4.25 shows the risk/reward profile of the OTM put ratio write adjustment and demonstrates how the adjustment outperforms the unadjusted short stock position with a greater bias to the downside than the ATM put ratio write adjustment. Moreover, the OTM put ratio write adjustment has a much lower downside breakeven point. Therefore, the graph shows that if you expect IBM to move sideways or slightly lower, the OTM put ratio write adjustment produces better returns than the ATM put ratio write adjustment.

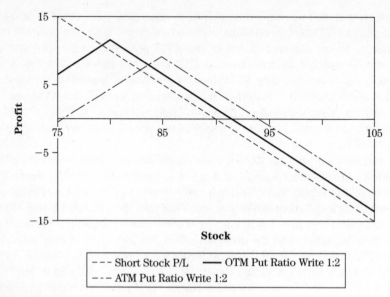

FIGURE 4.25 ATM versus OTM Put Ratio Writes

In addition to the use of ATM and OTM puts for a put ratio write adjustment, we can also use ITM puts. The ITM put ratio write has a tremendous bias to the upside, which we can use to our advantage in certain situations. If our short position has a profit and we have a strong feeling that the stock will reverse and move higher, then instead of simply closing out the position, we can add the ITM put ratio write to make even more money from the stock moving higher. Sometimes, our bearish outlook on the stock can change in midtrade, and the ITM put ratio write demonstrates a way to change the bias of our position by simply selling puts.

Assume that we shorted IBM at $90 and it has dropped to $85. Although we have a $5.00 unrealized profit, our analysis of IBM has changed, and we expect IBM to move back higher over the next month or so. At this point we could simply close out the short and take our profit—a choice that can never be criticized because taking a profit is always the best first choice. However, if we feel that the IBM puts are relatively expensive based on their implied volatility, we can change the bias of our trade without closing the short.

With IBM at $85, assume that 1-month ITM $90 Puts are trading at $6.50. We can create an ITM put ratio write by selling two $90 Puts at $6.50 each for a total credit of $13.00. Let's see the effect of using the ITM puts on our short position. If IBM is at $85 at expiration, then our short stock will be called away at $90 by one of the $90 Puts for no loss or gain on our short stock position. The remaining short $90 Put will be worth $5.00 and, when subtracted from our $13.00 in credit received, yields a net profit of $8.00. If IBM is at $80 at expiration, then we still have no profit or loss on our short position, which is closed by one of the short $90 Puts. The remaining short $90 Put is worth $10.00 and, when subtracted from our $13.00 credit received, yields an overall profit of $3.00. As IBM moves lower, the ITM puts reduce our overall profit. However, because we added the position expecting IBM to move back higher, let's see what happens when IBM does move back higher.

If IBM moves back to $90 by expiration, the two $90 Puts will expire worthless, for a $13.00 profit. Because we have no loss or gain on our short position with IBM at $90, our overall profit with IBM back to our original short price is $13.00. IBM has moved higher, and we have a greater profit on our combined position ($13.00) than if we had made no adjustment at all. Remember that our assumption was that IBM was going to move back higher and we were changing our bias on our IBM position. Therefore, our combined position will actually make more money if IBM moves back higher. The maximum profit is realized if IBM is at the short strike ($90) at expiration. However, if IBM moves above $90, we still make a good return on our short stock position. For example, if IBM moves back to $95, we will have a $5.00 loss on our short position, which will be offset by the $13.00 profit on the short puts expiring worthless, for an overall profit of $8.00.

As Figure 4.26 indicates, adding the ITM put ratio write in effect adjusts our short stock position into a slightly bullish trade. We will earn

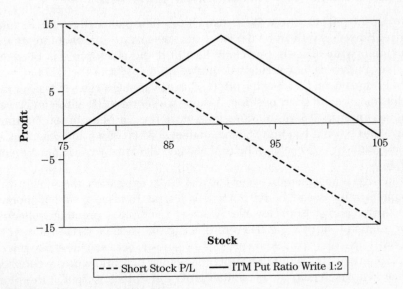

FIGURE 4.26 ITM Put Ratio Write

more money if IBM moves higher, and therefore we add the ITM put ratio write when our assumption has changed on where IBM will move. Instead of closing out the short and then opening a new position, we can simply add the ITM put ratio write. Because we have room for more downside movement in IBM to still make a profit, we also have a cushion in case we are wrong about IBM moving higher. The benefit we get from using options to make adjustments is that we have some sort of cushion in case we are wrong in our assumption.

Any of the foregoing put ratio writes can be adjusted further by increasing the ratio from 1:2 to 1:3 or to 1:4. However, with respect to short stock positions, we recommend sticking mostly with the 1:2 put ratio write, which has a more definable risk/reward pattern. Of course, the more naked puts you add to the position, the more premium you will take in, which will result in raising your breakeven point. However, the additional naked puts will also create a downside breakeven point that is much higher than if you selected a 1:2 put ratio spread. Although we recommend sticking with 1:2 ratio put spreads, you are free to use higher ratios if the premium collected and the risk/reward profile fit your risk tolerance and assumptions about where the stock price will move. For a detailed analysis of the effect of higher ratios, review the section on ratio writes in Chapter 3 on long stocks. Although the underlying is a long stock position, the analysis of the effect that adding more naked options has on the risk/reward profile is the same.

Stock Moves Lower—Variable Strike Ratio Write

We considered put ratio write adjustments selling puts with the same strike price. However, we can be flexible and use separate strikes to create the put ratio write. This is especially helpful if the stock price is between strikes and we cannot decide whether to use the OTM or the ITM put ratio write adjustment. Let's see the effect of using variable strikes in making the adjustment to our short position. Assume we shorted IBM at $90 and it has moved lower to $85. At the same time we observe a 1-month $90 Put trading at $6.00 and a 1-month $80 Put trading at $1.00. If we add the variable strike ratio write by selling the IBM $80 and $90 Puts, we bring in a credit of $7.00.

If IBM is anywhere between $80 and $90 at expiration, the $80 Put will expire worthless, and the $90 Put will be assigned and close out our short at $90 for no loss or gain. However, we keep the $7.00 in premium collected for a total profit of $7.00. Therefore, using the variable strike ratio write allows us to earn a consistent profit if the stock is between the strike prices at expiration. This is different from the regular put ratio writes we looked at earlier, which earn the maximum profit if the stock is right at the short strike at expiration. With the variable strike ratio write, we can earn the maximum profit over a wide range of stock prices at expiration.

If IBM moves outside the strike prices to the upside, that is, above $90, then both the $80 and $90 Puts will expire worthless, but we will have a loss on the short stock position. Our new upside breakeven point is $97 because the $7.00 loss on the short stock position at $97 will be offset by the $7.00 in premium collected from adding the variable strike ratio write. Therefore our adjustment has raised our upside breakeven point from $90 to $97. On the downside, if IBM is below $80 at expiration, the short $80 Put will reduce our $7.00 maximum profit by $1.00 for every $1.00 IBM moves below $80.

As Figure 4.27 indicates, the variable strike ratio write creates a very wide profit zone. If after our short stock position has moved lower, we expect IBM to move sideways, we can add this adjustment to create a profit zone over a wide range so that even if IBM does not stay right at $85, we still have the opportunity for a nice profit. Compare this adjustment to the ATM put ratio write example using the $85 Puts. The ATM put ratio write has a higher maximum profit, but only if the stock is right at $85 at expiration. With the variable strike ratio write, our maximum profit is slightly lower, but we have a better chance of obtaining this maximum profit because it can occur over a wider range.

There are numerous variations that can be created when considering variable strike ratio writes. The previous example used an ITM and an

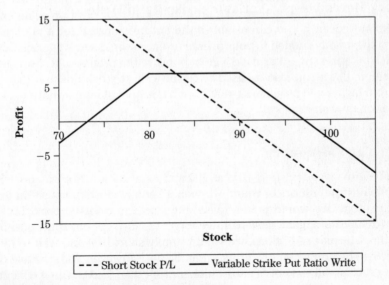

FIGURE 4.27 Variable Strike Put Ratio Write

OTM strike for the variable strike ratio write adjustment. You can select ATM and ITM strikes or ATM and OTM strikes. The choice depends on the risk/reward profile generated from the selection of the strike prices and whether the maximum profit and the range over which it is achieved fit your assumptions about where IBM will be at expiration. You also want to make sure that no matter which variable strike ratio write you establish, you have enough of a cushion in case your assumptions are wrong about where IBM will be at expiration. You always want some sort of a cushion to reduce your risk if you are wrong.

PUT RATIO SPREAD

A 1:2 put ratio spread is created by purchasing a put and selling two puts at a lower strike price. By itself, the put ratio spread will have a naked put because we are selling more puts than we are long. However, if we add a put ratio spread to a short stock position, then both short puts (in a 1:2 spread) are covered by the long put and the 100 shares of short stock. The benefit of adding a put ratio spread to our short stock position is that the put ratio spread acts as a profit lever and produces a greater return from a smaller move lower in the stock.

Because we are selling more puts than we are purchasing, we most likely can establish the spread for a net credit or at no cost. We recommend adding put ratio spreads only when they can be done for a net credit or no cost so that you can achieve the profit boost in your position at no extra cost. Moreover, if you can establish the put ratio spread for a net credit, then the credit is added to your overall profit. As we discuss later, not only can a put ratio spread provide a great boost to the profits on a short stock position, but it can also be used to repair a short stock position that has moved higher and produce a profit even if the stock does not move back to your original short price.

Opening Position

Assume we want to short IBM at $90 and expect it to drop to about $85 in the next month or so, where we would happily close the position for a $5.00 profit. We would prefer something closer to a $10.00 profit but we feel that $85 is a more realistic price target to close out our short position. Without the use of options, we would simply short IBM and wait to close out the position when our profit target is met. However, with the use of a put ratio spread, we could earn a higher profit than $5.00, even if IBM only moves lower to $85.

Assume that with IBM at $90, we observe a 1-month IBM $90 Put trading at $2.25 and a 1-month IBM $85 Put trading at $1.25. We can use these puts to add a put ratio spread to a short stock position and leverage our returns at no cost. When we short 100 shares of IBM at $90, we purchase the $90 Put for $2.25 and sell two $85 Puts at $1.25 each ($2.50 total) for a credit of $0.25. Initially, the addition of the credit of $0.25 adds to the potential profit of our overall position. For example, if IBM is at $90 at expiration, the puts will expire worthless, and we will have no gain or loss on our short position. However, we keep the $0.25 credit received from establishing the put ratio spread and therefore do have a profit of $0.25.

The benefit of adding the put ratio spread is seen when IBM is at the short strike ($85) at expiration. If IBM is at $85, we have a $5.00 profit on our short stock position. The short $85 Puts will expire worthless, but the long $90 Put will be worth $5.00 for a combined overall profit of $10.00. We also collect the $0.25 credit from establishing the put ratio spread. Therefore, the put ratio spread produces a $10.25 profit on our short stock position, which has only dropped $5.00. The adjustment levers up our position to be the equivalent of 200 short shares so that at $85 we have a profit of $10.25 as opposed to $5.00 on our unadjusted position.

The put ratio spread levers up the profit we can achieve on our short stock and caps out the maximum profit if IBM is below $85. Below $85, the long $90 Put and one of the short $85 Puts create a bear put spread with a maximum profit of $5.00. The remaining short $85 Put will close out our short at $85 for a $5.00 profit. Therefore, the short stock and put ratio spread combined will have a maximum profit of $10.25 (including the $0.25 credit) no matter how far below $85 IBM moves.

As Figure 4.28 indicates, the addition of the put ratio spread boosts our profit and outperforms the unadjusted position until IBM moves below $80. If IBM moves higher, we would have a loss just as if we did not make any adjustment at all to our short stock position. We did receive a net credit of $0.25 for establishing the position, but this credit is small and does not provide a true hedge in case IBM moves higher.

If we want a bigger credit to provide bigger profits and a partial hedge to the upside, we can add a 1:3 ratio put spread instead of a 1:2 spread. Using the same option prices, we can short IBM at $90, purchase the $90 Put for $2.25, and sell three $85 Puts for $1.25 each for a net credit of $1.50. The $1.50 in credit received raises our breakeven point from $90 to $91.50. The credit received also boosts our profit on IBM if it moves lower in price. For example, if IBM is at $85 at expiration, the $85 Puts expire worthless and the long $90 Put will be worth $5.00. Our short position will also be worth $5.00 for a total profit of $10.00. Once we add the $1.50 premium we collected for establishing the position, our overall profit is $11.50.

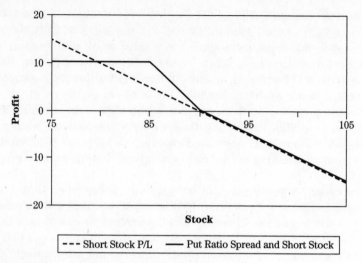

FIGURE 4.28 1:2 Put Ratio Spread and Short Stock

Unlike the 1:2 put ratio spread, the 1:3 put ratio spread does not have a locked-in maximum profit because the 1:3 spread has an extra uncovered naked put (Figure 4.29). Two of the short puts at $85 are covered by the 100 shares of short stock and the long $90 Put. The remaining short $85 Put is uncovered and therefore will reduce our overall profit if IBM moves

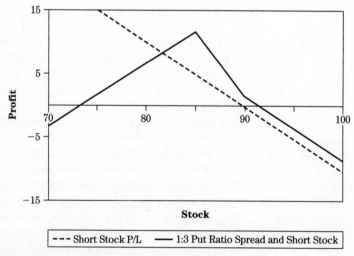

FIGURE 4.29 1:3 Put Ratio Spread and Short Stock

far below $85. For example, if IBM is at $80 at expiration, we have a profit of $11.50 on the short stock, the long $90 Put, and two of the short $85 Puts. The remaining naked $85 Put is worth $5.00, and therefore our overall position profit is $6.50.

As IBM moves lower, we eventually will hit a downside breakeven point, which is $73.50. At this point, our profit of $11.50 in our short stock and the bear put spread portion of the put ratio spread will be offset by the $11.50 value of the naked $85 Put. As the risk/reward graph in Figure 4.29 indicates, the 1:3 put ratio spread adjustment creates a wide profit zone boost for our short stock position over the unadjusted position. However, the addition of the third uncovered put begins to cut into our potential profits as IBM moves below $85 by expiration. Therefore, if you choose the 1:3 put ratio spread over the 1:2 spread as an adjustment to your initial short stock position, you should be aware of what happens to your potential profit if IBM moves lower than $85.

Basically, whether you choose the 1:2 or the 1:3 put ratio spread as an adjustment to an initial short stock position, the spread will provide a nice boost to the potential profits realized when the stock moves lower. The long strike selected should be as close to the short price of the stock as possible so that the profit lever works from the initial downward movement in the stock. Most important, we recommend adding put ratio spreads for a net credit or even whenever possible because the goal is to add a profit boost to your position at no cost.

Stock Moves Lower

You can still use put ratio spreads as a profit boost to a short stock position that has already moved lower for an unrealized gain. If you expect your short position to keep moving somewhat lower, then you can add the profit-boosting put ratio spread to leverage your return. Assume you shorted IBM at $90 and it has dropped in price to $85 for an unrealized gain of $5.00. If you feel that IBM will continue to move somewhat lower over the next month or so, you can add a put ratio spread to produce even greater profits from just a smaller move in the stock.

With IBM at $85, assume that a 1-month $85 Put is trading at $2.50 and a 1-month $80 Put is trading at $1.25. You expect IBM to continue to move lower but not by too much, so you want to add a put ratio spread adjustment to improve the potential performance of your position. With these option prices, you can purchase the $85 Put for $2.50 and sell two $80 Puts for $1.25 each ($2.50 total) for a total cost of $0.00. Therefore, you are able to make a cost-free adjustment to your short stock position that does not add any additional risk.

Remember that if IBM stays at $85 or moves higher, then the puts will expire worthless and your profit on the overall position will be whatever profit you make on the short stock. Because the put ratio spread does not provide any hedge against an upward movement in the price of IBM, you still need to practice good risk management and close out the position before it turns into a loss or make an appropriate adjustment to lock in a profit.

The benefit of the put ratio spread adjustment is felt if IBM moves below $85. For example, if IBM is at $80 by expiration, then the $80 Puts will expire worthless and the $85 Put will be worth $5.00. This $5.00 in profit is added to the $10.00 profit in your short stock position for a total profit of $15.00. Thus the addition of the put ratio spread has turned an unadjusted profit of $10.00 on your short stock position to $15.00—50% greater! The increase in your overall profit has also come at no additional cost to you nor added any additional risk to your position. As confirmed by the risk/reward profile of your adjusted position in Figure 4.30, options are a great tool that, when used appropriately, can improve your trading results.

If you want to provide a slight hedge against IBM moving higher while still boosting your overall profit should IBM move lower, you can add a 1:3 put ratio spread instead of a 1:2 spread to bring in a credit. With IBM at $85, you could purchase the $85 Put at $2.50 and sell three $80 Puts at $1.25 each ($3.75 total) for a net credit of $1.25. The $1.25 credit received from establishing the 1:3 spread is added to your overall profit and also reduces your risk slightly should IBM move back higher.

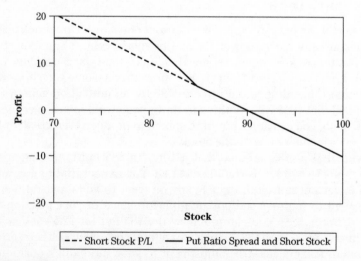

FIGURE 4.30 1:2 Put Ratio Spread after Stock Moved Lower

If IBM is at $85 at expiration, then your 1:3 put ratio spread expires worthless, and the $5.00 profit in your short position is increased to $6.25 by the premium you collected when you added the adjustment. The additional premium also boosts your profit when IBM moves lower. If IBM is at $80 at expiration, then your short $80 Puts will expire worthless and your overall profit will be $16.25 ($10.00 profit from short stock plus $5.00 profit from $85 Put plus $1.25 credit). Of course, the bigger the credit, the bigger is the boost in your overall profit from selling the third short put. However, selling the third put does reduce your profits to the downside if IBM falls beyond $80, the short strike in your put ratio spread. For example, if IBM is at $75 at expiration, the short stock has a profit of $15.00, your long $85 Put is worth $10.00, but your three short $80 Puts are worth $15.00 for a combined profit of $11.25 (adding in the credit received). Although you still have a nice profit, it is reduced slightly by the extra short put. If you do not expect IBM to fall too much further past $80 when you are considering the put ratio adjustment, then the 1:3 spread is a good potential choice.

Figure 4.31 compares the use of the 1:2 put ratio spread and the 1:3 put ratio spread against the unadjusted short stock position in IBM. As indicated, the 1:2 and 1:3 spreads both boost the overall profit to an extent as IBM moves lower. Sooner or later the 1:3 spread begins to decrease its profit potential due to the presence of the third naked put. When deciding between the 1:2 or 1:3 spread adjustment, you need to keep this figure in

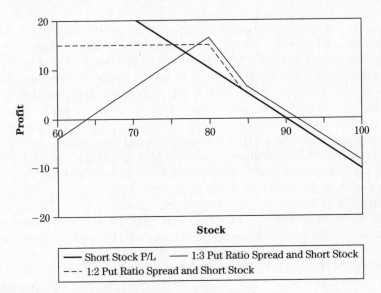

FIGURE 4.31 Variable Put Spreads and Short Stock

mind and select the adjustment that provides the best return, given your assumptions of where IBM will be at expiration.

Stock Moves Higher—Short Repair Strategy

The put ratio spread can be used on a short stock position that has moved higher to repair a losing position and actually turn a potential loss into a profit. Assume we shorted IBM at $90 and it has risen to $94. We feel that IBM will recover and move back lower, but maybe not all the way back to $90 or below for a profit. However, we do feel that IBM will move back lower. Normally we could just sit on our short and try to reduce our loss by closing out the position on any dip in price. Another option chosen by many "gamblers" is to short another 100 shares of IBM in order to raise the breakeven point so that if IBM does dip, they can get out even or perhaps with a small profit. The reason we use the term *gamblers* for traders who double down on a losing short stock position is that they are simply doubling their risk on an already losing position. If the ship is sinking, why add more water? Only gamblers in Las Vegas double down.

Efficient risk managers who trade options have a better solution. We can add a put ratio spread to our losing position and implement the short repair strategy, which will serve to raise our breakeven point and perhaps earn a profit on a position that if left alone would produce a loss. The short repair strategy can be implemented at no additional cost, which means we can adjust our position without spending more money and increasing our risk.

Before discussing the short repair strategy, we do want to make the reader aware that the short repair strategy only works if the stock is expected to move back lower to some extent by expiration of the puts in the put ratio spread. The strategy does not hedge against any further losses, should IBM continue to rise in price. Therefore, the short repair strategy should only be used when you are somewhat sure that the stock will move back lower, and you should be ready to pull the plug on the position to prevent any large losses if IBM does continue to move higher.

Assume as before that after shorting IBM at $90 the stock moved to $94, and you expect IBM to move back lower somewhat but maybe not all the way to $90 or below. At the same time, you observe a 1-month $95 Put trading at $3.00 and a 1-month $90 Put trading at $1.50. To apply the short stock repair strategy, purchase one ATM, or as near the money as possible, put for every 100 shares of stock you are short, and then sell twice as many puts at the next lowest strike. In the foregoing example, we would purchase the $95 Put for $3.00 and sell two $90 Puts for $1.50 each for a net cost of $0.00. Remember that the put ratio spread provides a profit lever if the stock moves lower. Here we are using that profit lever to make money as IBM pulls back and moves somewhat lower. The presence of the long $95 Put is similar to shorting another 100 shares of IBM at $95 to lower our breakeven point, and we financed the purchase of this put by selling two OTM puts. Both OTM puts are covered by the long $95 Put and the 100 shares of short stock, so we have no uncovered options.

Let's see how the addition of the put ratio spread "repairs" our broken short stock position. Assume that at expiration IBM has moved back lower to $91. At $91 we have a $1.00 loss in our short stock position. Our two $90 Puts will expire worthless but our $95 Put will be worth $4.00. Therefore, our overall profit on the repaired position with IBM at $91 is $3.00. The long $95 Put will produce a profit as IBM moves back lower and serve to offset or reduce any loss in the short stock position. More importantly, the adjustment can allow us to earn a profit on our short stock position even if IBM is still above our short price.

Because we have a profit with IBM at $91 at expiration, the put ratio spread has therefore raised our breakeven point above $90. Our new breakeven point is now $92.50. At $92.50, our $2.50 loss on the short stock position is offset by the $2.50 value in the long $95 Put (both $90 Puts expire worthless) for an overall profit of $0.00. As long as IBM only moves back lower to $92.50, we will have no loss on our short stock position, even though it is above the price at which we shorted it (Figure 4.32). Therefore, the addition of the put ratio spread allows us to raise our breakeven point at no cost and without any additional risk, such as what would occur if we were to double down and short another 100 shares of IBM at $94.

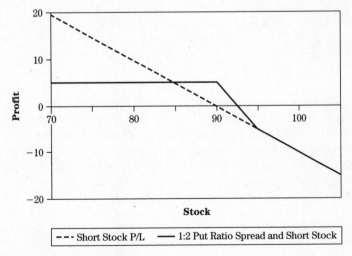

FIGURE 4.32 Repair Strategy

What happens if IBM moves back below $90? The long $95 Put and one of the short $90 Puts create a bear put spread with a maximum profit of $5.00 no matter how far IBM is below $90 at expiration. The remaining short $90 Put will be assigned and close out our short position at $90 for no gain or loss. Therefore, no matter how far below $90 IBM moves by expiration, the maximum profit on our "repaired" position is $5.00. Of course, we only added the put ratio spread because we felt that although IBM would recover and move lower, it might not get back to $90 or even move below $90. We used the adjustment to raise the breakeven point to get out of the position with no loss or even a profit. If the stock does end up dropping sharply in price, our adjustment still produces a limited $5.00 profit. Giving up potentially large profits in case IBM drops sharply by expiration is a small price to pay for raising our breakeven point at no extra cost.

When applying the short stock repair strategy to a short stock position that has moved higher, remember that first we should feel that the stock will move back lower. The strike price for the long put of the put ratio spread should be as close as possible to the current price of the short stock. We like placing the long put strike as close as possible to the price of the stock so that as soon as the stock moves lower, the long put is earning a profit to offset, either partially or totally, any loss in the short stock position. The strike for our short puts should be one strike below the strike of the long put. Using OTM options one strike away ensures that they will still have sufficient time value premium so that when they are sold they can completely cover the cost of the long put. Strike prices that are $10.00 apart can also be used if we expect a larger pullback in a stock and the put ratio spread can still be established for a net credit or at no cost.

CHAPTER 5

Calls and Puts

INTRODUCTION

Many investors begin trading options by using calls and puts alone. One can buy or sell a call or a put for a bullish or bearish, or even neutral, outlook on the underlying stock. However, many investors overlook the fact that after they open call or put positions, they can make many trade adjustments by adding more calls or puts, and even stock in some cases. These adjustments can have a great impact on the profit and loss of a call or put position because of the large trading leverage. Because there is potential for high returns when trading simple calls and puts, the adjustments can serve to boost those potential returns while hedging risk, reducing loss, or locking in profit.

Many of the trade adjustments for long calls are similar to those adjustments for long puts, and much of the background on the different long call trade adjustments is applicable to long puts. Therefore, we recommend that you read the long call section even if you are focusing only on adjustments to a long put position.

Naked calls and puts are extremely risky, and there are few adjustments that can be made to these types of positions. In Chapter 4, we were able to reverse many of the long stock trade adjustments to adjust short stock positions. The same cannot be said for long and short call or put positions. Therefore, the number of possible trade adjustments to naked option positions is far less than those on long call and put positions. Although we really do not recommend naked option positions, we do include possible trade adjustments to these positions with an appropriate discussion of the risks involved.

LONG CALL

Protective Put—Stock Moves Higher

One of the adjustments we discussed in Chapter 3 to a long stock position that has increased in price was to add a protective put in order to lock in a profit and still participate in the upside of the stock. Because a long call is a leveraged way to control 100 shares of stock and profits if the underlying stock moves higher, you can also add protective puts for long call positions that have moved higher. The protective put will lock in a guaranteed profit (if the total cost is less than the difference in the strikes) and allow you to participate in the upside if the stock keeps rising until expiration of the call.

Assume that Yahoo (YHOO) is trading at $45 and you purchased a 2-month $45 Call for $2.75, expecting YHOO to move higher by expiration. YHOO rises to $50, and you expect YHOO to keep moving higher until expiration. However, you are concerned that YHOO could drop in price still and wipe out your profits. Because you purchased the $45 Call for $2.75, your breakeven point is $47.75 (strike price + call premium). With YHOO at $50, the position will lose money if the stock falls below $47.75 by expiration. Therefore, you want to protect your profit from any drop in price and still make money if YHOO continues higher.

With YHOO at $50, assume that a $50 Put with the same expiration as your YHOO $45 Call is trading at $1.25. To lock in a minimum profit and hedge against YHOO moving lower, you could purchase the YHOO $50 Put. The $1.25 cost of the $50 Put is added to your original debit of $2.75 for the $45 Call for a total cost of $4.00. To see the benefits of adding the protective put, we will look at what happens at expiration for different prices of YHOO.

With the addition of the protective put, your new trade cost is $4.00. If YHOO does move higher and is above $50 at expiration, then the profit is simply the stock price minus the $45 Call strike price minus the $4.00 cost of the trade. For example, if YHOO is at $53 at expiration, the $50 Put will expire worthless, and the $45 Call will be worth $8.00 for a $4.00 profit. Without the adjustment, you would have a profit of $5.25 ($8.00 − $2.75). Thus, the adjustment gives up some profit on the upside for a locked-in profit on the downside.

If YHOO is anywhere between $45 and $50 at expiration, then the $45 Call and the $50 Put will be worth a combined $5.00. For example, if YHOO is at $47 at expiration, the $45 Call will be worth $2.00, and the $50 Put will be worth $3.00 for a total of $5.00. Because the combined position cost is $4.00, the profit if YHOO is between $45 and $50 is $1.00.

Below $45, the position will still have a profit due to the presence of the $50 Put, just as there is a profit above $50 from the $45 Call. For example, if YHOO is at $42 at expiration, the $45 Call will expire worthless and, the $50 Put will be worth $8.00 for a profit of $4.00.

By adding the protective put, you have locked in a minimum profit of $1.00 and still participate in the upside, should YHOO continue to move higher. An additional benefit of adding the protective put is that the YHOO position also results in additional profit if YHOO falls back below $45. The addition of the $50 Puts turns your long $45 Call that has moved higher into a nondirectional trade that profits if YHOO moves in either direction.

Looking at the risk/reward profile of the adjusted position in Figure 5.1, you can see how the shape resembles that of a strangle, except that there is no potential for a loss. The strangle shape of the risk/reward profile should come as no surprise because our combined position consists of a long call and a long put. Normally, a strangle consists of buying an out-of-the-money (OTM) put and an OTM call, but your adjustment creates a strangle legged into with an in-the-money (ITM) Call and an at-the-money (ATM) put.

To create a risk-free trade, you have to make sure that the total cost of the trade (put and call) is less than the difference between the strike prices of the options. In our example, the total cost of the $45 Call and $50 Put

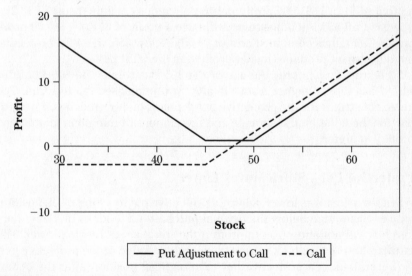

FIGURE 5.1 Protective Put Adjustment to Call

is $4.00, which is less than the $5.00 difference between the two strikes. As long as the total cost is lower than the difference between the strikes, you can lock in a guaranteed profit and still have a greater profit if YHOO continues to move higher or drops in price. Therefore, when considering adding a protective put to a long call position that has moved higher, you need to take into consideration the added cost of the protective put and the difference between the two strike prices. We recommend adding the protective put only when you can lock in a minimum profit.

If the stock moves more than one strike price away from your long call, then you can be more flexible in which strike price to choose for the protective put. For example, if after you purchase the YHOO $45 Call for $2.75, YHOO moves to $55, then you can look at the $50 Put or the $55 Put. Assume that with YHOO at $55, the $55 Put is trading at $1.25 and the OTM $50 Put is trading at $0.50. Purchasing the $55 protective put locks in a minimum profit of $6.00 (combined position cost of $4.00 from purchase of $45 Call and $55 Put subtracted from difference in strike prices). If YHOO is anywhere between $45 and $55 at expiration, the combination will be worth $10.00 for a guaranteed minimum profit of $6.00.

If you decide to choose the OTM $50 Put instead for lower cost protection, you would pay $0.50 for a total combined cost of $3.25. If YHOO is anywhere between $45 and $50 at expiration, then the position will have a guaranteed minimum profit of $1.75. Although this minimum profit is lower than if you selected the $55 protective put, the lower cost of the combined position results in higher profits if YHOO moves above $55. For example, if YHOO is at $60 at expiration, the $45 Call/$50 Put adjustment will have a profit of $11.75 ($15.00 profit on $45 Call minus combined cost of $3.25). The $45 Call/$55 Put adjustment will have a profit of $11.00 ($15.00 profit on $45 Call minus combined cost of $4.00). Below $55, the ATM protective put adjustment produces higher profit than the OTM put.

Figure 5.2 compares the use of the $55 Put versus the $50 Put after YHOO has moved higher from $45 after you purchased the $45 Call. The choice of strikes for the protective put depends on how much you want to pay for the additional insurance and the amount of minimum guaranteed profit you prefer.

Protective Put—Stock Moves Lower

When a stock moves lower, adding a protective put to a long stock position with a strike price below the original purchase price locks in a minimum loss but will not allow you to profit if the stock keeps moving lower. The growing loss in the stock offsets the increased value of the protective put. However, adding a protective put to a long call position after the underlying stock has moved lower is different. As the stock drops in value, the

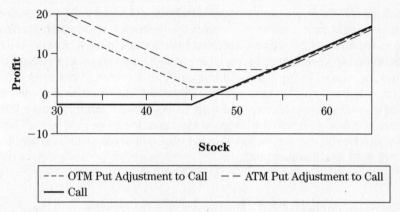

FIGURE 5.2 Comparison of Different Strikes for YHOO Protective Put

call eventually becomes worthless and the maximum loss is the debit paid. Once the long call becomes worthless, the protective put can still produce a profit as the stock drops.

Therefore, even if a stock moves lower when you own a long call, you can still consider adding a protective put if you expect more movement in the stock but are not sure of the direction. Calling this type of put a "protective put" is something of a misnomer because there is no profit to protect by adding the put to a long call where the underlying stock has moved lower. However, the put allows you to roll your losing long call position into one that could become profitable if a large move in the underlying stock is expected. If the stock moves back higher, you can realize a profit on your long call, and if the stock continues moving lower, you can realize a profit on your long put, just like a strangle, which is what your position has now become. Remember that the stock movement has to be large enough to cover the cost of the combined position.

Assume that with YHOO at $45 you purchased a $45 Call for $2.75 and YHOO has since dropped to $42. You feel that YHOO could reverse from the temporary decline but you have a concern for a continued drop in price. If you feel the potential movement in YHOO could be large but you are no longer sure about the direction, then you could add the protective put to convert the position into a strangle. Assume that an OTM $40 Put with the same expiration date as the $45 Call is trading for $1.00. You can add the $40 Put to the $45 Call for a combined position cost of $3.75. The new breakeven points, calculated by adding the total debit paid to the call strike and subtracting it from the put strike, are $48.75 and $36.25.

The addition of the $40 Put adds another $1.00 of risk to your position without any guarantee of a profit and adds to your previous breakeven point of $47.75. We do not recommend adjustments that increase your risk and require a greater move in the underlying stock for you to profit. However, we do want to present different possible trade adjustments. We do not recommend adding the protective put to a long call position where the stock has moved lower in price unless you truly feel that a large price swing is expected and you are unsure of the direction. The breakeven points created by adding the protective put with YHOO at $42 require at least a $6.00 move in either direction for the combined position to be profitable. Therefore, unless you feel a significant price swing will occur prior to expiration, avoid this type of adjustment.

Call Replacement

Assume that you purchase a long call on a stock you expect to move higher and it does in fact move higher. You have a nice profit in your position, but you expect the stock to continue to move higher. However, you still cannot help getting nervous that the stock could still move back lower toward your breakeven point and your profit could disappear. Of course, you could always take your profit by selling the call, but you do not want to miss out on further profit because your analysis tells you that the stock could move much higher. For a long stock position, we recommended call replacement therapy, where you sell the stock to lock in your profit and replace the position with a long call to continue to participate on the upward movement of the stock. You can use the same therapy for a long call that has gone up in value because the underlying stock has increased in price.

Assume that with YHOO at $45 you purchased a 3-month $45 Call for $3.50 and YHOO rises to $53. With 2 months left to expiration, assume that your $45 Call is now worth $9.00 for an unrealized profit of $5.50. At this point, you could sell the $45 Call for an excellent return on your original purchase price of $3.50. However, what if you feel that YHOO can continue to move higher but you do not want to give up all of your profit should YHOO reverse and start falling by expiration? You could use the call replacement strategy and sell your long $45 Call and replace it with a higher strike call. You lock in a profit and still make money if YHOO moves higher.

If a 1-month YHOO $55 Call is trading for $1.00, you can sell your $45 Call for a profit of $5.50 and use $1.00 of your profit to purchase the $55 Call. You have a locked-in profit of $4.50 and have a long $55 Call at no cost (because it was paid for with your profits). If YHOO continues to climb higher by expiration, your position has the potential for higher gains without risking your locked-in profits. Figure 5.3 shows how using the call replacement strategy in effect shifts the risk/reward profile of your original long call above the $0 line to create a risk-free trade. You can reinvest the

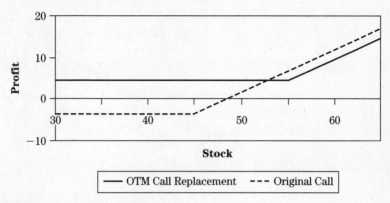

FIGURE 5.3 Call Replacement Strategy

$4.50 profit somewhere else and have your money working in two different trades at the same time.

We recommend using ATM or OTM calls for the call replacement strategy. In the foregoing example, we used the OTM $55 Call with YHOO at $53. Assume that with YHOO at $53, a $50 Call is trading at $4.25 and your original $45 Call is trading at $9.00. You could sell the $45 Call at $9.00 for a profit of $5.50 (purchase price of $3.50) and use $4.25 of your profit to purchase the $50 Call. The remaining $1.25 is your locked-in profit, which you keep no matter what happens to your replacement $50 Call. The locked-in profit is smaller than with the $55 replacement call because the $50 Call is ITM and has a higher cost.

Although the locked-in profit is smaller using the ITM replacement call, the potential profits on the upside will be higher because the $50 Call already has intrinsic value. If the stock moves sideways or higher by the expiration of the $50 Call, then the overall profit will be higher than if you used the $55 replacement call. For example, if YHOO is at $55 at expiration, the $50 Call will be worth $5.00. When added to the locked-in profit of $1.25, this gives an overall profit of $6.25. Compare this profit to the profit realized if the $55 replacement was used instead. Remember that with the $55 Call, you locked in a profit of $4.50. With YHOO at $55 at expiration, the $55 replacement call will expire worthless for an overall profit of $4.50, lower than the $6.25 profit realized using the ITM $50 Call. Figure 5.4 compares the potential profit of the ITM replacement call versus the OTM replacement call.

The ITM replacement call allows for greater overall profits than the OTM replacement call, should YHOO continue moving higher. The OTM replacement call locks in a higher minimum profit. These two factors are important to consider when deciding on which replacement call to use. If

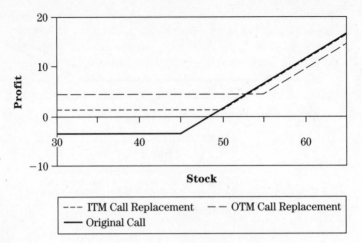

FIGURE 5.4 Comparison of ITM versus OTM Call Replacement Strategy

you expect the stock to keep moving higher but want to ensure a minimum profit, then you would use the ITM replacement call, which will allow for a greater return as YHOO moves higher. On the other hand, if you feel that YHOO will move higher but are truly concerned that YHOO could drop in price, then you would be more inclined to lock in a larger minimum profit and therefore would use the OTM replacement call.

If YHOO is right at a strike price when you are considering replacing the long call position with another call, then you can compare the use of the ITM, ATM, and OTM replacement call strategies. Basically, you should review the minimum locked-in profit versus the potential for profits should YHOO continue to move higher and select the replacement call that best fits your risk/reward requirements. As long as you locked in a minimum profit, there is no incorrect choice.

Remember that if your replacement call moves higher, you still have the choice of continuing to replace your long call with higher strike calls and adding to your guaranteed profit. For example, assume that after YHOO moves from $45 to $53, you selected the OTM $55 replacement call for $1.00 and locked in a profit of $4.50 on your $45 Call, as described in the foregoing example. If YHOO continues moving higher to $59, your $55 Call could be worth $5.00 with 1 month to expiration. If a 1-month $60 Call is trading for $1.00, you could close the $55 Call for $5.00 and use $1.00 of your profit to purchase the $60 Call. The remaining $4.00 profit on the $55 Call is added to your original locked-in profit of $4.50 for an overall profit of $8.50. In addition to the overall locked-in profit, you now have a long $60 replacement call.

If YHOO continues moving higher, your overall profit increases, and if YHOO reverses and moves lower by expiration, then you still have a guaranteed profit of $8.50. Rolling into one replacement call after another as the stock keeps moving higher allows you to increase your guaranteed profit and make more money as the stock moves higher. If the stock ever drops sharply in price by expiration, you will have no loss as long as you locked in a profit.

Rolling into a Bull Call Spread—Stock Moves Higher

A bull call spread is established by simultaneously purchasing a call and selling another at a higher strike for a net debit. However, you can also establish a bull call spread by legging into one as an adjustment to a long call position when the underlying stock has moved higher. If you sell the call for the same price or greater than the cost of your long call, then you will have a bull call spread at no cost, or perhaps even for a credit, with the potential for a risk-free profit.

Assume that with YHOO at $45 you purchased a $45 Call for $1.25. YHOO rises to $49, and your $45 Call is now worth $5.00 for a profit of $3.75. You could sell the call to collect your profit, but you might be reluctant to close your position if you felt that YHOO will move higher by expiration. However, you do have some concerns that YHOO could move back lower and you do not want to give back your profits. Assume that you feel that YHOO could move somewhat higher, over $50, and you would like to increase your profits slightly without risking your unrealized profits. If a $50 Call with the same expiration date as the $45 Call is trading for $2.00, you can roll your long call into a bull call spread for a net credit. By selling the $50 Call, you receive $2.00 in credit. Your $45 Call cost $1.25, so the premium you collected not only covers your initial trade cost but also provides a credit of $0.75.

What does rolling into the bull call spread do to your initial long call trade? First, rolling into the bull call spread after the stock has moved higher allows you to sell the call at a price higher than what you paid for your long call. Therefore, you can recover the cost of your long call and create a risk-free trade. If the premium collected from the short call is greater than the cost of the long call, then the extra premium is a credit received and is a guaranteed profit, no matter what YHOO does by expiration. If both calls expire worthless, you keep the credit received. In the foregoing example, rolling into the bull call spread brought in a credit of $0.75. Therefore, your adjustment has guaranteed a minimum profit of $0.75.

The bull call spread has a maximum profit of the difference between the strikes minus the net debit paid for establishing the position. However, when you roll into the bull call spread after the stock has moved higher, you are creating a bull call spread for no cost or a net credit. Therefore, the maximum profit is the difference between the strikes plus any credit received. Because you rolled into a $45/$50 bull call spread for a net credit of $0.75, your maximum profit if YHOO is at $50 or above at expiration is $5.75. Therefore, rolling into the bull call spread takes the risk out of the trade by guaranteeing a minimum profit of $0.75 and allowing for a maximum profit of $5.75 if YHOO moves higher as expected and is above $50 at expiration.

As Figure 5.5 demonstrates, rolling into the bull call spread creates a risk-free trade with the potential for significant limited profits. Remember that at the time you adjusted the long $45 Call, you had an unrealized profit of $3.75. Because you felt that YHOO would continue to move somewhat higher, rolling into the bull call spread allows you to have a maximum profit of $5.75 if YHOO is at $50 or above. Although the bull call spread does limit your potential profit should YHOO move significantly higher, this is the trade-off for turning the $45 Call into a risk-free trade.

Even if YHOO is expected to move significantly higher, rolling your long call into a bull call spread is still a viable adjustment. Assume that, as before, you rolled your long $45 Call into a $45/$50 bull call spread for a credit of $0.75. You turned your long $45 Call into a free trade, and you can still invest more money in YHOO calls if you expect the stock to continue to move higher. Assume that with YHOO at $49 after rolling into the bull call spread, a $55 Call is trading at $0.50. You can add the $55 Call to your bull call spread position and use the $0.75 credit to help cover the cost of the additional call. Because the $55 Call costs $0.50, you can use the net

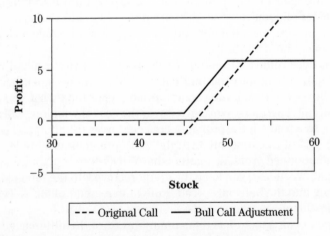

FIGURE 5.5 Rolling into Bull Call Spread Adjustment

credit you already received to pay for it and still have a locked-in profit of $0.25. Now you have a $45/$50 bull call spread and a YHOO $55 Call with the same expiration dates, and it has cost you nothing. In fact, you have pocketed $0.25! If YHOO stays above $50, then you have a $5.25 profit on the bull call spread; if YHOO moves above $55 by expiration, your $5.25 profit is increased by the value of the $55 Call.

Therefore, rolling into the bull call spread and buying another long call allows you to double up on your YHOO position at no cost or risk at all. If you are using long-term calls in an upward-trending stock, you can keep rolling into bull call spreads to create free trades and add additional calls at a higher strike at no cost. As the stock moves even higher, you then roll the long calls into bull call spreads and repeat the process as often as possible. After a while, you can establish multiple long positions in an underlying security at no cost and generate significant profits when the positions eventually reach expiration and the stock stays higher.

Even if the initial adjustment of rolling into the bull call spread is done at even cost—that is, no credit—then you can still add additional calls for the same amount of money you spent on the initial long call. For example, if, as before, you purchased the long YHOO $45 Call for $1.25 and you rolled into a bull call spread by selling the $50 Call for $1.25, you still have a free trade because the short call covers the cost of your long call. If the next higher strike call is trading at $1.25, then you can purchase that long call, and for the same cost of your original trade, you have a bull call spread and a long call together. Although you have no net credit or locked-in guaranteed profit, you have multiplied the number of bullish positions in YHOO at no extra cost. For your original debit of $1.25, you now own a bull call spread and a long call.

Rolling into a Bull Call Spread—Stock Moves Lower/Call Repair Strategy

Assume that after you purchase a long call, the underlying stock moves lower. When the underlying stock moves lower, you cannot necessarily roll into a bull call spread for no cost or a net credit. The next highest strike call from the one you purchased will also decrease in value and therefore will not have enough premium to convert the position into a risk-free trade.

You will most likely be more concerned with the ability of the stock to move back higher; otherwise, your long call will result in a loss. If you could, you would like to lower your breakeven point without purchasing more calls or adding more capital and risk to the trade. By rolling your long call into a lower strike bull call spread, you can lower your breakeven point, and in most cases, you can do it at no cost. Therefore, you can repair your losing position and give it a chance for a profit if the stock recovers somewhat.

With YHOO at $45, assume that you purchased a 2-month $45 Call for $2.50. The breakeven point on your position is $47.50 (strike price + debit paid). A few weeks later, YHOO drops in price to $42.50, and your $45 Call is now worth $1.50. YHOO will have to move all the way back to $47.50 for you to just break even on the trade. You still feel YHOO will move back higher but most likely not all the way back above $47.50. Instead of taking the loss and closing the position, you can lower your breakeven point by rolling down into a bull call spread.

Assume that with YHOO at $42.50, a YHOO $40 Call with the same expiration as your $45 Call is trading at $3.00. To roll down to a bull call spread, you sell two $45 Calls at $1.50 each for a total credit of $3.00 and simultaneously purchase the $40 Call for $3.00 for no additional cost. By selling two $45 Calls, you are closing your long $45 Call and opening another short $45 Call to combine with the long $40 Call for a $40/$45 bull call spread. The credit from selling the two calls covers the cost of the long call and allows you to roll down into a lower strike bull call spread at no additional cost.

Your new $40/$45 bull call spread has the same cost basis as your $45 call—$2.50—because rolling down cost you nothing. Therefore, with the $40/$45 bull call spread, your new breakeven point is now $42.50, $5.00 lower than your previous breakeven point of $47.50. YHOO just has to move higher from its current price of $42.50 by expiration for you to realize a profit. For example, if YHOO moves back to $45, you will have a profit of $2.50 for a return of 100% as opposed to a loss of $2.50 on your original position (Figure 5.6).

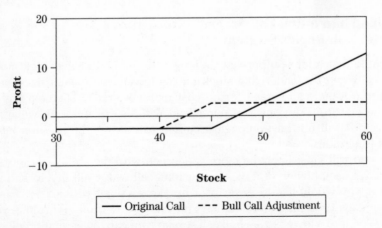

FIGURE 5.6 Rolling Down into a Bull Call Spread Adjustment

Rolling into a Bear Call Spread

In the previous section, we demonstrated how to roll down to a bull call spread after you purchased a call and the underlying stock moved lower. You roll down to the bull call spread to lower your breakeven point if you expect the stock to recover somewhat and move higher. However, what if your analysis changes, and you expect the stock to continue to move lower? One choice is to simply close out the long call for a loss. Another choice is to adjust the position into a bear call spread for a net credit and convert your bullish trade into a bearish one.

Assume that you purchased a YHOO $45 Call for $2.25 with YHOO at $45 and it subsequently drops to $43. The $45 Call you purchased is now worth $1.50. Your opinion on YHOO changes, and you expect the stock to keep on dropping in price and move below $40. You could close out your long call and take the loss or convert the position to a bearish one.

Assume that the $40 Call with the same expiration date as the $45 Call is trading at $3.75. If you sell the YHOO $40 Call, you will bring in $3.75 in premium, which will cover your initial debit paid of $2.25 and provide a net credit of $1.50. The resulting position will be a short $40 Call and a long $45 Call for a net credit of $1.50—a bear call spread. The maximum reward on the bear call spread is the credit received. Therefore, you would want YHOO to be at $40 or below by expiration so that both calls expire worthless and you keep the net credit. The maximum risk on the bear call spread is the difference between the strikes ($5.00) minus the credit received ($1.50), which is $3.50.

The rationale for rolling into the bear call spread is that you expect YHOO to continue moving lower and be below the short strike of the $40 Call by expiration. As Figure 5.7 indicates, the bear call spread has a higher risk than the long $45 Call and also has a limited reward of $1.50. Therefore, you should be aware that rolling into the bear call spread adds risk to your position in exchange for limited reward. Usually we demonstrate how reducing your risk lowers your reward, but this position accomplishes the opposite. It is an adjustment that is recommended only when you truly feel that the stock will continue to move lower.

With a net credit of $1.50, your new bear call spread has a breakeven point of $41.50. You rolled into the bear call spread when YHOO was at $43. Thus, you will need the stock to fall another $1.50 before you can start making a profit. This trade adjustment is not appropriate in all situations, and you should use it only when you can roll into the spread for a net credit and you feel that the stock will move below the short strike of the bear call spread by expiration. If these conditions exist, however, rolling into the bear call spread is a great way to turn your bullish long call position into a bearish call spread.

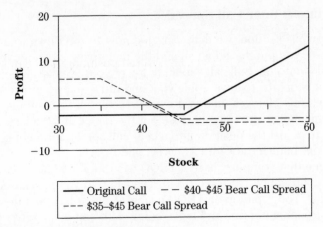

FIGURE 5.7 Rolling Down into Bear Call Spreads

If your opinion turns extremely bearish, then you can convert your $45 Call into a bear call spread using a lower strike price for the short call. You will take in more premium for a higher net credit and therefore have the potential for increased profits. Assume that when YHOO dropped from $45 to $43 after you purchased the $45 Call for $2.25, the YHOO $35 Call is trading at $8.25. Instead of selling the YHOO $40 Call to convert your position to a bear call spread, you can sell the YHOO $35 Call for $8.25 if you are more bearish; that is, you expect YHOO to fall even further in price.

The $8.25 in credit received for selling the $35 Call will cover the $2.25 cost of your $45 Call and result in a credit of $6.00 for the $35/$45 bear call spread. Your new breakeven point is now $41. Just as with the $40/$45 bear call spread adjustment, you expect YHOO to move lower below $40. However, the $35/$45 bear call spread has the potential for greater profits. If YHOO is below $40 at expiration, the $40/$45 bear call spread will earn a maximum reward of $1.50. The $35/$45 bear call spread can earn a maximum reward of $6.00 if YHOO moves below $35. Therefore, the $35/$45 trade adjustment has more of a bearish bias than the $40/$45 adjustment. The choice between the two depends on how bearish your opinion of YHOO has become (Figure 5.7).

Short Stock

The combination of a long call and a short stock creates a protective call position. On the upside, the long call limits the risk on the short stock because you can exercise the call at any time to close out the short. On the downside, your short position is free to run and produce a profit as long as the price of the long call is covered. A long call, therefore, is a possible adjustment to a short stock position. You can also add short stock to a long call position to create a possible risk-free trade. Remember that adding a short stock to a long call creates a covered position; that is, the long call hedges against unlimited loss in the short stock position. However, you will most likely have a margin requirement, which should be taken into consideration before shorting the stock.

Assume you purchased a YHOO $45 Call for $2.50 with YHOO at $45. YHOO climbs to $51, and your call is now worth $6.25 for an unrealized profit of $3.75. If you are an investor who likes to trade price swings and expects YHOO to move back lower temporarily, you can short 100 shares of YHOO at $51 to profit from a YHOO price movement lower. First, let's see what happens if you are wrong and YHOO keeps climbing higher. No matter how high YHOO climbs before expiration, you can exercise the long call at any time to cover the short stock at $45 for a profit of $6.00 (stock was shorted at $51). Although you expected the stock to move back lower, even if you are wrong, shorting the stock locks in a minimum profit of $3.50 ($6.00 short stock profit minus $2.50 cost of $45 Call).

If YHOO begins moving lower than $51, then the short stock position will produce a profit. For example, if YHOO slides back to $47, you will have a $4.00 unrealized profit in the short stock position. Assume that with YHOO at $47, the $45 Call is now worth $2.75. At this point, you have several choices. If you added the short stock because you wanted to trade the price swings, you could simply close out the short for a $4.00 profit and hold on to the long $45 Call if you expect YHOO to move back higher, locking in a minimum profit of $1.50 after deducting the original cost of $2.50. Another choice is to close out the long call position when you close out the short stock, bringing in $6.75 for an overall profit of $4.25 when the original cost of $2.50 is subtracted.

Finally, you could just leave the position as it is with the short stock and long $45 Call. If YHOO is above $45 at expiration, you can exercise the call to close out the short stock position at $45 for a $6.00 profit on the short stock for an overall profit of $3.50 (when the $2.50 cost of the call is subtracted). Therefore, the position will earn $3.50 no matter how far above $45 the stock moves. If YHOO instead moves below $45 by expiration, the overall profit will increase as the short stock produces a larger profit and the $45 Call expires worthless. Figure 5.8 shows the risk/reward profile of the long $45 Call position after adding the short stock at $51. As the chart indicates, adding the short stock locks in a minimum profit and allows for potentially higher profits, should YHOO reverse and move lower.

The risk/reward profile of the long call/short stock should look familiar. In Chapter 2, when we discussed synthetic positions, we demonstrated how a long call/short stock combination created a synthetic put; that is, it

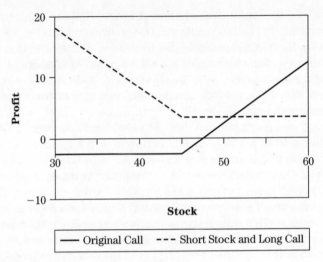

FIGURE 5.8 Short Stock Added to Long Call

has the same risk/reward profile as a long put. Adding the short stock after your long $45 Call has increased in value creates a position equivalent to a $45 Put established for a credit of $3.50, thus producing a risk-free trade.

Rolling into a Synthetic Straddle

A synthetic straddle is created by shorting a stock and buying twice as many calls at the same strike price. Remember from Chapter 2 that a synthetic put is created from shorting stock and purchasing a long call. Therefore, one of the long calls combines with the short stock to create a synthetic put. This synthetic put is combined with the other long call to create a synthetic straddle that will realize a profit if the stock makes a significant move in either direction. Straddles and synthetic straddles allow you to profit from a significant move in the stock without picking direction. Therefore, if you purchase a number of long calls, then you can adjust your position to convert it to a synthetic straddle by shorting 100 shares for every two calls you are long.

We do not recommend synthetic straddles over straightforward straddles as opening positions. On the other hand, converting a position of long calls into a synthetic straddle can create a risk-free trade if the adjustment is made after the underlying stock has moved higher and the calls have increased in value. The locked-in minimum profit in this type of adjustment is sufficient to outweigh the negative aspects of shorting stock, and the adjustment produces a position that has the potential for greater profits in either direction.

Assume that YHOO is trading at $45 and that because you are bullish on YHOO, you purchase two 5-month $45 Calls for $4.00 each. One month later, YHOO moves higher to $53, and your two $45 Calls are now worth $9.50 each. With 4 months left to expiration, you might be inclined to hold on to the two $45 Calls in case YHOO continues to rise. However, you are concerned that over the next 4 months an unexpected event could occur that will send YHOO falling, and your profit will disappear. To lock in a minimum profit and make money no matter which direction YHOO moves until expiration, you can convert your long calls into a synthetic straddle by shorting 100 shares of YHOO at $53.

If YHOO is back at $45 at expiration, both of the $45 Calls will expire worthless, but the short stock will have a profit of $8.00. Because the two $45 Calls cost $8.00 total, the overall position has no loss or profit. If YHOO is below $45 at expiration, the two $45 Calls expire worthless, but the short stock position produces a profit of $1.00 for every dollar YHOO moves below $45. If YHOO keeps moving higher from $53, then your profit will increase because of the presence of the two calls, which offset the loss in the short stock. For example, if YHOO is at $60 at expiration, the two $45 Calls will be worth $15.00 each for a total of $30.00. After subtracting the $8.00 cost of the two calls and the $7.00 loss on the short stock position, the overall profit is $15.00.

As Figure 5.9 demonstrates, adding the short stock to your long calls turns a bullish strategy into a nondirectional trade. Because there is no possibility of a loss from the movement of the stock, you can relax for the

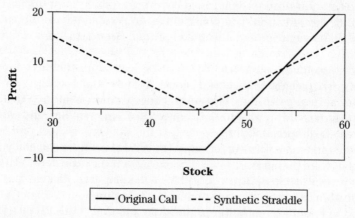

FIGURE 5.9 Rolling Long Calls into Synthetic Straddle

remaining 4 months of the life of the two YHOO calls and let the position run either higher or lower. Even if you are forced out of your short stock early, you can either cover the short if the stock moved lower or exercise one of the calls to cover the position if the stock has moved higher after you shorted it.

Rolling into a Calendar Spread

A calendar spread consists of purchasing a long-term call and selling a short-term call with the same strike price. The premium received from the sale of the short-term call reduces the cost of the long-term call.

Although calendar spreads can be initiated by using ITM, ATM, or OTM strikes, the objective is to have the short option expire worthless. When the short option expires worthless, you then have the long option at a lower cost. You could then hold the option until expiration or sell the next short-term option to bring in more premium and further reduce your cost and risk. With calendar spreads, you expect the stock to move sideways in the short term and then make a significant move higher or lower, depending on whether you use all calls or all puts. When you have a long call position with a long time to expiration, you can take advantage of short-term sideways trading patterns by rolling your position into a calendar spread to reduce the cost of your trade, lower your risk, and even create a risk-free trade in certain situations.

Assume that you purchased a 6-month YHOO $45 Call for $5.50 with YHOO at $45. Your breakeven point is $50.50 (strike price + debit paid). You expect YHOO to make a significant move higher over the long term, and therefore you purchased a call with plenty of time to expiration. After you open the position, your analysis of YHOO tells you that the stock is entering a short-term trading range hovering around your purchase price of $45. In this situation, you could either do nothing or use the calendar spread adjustment to take advantage of this short-term sideways trading pattern.

After deciding that YHOO will trade sideways for the next couple of weeks or so, you notice that the 1-month ATM $45 Call is trading for $1.75. To take advantage of the short-term sideways movement in YHOO, you could sell the short-term $45 Call, collect $1.75 in premium, and establish a call calendar spread. Your hope is that the sideways trading pattern will eat away at the time value premium in the ATM short-term call and you can keep the entire premium of $1.75. For example, if the short-term YHOO $45 Call expires worthless, then you still have the long-term call but at a lower cost of $3.75 ($5.50 original cost minus $1.75 in premium collected).

Assume that at expiration of the short $45 Call, YHOO is at $44. The short call will expire worthless, and you keep the $1.75 premium, and as stated before, you reduce the cost of your long call to $3.75. Assume that your long $45 Call with now 5 months left to expiration is worth $5.00. Your adjustment has lowered your overall cost and risk in your long call trade, and now with 5 months to expiration, you have three choices. First, you could simply hold on to your long call at a reduced cost for the remaining 5 months to profit from the expected move higher by YHOO. Your previous breakeven point of $50.50 has been lowered to $48.75.

Second, you could simply close out your long $45 Call at $5.00 for a profit of $1.25. Although your intent was to hold the $45 Call for a long period of time, you have a profit after 1 month, and you are certainly entitled to take your money now and look for another trade opportunity. Third, if you felt that YHOO will trade sideways or slightly lower for another couple of weeks, you could sell the next-month $45 Call to bring in more premium and lower your cost even more.

After the expiration of the first short $45 Call with YHOO at $44, you feel that YHOO will stay around $45 or so, or perhaps move a little lower. Overall, you still expect YHOO to move higher in a few months, but you are anticipating another short-term quiet period. Assume that with YHOO at $44, the next 1-month $45 Call is trading at $1.50 and you want to sell the short-term $45 Call to roll your long call into another call calendar spread. By selling the short $45 Call, you bring in another $1.50 in premium and further lower the cost of the long $45 Call from $3.75 to $2.25.

If YHOO stays below $45, the short-term $45 Call expires worthless; then, you keep the $1.50 in premium collected. With 4 months left to expiration, you will again be presented with the same three choices as before: hold the long $45 Call until expiration, close the long $45 Call if it is worth more than your reduced purchase price, or roll into another short-term $45 Call if you still expect YHOO to stay below $45 by expiration of the short call.

What is the potential loss if YHOO does not stay below the short strike by the expiration of the short call in your calendar spread? If YHOO moves above $45 before expiration of the short call, then both your short-term and your long-term call will be ITM. The more ITM both calls are, the narrower the spread between the two. As options move deeper ITM, the time value begins to disappear, and the option is mostly intrinsic value.

For example, if YHOO moves higher to $49, assume that the short-term $45 Call is around $4.25 and the long-term $45 Call is around $5.25. If you close the spread, you receive $1.00. No matter which reduced cost figure you use from these examples, you will have a loss. A loss will also occur if you are assigned on your short call. If you are assigned, you will be short 100 shares of YHOO at $45, and you can exercise your long $45 Call to cover the short at no loss or profit. However, you do lose the debit paid for the spread, and therefore, the position results in an overall loss.

Therefore, when you roll your long $45 Call into a call calendar spread, you have to watch the position closely if the stock moves above $45. If the stock is just above $45 as expiration approaches, then the short-term call will have little intrinsic value and little time value. You can buy back the short call for a lower amount than what you sold it for to remove the short call and still hold on to your long $45 Call. With call calendar spreads, you do have to be ready to act when the stock moves above the short strike. Possible adjustments to call calendar spreads are covered in Chapter 7.

The call calendar spread, therefore, is a way to bring in some premium on a long call position where the underlying stock is expected to move sideways or slightly lower in the short term. You can take advantage of this sideways movement by selling short-term calls without adding any risk to your position. On the contrary, the sale of the short-term call actually reduces your initial debit and therefore lowers your risk and breakeven point. You just have to watch the position carefully because if the stock moves above the short strike price, you should be prepared to make a follow-up adjustment to realize a profit.

Rolling into a Ratio Spread

One of the adjustments discussed in this chapter for a long call position is rolling into a bull call spread by selling a call at a higher strike with the same expiration date. The short call brings in extra premium, which lowers the cost of your long call, and possibly produces a risk-free trade if the premium taken in is greater than the cost of the trade. The bull call spread adjustment involves selling the same number of calls as you are long. If you sell more calls than you are long, then the adjustment is a call ratio spread and can provide many opportunities to boost the return on your long call.

Because a call ratio spread involves selling more calls at a higher strike than your long call, it has naked calls. The position can produce a significant loss if the stock climbs higher than the short strikes. The maximum reward occurs when the stock is right at the short strike price at expiration so the short calls will expire worthless and the long call will have pure intrinsic value. Therefore, the expectation is that the stock will be right at the short strike at expiration or as close to it as possible. The benefit of establishing the position for a net credit is that if the stock moves lower below the long strike price, you still have a profit.

Assume you purchased a 2-month YHOO $45 Call for $2.75 with YHOO at $45. A few weeks later, YHOO climbs to $49, and your $45 Call is worth $5.00 and the YHOO $50 Call is worth $1.75. The premium in the $50 Call is not large enough to roll your long call into a bull call spread for a net credit, and therefore you cannot create a risk-free trade. However, you can sell two YHOO $50 Calls and bring in $3.50 in premium, which covers your cost of $2.75 and brings in a credit of $0.75. This is a 1:2 call ratio spread.

If YHOO suffers a drastic drop in price back below $45, all the calls will expire worthless, and you keep the net credit of $0.75. Therefore, you have guaranteed a minimum profit in case YHOO moves back lower. Between $45 and $50, the $50 Calls will expire worthless, and your profit will be the value of your $45 Call, depending on where YHOO is at expiration. For example, if YHOO is at $47 at expiration, the $50 Calls expire worthless, and the $45 Call will be worth $2.00 for an overall profit of $2.75 (when the net credit is added). The maximum reward occurs when YHOO is at the short strike at expiration. If YHOO is at $50 at expiration, the $50 Calls will expire worthless and the $45 Call will be worth $5.00 for an overall profit of $5.75.

As YHOO moves above $50, the two short calls move further ITM, and the position will result in a loss if YHOO moves far enough above the short strike. The upward breakeven point is calculated by adding the difference between the strike prices ($5.00) to the short strike ($50.00) plus the credit received ($0.75), resulting in $55.75. At $55.75, the overall position will have a profit of $0.00. Figure 5.10 shows the risk/reward profile of your adjusted call position. Compared with the long call alone, the call ratio spread adjustment boosts the profit of the overall position right around the short strike price. Therefore, whenever you roll the long call position into a call ratio spread, the short strike you select for selling calls should be a sort of target for expiration. You should expect the stock to be near the short strike at expiration and avoid this adjustment if you feel there is a good chance the stock will move substantially higher.

If you are very confident that the stock will be near the short strike price at expiration or move lower, then you can increase the potential profit of your long call adjustment by using a 1:3 call ratio spread and sell three calls against your long call position. Selling a third call brings in more premium, but it also increases your risk to the upside. Therefore, the 1:3 call ratio spread adjustment should be used only when you feel that the stock will not move much higher than the short strike price.

Assume as before that you purchased a 2-month YHOO $45 Call for $2.75 with YHOO at $45. A few weeks later, YHOO climbs to $49, and you feel that YHOO is going to trade sideways or perhaps drift lower, but there is little chance the stock will move much higher. You observe the YHOO $50 Call with the same expiration as your long call trading at $1.75. To roll your long $45 Call into a 1:3 call ratio spread, sell three YHOO $50 Calls at $1.75 each for a total of $5.25. The credit of $5.25 collected from selling the three $50 Calls covers the initial cost of your $45 Call ($2.75) and results in a net credit of $2.50 (compare this with the $0.75 net credit in the 1:2 ratio spread adjustment).

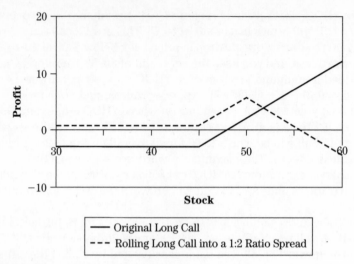

FIGURE 5.10   Rolling Long Call into a 1:2 Ratio Spread

If YHOO is right at the short strike price of $50 at expiration, then the three $50 Calls expire worthless, and your long $45 Call is worth $5.00 for an overall profit of $7.50 (do not forget to include the net credit received from establishing the position). If you simply kept your long $45 Call at $2.75, your profit with YHOO at $50 at expiration would be only $2.25. This profit boost over the long call, however, disappears if YHOO makes a significant move above $50.

Because you have two naked calls (one short call is covered by your long $45 Call), the profit will disappear quickly as YHOO moves higher. The upside breakeven point is $53.75. At $53.75, the long $45 Call will be worth $8.75, and the three $50 Calls will be worth $3.75 each for a total of ($11.25). When combined, the calls have a net loss of $2.50 ($11.25 minus $8.75), which is offset by the net credit collected of $2.50 for an overall loss of $0.00. When compared to the breakeven point of $55.75 for the 1:2 call ratio spread adjustment, you see how the 1:3 adjustment increases your risk slightly by producing a loss quicker if YHOO continues to move higher. Before adjusting the long $45 Call position with a 1:3 ratio spread, calculate the breakeven point to determine if you are comfortable with the potential risk.

An added benefit of using the 1:3 ratio spread adjustment, and why it is preferable if you feel that in addition to moving sideways, the stock could also move back lower, is that the large credit provides a nice return even if YHOO reverses and drops significantly in price. If YHOO is below $45 at expiration, you still have a profit of $2.50 from the net credit received.

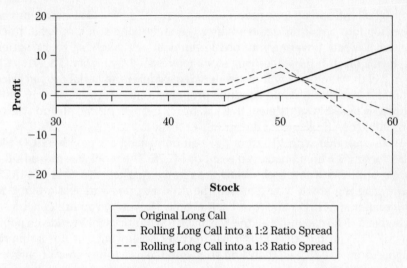

FIGURE 5.11 1:2 Ratio Spread Rolling Long Call into a 1:3 Ratio Spread

Figure 5.11 compares the 1:2 and 1:3 ratio spread adjustments to the original long $45 Call purchase.

Moving from the 1:2 ratio spread adjustment to the 1:3 ratio spread adjustment raises the profit line on the left side of the chart (i.e., below $45) in exchange for narrowing the profit zone around the short strike ($50). Remember, there is always a risk/reward trade-off. Increasing potential profits usually involves increasing the potential losses. Although you could theoretically use a higher ratio, such as 1:4—that is, sell four $50 Calls against your long $45 Call—we feel that the added risk is too high because the breakeven point will be even closer to the $50 strike price. If you truly feel that the stock will move sideways or lower, the 1:4 ratio spread adjustment may seem like a reasonable adjustment, but we do not recommend it, given the sufficient rewards from the 1:3 ratio spread adjustment. If the 1:3 ratio spread adjustment does not provide a sufficient net credit for your preferences, then another possible adjustment may be better.

Stock Moves Lower—Call Repair Strategy

In the bull call spread section in this chapter, we demonstrated how you could roll your long call into a bull call spread at a lower strike price to lower your breakeven point when the underlying stock has dropped in price and repair your position. The adjustment was done at no cost and therefore increased your chances of turning a profit if the stock recovered even somewhat, without increasing your risk. What if you cannot roll down into a bull call spread for a net credit or no cost? You can also roll a long call position into a call ratio spread after the underlying stock drops in price for a net credit, lowering your breakeven point and allowing your position to turn a profit if the underlying stock moves slightly higher. Therefore, if you feel that the stock will recover somewhat after the initial drop in price and still fear that it could continue dropping a little further, the call ratio spread is possible adjustment that can turn a losing long call position into a profitable one.

Assume that with YHOO at $45 you purchased a 2-month YHOO $45 Call for $2.75 with a breakeven point of $47.75. The stock has moved sideways, and after a few bad trading days in the market, YHOO is at $41.75. Analyzing the stock, you feel that the drop in price was just a bump in the road and YHOO can move back higher. However, you are concerned whether YHOO can move all the way back to your original breakeven point of $47.75. You feel that YHOO will recover somewhat but not so much higher from $41.75, and therefore you would like to lower your breakeven point and realize a profit if YHOO does move somewhat higher. You can roll your long call into a call ratio spread and repair your losing position.

With YHOO down to $41.75, assume that your $45 Call is now worth $1.25 with just over 1 month to expiration. You also observe that a YHOO $40 Call with the same expiration date is trading at $2.75. If you decide to roll down your position into a bull call spread, sell two $45 Calls for a total of $2.50 ($1.25 each) and purchase the $40 Call for $2.75 for a net debit of $0.25. Because you originally paid $2.75 for the long $45 Call, the net debit in rolling to the bull call spread increases your cost from $2.75 to $3.00. Your new breakeven point is $43.00. Although lower than the original $47.75 breakeven point, you can further reduce that number by rolling into a call ratio spread.

To roll into a 1:2 ratio spread, sell three YHOO $45 Calls at $1.25 for a credit of $3.75. When rolling to a ratio spread, always sell one more call than the ratio spread calls for, because one of the calls sold is actually closing out your long $45 Call. The other two $45 Calls form part of the 1:2 spread. With $3.75 in premium, you simultaneously purchase the YHOO $40 Call at $2.75 for a net credit of $1.00. You have now rolled into a $40/$45 1:2 call ratio spread at a credit of $1.00, and this credit reduces your original trade cost on the long $45 Call from $2.75 to $1.75. Therefore, your breakeven point is now $41.75. At $41.75, the short $45 Calls will expire worthless, and the long $40 Call will be worth $1.75, which offsets the reduced trade cost of $1.75. Because YHOO was at $41.75 when you rolled into the 1:2 ratio spread, the stock has to move only slightly higher by expiration for you to realize a profit.

The maximum reward on the converted position occurs when the stock is right at the short strike price at expiration. If YHOO is at $45 at expiration, the $45 Calls will expire worthless, and the $40 Call will be worth $5.00 for a profit of $3.25 on the reduced trade cost of $1.75. The call repair strategy therefore lowers your breakeven point and produces a significant profit if the underlying stock simply moves back to the original price where you first opened your long call position.

On the upside, if YHOO moves too much higher, then the position could produce a loss. Because your adjusted long call position still has an overall net debit, there is a downside and an upside breakeven point. We calculated the downside breakeven point previously. The upside breakeven point occurs when YHOO moves above the $45 short strike. As we said, the maximum reward occurs when YHOO is right at the short strike price at expiration, but if YHOO moves higher than that, the additional naked call starts to produce a loss. Your new upside breakeven point is $48.25 at expiration. At $48.25, the long $40 Call will be worth $8.25, and the two short $45 Calls will be worth $6.50 ($3.25 each) for a combined profit of $1.75. However, this profit is offset by the $1.75 reduced debit paid for the overall position for a net profit of $0.00.

The best way to see how converting the long $45 Call into the $40/$45 1:2 ratio spread can repair your long call when the underlying stock drops in price is to compare the risk/reward profiles in Figure 5.12. As the chart indicates, the adjusted position will produce a profit if YHOO is anywhere between $41.75 and $48.25 at expiration. This is a wide profit zone that gives you plenty of room to the upside should YHOO recover in price. With YHOO at $41.75 when you adjusted your long $45 Call, YHOO has to move only slightly higher to realize a profit. Left unadjusted, your long call will

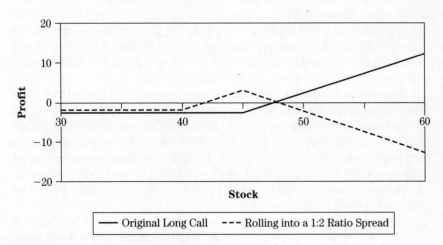

FIGURE 5.12 Call Repair Strategy

not produce a profit at all unless YHOO moves all the way beyond $47.75. Therefore, you lowered your breakeven point and can still realize a profit, even if YHOO does not get back to its original price when you first opened your position.

The benefit of the adjustment is that you were able to convert to a call ratio spread at no cost. Even better, you made the adjustment for a net credit, which reduced your initial trade cost and therefore lowered your risk to the downside. Although there is risk to the upside, you have a large cushion because YHOO would have to move above $48.25 before a loss occurs. The adjustment creates a wide profit zone at lower stock prices and therefore repairs your losing call position. Remember that even though the adjustment reduces your risk to the downside, there is still a potential for loss if YHOO moves below the lower breakeven point.

If you feel that YHOO will recover only slightly and you want to improve the potential profit from the repair of your long call, you can roll into a 1:3 call ratio spread instead of the 1:2 spread. Assume as before that you purchased a 2-month YHOO $45 Call for $2.75 when YHOO was at $45 and the stock has fallen to $41.75. Your $45 Call is now worth $1.25, and you observe that the YHOO $40 Call with the same expiration date is trading at $2.75. To repair your long call position and convert it into a 1:3 call ratio spread, sell four YHOO $45 Calls for $1.25 each and collect $5.00 in premium. Simultaneously, purchase the YHOO $40 Call for $2.75 for a net credit of $2.25. The credit of $2.25 received will reduce your initial trade cost of the $45 Call from $2.75 to $0.50.

Because your total trade cost has been reduced to $0.50, your new breakeven point is $40.50. At $40.50, the three $45 Calls will expire worthless, and the $40 Call will be worth $0.50, which will offset the reduced cost of the trade. Below $40.50, the maximum loss is only $0.50. If YHOO is at $45 at expiration, the three $45 Calls will still expire worthless, but the $40 Call will be worth $5.00 for a profit of $4.50. The repaired long $45 Call will have a significant profit if the stock moves back only to $45, whereas the unadjusted long $45 Call would have a loss of $2.75.

Because there are two naked calls in the 1:3 call ratio spread, the position will result in a loss if YHOO moves too far above the short strike ($45) by expiration. The upside breakeven point is $47.25. At $47.25 the $40 Call will be worth $7.25, and the three short $45 Calls will be worth $2.25 each for a total of $6.75, for a profit of $0.50. This profit is offset by your reduced trade cost of $0.50 for an overall profit of $0.00. Therefore, the repair call ratio spread adjustment has a profit range between $40.50 and $47.25, as indicated in Figure 5.13.

Figure 5.13 also compares the 1:2 ratio spread adjustment with the 1:3 ratio spread adjustment. Both repair strategies create a wide profit zone

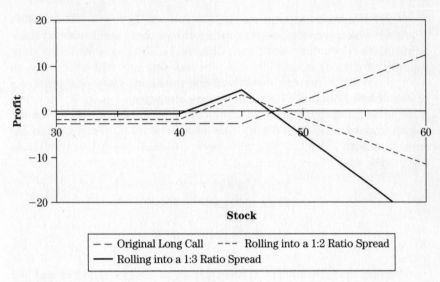

FIGURE 5.13 Call Repair Strategy: Rolling into 1:2 versus 1:3 Call Ratio Spread

at lower stock prices, so that if YHOO moves only slightly higher, you still have a profit. The 1:3 spread has a higher potential profit and lower downside risk than the 1:2 spread but does have a lower upside breakeven point. The choice between them depends on where you expect YHOO to be at expiration and the amount of upside and downside risk you are willing to accept. However, both are good adjustments to repair a long call position where the underlying stock has dropped in price. The adjustment can lower your overall trade cost and provide a bigger profit boost, even if the stock does not move back to its original price when you first initiated the long call purchase.

SHORT CALL

The sale of a short call is very risky strategy. The seller of the naked call has the obligation to deliver 100 shares at the strike price, and the maximum risk is theoretically unlimited because a stock can climb higher and higher. Under the principles of good risk management, we do not usually recommend naked calls alone as a trading strategy due to the enormous risk. Moreover, even if you are willing to accept the risk of naked calls, there are not many possible trade adjustments that can be made as with similar strategies, such as shorting stock.

If you are assigned on a naked call, you will be short 100 shares of stock. Once you are assigned on your short call, there are numerous trade adjustments that can be made (see Chapter 4). The naked call itself does not allow for many possibilities, as most adjustments will either take up most, if not all, of the credit received and thus take away your profit potential or add even more risk than you are already undertaking. However, if the underlying stock makes a significant move, there are some limited opportunities to lock in a profit or hedge against a loss. For example, assume that with YHOO at $45, you observe the following 1-month YHOO call prices:

YHOO @ $45
YHOO $40 Call	$5.50
YHOO $45 Call	$1.75
YHOO $50 Call	$0.75

Assume that you expect YHOO to trade sideways or lower and sell the YHOO $45 Call short for a credit of $1.75. If YHOO drops to $42, the short $45 Call could be worth $1.00 for an unrealized profit of $0.75. If you feel that YHOO will not move back above $45 by expiration, then you could simply leave the position open and let time decay work in your favor (that is why we always recommend short-term options if you are going to sell naked calls). If you wanted to lock in the $0.75 profit or some other minimum guaranteed profit, there is no sensible adjustment that will do so. The only way to lock in the $0.75 profit is to close the position and take your money and risk off the table.

The same is true if you shorted the OTM YHOO $50 Call at $0.75 and the stock dropped to $42. Without an effective way to lock in a profit, the best strategy is to close out the position as soon as possible or, if the short option has become deep OTM, keep a tight watch over the position and be ready to close it out if the stock begins to get close to the strike price.

The only situation where an adjustment to a naked call can lock in a guaranteed profit or significantly hedge the risk of unlimited loss is when the short call is ITM. Selling a naked deep ITM call is very similar to holding a short stock position because deep ITM options have mostly intrinsic value and very little time value, especially with calls that have 1 month to expiration. For example, with YHOO at $45, you could sell the $40 Call and receive $5.50 in premium. The breakeven point is $45.50, where the value of the $40 Call at expiration will equal the premium collected. If a few days later YHOO drops sharply to $41, the long $40 Call may be worth about $1.50. Assume that the $45 Call with the same expiration is currently trading at $0.50. With your short $40 Call at $1.50, you could close out the position for a profit of $4.00. However, if you feel that YHOO will continue to move below $40 at expiration, you could purchase the $45 Call for $0.50 and convert the short call position into a bear call spread with limited risk. You received $5.50 in credit for selling the $40 Call and paid $0.50 for the $45 Call. Therefore, your net credit is reduced to $5.00, and your new breakeven point is $45. Although the breakeven point is lowered, you will no longer be susceptible to unlimited risk.

If YHOO moves below $40 by expiration, then all calls will expire worthless, and you keep the $5.00 net credit as profit. With YHOO between $40 and $45 at expiration, you still have a profit because the breakeven point is $45. What happens if YHOO moves above $45? Remember that you now have a $45/$40 bear call spread. If YHOO moves above $45, then the value of the long $45 Call will offset the loss in the short $40 Call. The maximum risk in a bear call spread is the difference between the strikes minus the credit received. In your adjusted bear call spread, you have a credit of $5.00, and the difference between the $45 and $40 strikes is $5.00. Therefore, there is no risk at all in this position. If YHOO is above $45 at expiration, the long $45 Call covers the short $40 Call, and the net profit/loss will be $0.00. Your adjustment has guaranteed that you will not lose any money on the position. If YHOO is below $40 at expiration, you will have a profit of $5.00.

Therefore, in certain unique situations, there may be a way to hedge naked call positions. However, more often than not, any possible adjustment will either involve a large capital outlay (such as purchasing 100 shares of stock to "cover" the naked call) or increase your overall risk (rolling your short call higher if the stock continues to rise by shorting even more calls to repurchase your now ITM naked call). For these reasons, we do not recommend naked calls alone unless they are part of another strategy, such as ratio writes or ratio spreads, where other components of the position serve to somewhat reduce the risk of the naked calls.

There are some people who advocate the "roll up and out" strategy when selling naked calls. Using the previous example, you sold the 1-month YHOO $45 Call for $1.75. After a few days, YHOO has begun to move higher from $45 to $48, and the short call is now worth about $3.25 for an unrealized loss of $1.50 with the potential for more losses if YHOO keeps moving higher. Often in these situations, traders feel that they will eventually be proven right but just need more time since expiration is approaching. In that case, they will buy back the $45 Call at $3.25 and then roll the call up to a higher strike and go to an expiration month further out in time to get more option premium to cover the cost of buying back the original call—thus the name "roll up and out."

The problem with this "adjustment" is that it fails to recognize or acknowledge that the original position may have simply become a bad trade that needs to be closed to limit losses. It may also create a false hope that if you just had more time, you would be proven right and ultimately earn a profit. Not every trade is a winner, and it is quite reckless to trade naked options, which have significant risk, and not cut your losses when you can. Moving the short call out to a later expiration month simply gives the position more time to move against you and also negates any benefits of time decay. Moreover, depending on the credit you receive, you may be locking in a lower maximum profit for the increased risk or, even worse, locking in a loss. Rarely does it make sense to take a losing position and worsen the odds against you through an adjustment. Therefore, instead of rolling up and out, it is often better to close out the position, take the limited loss, and then simply reevaluate the situation with the understanding that giving yourself more time will not ensure a profit.

LONG PUT

Many of the trade adjustments that can be made to a long put position are similar to those that can be made to a long call position. The actual components of the adjustments will be different—that is, using puts versus calls—but in essence will involve the same factors and reasoning. Therefore, much of the detailed rationale for each adjustment will not be repeated, and we will focus directly on the possible trade adjustment that can be made to a long put position.

Protective Call

Underlying Stock Moves Lower   When a long put you purchased has increased in value—that is, the underlying stock has dropped in price—you might not want to close out the position yet because you feel that the stock will continue to drop. However, you also do not want to give back all your unrealized gain. Therefore, if the underlying stock has made a significant move lower, you can add a protective call to your long put position to lock in a guaranteed minimum profit, continue to make even more money if the stock continues to drop before expiration, and, as an added benefit, also increase your profit if the stock reverses and makes a significant move back higher from where it was when you first purchased the long put.

Assume that with YHOO at $45 you purchased a 2-month YHOO $45 Put for $2.50. A few weeks later, YHOO has dropped in price to $41, and you expect the stock to keep on falling. However, a move back to $45 could wipe out your profits, and you wish to hedge against such a move. If a YHOO $40 Call with the same expiration date as the put is trading at $1.50, you could purchase the $40 Call as a protective call and lock in a guaranteed minimum profit.

By purchasing the YHOO $40 protective call, your new trade cost is now $4.00 ($45 Put for $2.50 plus $40 Call for $1.50). If YHOO is between $40 and $45 at expiration, your long put and protective call will combine for a value of $5.00. For example, if YHOO is at $43, the $45 Put will be worth $2.00, and the $40 Call will be worth $3.00 for a combined $5.00. Because your trade cost is now $4.00, your overall profit is $1.00. Thus, between $40 and $45, you have a guaranteed profit of $1.00.

If YHOO moves lower below $40, then the protective $40 Call will expire worthless, and your profit will be the $45 Put strike price minus the price of the stock, reduced by your $4.00 trade cost. For example, if YHOO is at $38 at expiration, the $45 Put will be worth $7.00 for an overall profit of $3.00. Therefore, you will still make more money if YHOO continues to move lower below $40. The potential profit is reduced by the increased cost of the trade from the adjustment, but because the adjustment has created a risk-free trade, the reduced return is still guaranteed money. Remember, when we reduce the risk, we also reduce the return. However, in the example with YHOO at $38, your $3.00 profit is realized with no capital at risk, and only options can provide such opportunities.

An added benefit of the protective call is that your position can still make more money if YHOO reverses and moves back above $45 by expiration. Although your initial long $45 Put will expire worthless, the long $40 protective call will increase in value. For example, if YHOO moves back to $49 by expiration, the long $45 Put will expire worthless, but the long $40 Call will be worth $9.00 for a profit of $5.00 (after subtracting $4.00 trade cost).

Figure 5.14 demonstrates how your adjusted long put position now has the nondirectional look and characteristics of a long strangle. This should come as no surprise because a long strangle consists of a long put and a long call, just as with your long put and protective call adjusted position. The main differences are that a long strangle has risk limited to the initial debit paid and in your adjustment you have no risk, and a long strangle usually uses OTM calls and puts, while your adjusted position uses an ITM put and call.

We have no preference for which strike price you select for the protective call as long as the adjusted position meets one criterion—it becomes a risk-free trade. There is a formula for ensuring that you are picking the right strike price for the protective call adjustment. As Figure 5.14 demonstrates, the locked-in minimum profit occurs between the strike prices of the protective call and the long put. Therefore, the total trade cost should be less than the difference between the two strike prices. In the foregoing example, the $40/$45 strike prices used for the protective call and long put have a difference of $5.00 and your total trade cost was $4.00, locking in a $1.00 guaranteed profit. If the total adjusted trade cost was greater than

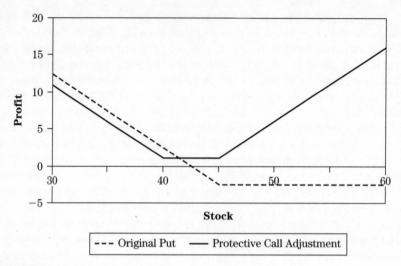

FIGURE 5.14 Protective Call Adjustment to Long Put

$5.00, then you would have a loss if the stock was between $40 and $45 at expiration. So you can quickly determine whether a proposed protective call is an appropriate adjustment by simply taking the difference between the strike prices and subtracting the total cost of the adjusted trade.

If YHOO moves significantly lower after you purchase the long $45 Put, you will have more choices as to what strike price to use for the protective call. For example, assume that after purchasing the YHOO $45 Put at $2.50, YHOO drops in price from $45 to $37. Now you can choose either the $40 strike or the $35 strike for your protective call with the same expiration date as the $45 Put.

Assume that with YHOO at $37, the OTM $40 Call is trading at $1.00 and the ITM $35 Call is trading at $2.75. With the OTM $40 protective call, your adjusted trade cost is $3.50 ($2.50 for $45 long put and $1.00 for $40 protective call). Your locked-in minimum profit is the difference between strike prices ($5.00) minus the adjusted trade cost ($3.50). However, if you select the ITM $35 protective call for $2.75, then your adjusted trade cost is $5.25 and the guaranteed minimum profit is $4.75. The use of the ITM protective call has a higher guaranteed minimum profit over a wider range of stock prices. This difference can be seen clearly from the comparison of the two protective call positions in Figure 5.15.

Underlying Stock Moves Higher   When the underlying stock moves higher after you purchase a long put, a protective call does not lock in a guaranteed minimum profit. The reason may seem obvious enough, but

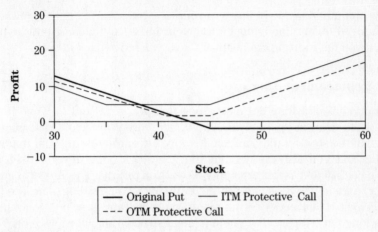

FIGURE 5.15 Comparison of ITM and OTM Protective Calls

there is no guaranteed minimum profit because the long put position it-self does not have a profit if the underlying stock moves higher. However, you can still use a protective call to convert the long put position into a non-directional strangle if, after the stock moves higher, you expect a significant move in the underlying stock but you are no longer certain of the direction.

Assume that with YHOO at $45, you purchased a 2-month YHOO $45 Put for $2.50. A few days later, YHOO makes a sudden move higher to $48. Your analysis changes slightly, and you feel that YHOO will make a significant move by expiration, but now you are not as sure of the direction as you were when you purchased the long put, expecting the stock to move lower. You observe that the YHOO $50 Call with the same expiration as your $45 Put is trading for $1.25. If you wish to convert your long put position into a nondirectional strangle, you could add the OTM $50 Call for $1.25 and increase your adjusted trade cost to $3.75.

With a trade debit of $3.75, your adjusted strangle will have an upside breakeven point of $53.75 (OTM call strike + total debit paid) and a down-side breakeven point of $41.25 (OTM put strike – total debit paid). If YHOO is anywhere between these breakeven points, you will lose $3.75.

Because of the wide range between the breakeven points, YHOO has to make a significant move for you to realize a profit. Adding the long OTM $50 Call adds risk to your position and requires the stock to make an even larger move for you to recover your higher trade cost. We do not recommend such a trade adjustment, but we present it in case there is that unique situation where you expect the underlying stock to make such a significant move for this adjustment to be profitable and worthwhile. If not, then there are better adjustments to make to your long put after the underlying stock has moved higher, including cutting your losses and closing out the position if you have strong doubts that YHOO can move back lower.

Put Replacement Therapy

You purchased a long put on a stock that you expected to move lower, and it did drop in price, giving you a nice unrealized profit. Assume you feel that the stock could continue to move lower, increasing your potential profits, but you also are nervous that the stock could reverse itself and move back higher, wiping out your unrealized returns. This anxiety usually leads to trade paralysis and drifting away from your trading plan. The best medicine for this anxiety is put replacement therapy, in which you replace your long put with another put at a lower strike. This put replacement can allow you to lock in a profit and still make more money if the underlying stock keeps moving lower.

Assume that you purchase a 2-month YHOO $45 Put at $2.50 with YHOO at $45. Shortly thereafter, YHOO drops to $38, and your $45 Put is now worth $7.75 for a profit of $5.25. You could simply close out your position and take your profit, but what if you have plenty of time to expiration and expect YHOO to continue moving lower? You want to keep your long put, but you are also worried that YHOO could move back higher and erase your unrealized profit. You could sell your profitable long $45 Put and replace it with a lower strike put so that you can lock in a profit and still make money if YHOO continues moving lower.

With YHOO at $38, assume that an ITM $40 Put is trading at $3.00 and an OTM $35 Put is trading at $1.00, both with the same expiration as your long $45 Put. Selecting the ITM $40 Put, you could sell your $45 Put for a profit of $5.25 and use $3.00 to purchase the $40 replacement put. The remaining $2.25 from your $45 Put profit is pocketed and is your guaranteed profit. If YHOO moves back above $40 by expiration and your replacement $40 Put expires worthless, you still keep the $2.25 profit.

If you want to lock in a higher minimum profit, you could use the lower cost OTM $35 replacement put instead. Sell the $45 Put for a profit of $5.25, and purchase the $35 Put for $1.00, locking in a minimum profit of $4.25. If YHOO is above $35 by expiration, your $35 replacement put expires worthless, and you keep the $4.25 in profit. However, if YHOO moves below $35, your overall profit will increase. For example, if YHOO is at $33 by expiration, your replacement $35 Put will be worth $2.00 and increase your overall profit to $6.25.

Figure 5.16 shows the advantage of using the put replacement therapy when your long put has a nice unrealized profit. Turning the position into a risk-free trade allows you to commit the pocketed profit to another trade

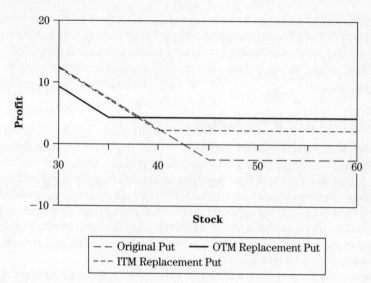

FIGURE 5.16 Comparison of ITM and OTM Replacement Puts

while still having the potential for increased profits, should YHOO continue to move lower. The choice between the OTM and the ITM replacement put depends on the amount of locked-in profit you wish to have and whether you feel that YHOO can continue moving lower. The ITM replacement put has a lower locked-in profit due to the higher cost, but if YHOO stays where it is or moves lower, your overall profit will increase with the value of the ITM put at expiration. The OTM put has a higher locked-in profit, but YHOO will have to move much lower before the replacement put can add to your overall profit. You have to decide what your preference is, given the potential for YHOO to move lower and how much profit you want to take now versus potential profit later.

Whether you choose the OTM or the ITM put, if YHOO does make a significant move lower, you can use the put replacement therapy again to close out your new put and replace it with another put at a lower strike. For instance, assume that you select the ITM replacement put from the foregoing example. With YHOO at $38, you sell your $45 Put, purchase the $40 Put for $3.00, and lock in a profit of $2.25. Assume that YHOO keeps running lower and is at $34 a few weeks later, the $40 Put is worth $6.50, and the $35 Put is trading at $2.00.

You could close the $40 Put and add the $6.50 in premium to your overall profit of $2.25. On the other hand, if you expect YHOO to continue moving lower but do not want to give back all of your additional profits, you could sell the $40 Put for $6.50, purchase the $35 Put for $2.00, and pocket an additional $4.50 in profit. Your new overall profit is $6.75, and you now have the $35 Put to add more profit, should YHOO continue to move lower. Because you can never have a loss after locking in a guaranteed profit, you can keep rolling down into replacement puts and adding to your profits until expiration.

Rolling into a Bear Put Spread

Underlying Stock Moves Lower   A bear put spread is established by purchasing a put and selling another put at a lower strike price to reduce the cost of the long put. The position is established for a net debit, and therefore there is risk of losing money if the stock moves higher instead of lower. However, you can also leg into a bear put spread as a trade adjustment to a long put position. If the underlying stock drops in price after you purchase the long put, then you could sell the lower strike put and convert your long put into a risk-free trade.

Assume you purchase a 2-month YHOO $45 Put for $2.50 with YHOO at $45. Shortly thereafter, YHOO drops sharply in price to $38. YHOO could continue moving lower, but there is always a risk that it will move back higher and your unrealized gains will disappear. You would like to still hold the position, but you do have some concerns that YHOO will move back higher by expiration. You would like to lock in some profit but still allow for increased gains should YHOO continue moving lower. With YHOO at $38, you observe that the YHOO $40 Put with the same expiration date as your $45 Put is trading at $3.25.

To convert your YHOO $45 Put into a bear put spread, sell the YHOO $40 Put for $3.25. The $3.25 in premium collected covers the $2.50 cost of your long $45 Put and leaves a net credit of $0.75, which is your guaranteed minimum profit. No matter what YHOO does until expiration, you will make a minimum of $0.75. If YHOO moves all the way back to $45 by expiration, all the puts will expire worthless, and you keep the $0.75 credit received from converting your long put to a bear put spread. Therefore, you have removed all the risk from your position. If YHOO is between $40 and $45, then the short $40 Put will expire worthless, and your profit will be the value of the $45 Put plus the $0.75 credit. For example, if YHOO is at $42 at expiration, the $40 Put will expire worthless, and the $45 Put will be worth $3.00 for an overall profit of $3.75.

If YHOO is below $40 at expiration, then the $45/$40 bear put spread will reach its maximum reward, which is the difference between the strikes plus the $0.75 credit. For example, if YHOO is at $39, the $45 Put will be worth $6.00, and the short $40 Put will be worth $1.00 for a net profit of $5.00. Your overall profit will be $5.75 once the credit received is added. Therefore, if you can roll into a bear put spread by selling the lower strike

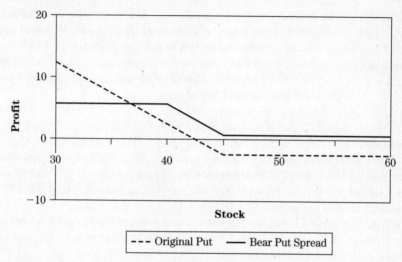

FIGURE 5.17 Rolling into a Bear Put Spread

put for more than you paid for your original long put, you can create a risk-free trade. Figure 5.17 demonstrates how the adjusted long $45 Put creates a risk-free trade with a maximum profit of $5.75. Although you give up additional profit on the downside if YHOO makes a significant move lower, you have removed all risk from your trade in exchange for the limited profit.

Because you now have a free trade, you can increase your position in YHOO by purchasing additional puts if you feel that YHOO will move lower. For example, after rolling your position into a free trade with YHOO at $38, assume an OTM $35 Put is trading at $0.75. Remember that you received a net credit of $0.75 when you rolled your long $45 Put into a bear put spread. You can use the net credit and purchase a long $35 Put and add that to your $45/$40 bear put spread. Therefore, you will have two positions in YHOO at no cost at all.

If YHOO is below $40 at expiration but above $35, you will earn $5.00 from the $45/$40 bear put spread. However, if YHOO moves much lower than $35, then your overall profit will be increased by the value of the $35 Put. For example, if YHOO is at $33 at expiration, then your $35 Put will be worth $2.00 and the bear put spread will be worth $5.00 for a total profit of $7.00. Rolling down into the bear put spread therefore allows you to double your position in YHOO with no risk.

Underlying Stock Moves Higher—Put Repair Strategy Assume that after you purchase a YHOO $45 Put for $2.50, YHOO climbs to $48 and your $45 Put shrinks in value to $1.50. Your original breakeven point is $42.50 (strike price minus debit paid), and YHOO will have to make a significant move lower just to get to your breakeven point. You feel that YHOO will move back slightly lower but not far enough for you to break even on your position. Therefore, you want to repair your position by raising your breakeven point to realize a profit with only a slight move lower in YHOO, without adding any additional risk.

With YHOO now at $48, assume that a $50 Put with the same expiration date as the YHOO $45 Put is trading at $3.00. The way you can repair your position is by rolling up from your $45 Put to a bear put spread. First, you sell two $45 Puts, now at $1.50, for a total credit of $3.00. Simultaneously purchase a $50 Put at $3.00. Therefore, your new position is a long $50 Put and a short $45 Put—a bear put spread. You rolled from the long put into a bear put spread at no cost.

The breakeven point on the bear put spread is the long strike minus the debit paid. Your initial debit from the long $45 Put was $2.50, and because you rolled into the bear put spread at no cost, your initial debit is still $2.50. Therefore, your new breakeven point on the bear put spread is $47.50. Compare this with your original breakeven point of $42.50. Your adjustment has repaired your position and raised your breakeven point from $42.50 to $47.50 at no cost. If YHOO moves back to $45 by expiration, then the bear put spread will have a profit of $2.50 as opposed to a $2.50 loss on your original $45 Put position. The repaired long put compared with the unadjusted position is shown in Figure 5.18.

The repaired long put does not have the potential for large returns if YHOO moves significantly lower, as did the unadjusted long put. Raising

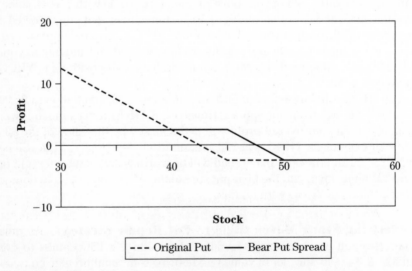

FIGURE 5.18 Rolling into a Bear Put Spread

the breakeven point by rolling into the bear put spread was done at no cost, but there is a price to pay—limiting potential profits should YHOO move much lower. However, the ability to raise your breakeven point in the repaired position and to salvage a profit is worth the limited reward. When rolling into the bear put spread, it is preferable to do so at no cost so that you raise your breakeven point without assuming any additional risk.

Rolling into a Bull Put Spread

If you purchase a long put and the stock moves higher instead of lower, you need to decide in which direction the underlying stock will continue to move by expiration. If you feel that the underlying stock is going to continue to move higher, then you will lose money if you hold on to your long put. However, you can convert your bearish long put into a bullish strategy and profit from the rise in the underlying stock.

Assume that you purchase a YHOO $45 Put for $2.25 with YHOO at $45. A few weeks later, YHOO climbs to $47, and your analysis of YHOO changes as your $45 Put shrinks in value. You now expect YHOO to continue to move higher and move past $50 by expiration. With YHOO at $47, you observe a YHOO $50 Put with the same expiration trading at $3.50. Instead of closing out your long $45 Put for a loss, you could simply sell the $50 Put for $3.50, converting your long put into a bull put spread that will realize a profit if YHOO does move above $50.

The $3.50 in premium collected from selling the $50 Put covers the $2.25 cost of your long $45 Put and results in a net credit of $1.25. The breakeven point on this bull put spread is the short strike ($50) minus the net credit received ($1.25), which is $48.75. Therefore, YHOO will have to move above $48.75 for the adjusted position to realize a profit. The maximum reward on the bull put spread, however, is limited to the net credit received ($1.25), and the maximum risk is the difference between the strike prices minus the net credit received ($5.00 − $1.25 = $3.75).

As Figure 5.19 indicates, the bull put spread has a higher risk than reward. You want YHOO to be above $50 at expiration so that both puts expire worthless and you keep the net credit of $1.25. If you are wrong about the direction of YHOO, and it moves back below $45, then you will have a loss of $3.50—greater than the potential $2.25 loss on the original long $45 Put position. Therefore, before rolling the long put into a bull put spread, you should be confident that YHOO will indeed continue to move higher and be above the breakeven point at expiration.

If you feel that YHOO will make a significant move higher, then you can sell a higher strike put to roll into the bull put spread to collect more premium and have a bigger potential reward, should YHOO move much higher by expiration. As in the previous example, assume that you purchased a YHOO $45 Put for $2.25 and YHOO subsequently moves higher to

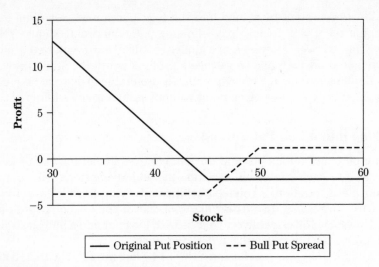

FIGURE 5.19   Rolling Long Put into a Bull Put Spread

$47. In addition to the YHOO $50 Put trading at $3.50, you also observe the YHOO $55 Put trading at $8.25. Your analysis now is that YHOO will continue to run higher and most likely will be near $55 at expiration. Instead of selling the $50 Put to convert your position into a bull put spread, you can choose the deeper ITM strike and sell the $55 Put for $8.25.

The $8.25 in premium collected from selling the $55 Put covers your cost of $2.25 for the long $45 Put and results in a net credit of $6.00. The breakeven point for your $45/$55 bull put spread is $49 (short strike minus net credit). The maximum reward, limited to the net credit received, is $6.00, and the maximum risk, limited to the difference between the strike prices ($10.00) minus the net credit received ($6.00), is $4.00. As Figure 5.20 shows, using the deeper ITM put to roll to the bull put spread creates a position with a higher reward than risk, but YHOO will have to move higher to get above the breakeven point than with the $45/$50 bull put spread adjustment. Therefore, we recommend using the deeper ITM put to roll into a bull put spread when you feel strongly that the underlying stock will make a significant move higher.

Long Stock/Synthetic Straddle

One of the trade adjustments we discussed with respect to long calls earlier in the chapter was adding a short stock position to either lock in a minimum profit or create a nondirectional strategy called a synthetic straddle. The addition of short stock to a long call position does not require any capital outlay but does have a margin requirement, which can usually be

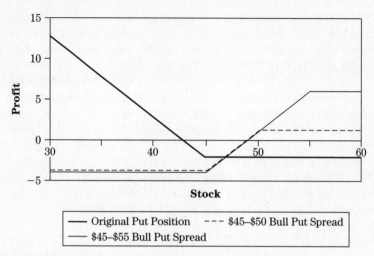

FIGURE 5.20 Rolling into Bull Put Spreads Using $50 and $55 Puts

satisfied by cash and/or securities already in your account. Similar adjustments can be made to a long put position, but instead of shorting stock, you would purchase stock to combine with your long put.

Although the purchase of stock combined with long puts can also achieve the results of locking in a profit and creating a nondirectional synthetic straddle position, the purchase of stock will entail a large capital outlay, even if the stock is bought on margin, and tie up that capital until you close out the position or the options expire. The more puts you own, the more stock you would be required to purchase and the more capital is tied up in your option position. Options are preferred because of the relatively small use of capital required and the leverage they provide. Therefore, adding long stock to a long put position may not always be the preferred trade adjustment, given that other adjustments discussed in this chapter can achieve similar results while tying up less of your capital. However, many traders may feel comfortable adding long stock to a long put position as a trade adjustment or may want to add the benefits of stock ownership (i.e., dividends, voting rights, etc.). Others may use the addition of long stock as a way to trade price swings higher against their long put position. Therefore, we will demonstrate the use of long stock as a trade adjustment to a long put position and how to convert a long put into synthetic straddle.

Assume you purchase a YHOO $45 Put for $2.50 with YHOO at $45. A few weeks later, YHOO drops to $40. Assume that you want to hedge your profit because YHOO may move back higher in the short term, and in case YHOO stays higher, you want some profit locked in. Because you expect that YHOO will have a short-term bounce higher, you wish to trade that upward movement for additional returns while locking in a minimum profit.

To hedge your profit and trade the upward price swing, you could purchase 100 shares of YHOO at $40. The purchase of the long stock hedges your profit because you own a long $45 Put. If you are wrong about YHOO short-term price movement and the stock continues to drop in price, you can always exercise the put to sell your long stock at $45 for a profit of $5.00. However, because you purchased the YHOO $45 Put originally for $2.50, your overall profit is $2.50. No matter how far YHOO drops in price by expiration, you will be able to exercise your $45 Put and lock in a profit of $2.50 guaranteed. Guaranteeing this profit means that you do not have the significant profits that can be realized on the unadjusted long $45 Put. However, guaranteeing a return is the trade-off for limiting your potential profit on the downside.

Assume that after you purchase 100 shares of YHOO at $40, YHOO climbs back to $44 and your long $45 Put is worth $1.75. There are three choices you can make to guarantee a profit. One choice is to sell the stock, take your $4.00 profit, and leave the $45 Put in place. Assume that after trading the upward movement in YHOO, you expect the stock to move back lower; perhaps you are not sure whether YHOO will move back lower, but you want to lock in the profit in your long stock position. Because you received $4.00 from the stock sale and the cost of your initial $45 Put was $2.50, your stock profit can pay for the long $45 Put and leave you with $1.50 in a minimum guaranteed profit no matter what YHOO does by expiration. If YHOO moves higher by expiration and the $45 Put expires worthless, then your $1.50 overall profit is already locked in. If YHOO moves lower, then your overall profit will be increased by the value of the $45 Put at expiration. For example, if YHOO is at $41 at expiration, the $45 Put will be worth $4.00 and increase your overall profit to $5.50.

A second choice is to close out the long $45 Put at the same time you close out the long stock at $44. Remember that with YHOO at $44, your long $45 Put is assumed to be $1.75. You can sell the stock for a $4.00 profit and simultaneously sell the $45 Put for $1.75 for a total of $5.75. After subtracting the initial debit cost of the $45 Put of $2.50, your overall profit is $3.25. If you want to take your stock profit and free up your committed capital in the long stock position, as well as collect any remaining premium in the long $45 Put, then closing out of both positions at the same time would be best.

The third choice is to simply do nothing because your position is completely hedged. You can hold your long stock and long $45 Put until expiration because you are guaranteed a profit no matter where YHOO is at expiration. If YHOO drops below $40, your stock purchase price, you can always exercise your long $45 Put and sell the stock at $45 for a profit of

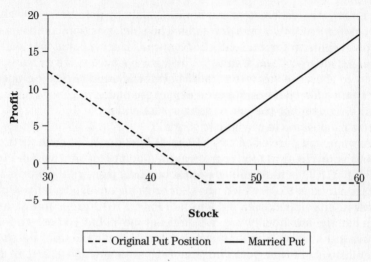

FIGURE 5.21 Long Stock Added to Long Put

$5.00. However, because you paid $2.50 for the $45 Put, your overall profit is $2.50. If YHOO is between $40 and $45, then the combined long put and long stock will be worth $5.00 for a profit of $2.50. For example, if YHOO is at $43 at expiration, the long stock will have a profit of $3.00 and the long $45 Put will be worth $2.00 for a total of $5.00. After you subtract the initial trade cost of $2.50, the overall profit is $2.50. If YHOO climbs above $45, then your profit is unlimited because your long stock will increase in value. Figure 5.21 shows the risk/reward profile of your long $45 Put combined with long stock.

The risk/reward profile of the married put in Figure 5.21 looks the same as a long call graph with a guaranteed profit of $2.50 if YHOO is at $45 or below. The combination of a long put and a long stock creates a synthetic call. Adding the long stock to the $45 Put after YHOO has dropped to $40 is equivalent to establishing a synthetic call for a credit of $2.50. Thus, the position has unlimited profit potential to the upside and a guaranteed minimum profit to the downside. Therefore, if you are willing to make the large capital outlay to add long stock to your long put position, you can guarantee a profit and make even more money if the stock moves higher. This adjustment can be used when a long put has become profitable but there is a chance the stock could rally strongly. Thus, the adjustment gives a bullish bias to your bearish position.

You can also add long stock to your long put position to create a synthetic straddle. The synthetic straddle is a nondirectional strategy designed to profit from a significant move of the underlying stock in either direction.

Using puts, you can create a synthetic straddle by purchasing 100 shares of stock for every two puts you hold. The stock position combines with one of the puts to form a synthetic long call. The synthetic long call and remaining long put form a straddle. You always have twice as many puts as you do shares of stock to form the synthetic straddle. If after opening your bearish long put position, you expect the underlying stock to make a significant move but you are no longer sure about the direction, you can convert the position to a synthetic straddle.

Assume you purchased two YHOO $45 Puts at $2.50 each for a total of $5.00 with YHOO at $45. Your breakeven point on your two $45 Puts is $42.50. If YHOO is at $42.50 at expiration, both puts will be worth $2.50 each for a total of $5.00, which was your original combined purchase price. Shortly after you purchase the long $45 Puts, YHOO drops to $40, and it looks like the stock will make a significant move, but you are no longer positive that it will be lower. You are concerned that if the stock does move higher instead of lower, your two puts will lose money and your unrealized gain will disappear. Therefore, you can convert the position into a synthetic straddle so that when the significant move occurs, you have the potential to make even more money regardless of the direction of the move. Assume that with YHOO still at $40, you convert your two $45 Puts into a synthetic straddle by purchasing 100 shares of YHOO at $40.

Because the stock purchase price is at $40, your synthetic straddle position will have no risk of loss and the potential for significant profits if YHOO moves in either direction. For example, if YHOO is still at $40 at expiration, the stock position will have no profit or loss, but the two $45 Puts will be worth a total of $10.00 for a profit of $5.00 overall. With YHOO at $45 at expiration, the two $45 Puts will expire worthless, but the long stock position will have a $5.00 gain for an overall profit of $0.00. If YHOO moves higher, then the overall profit will increase with the price of YHOO. Therefore, your converted position now has no risk of loss, as demonstrated in Figure 5.22.

Adjusting the long puts into a synthetic straddle does require a large capital outlay. However, adding the long stock turns your long put position into a risk-free trade. If you have a long time until expiration of the long puts and can tie up your capital, then the synthetic straddle has the potential for huge returns if the stock is above or below $45 at expiration. As long as the long stock position is added when your long puts already have an unrealized gain, you can create a risk-free trade.

Put Calendar Spread

A put calendar spread is established by selling a short-term put while simultaneously purchasing a long-term put with the same strike price. The

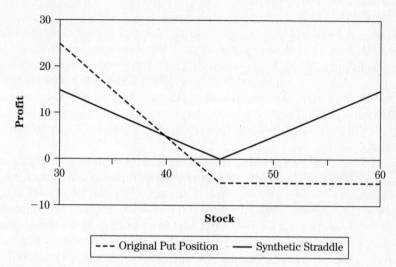

FIGURE 5.22   Rolling Long Put into a Synthetic Straddle

sale of the short-term put helps reduce the cost of the long-term put, and the position is meant to take advantage of short-term sideways movement in the underlying stock, followed by a large downward movement after expiration of the short-term put. Whether you choose ITM, ATM, or OTM strikes for the calendar put spread, your goal is to have the short-term option expire worthless, that is, OTM, so that you retain your long put at the reduced price.

Therefore, you want the stock to essentially move sideways to hover at or above the short put strike until expiration of that option. If you own a long-term put, you can convert your position into a put calendar spread if you expect the underlying stock to move sideways in the short term. You can sell the short-term put at the same strike and use that sideways movement to your advantage to reduce your long put cost, lower your risk, and even possibly create a risk-free trade.

Assume you purchased a 4-month YHOO $45 Put for $3.75 with YHOO at $45 because you expect YHOO to move lower by expiration. After opening your position, your analysis leads you to conclude that for the next couple of weeks, YHOO will be in a tight sideways trading pattern. You also observe that a 1-month YHOO $45 Put is trading at $1.50 and decide to take advantage of the expected sideways movement of YHOO in the short term. To convert your position into a put calendar spread, sell the short-term YHOO $45 Put for $1.50. The $1.50 in premium received reduces the cost of your long-term $45 Put from $3.75 to $2.25, which also reduces your risk because the maximum loss on a calendar spread is the debit paid.

If YHOO is right at $45 or above at expiration of the short-term $45 Put, then the short-term put expires worthless, and you still hold the long-term $45 Put at a reduced cost of $2.25. If YHOO is right at $45, then your long-term put will still have plenty of time to expiration, as well as time value premium. Assuming that there is now 3 months left to expiration with YHOO at $45, your long-term put may now be worth $3.50. Because your cost has been reduced to $2.25, you can hold on to the put if you expect YHOO to move lower or even close the long put at $3.50 for a profit of $1.25.

Another viable choice is selling the next short-term $45 Put if you still expect YHOO to move sideways and remain at or above $45 by expiration of the short-term put. For example, if the next 1-month YHOO $45 Put is trading at $1.25, you can sell that option, and the $1.25 in premium collected will reduce your long-term put cost from $2.25 to $1.00. If that short-term option expires worthless, you will then have a 2-month $45 Put at a cost of $1.00. The lower cost means a much lower risk and the potential for large profits if YHOO makes a move below $45. If YHOO is still above $45 at expiration of the short-term option, you may consider selling the next 1-month option as well. If that $45 Put is worth more than $1.00, then the sale of the short-term puts has covered the cost of your trade and even provided a net credit. For example, if you sell the next 1-month $45 Put for $1.25, the premium will cover the $1.00 reduced cost of your trade and leave you with a net credit of $0.25. Now your position will not result in a loss and has the potential for significant profits if the short put expires worthless. Your remaining long $45 Put will provide additional profits if it has any value left and if YHOO makes a move below $45 before expiration of the long option.

Even if you only convert your long put position into a calendar spread for 1 month, the reduced cost of your trade as a result of selling the short-term put will reduce your overall risk. If YHOO makes a strong move higher, before expiration of the short-term put, both the long-term and short-term puts will be deep OTM. Deep OTM puts tend to lose most of their time value premium and therefore, despite the difference in expiration dates, both puts will be almost worthless. Because the spread between the two will shrink to almost $0 (not quite $0, because the long-term option will still have a slight time value premium), your maximum loss on the position will be the debit paid. Therefore, your maximum loss will be your reduced debit of $2.25 (assuming you sold only 1 month of premium in the foregoing calendar spread).

You will also suffer a loss if YHOO makes a large move lower before expiration of the short-term option. If YHOO drops sharply in price, both the short-term and long-term options will be deep ITM. Deep ITM options tend to lose most of their time value and have mostly intrinsic value. Therefore, the short-term and long-term $45 Puts will be trading at almost the same price, and the spread between the two will be close to $0 (not exactly $0, because the long-term $45 Put will still have a slight time value premium). Therefore, whether you are assigned on your short put (in which case you simply cover the position with the long put) or are forced to close out the spread altogether, your maximum loss is still limited to the debit paid.

As indicated, your calendar spread position will suffer a loss if the stock moves too far down before expiration of the short-term option. Although you were right about YHOO moving lower, converting into a calendar spread will not allow you to profit from such a move because of the existence of the short put. Therefore, consider rolling into the calendar spread when you own a long-term put only if you truly expect the stock to move sideways or slightly higher in the short term and do not expect any large moves lower prior to expiration of the short put.

Put Ratio Spread

Underlying Stock Moves Lower   Earlier in the chapter, we discussed rolling a long put position into a bear put spread after the underlying stock has moved lower in order to create a risk-free trade if done for a net credit or, if the premium collected is not enough to cover the entire cost of the long put, then to reduce the trade cost and overall risk. You always sell the same number of puts as you are long when rolling into a bear put spread. If you sell more puts than you are long, you will bring in even more premium, and the trade adjustment is then a put ratio spread.

The put ratio spread has more short puts than long and therefore has naked options. The position can therefore produce significant losses if the underlying stock moves too far down and the naked puts are deep ITM. The maximum reward from such a position occurs when the stock is right at the short strike at expiration because the short puts will expire worthless and the ITM long put will have significant value. Therefore, when establishing the put ratio spread adjustment, the expectation should be that the stock will be at or as near as possible to the short strike at expiration. The added benefit of establishing the position for a net credit is that if the stock is between the long and short strikes, then your overall profit is increased by the net credit received, and if the stock rallies higher and all the puts expire worthless, you still have a profit. Thus, there would be no risk to the upside as there would be in your unadjusted long put position.

Assume you purchase a 2-month YHOO $45 Put for $2.50 with YHOO at $45. A few weeks later, YHOO slides down to $42, and you observe that the $40 Put with the same expiration is trading at $1.50. You expect YHOO to continue to move lower but feel that YHOO will be around $40 by expiration. Of course, there is always the concern that YHOO could move back higher, wiping out all your unrealized profit and even produce a loss. To take advantage of the movement in YHOO and hedge against a reversal higher in the stock, you could sell two $40 Puts at $1.50 each for a total of $3.00 and convert your long put into a 1:2 put ratio spread.

The $3.00 in premium received from selling the two $40 Puts will cover the $2.50 cost of your long $45 Put and result in a net credit of $0.50. The benefit of this credit is that if YHOO reverses and moves higher above $45 by expiration, the puts will expire worthless, and you will still have an overall profit of $0.50. Therefore, rolling into the put ratio spread for a net credit removes all risk to the upside. The net credit will also boost any profits realized from the position.

The maximum reward on the put ratio spread is achieved when the stock is at the short strike at expiration. If YHOO is at $40 at expiration, then the short $40 Puts will expire worthless, and the long $45 Put will be worth $5.00 for an overall maximum profit of $5.50 (adding back the net credit). Between $45 and $40, the short puts will expire worthless at expiration, and the profit is the net credit of $0.50 added to the value of the long $45 Put.

If YHOO makes a significant move lower below $40, then the naked put will move deeper ITM and can produce a loss. The downside breakeven point for the 1:2 ratio spread is calculated by subtracting the difference between the strikes ($5.00) from the short strike ($40), which results in $35, and then subtracting the net credit ($0.50) to get a breakeven point of $34.50. Therefore, if YHOO moves below $40 but stays above $34.50, the position will still have a profit.

As Figure 5.23 indicates, rolling your long put into a 1:2 put ratio spread will provide a profit boost to your overall position as long as YHOO does not fall too far past the short strike price of $40. Therefore, the short strike price used in establishing the put ratio spread should be used as a price target. If the stock is expected to move much below the short put strike price, then do not roll into the put ratio spread.

If you are very confident that the stock will be near the short strike price at expiration or have concerns that YHOO could move back higher by expiration, then you can look into selling three $40 Puts instead of two to create a 1:3 put ratio spread. The 1:3 spread brings in more premium and therefore has a higher net credit. However, the presence of the additional naked puts raises your downside breakeven point slightly, and therefore you do not want to roll into the 1:3 put ratio spread if there is potential for a significant drop in the price of YHOO below the short strike.

Therefore, instead of selling two YHOO $40 Puts at $1.50 each, sell three $40 Puts for a total of $4.50 and establish a 1:3 put ratio spread at a net credit of $2.00 when the original trade cost of $2.50 is subtracted. The net credit means that the position will not suffer a loss if YHOO should rally

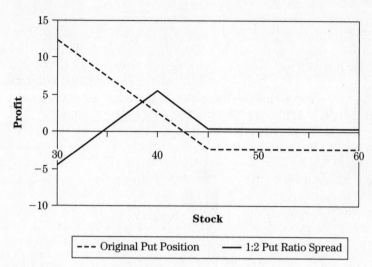

FIGURE 5.23 Rolling Long Put into a 1:2 Put Ratio Spread

and move above $45 by expiration. The maximum reward of the 1:3 spread is also realized when the stock is right at the short strike at expiration. For example, if YHOO is at $40 at expiration, the three $40 Puts expire worthless, and the $45 Put will be worth $5.00 for an overall profit of $7.00 when the net credit is added. Compare this with the maximum reward of $5.50 on the 1:2 put ratio spread adjustment.

Because the 1:3 put ratio spread adjustment has two naked puts, the downside breakeven point will be higher than the 1:2 put ratio spread adjustment. The downside breakeven point of the 1:3 put ratio spread is $36.50, compared with the breakeven point of $34.50 for the 1:2 ratio put spread adjustment. At $36.50, the long $45 Put is worth $8.50 and the three short $40 Puts are worth $3.50 each, for a total of $10.50, for a net loss of $2.00. However, this net loss is offset completely by the $2.00 net credit received.

Comparing the 1:2 and 1:3 put ratio spreads in Figure 5.24, you see that the 1:3 has a higher maximum reward potential at the short strike than the 1:2 spread due to the higher net credit. However, because the 1:3 adjustment has a higher breakeven point on the downside, it should be used only when the stock is not expected to fall that much further below $40 at expiration. Also, the higher net credit provides a nice profit even if you are wrong and YHOO rallies higher above $45.

Most traders who consider the 1:3 put ratio spread adjustment might also feel inclined to use a 1:4 adjustment to bring in more premium and provide an even higher profit at the short strike. However, adding the

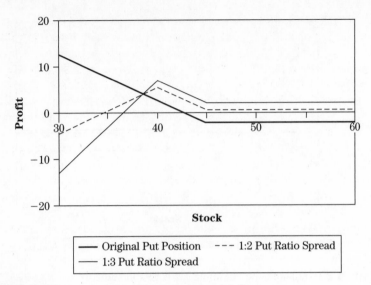

FIGURE 5.24 1:2 versus 1:3 Put Ratio Spread Adjustment

additional naked put also raises the breakeven point closer to the short strike and leads to potentially large losses if YHOO drops lower in price. The 1:2 and 1:3 adjustments provide sufficient risk/reward profiles, given the risk of the naked options, and we feel that the 1:4 adjustment adds too much risk to the downside despite the higher reward. Therefore, we do not recommend that traders consider put ratio adjustments greater than 1:3.

Underlying Stock Moves Higher—Put Repair Strategy   Earlier in the chapter, we demonstrated how to roll a long put into a higher strike bear put spread to repair a losing put position where the underlying stock has moved higher and to raise your breakeven point. If the stock recovered somewhat and moved back lower, you could still turn a profit because you raised your breakeven point. The key to the bear put spread adjustment is that it has to be done at no cost or for a net credit to make it worthwhile. (This is not to say that you cannot do it for a net debit, but although it will still raise your breakeven point, it will also increase your risk.) If the option prices do not allow you to roll your losing long put into a bear put spread at no cost or for a net credit, then you can roll into a put ratio spread instead. By selling more puts than you are long, you can take in more credit and therefore make the repair adjustment at no cost or possibly for a net credit.

Assume that you purchased a $45 Put at $2.50 with YHOO at $45. Your breakeven on the long put is $42.50. A few weeks later, YHOO moves higher to $48, and your $45 Put has decreased in value to $1.50 for an unrealized loss of $1.00. You still feel that YHOO could move back lower, but not all the way back below $42.50 from $48. Instead of closing out the losing position, you want to repair it and raise your breakeven point so that if YHOO does move back somewhat lower, you can realize a profit on your position.

Assume that a $50 Put with the same expiration is trading at $4.25. You feel that YHOO will move somewhat lower but not by much and therefore want to roll into a put ratio spread for a large credit to raise your breakeven point as much as possible. To roll into a 1:2 put ratio spread, first sell three $45 Puts at $1.50 each for a total credit of $4.50. Always sell one more put than the ratio spread requires because one of the sold puts is actually closing out your original long $45 Put. Simultaneously, purchase the $50 Put for $4.25, and you have $0.25 left over for a net credit. This net credit adds another benefit in that it reduces your initial trade cost from $2.50 to $2.25. Therefore, the adjustment already lowers your risk by reducing your initial debit.

Your adjusted position is now a long $50 Put and two short $45 Puts, and the new breakeven point is $47.75. At $47.75, your short $45 Puts will expire worthless, and the $50 Put will be worth $2.25, which offsets your reduced trade cost of $2.25. Compare this new breakeven point of $47.75 with the prior breakeven point of $42.50. Rolling into the 1:2 put ratio spread has raised your breakeven point by more than $5.00. Even if YHOO moves only slightly lower, you will still have a profit on your position. For example, if YHOO is at $47, the short $45 Puts will expire worthless, and the $50 Put will be worth $3.00 for a profit of $0.75.

The maximum profit is reached when the stock is at the short put strike at expiration. At $45, the $45 Puts will expire worthless, and the $50 Put will be worth $5.00 for a profit of $2.75. To further emphasize how you repaired your position, the unadjusted long put instead would have a loss of $2.50 with YHOO at $45 at expiration instead of the $2.75 profit from the repaired position.

Because you have a naked put, the position will produce a loss if YHOO moves too far below $45. The downside breakeven point is $42.25. At that price, the long $50 Put will be worth $7.75, and the two short $45 Puts will be worth $2.75 each for a total of $5.50, for an overall profit of $2.25. This profit of $2.25 is offset by your reduced trade cost of $2.25, to result in no loss or profit. Therefore, the adjusted put ratio spread has an upper breakeven point of $47.75 and a lower breakeven point of $42.25, as indicated in Figure 5.25.

With YHOO at $48 when you made the repair adjustment, YHOO has room to move somewhat lower and still result in a profit. The only additional risk from the original position occurs if YHOO moves below $42.25, where the loss can be significant if YHOO makes a large move lower. On

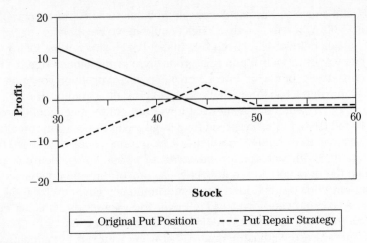

FIGURE 5.25   Put Repair Strategy: Rolling into a Put Ratio Spread

the upside, the net credit received from making the repair adjustment actually reduces your trade cost and thus lowers your risk, should YHOO move higher and your puts expire worthless. Because there is potential for significant losses on the downside, this repair strategy is appropriate only when you expect the stock to recover somewhat. If you expect a major price reversal downward, then you are better off simply letting your long $45 Put run until expiration.

If you are really concerned that YHOO will move only slightly lower and want a higher breakeven point, then you could convert your long $45 Put into a 1:3 put ratio spread to collect more premium. If your long $45 Put is at $1.50 and the $50 Put is at $4.25 with YHOO at $48, you can sell four YHOO $45 Puts at $1.50 each for a total credit of $6.00. Simultaneously, purchase the $50 Put for $4.25, leaving a net credit of $1.75. This net credit of $1.75 reduces your initial trade cost of $2.50 to a net debit of $0.75. The upside breakeven point is raised to $49.25.

If YHOO is above $50 at expiration, then all the puts will expire worthless, and you lose the net debit of $0.75. Therefore, your repair has reduced your loss. The maximum reward occurs when the stock is at the short strike at expiration. If YHOO is at $45 at expiration, then the short $45 Puts will expire worthless, and the $50 Put will be worth $5.00 for an overall profit of $4.25 when the net debit of $0.75 is subtracted.

Because there are two naked puts in the 1:3 put ratio spread, the position could produce losses if YHOO moves well below $45. The downside breakeven point is $42.875. At that price, the three $45 Puts will be worth

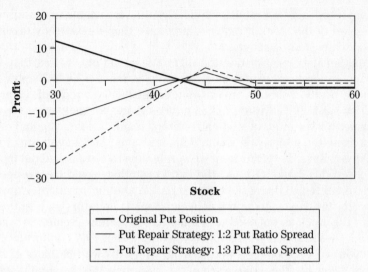

FIGURE 5.26 Put Repair Strategy: 1:2 versus 1:3 Put Ratio Spread

$2.125 each for a total of $6.375, and the long $50 Put will be worth $7.125, for a profit of $0.75, which will be offset by the net debit of $0.75. Therefore, as long as YHOO is between $42.875 and $49.25 at expiration, the repaired position will produce a profit. Figure 5.26 compares the use of the 1:2 put repair ratio spread versus the 1:3 put repair ratio spread.

SHORT PUT

The sale of a naked put creates an obligation on the seller to purchase the underlying stock at the strike price of the short put. This strategy can be very risky and lead to significant losses, should the stock make a large move below the strike price. Although many investors equate the risk in naked puts with that in naked calls, they are two distinct strategies. First, naked calls have theoretically unlimited risk, whereas naked puts have substantial but not unlimited risk because the stock can only fall to $0. Therefore, you know exactly how much cash you will need to cover the short put in case you are assigned, and as a result, the margin requirements are less stringent than for naked calls. Also, naked puts can be used as a means to acquire stocks at prices better than the current market. For example, you might get assigned on the short put at an effective purchase price lower than the market price. In other words, despite the risks of naked puts, investors may not mind such risks as they are willing to actually take possession of the stock if assigned and have therefore already taken the stock price cost into account.

Another important distinction regarding naked puts is that they have the same risk/reward profile as covered call strategies (see Chapter 2 on synthetic positions). Many investors regard using covered calls as a conservative strategy and using naked puts as risky, but they are in essence the same. However, a covered call strategy requires a large capital outlay to purchase the underlying stock, whereas naked puts have a small margin requirement. Therefore, it may be preferable to use a naked put instead of a covered call and then use the extra cash that would have otherwise been committed to doing the covered call in another position elsewhere. However, this choice is up to you because many investors may still prefer to own the stock as opposed to trading naked options. Remember that in Chapter 1 we said that you should trade only within your comfort level.

If you are assigned on your naked put, you will own 100 shares of stock at a price equal to the strike price of the put minus the premium received. Once you own the stock, there are numerous trade adjustments that can be made (see Chapter 3). However, there are not many possible trade adjustments for a naked put. For short-term naked puts, the premium received for ATM and OTM short puts is very small, and therefore any adjustment that requires purchasing another option could wipe out any potential profit, should the puts expire worthless. The best adjustment in the case of short ATM and OTM puts is to have a good exit strategy and close out the position before your naked put becomes deep ITM unless you are willing to take possession of the stock.

For example, assume that with YHOO at $45, you observe the following 1-month put prices:

YHOO @ $45

YHOO $40 Put	$0.50
YHOO $45 Put	$1.75
YHOO $50 Put	$5.50

If you sell the ATM $45 Put or the OTM $40 Put, the premium received will be small, and there is no way to hedge that profit, even if YHOO moves higher, without possibly spending more money than the credit you received. That will wipe out your profit and therefore is not a good adjustment. For example, if you sell the OTM $40 Put for $0.50 and the stock moves higher, the only way to lock in a profit is to close the position because the premium received is so small. The same holds with the $45 Put selling for $1.75.

However, if you sell the ITM, then there are a few ways to hedge your position if the stock moves higher. If you sell the $50 Put for $5.50 and YHOO moves from $45 to $49, the $45 Put may be selling at $0.50. If you fear that YHOO may drift lower instead of moving over $50 as you had expected, you could purchase the $45 Put for $0.50 and convert your naked put into a bull put spread for a credit of $5.00 ($5.50 initial credit minus $0.50 for purchasing $45 Put). Your $45/$50 bull put spread has a maximum risk of the difference between the strike prices minus the credit received. Because you received a credit of $5.00 after rolling into the position and the difference between the strikes is $5.00, you have no risk at all. If the stock is above $50 at expiration, you keep the entire $5.00 credit. If YHOO is below $45, your profit and loss are $0. Anywhere between $45 and $50, you will still have a profit. Therefore, rolling into the bull put spread turned your risky naked put into a risk-free trade.

In certain situations like this, there may be a way to adjust a naked put position. However, we mainly recommend that with naked options, when you have a profit, take it. Waiting to squeeze the last $0.10 or so out of a naked option as expiration approaches will eventually cause you to have significant losses that one time the stock makes a sudden huge move against you. Therefore, we do not recommend overtrading or searching for complicated adjustments to a naked put position with an unrealized profit. Sometimes the best way to guarantee an unrealized profit is take it at that moment and move on to the next position.

Now, as noted before, naked puts do differ from naked calls in which the seller is willing to take possession of the underlying stock if assigned. Many investors use naked puts not only as a neutral-to-bullish strategy on a stock but also as a way to purchase the stock at a price lower than the market price if assigned. In these instances, the sellers are often aware of the full risks of the position since they either have set aside the cash to fund the purchase or are aware of the cash required should they be assigned. Therefore, traders might not wish to close their position so fast if the stock does drift lower because taking ownership of the stock is a consequence they are prepared for.

We still advocate that when selling a put, there are not many sensible adjustments available because of the possibility of losing all the profit potential by eliminating your credit or adding significant risk. However, when you short a put with the intent to collect premium to use to reduce the purchase price of a stock if assigned, then you might have a little more leeway to let the position run and not be in such a hurry to adjust. In this case, time is not your friend, and you certainly do not want lots of time to expiration for the stock to run against you. Therefore, not only do we advocate for the most part that you sell puts with at most 1 month to expiration but also rolling down and out to a later expiration month might not work to your advantage by giving the position more time to work against you.

Some traders feel that if the original intent in selling the puts was to eventually take ownership of the stock, then rolling down a strike and out an expiration month is not a bad adjustment since you get more premium and more time to wait and see if the stock can reverse. If it does not move back higher, then the stock stays below your strike price, and you eventually get assigned as you originally intended. We view this thinking as flawed for several reasons. First, if the stock is moving lower and your original intent is to get assigned and take delivery at some point, then why even bother rolling down and out if the option has now moved against you and assignment is likely? The short put will show an unrealized loss, and you might be assigned at a stock price above the current market, resulting in a losing position; but if your intent was to own the stock, then there has to be some rationale for the long-term prospects of the stock to move higher.

In the preceding YHOO put premiums, if you sold the 1-month $45 Put for $1.75 while YHOO was at $45, and now the stock is at $42 with about a week to go to expiration, your put will most likely be worth about $3.25, for an unrealized loss of $1.50. If YHOO stays there until expiration, you will be assigned on the short $45 Put for an effective purchase price of $43.25 with the market at $42, for an initial paper loss of $1.25. If you were willing to take possession of the YHOO stock at $43.25, then it should be based on your expectation that YHOO would be higher in the future. If YHOO has dropped to $42 and your short put has increased in value, you should ask whether your fundamental view of YHOO has changed. If your fundamental view of YHOO has not changed, then it is still a good buy even if you are getting it at a slightly higher price. We want to get the lowest and best possible price, but that is not always easy to do. Therefore, if you believe that YHOO is still a good buy, then a slightly higher price than the current market price should not change your opinion.

Now, given the preceding situation, the question is whether it is a logical adjustment to buy back the YHOO $45 Put for $3.25 and then sell a YHOO $40 Put in the next expiration month as an adjustment. Our problem with this adjustment is that in this case the $40 Put in the next expiration month might be worth less than $3.25 and perhaps closer to $1.50 or so. So you would buy back the $45 Put for $3.25, sell the next month $40 Put for $1.50, and end up with a net debit of $1.75. You originally collected $1.75 in premium for selling the front month $45 Put and now own a short $40 Put with one more month to go until expiration for a net credit of $0.00. So you gave yourself more cushion to possibly get YHOO at a lower price, but you ended up eliminating your entire credit collected. You still have the significant risk of a short put, but you gave up your reward (premium), and now your position has even more time to move against you. If you felt that YHOO would recover somewhat anyway, then the best move to match your expectations is to simply hold the short put with a tight stop loss in case you are wrong or take assignment and play the long stock for the expected move higher.

Some may consider the roll-down-and-out adjustment for the naked put more worthwhile if you can collect a larger credit as a result of the adjustment. In our experience, the only way to do that is to roll out to a much further in time short put, which increases your potential risk by giving the position more time to move against you and taking away time decay as an ally. There may always be unique cases where rolling down and out works in a certain set of facts. For the most part, we still believe that if the position moves against you, it is best to either leave the position alone, take assignment, or cut your losses by closing the short put, and reevaluate.

CHAPTER 6

Spreads

INTRODUCTION

A spread involves the simultaneous purchase of one option and sale of another option of the same type on the same underlying security. The two options can have different expiration dates and/or different strikes. Spreads involve limited risk and limited reward, although there are still many possible trade adjustments to the position.

The first section of this chapter covers bull call and bear call spreads, as well as bear put and bull put spreads. Because the adjustments for these types of call spreads are the same as those for the put spreads, we focus on the call spread adjustments and include examples for the put spreads. The second half of the chapter covers other types of spreads, such as calendar spreads and ratio spreads using calls, with put spreads included for illustrative purposes.

BULL CALL SPREADS/BEAR PUT SPREADS

A bull call spread is established by purchasing a call and selling another at a higher strike with the same expiration date. The sale of the higher strike call reduces the cost of the long call and therefore reduces the risk. In exchange for the reduction in risk, the maximum reward is limited to the difference between the strikes minus the net debit paid to establish the spread. For the spread to reach its maximum value, the stock must be at or above the short strike at expiration.

Protective Puts/Protective Calls

Bull Call Spread—Protective Put   A protective put is used to hedge a long stock position or a long call position to lock in a profit and still allow the position to earn more money, should the underlying stock continue to move higher. You can also add a protective put to a bull call spread position for the same reasons. One downside to using a bull call spread is that as the stock moves higher, the short strike call increases in value along with the long call at the lower strike. Although the spread will widen to its maximum value as the stock moves higher, the spread will usually not reach its maximum value until expiration is close because both the short call and the long call will have a time value premium. Therefore, investors who use bull call spreads sometimes need to wait until expiration approaches for the spread to widen and the time value premiums to erode. However, a protective put adjustment can help to lock in a profit and remove all risk from the position.

Assume that Costco (COST) is trading at $35 and you expect the stock to move just above $40 over the next few months. You observe a 3-month COST $35 Call trading at $2.50 and a $40 Call with the same expiration at $0.75. You feel that COST will move to $40 and decide to establish a bull call spread by purchasing the $35 Call for $2.50 and selling the $40 Call for $0.75, for a net debit of $1.75.

One month later, COST is at $41, and the spread has widened to $3.75. Although the stock has moved as expected, the time value premium in the short $40 Call will prevent the spread from being worth the full $5.00. You will have to wait until expiration approaches before realizing the maximum profit, but you are afraid that while waiting for the spread to widen, the stock could reverse, move lower, and wipe out any chance for profit. You can use a protective put to lock in a guaranteed profit so that as you wait for expiration to approach, not only will your profit be secured but also there is a possibility of even greater returns than the original maximum reward.

Assume that with COST at $41, a $40 Put with the same expiration as the bull call spread is trading at $1.25. To lock in a profit in the bull call spread, purchase the COST $40 Put for $1.25. Your new total trade cost is $3.00 ($1.75 bull call spread plus $1.25 for $40 Put), and the protective put now acts as a perfect hedge against the stock moving lower by expiration. To see how this hedge works, let's analyze the profit and loss in the position at expiration for different stock prices.

If COST is above $40 at expiration, the $35/$40 bull call spread will be worth the maximum reward of $5.00 for a profit of $2.00 when the $3.00

trade cost is subtracted. Between $35 and $40, the short $40 Call will expire worthless, and the long $35 Call and long $40 Put will combine for a value of $5.00. For example, if COST is at $37 at expiration, the $35 Call will be worth $2.00, and the $40 Put will be worth $3.00, for a total of $5.00. Once the $3.00 trade cost is subtracted, your profit is $2.00. Therefore, if COST is at $35 or above at expiration, your adjusted position has a locked-in profit of $2.00.

The added benefit of adjusting your bull call spread with the protective put is that you can earn more than the guaranteed profit of $2.00 if COST moves back below $35. For example, if COST reverses and drops sharply in price to $33 by expiration, your calls will expire worthless, and the $40 Put will be worth $7.00, for a profit of $4.00. The further COST falls below $35, the larger the profits.

As Figure 6.1 indicates, adding the protective put to your bull call spread after the underlying stock has moved higher creates a risk-free trade. Moreover, the protective put gives you the opportunity to earn even more money if the stock drops sharply by expiration. The key to locking in a risk-free return is to ensure that the total cost of the combined position is less than the difference between the strikes used in the bull call spread. In the example just given, the $3.00 combined cost is less than the $5.00 difference between the $35 and $40 strikes, locking in a minimum $2.00 risk-free profit.

The protective put adjustment can also be added when you actually expect the stock to turn around and move lower. Most investors would simply close their bull call spread and establish a bearish position to profit from the stock moving back lower. However, you could simply add the protective put, and if COST does move back lower, you can make significant

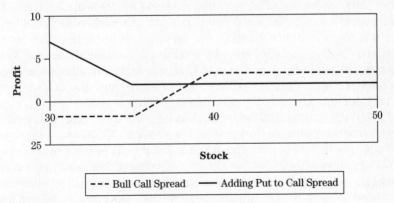

FIGURE 6.1 Adding Protective Put to a Bull Call Spread

profits. On the other hand, if you are wrong and COST keeps moving higher, you will not have a loss because you locked in a guaranteed profit.

Bull Call Spread—Protective Put Spread   If you want to guarantee a higher minimum profit or if the addition of the protective put does not lock in a guaranteed profit at all (i.e., the protective put is too expensive or the prospective combined cost of the position is greater than the difference between the strike prices), then you can consider a protective put spread instead of a single protective put. In the foregoing example, you purchased the $35/$40 bull call spread for a net debit of $1.75, and with COST at $41, the $40 Put is trading at $1.25.

Assume that you wish to add the protective put but want to reduce the cost of your protective put to boost your profits. You can sell a $35 Put with the same expiration and use those proceeds to reduce the cost of your long $40 Put. If the COST $35 Put is trading at $0.50, you can purchase the $40 Put for $1.25 and simultaneously sell the $35 Put to establish a bear put spread with a net debit of $0.75. The addition of the bear put spread makes your combined trade cost equal to $2.50 ($1.75 net debit for the bull call spread and $0.75 net debit for the addition of the bear put spread).

The difference between the protective put and the protective put spread is that there no longer is the potential for significant profits to the downside. Because the adjustment involves a bear put spread, the reward is limited. The combination of the bull call spread and the bear put spread with the same strike prices is called a box spread. The maximum profit on a box spread is simply the difference between the strikes minus the net debit. For example, if COST is at $37 at expiration, the short $40 Call and the short $35 Put will expire worthless, and the long $35 Call and the long $40 Put will combine for a value of $5.00 ($2.00 for the $35 Call and $3.00 for the $40 Put with COST at $37). The net profit will be $2.50.

If COST is below $35, the call spread will expire worthless, and the bear put spread will be worth the maximum value of $5.00. Likewise, if COST is above $40 at expiration, the bear put spread will expire worthless, and the bull call spread will be worth the maximum value of $5.00. Because the combined position cost $2.50, the locked-in guaranteed profit is $2.50, no matter where COST is at expiration, because the $2.50 cost will be subtracted from the $5.00 value of the position.

The risk/reward profile of your adjusted position in Figure 6.2 demonstrates that your profit is the same no matter where COST is at expiration. Although the locked-in minimum profit is lower than the maximum reward of the unadjusted bull call spread, the adjustment has removed all risk from your position. Therefore, even though the reward is less after making the adjustment, you are guaranteed to receive the profit no matter what happens to COST by expiration.

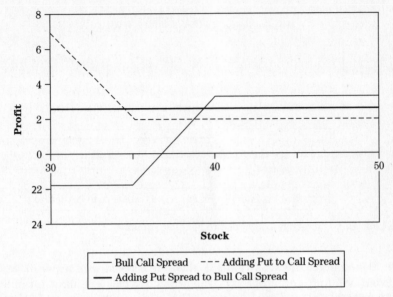

FIGURE 6.2 Protective Put Spread with Bull Call Spread

Bear Put Spread—Protective Call You can also lock in a profit in a bear put spread by using a protective call in the same way as the protective put locks in a profit and provides for increased returns in the bull call spread. With COST at $35, assume you purchased a 3-month COST $35 Put for $2.50 and sold a 3-month COST $30 Put for $0.75 to establish a bear put spread for a net debit of $1.75. Assume that 1 month later, COST is at $31 and the COST $30 Call with the same expiration is trading for $1.75. You expect COST to keep moving lower, but you are also concerned that COST may rebound by expiration and be above $35, wiping out your unrealized gain.

To lock in a minimum profit, you can add a protective call to your bear put spread by purchasing the COST $30 Call for $1.75. Your new cost of the combined position is $3.50 when the bear put spread net debit and protective call positions are added together. If COST moves below $30 at expiration, your $35/$30 bear put spread will have a maximum value of $5.00 and your $30 Call will expire worthless for a profit of $1.50 when the $3.50 cost is subtracted. Between $35 and $30, the combined position will have a profit of $1.50 as well. For example, if COST is at $33, the $30 Call will be worth $3.00, and the $35 Put will be worth $2.00 for a combined value of $5.00.

If COST is above $35 at expiration, then all the puts will expire worthless, and the total profit will be the value of the call minus the total trade

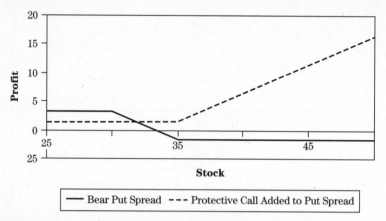

FIGURE 6.3 Protective Call Added to Bear Put Spread

cost. For example, if COST is at $38, then the $30 Call will be worth $8.00 at expiration for a profit of $4.50. The protective call will allow for unlimited profits if COST makes a substantial move higher by expiration. As long as the combined cost of the adjusted position is less than the difference between the bear put spread strikes, you will have a risk-free position.

As with the protective put adjustment, the addition of the protective call can also be considered when you expect the stock to turn around and move significantly higher. Instead of closing out the bear put spread and entering into a bullish position, you can add the protective call to your bear put spread to allow for profits to the upside as indicated in Figure 6.3. The benefit from this combined position is that you are hedged in case you are wrong because if the stock moves lower instead of higher, you have a guaranteed profit locked in.

Bear Put Spread—Protective Call Spread To lower the cost of adding the protective call to your bear put spread, you can also sell a higher strike call to create a bull call spread combined with your bear put spread. You originally purchased a COST $35/$30 bear put spread for a net debit of $1.75. With COST at $31, the $30 Call with the same expiration is trading at $1.75, and the $35 Call is trading at $0.75. To add the protective call spread to your position, purchase the $30 Call and sell the $35 Call for a net debit of $1.00. The combination of the bear put spread for $1.75 and the bull call spread for $1.00 results in a total trade cost of $2.75.

The maximum profit on the combination of a bear put spread and a bull call spread with the same strike prices is the difference between the strike prices ($5.00) minus the net debit ($2.75), which is $2.25. If COST is above $35 at expiration, the puts will expire worthless, and the bull call

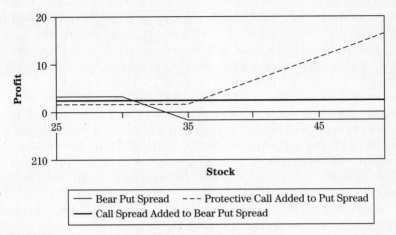

FIGURE 6.4 Call Spread Added to Bear Put Spread

spread will be worth $5.00, and if COST is below $30, the calls will expire worthless, and the bear put spread will be worth $5.00. On the other hand, if COST is between $30 and $35, then the combination of the long call and the long put will result in a total of $5.00 as well. Therefore, no matter where COST is at expiration, the spread will be worth $5.00 for a profit of $2.25 (Figure 6.4).

Adding the protective call spread is a good way to remove all doubt of a profit while waiting for expiration. Although the locked-in profit is lower than the maximum profit of the bear put spread, you know for sure that you will receive that profit no matter what. Sometimes it is worth giving up a little reward in exchange for removing all risk.

Convert to Ratio Spreads

Bull Call Spread—Stock Moves Higher A bull call spread involves the same number of short calls as you are long. The call ratio spread involves selling more calls at a higher strike than you are long. It is very easy to convert a bull call spread into a call ratio spread simply by adding more short calls to your position. Because a call ratio spread has naked calls, you would convert your limited-risk bull call spread into a potentially risky call ratio spread only after the underlying stock has moved higher and you expect the stock to move sideways or back lower by expiration. The additional premium collected from selling the extra calls will boost your profits and hedge against the stock moving below the long strike of your bull call spread by expiration.

Assume that with COST at $35, you purchased a 3-month $35/$40 bull call spread for a net debit of $1.75. One month later, COST runs higher to $41, and you feel that the stock will move sideways or back lower, but you do not want to close your position because the spread has not reached its maximum reward and your profit is not as high as it should be if it were near expiration. Because you feel that COST will move sideways or lower, you are concerned that there is a chance that while you are waiting for expiration to approach, the stock could drop significantly lower, below $35, and wipe out your unrealized profit. Therefore, you can convert your position into a call ratio spread to bring in premium to reduce the cost of the spread or perhaps collect a net credit and remove the risk of the underlying stock moving lower.

With COST at $41, assume that a $40 Call with the same expiration date as your bull call spread is trading at $2.00. To convert your position to a 1:2 call ratio spread, sell another $40 Call and collect $2.00 in premium. The $2.00 covers your initial bull call spread cost of $1.75 and leaves you with a net credit of $0.25 for your new 1:2 $35/$40 call ratio spread. To understand the benefits of converting your bull call spread into a call ratio spread, let's look at the potential profit and loss on the position at expiration.

If COST is below $35 at expiration, all your calls will expire worthless, and your overall profit will be the $0.25 net credit you received from rolling your spread into a call ratio spread. Therefore, your trade adjustment has taken out all the downside risk that existed in the unadjusted bull call spread. If COST is between $35 and $40, the short $40 Calls will expire worthless, and the long $35 Call will be worth its intrinsic value, depending on where COST is at expiration. For example, if COST is at $37, the long $35 Call will be worth $2.00, for an overall profit of $2.25 when the net credit is added in. The maximum profit is reached when COST is right at the short strike at expiration. If COST is at $40, the short $40 Calls will expire worthless, and the long $35 Call will be worth $5.00, for an overall profit of $5.25 when the net credit is added in.

If COST moves above $40, the presence of the naked call will begin to reduce the overall profit of the position until it hits the upside breakeven point. The upside breakeven point for a 1:2 call ratio spread is calculated by adding the difference between the strike prices ($5.00) to the short strike price ($40) plus/minus the net credit/net debit ($0.25 credit), which is $45.25. As COST moves above $45.25, the position will begin to produce a loss, as indicated in the risk/reward profile of the adjusted position in Figure 6.5.

As Figure 6.5 demonstrates, the converted call ratio spread has the potential for significant losses, should COST make a large move higher before expiration. Therefore, the adjustment should be considered only if you

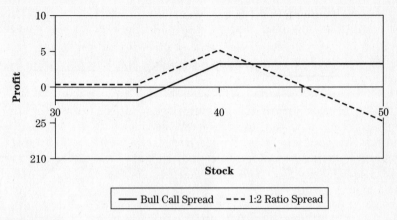

FIGURE 6.5 Converting Bull Call Spread into 1:2 Ratio Spread

do not expect COST to move much higher, at least not that much closer to the breakeven point. You actually prefer COST to be right at the short strike price at expiration for the maximum reward of $5.25. Therefore, with COST at $41, you prefer to have the stock move sideways, or at worst move slightly higher, and you are hedged no matter how far down it moves.

What if you feel very strongly that COST will move sideways or lower and want to boost your potential profit and hedge against the stock moving lower by expiration? Instead of converting your position to a 1:2 call ratio spread, you can roll it into 1:3 call ratio spread by selling two $40 Calls with COST at $41 to add to your existing $35/$40 bull call spread.

To convert your $35/$40 bull call spread into a 1:3 call ratio spread with the COST $40 Call trading at $2.00, sell two $40 Calls and bring in $4.00 in premium. The $4.00 covers the $1.75 net debit of your initial bull call spread and leaves a net credit of $2.25. This credit provides a locked-in profit even if COST falls below $35 by expiration. It also boosts your profit if COST is anywhere between $35 and $40 at expiration. For example, if COST is at $37, the $40 Calls will expire worthless, and your long $35 Call will be worth $2.00, for an overall profit of $4.25 when the net credit of $2.25 is added. The maximum profit is realized when COST is at the short strike at expiration. With COST at $40, the short $40 Calls will expire worthless, and the long $35 Call will be worth $5.00 for an overall profit of $7.25.

The addition of the two naked calls to your bull call spread adds risk to the position if COST moves too far above $40. The upside breakeven point is $43.625. At $43.625, your long $35 Call will be worth $8.625, and your three short $40 Calls will be worth a combined $10.875, for a net loss of $2.25, which is offset by the $2.25 net credit collected from establishing the position.

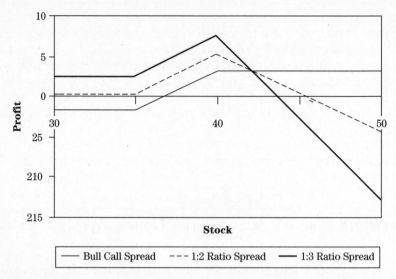

FIGURE 6.6   Converting Bull Call Spread into 1:2 versus 1:3 Ratio Spread

As Figure 6.6 indicates, the 1:3 call ratio spread adjustment has a higher reward at the maximum profit point (short strike price) and also provides a larger profit if COST should fall below $35 by expiration. However, the position also has a lower breakeven point due to the existence of the extra short calls. Therefore, you should consider the 1:3 ratio spread adjustment only when you really do not feel that the stock will move much higher and expect it to move sideways or lower by expiration.

Bull Call Spread—Stock Moves Lower/Repair Strategy   Assume that after you establish the COST $35/$40 bull call spread for a net debit of $1.75 with COST at $35, the stock slides lower to $32. You feel that COST will recover somewhat by expiration but perhaps not back to your bull call spread breakeven point of $36.75. You therefore would want to lower your breakeven point so that if COST does recover somewhat, you can still realize a profit on your position. We discussed in Chapter 5 how to repair a long call by rolling into a bull call spread at lower strikes. Because your position is already a bull call spread, you can roll down into a call ratio spread. However, if the idea of significant losses if COST makes a large move higher before expiration is troubling, we will also demonstrate how to roll down into a lower bull call spread, although it requires an additional small capital outlay.

With COST down to $32, assume that your long $35 Call is now trading at $1.25, and your short $40 Call is now trading at $0.40. You also observe that a $30 Call with the same expiration is trading at $2.50. To lower your breakeven point and roll down your position, first sell two $35 Calls at $1.25 each for a total of $2.50. Basically, you have closed your long $35 Call and opened an additional short $35 Call. With the $2.50 in premium collected, you simultaneously purchase the $30 Call for $2.50. The result is that you now have a long $30 Call, a short $35 Call, and a short $40 Call, all for the same original net debit of $1.75 because the conversion did not cost any additional money.

The combination of the long $30 Call and the short $35 and $40 Calls creates a type of 1:2 ratio spread called a Christmas tree. The difference between this spread and regular call ratio spreads is that the short calls are at different strike prices. We will examine the different profit and loss scenarios to see how rolling down into a Christmas tree spread can repair a losing bull call spread if you expect the stock to recover somewhat.

If COST continues to fall and is below $30 at expiration, then all the calls will expire worthless, and your loss is limited to your initial debit of $1.75. You are no worse off than you were if you did not make the adjustment if COST is below $30 at expiration. On the downside, your new breakeven point is $31.75, which is the initial debit of $1.75 added to your new long $30 Call. Compare this breakeven point with your original breakeven point of $36.75—a reduction of $5.00. On the upside, the breakeven point is $43.25. The maximum profit is the difference between the strikes ($35 − $30) minus the initial debit ($1.75), which is $3.25. This maximum profit of $3.25 is realized when COST is between $35 and $40 at expiration. As COST moves above $40, the additional naked call will begin to cut into your profits until the upside breakeven point, which is the upper short strike plus the maximum profit.

The effect of the repair adjustment is seen clearly in Figure 6.7. The adjustment has lowered your breakeven point while still allowing for a profit should COST move higher. Although there is the potential for significant losses if COST makes a very large move back higher above $40, there is more than enough cushion to absorb a price increase before the position turns negative. Because COST was at $32 when you made the repair adjustment, the stock would have to move more than $10.00 by expiration for a loss on the upside to occur. If COST is anywhere between $31.75 and $43.25, your repaired position will have a profit.

The adjustment above is a 1:2 multiple strike ratio spread. If you feel that COST will recover only somewhat and that it is very unlikely that the stock will surge much higher by expiration, you can roll your bull call spread into a 1:3 ratio spread to lower your breakeven point even more because you will receive a larger credit for making the adjustment. To roll your bull call spread down to a 1:3 ratio spread, sell three $35 Calls at $1.25

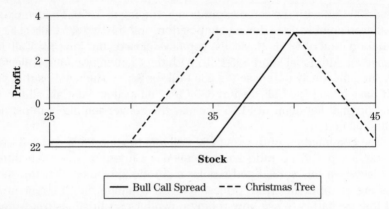

FIGURE 6.7 Bull Call Spread Repair Strategy

each for a total of $3.75, and purchase the $30 Call for $2.50 for a net credit of $1.25. The net credit of $1.25 will reduce your original net debit cost of $1.75 down to a net debit of $0.50.

Your new position will be long the $30 Call, short two $35 Calls, and short the $40 Call for a new cost of $0.50. Because your trade cost is lower, your downside risk is now lower as well. Your new breakeven point on the downside is $30.50 (lower $30 Call strike plus trade cost). The maximum reward occurs when COST is at the short strike at expiration ($35 in this case). If COST is at $35, all the short calls will expire worthless, and the $30 Call will be worth $5.00 for a profit of $4.50. Your upside breakeven point is $39.50. At $39.50, the $40 Call will expire worthless, the two $35 Calls will be worth $9.00 total, and your $30 Call will be worth $9.50, for a profit of $0.50, which is offset by the reduced trade cost of $0.50. Therefore, the adjusted position will be profitable if COST is between $30.50 and $39.50 (Figure 6.8).

If you are uncomfortable rolling your bull call spread into a call ratio spread, or you do not want to pay the margin required for the naked calls in the ratio, you can make a slight change to the foregoing repair adjustment to roll your bull call spread into a lower strike bull call spread.

First, follow the same steps as before to move from the $35/$40 bull call spread into a long $30 Call, a short $35 Call, and a short $40 Call ratio spread. Simultaneously, close out the $40 Call by purchasing it at $0.40 (assumed price). By repurchasing your short $40 Call for $0.40, your remaining position is now long the $30 Call and short the $35 Call for a $30/$35 bull call spread.

The repurchase of the $40 Call for $0.40, however, increases your total trade cost from $1.75 to $2.15. Therefore, your new breakeven point is $32.15, much lower than the original breakeven point of $36.75 and slightly

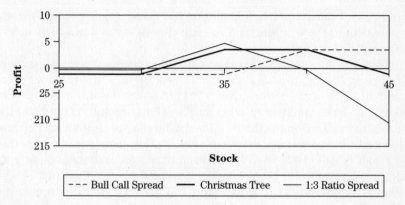

FIGURE 6.8 Rolling Bull Call Spread into Repaired 1:2 versus 1:3 Ratio Spread

higher than the repaired breakeven point from rolling into the multiple strike ratio spread of $31.75. The maximum profit on the $30/$35 bull call spread is the difference between the strikes ($5.00) minus the net debit ($2.15), which is $2.85 (Figure 6.9).

Although rolling down to the lower strike bull call spread involves re-purchasing the long $40 Call and adding slightly more risk to your position, you get to lower your breakeven point and profit if COST should recover somewhat by expiration. The choice between rolling down to a multiple call ratio spread or a lower strike bull call spread depends on your preference. The multiple strike call ratio spread has a lower breakeven point and a wide profit zone, which gives COST room to move higher and still realize a profit. However, if you are concerned about the potential for losses

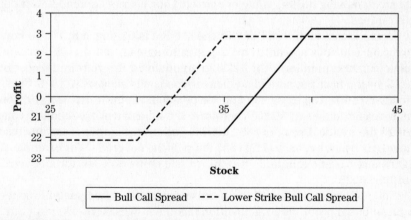

FIGURE 6.9 Rolling Bull Call Spread into Lower Strike Bull Call Spread

should COST move too much higher or you do not want to add a margin requirement to the position, then you can choose to roll down to the lower strike bull call spread.

We made the assumption that you are able to make a repair adjustment for a net credit or at no additional cost. Depending on where the stock price is and the price of the options, you might not always be able to repair your position at a net credit or at no cost. Therefore, we still recommend the repair strategies as long as the additional debit required is minimal because adding cost increases your risk somewhat. The key in determining whether the repair is still viable even if you have to roll for additional debit is to calculate the new lower breakeven point and see whether the stock has the potential to move above it by expiration. Either way, your new breakeven point will be much lower than your original breakeven point, and that is the purpose of the repair strategy.

Bear Put Spread—Stock Moves Lower   The analysis behind adjusting your bear put spread into a put ratio spread after the stock has moved lower is the same for the call ratio spread adjustments we discussed for bull call spreads. Therefore, we simply review the techniques for making the adjustments using our COST example. Assume that you purchased a 3-month COST $35/$30 bear put spread for a net debit of $1.75. One month later, COST moves lower to $30. Your bear put spread has a small profit but has not yet reached the maximum value because both options have significant time value premiums. You wish to hold onto your position longer. You do not expect the stock to continue moving lower, but instead expect it to move sideways. Of course, you do have concerns that the stock could move back higher and wipe out your unrealized gains. To take advantage of the sideways movement of the stock until expiration and hedge against the stock moving higher, you can convert your bear put spread into a put ratio spread.

Assume that with COST at $30, the $30 Put is trading at $2.00. To convert your bear put spread to a 1:2 put ratio spread, sell the $30 Put and collect $2.00 in premium. The $2.00 in premium covers your initial cost of $1.75 for the bear put spread and leaves you a net credit of $0.25. If COST moves above $35 by expiration, all the puts will expire worthless, and you keep the net credit of $0.25. Therefore, the adjustment has hedged your risk to the upside. Between $35 and $30, your overall profit is the intrinsic value of the in-the-money (ITM) $35 Put plus the net credit. For example, if COST is at $32 at expiration, the $35 Put will be worth $3.00 for an overall profit of $3.25.

As COST moves below $30, the existence of the naked put will reduce your potential profit until the position hits the downside breakeven point. The downside breakeven point in a 1:2 put ratio spread is the lower strike

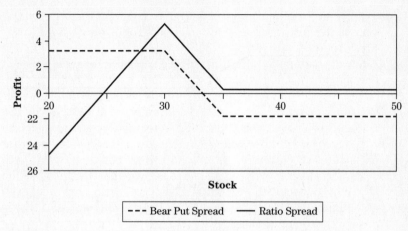

FIGURE 6.10 Converting Bear Put Spread into 1:2 Put Ratio Spread

($30) minus the difference between the strikes ($5.00) minus the net credit received ($0.25), which is $24.75. Although there is the potential for significant losses should COST move too far below $30, the breakeven point of $24.75 gives the stock plenty of room to move lower before a loss occurs.

As Figure 6.10 demonstrates, the adjustment provides a profit boost to your position and hedges against a loss, should COST move back higher above your long put strike. There is the potential for a loss on the position if COST moves below $24.75, and that should be taken into consideration when you are rolling into the 1:2 put spread.

If you are very confident that COST will not move much lower, and you want a bigger hedge in place should COST move higher, you can convert your bear put spread into a 1:3 put ratio spread instead of the 1:2 put ratio spread. Instead of selling one $30 Put at $2.00, sell two $30 Puts for a credit of $4.00. The $4.00 credit covers your initial trade cost of $1.75 and results in a net credit of $2.25. Because the credit is larger, you will have a better hedge to the upside should COST move above $35 by expiration. Also, your overall profit between $35 and $30 will be much higher because of the higher net credit. For example, if COST is at $32, the $30 Puts will expire worthless, and the $35 Put will be worth $3.00, for an overall profit of $5.25.

The maximum profit occurs when COST is at the short strike of $30 at expiration. With COST at $30, the short puts will expire worthless, and the long $35 Put will be worth $5.00, for an overall profit of $7.25. Because you have two naked puts in the adjusted position, your downside breakeven point will be higher than with the 1:2 put ratio spread. Your new downside breakeven point for the adjusted position is $26.375. At $26.375, the long

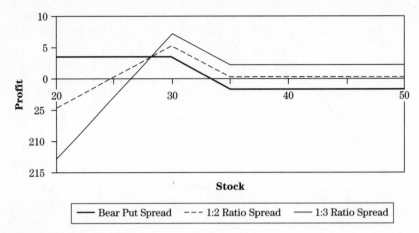

FIGURE 6.11 Converting Bear Put Spread into 1:2 versus 1:3 Ratio Spread

$35 Put will be worth $8.625, and the three $30 Puts will be worth $3.625 each, for a total of $10.875, which results in a net loss of $2.25. This net loss will be offset by the net credit of $2.25 received for rolling into the 1:3 put ratio spread, for an overall profit/loss of $0.00.

The 1:3 ratio spread adjustment has a higher profit potential than the 1:2 adjustment, as indicated in Figure 6.11, but does have a higher breakeven point ($26.375 vs. $24.75). The choice of whether to use the 1:2 or 1:3 put ratio spread depends on where you expect COST to be at expiration.

If you expect COST to move sideways and not much higher or lower, then the 1:2 spread produces a nice profit and has a wide cushion to the downside in case COST breaks out lower. However, if you feel strongly that COST will not only move sideways but could reverse and move higher, then the 1:3 spread adjustment provides an added profit boost and still produces a nice profit if COST moves back higher because of the large net credit.

Bear Put Spread—Stock Moves Higher/Repair Strategy   You can repair a bear put spread in the same way as we discussed for a bull call spread if the stock moves higher after you open your bear spread position. You can roll the position into a ratio spread to raise your breakeven point and realize a profit if the stock moves back lower somewhat for no additional risk. Assume that with COST at $35 you purchased a 3-month $35/$30 bear put spread for a net debit of $1.75. Your breakeven point is $33.25, which is the long $35 Put minus the net debit of $1.75. One month later, COST rises to $39, and you expect COST to recover and move back lower somewhat, but not necessarily back down to your original breakeven point of $33.25. Therefore, you want to repair your position and raise your breakeven point so that if COST does recover somewhat, you can still make a profit.

With COST at $39, assume that the $35 Put is now trading at $1.00 and the $40 Put is trading at $2.00. To repair your $35/$30 bear put spread, first sell two $35 Puts for a credit of $2.00. The transaction closes your long $35 Put and opens a new short $35 Put. With the credit of $2.00, simultaneously purchase the $40 Put for $2.00. Your resulting position is long the $40 Put, short the $35 Put, and short your original $30 Put for a multiple strike 1:2 ratio spread. Because the adjustment was done at no cost, your total trade cost is still $1.75.

Your new breakeven point is $38.25, which is calculated by subtracting the trade cost from the long $40 Put. Compare this repaired breakeven point with your original breakeven point of $33.75. The higher breakeven point means that COST has to move back lower only a smaller amount for the position to break even. The maximum reward is at the short strike of the bear put spread portion of the ratio spread, which is $35. At $35, the short puts expire worthless, and the $40 Put will be worth $5.00, for an overall profit of $3.25 when the net debit is subtracted. If COST moves below $35 but is above $30, then the overall profit is still $3.25 because the $30 put will expire worthless.

As COST moves below $30, the naked put will reduce the overall profit of your repaired position until COST hits the downside breakeven point. The new downside breakeven point is $26.75. At $26.75, the $3.25 loss on the short $30 Put will offset the $3.25 profit from the $40/$35 bear put spread portion of the adjusted ratio spread. Therefore, as indicated in Figure 6.12, the adjusted position will have a profit if COST is between $38.25 and $26.75 at expiration. The repair strategy will work only if COST is expected to move somewhat lower. If COST instead continues to move back higher, then you will still lose your initial debit of $1.75. The repair strategy, therefore, does not limit your risk but does give your position a chance to turn a profit without having to move all the way back to your original breakeven point.

If you are not very confident that COST can move to your new adjusted breakeven point, you can raise the breakeven point even more, as well as reduce your trade cost and upside risk, by converting your bear put spread into a 1:3 multiple strike ratio spread instead. Remember that with COST at $39, the $35 Put is trading at $1.00 and the $40 Put is trading at $2.00. To repair your position with the 1:3 multiple strike ratio spread, sell three $35 Puts at $1.00 each for a credit of $3.00. Simultaneously, purchase the $40 Put for $2.00 and have a net credit of $1.00. The leftover net credit of $1.00 will reduce your initial trade cost from $1.75 to $0.75. Remember that your position now is long a $40 Put, short two $35 Puts, and short a $30 Put.

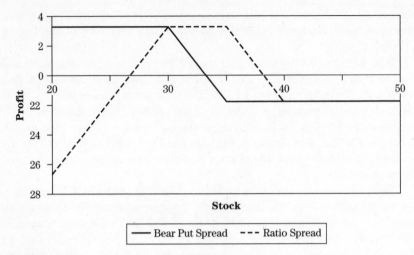

FIGURE 6.12 Bear Put Spread Repair Strategy

Because your trade cost is lower, your upside risk is reduced. If COST moves higher and is above $40 at expiration, all your puts will expire worthless, and your position will have a loss of $0.75, which is your reduced trade cost. With a lower trade cost, you will have a much higher breakeven point. Your new breakeven point is $39.25, which is the $40 Put minus the reduced trade cost of $0.75. Compare this with your original breakeven point of $33.25 and your adjusted breakeven point of $37.25 using the 1:2 ratio spread repair strategy. Because COST was at $39 when you made the adjustment, your position will make a profit even if COST moves sideways.

The maximum profit occurs when COST is at the short strike of $35 at expiration. With COST at $35, all the short puts will expire worthless, and the $40 Put will be worth $5.00, for an overall profit of $4.25 when the reduced cost of $0.75 is subtracted. As COST moves below $35, the extra naked put at $35 will begin to reduce your overall profit until COST hits the downside breakeven point. Your new downside breakeven point is $30.75. At $30.75, the $40 Put will be worth $9.25, and the two $35 Puts will be worth $4.25 each for a total of $8.50, resulting in a profit of $0.75, which is offset by the initial trade cost of $0.75.

If COST moves below $30, then there is the potential for significant losses as a result of the presence of two naked puts on your adjusted position, as indicated in Figure 6.13. The 1:3 ratio spread adjustment raises your breakeven point and reduces your trade cost and risk to the upside. However, it raises your lower breakeven point as well. Therefore, although there is a large cushion between the current price ($39) and the downside breakeven point ($30.75), you should still be aware of the potential risk.

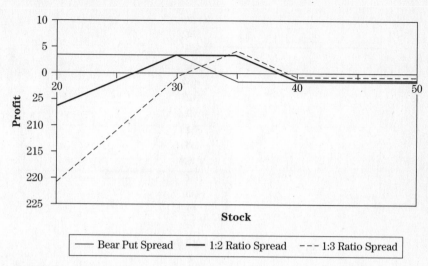

FIGURE 6.13 Rolling Bear Put Spread into 1:2 versus 1:3 Ratio Spread

If you wish to repair your bear put spread position but do not want the margin requirements or potential for large losses in the ratio spread adjustment, you can roll your bear put spread into a higher strike bear put spread by using the same technique we described previously, with one slight change. In rolling from the bear put spread into the 1:2 multiple strike ratio spread, you turned your $35/$30 bear put spread into a long $40 Put/short $35 Put/short $30 Put ratio spread. You can instead roll into a $40/$35 bear put spread by purchasing the $30 short call to close it out when making the adjustment.

Remember that when you made the repair adjustment (we will use the 1:2 adjustment as our example) you sold two $35 Puts for $1.00 each and purchased the $40 Put for $2.00 for a no-cost adjustment. Assume that the $30 Put is trading at $0.25 at the same time you made the adjustment. When adding the $40 Put, you could also simultaneously purchase the $30 Put for $0.25 to close out your additional short Put, and the result is a $40/$35 bear put spread. Because you spent an additional $0.25 to close out the short $30 Put, your new trade cost rises from $1.75 to $2.00.

The additional cost of rolling into the $40/$35 bear put spread as opposed to a 1:2 ratio spread adds slightly to your risk but raises your breakeven point and takes away the potential for significant losses if COST drops sharply before expiration. The maximum profit on the $40/$35 bear put spread is the difference between the strike prices ($5.00) minus the new trade cost ($2.00), which is $3.00 if COST is at or below $35 at expiration. Your new breakeven point is $38, which is the $40 Put strike minus

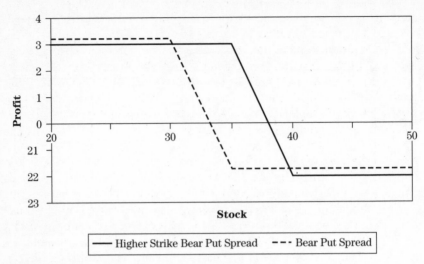

FIGURE 6.14   Rolling into Higher Strike Bear Put Spread

the new trade cost of 2.00. Compare this with your original breakeven point of $33.25 (Figure 6.14).

Although the adjustment adds another $0.25 to your trade cost, the position still has limited risk, raises your breakeven point, and takes away the significant risk potential from the put ratio spread adjustments. Because the underlying stock has moved higher instead of lower, the (OTM) short put in the initial bear put spread will drop in value and can be bought back at a lower cost. As long as that cost is minimal, you can roll into the higher strike bear put spread and achieve the same results of raising your breakeven point without adding too much risk to your position.

Convert to Butterflies

A butterfly is a position that can be seen as the combination of other strategies (for details on butterflies, see Chapter 2). For example, with respect to long butterflies using calls, the position is a combination of a bull call spread and bear call spread with the short option in each position at the same strike price. Another way to establish a long butterfly using calls is to enter into a 1:2 call ratio spread and simply add another long call at the next higher strike.

The reason we highlight these components of the long butterfly is that it will be easier to understand how we can convert a bull call or bear put spread into a butterfly, especially because the adjustment will in some ways build on the previous section, where we covered rolling into a ratio spread. For example, when rolling a bull call spread into a 1:2 call ratio spread, simply add another call at the next higher strike price to make the adjustment a butterfly. A butterfly has limited risk and limited reward, which may be preferred over the ratio spread adjustment, which can potentially have unlimited or significant risk. Moreover, the butterfly adjustments we demonstrate can also be used to change the direction or bias of your original position without adding any significant risk.

Bull Call Spread The reasons for converting a bull call spread into a long butterfly are the same as those for rolling your position into a call ratio spread. The underlying stock has moved higher but your spread has not widened to the full value, and you expect the stock to move sideways until expiration. However, you do not want the margin requirement or potential for large losses that come with the call ratio spread and the presence of the naked call. Therefore, you decide to roll your bull call spread into a butterfly, which has limited risk. Another benefit of rolling into the long butterfly is that doing so will most likely bring in a credit, which will reduce your trade cost and your overall risk.

Assume that with COST at $35 you entered into a $35/$40 bull call spread for a net debit of $1.75. COST moves higher to $39, and you expect the stock to move sideways until expiration. You do not feel that the stock will move much higher but are concerned that it could move back lower and wipe out your unrealized gain. Assume that with COST at $39, the $40 Call is trading at $1.25 and the $45 Call is trading at $0.25, both with the same expiration as your bull call spread. To convert your $35/$40 bull call spread into a long butterfly, sell another $40 Call for $1.25 and purchase the $45 Call at $0.25 for a net credit of $1.00.

Your new position is a long $35 Call/short two $40 Calls/long $45 Call butterfly. Your initial trade cost is reduced from $1.75 to $0.75 as a result of the $1.00 credit received from making the long butterfly adjustment. The adjustment has lowered your risk by reducing your trade cost. This reduction in trade cost also boosts your potential profit. A long butterfly, like a call ratio spread, has its maximum reward when the stock is at the short strike at expiration. If COST is at $40 at expiration, the short calls and the $45 Call will expire worthless, and the long $35 Call will be worth $5.00. Because your trade cost is $0.75, your overall profit is $4.25. If COST moves below $35 by expiration, all the calls will expire worthless and your total loss will be $0.75, which is less than your initial $1.75 at risk with your $35/$40 bull call spread.

If COST moves above $45 at expiration, then your position will still only produce a loss of $0.75. The reason is better understood by looking at the components of your long butterfly: a $35/$40 bull call spread and a

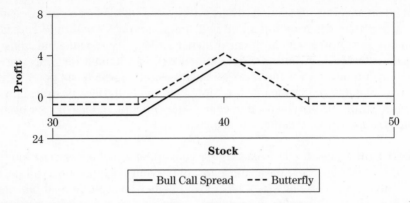

FIGURE 6.15 Rolling a Bull Call Spread into a Long Butterfly

$45/$40 bear call spread. With COST above $45 at expiration, the bull call spread will be worth $5.00 and the bear call spread will be worth $5.00, so they cancel each other out. Therefore, your loss will be limited to your reduced trade cost of $0.75.

A long butterfly has two breakeven points, which are calculated by adding the spread cost to the lowest long strike and subtracting it from the highest long strike. Using the trade cost of $0.75, we find the downside breakeven point to be $35.75 and the upside breakeven point to be $44.25.

The risk/reward profile of the adjusted bull call spread in Figure 6.15 shows how the adjustment creates less risk on the downside and greater profit potential at the short strike. The only downside is if COST does move much higher, where the adjusted long butterfly will produce a loss, whereas the bull call spread will still have a profit. Therefore, you would adjust your spread to a long butterfly only if you expect the stock to move sideways until expiration and especially if you do not expect the stock to move much higher.

Bear Put Spread   The reasons for rolling a bear put spread into a long put butterfly are the same as those for converting a bull call spread into a long call butterfly: The underlying stock has moved lower and is near your short strike, and you expect it to move sideways until expiration. Because you want to avoid the margin requirements of a ratio spread adjustment, as well as the potential for significant risk, you would roll your bear put spread into a long put butterfly. Moreover, because you most likely will be able to roll into the put butterfly for a net credit, you will reduce your position cost and thus your overall risk.

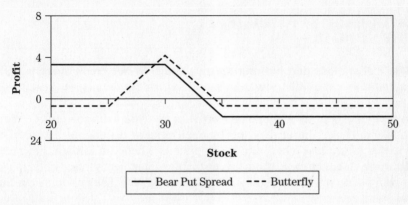

FIGURE 6.16 Bear Put Spread Butterfly

Assume that you entered into a $35/$30 bear put spread with COST at $35 for a net debit of $1.75. Subsequently, COST drops to $30, and you expect the stock to trade sideways until expiration. You also observe that the $30 Put is trading at $1.25 and the $25 Put is trading at $0.25. To convert your bear put spread into a put butterfly, sell another $30 Put for $1.25 and purchase the $25 Put for $0.25 for a net credit of $1.00. Your resulting position is a put butterfly with a long $35 Put/two short $30 Puts/long $25 Put. Because you received a net credit of $1.00 for making the adjustment, your initial trade cost is reduced from $1.75 to $0.75. Therefore, the adjustment immediately reduces your risk by lowering your trade cost (Figure 6.16).

The maximum reward on your put butterfly occurs when the stock is right at the short strike at expiration. If COST is at $30, the $25 and $30 Puts will expire worthless, and the $35 Put will be worth $5.00, for a profit of $4.25 when the reduced trade cost of $0.75 is subtracted. The two breakeven points on the put butterfly, calculated by adding the net debit to the lower long strike price and subtracting it from the upper long strike price, are $25.75 and $34.25.

As the risk/reward profile of the adjusted position shows, the maximum loss on the converted position is the reduced trade cost of $0.75. Because the position was adjusted with COST at $30, you want the stock to move sideways, or at worst slightly higher or lower, until expiration to realize the maximum profit. The only downside in comparison with the unadjusted bear put spread position is that if COST does continue to move below $25, then the bear put spread will still have its maximum reward, whereas the put butterfly will produce a loss. Therefore, the conversion to a put butterfly is not recommended when there is a good chance for the stock to continue moving lower.

BEAR CALL SPREADS/BULL PUT SPREADS

Bear call spreads and bull put spreads are both net credit spreads with limited risk and limited reward. (See Chapter 2 for details on these types of credit spreads.) The goal is to have your spread be OTM at expiration so that your options will expire worthless and you keep the entire credit collected. The credit received can be small or large, depending on the strike prices selected and where the stock price is when you initiate the trade. However, in either case, there are no viable adjustments that can be made to your position without significantly increasing your risk or wiping out the net credit received.

For example, with COST at $35, assume you create a bear call spread by selling the $35 Call for $1.25 and purchasing the $40 Call for $0.25 for a net credit of $1.00. We offer the same advice we offered for naked call and naked put positions—if the stock moves as expected and you have an unrealized gain, the best and safest way to lock in that gain is by closing the position. Purchasing an additional option or spread, whether a call or a put, will not guarantee any profit in your bear call spread, and if the cost of adding such a position is greater than $1.00, then you will wipe out your net credit. Selling additional options will only increase your risk and remove the limited risk characteristics of the credit spread.

The best adjustment that can be recommended is to simply set profit and loss targets so that you can close out the position. In this example, the maximum profit is $1.00 and the maximum risk is $4.00. If you are willing to accept the maximum risk, then you can simply wait until expiration to give the stock a chance to move below the short strike by expiration. If not, you should establish an exit point as recommended under the SCORE trading formula.

CALENDAR SPREADS

Calendar spreads involve the sale of a short-term option and the purchase of a long-term option at the same strike price for a net debit. The strategy can have a bearish, bullish, or neutral bias, depending on what strike prices you select. Either way, the initial maximum profit occurs when the stock is at the short strike at expiration of the short option. Once that option expires, if you still own the long-term option, your potential profit can be quite significant. Because the spread involves a long option and a short option at different expiration dates, there are various adjustments that can be made if the underlying stock is above or below the short-term option strike price at expiration. The possible trade adjustments that can be made for call calendar spreads are the same for put calendar spreads, and therefore we cover both together.

Call Calendar Spread

Stock Moves Higher—Rolling into a Bull Call Spread If you purchase a call calendar spread, you want the stock to be at or below the short-term option strike price at expiration of the short call. If the stock moves too far above the short-term call strike price, then the spread will shrink in value to almost $0 and your short call is in danger of being assigned. If you are assigned, then you will be forced to exercise your long-term call, close out your position, and lose your initial debit paid. However, if the stock does move above the short-term call strike price and you expect it to keep on moving higher, then you can roll the entire position into a long-term vertical bull call spread to profit from the rising price of the underlying stock.

Assume that with COST at $34, you enter into a $35 call calendar spread for a net debit of $1.25. You expect COST to trade sideways for the next month and then move significantly higher. Therefore, you want COST at $35 or slightly below at expiration of the short $35 Call so that it will expire worthless and you will own your long-term $35 Call at a reduced price. Assume that close to expiration of the short term call, COST rises to $37, your short $35 Call is trading at $2.10, and your long $35 Call is trading at $3.00. Your spread has narrowed to $0.90 for an unrealized loss of $0.35, and if you are assigned on your short $35 Call, then you will realize the full loss of $1.25.

If you expect COST to keep rising, then you must close out your short call to avoid a loss, especially as expiration approaches and all time value premium disappears from your short call. Instead of buying back your short call and adding more capital to your position, you can simply roll your calendar spread into a long-term vertical bull call spread. Assume that a $40 Call with the same expiration date as your long $35 Call is trading at $1.50. To roll into a long-term vertical bull call spread, repurchase the short $35 Call for $2.10 and simultaneously sell the long-term $40 Call for $1.50 for a net debit of $0.60. Your new position is now long a long-term $35 Call and short a long-term $40 Call for a $35/$40 vertical bull call spread with a combined trade cost of $1.85 (original net debit of $1.25 plus trade adjustment cost of $0.60).

Your new vertical bull call spread has a breakeven point of $36.85 (long strike plus net debit) and a long time left until expiration. As long as COST continues to move higher, your spread has a maximum profit of $3.15 (difference between strikes minus net debit). The adjustment removes the potential for loss on your calendar spread and gives your position time to realize a profit as long as COST continues to move higher. Therefore, you should only roll up to the long-term bull call spread if the underlying stock has moved above the strike price of your calendar spread and you expect it to continue rising in price.

Stock Moves Higher—Rolling into a Diagonal Ratio Spread   Assume as before that you entered into a $35 calendar spread for a net debit of $1.25 and COST has moved to $37 as expiration approaches on your short $35 Call. If you feel that COST will continue to move somewhat higher in price and possibly move sideways, then you can roll into a diagonal call ratio spread. A diagonal call ratio spread consists of a long-term call and a greater number of short-term calls at a higher strike price. It is the same as a regular call ratio spread except that the short calls at the higher strike are at an earlier expiration date than the long call. The diagonal ratio spread allows you to sell front month calls at a higher strike price to take advantage of time decay and still allow for a profit if the underlying stock moves higher.

With COST now at $37, assume that your short $35 Call is now trading at $2.10 and that a $40 Call with 2 months to expiration (but still less time to expiration than your long $35 Call) is trading at $1.10. To roll into a bullish call diagonal ratio spread, repurchase your short $35 Call for $2.10 and sell two of the mid-term expiration $40 Calls for $1.10 each, for a total of $2.20. The $2.20 premium collected from selling the two $40 Calls will pay for the repurchase of the short $35 Call for $2.10 and leave a net credit of $0.10. Your resulting position is a long $35 Call and short two mid-term $40 Calls for a reduced net debit of $1.15 (your original $1.25 debit reduced by the $0.10 net credit for making the adjustment).

You want COST to be right at the short strike of $40 at expiration of the short calls. If COST is at $40, then the short calls will expire worthless and your long $35 Call will be worth at least $5.00. We say at least $5.00 because the long $35 Call still has time to expiration, and so it will have time value in addition to its intrinsic value of $5.00. With your adjusted trade cost of $1.15 and a minimum value in your long $35 Call of $5.00, you will therefore have a minimum profit of $3.85.

If COST moves above $40 by expiration, then just as with a regular call ratio spread, the presence of the naked $40 Call will begin to reduce your profits until the stock hits the upside breakeven point. In the foregoing example, the estimated upside breakeven point at expiration would be $43.85. At that price, the two $40 Calls will be worth $3.85 each for a total of $7.70, and the long $35 Call will be worth a minimum of $8.85 (minimum because of the potential time value premium still on the long $40 Call) for a net profit of $1.15, which will be offset by the initial spread cost of $1.15. Because the long $35 Call may still have some time value premium left even though it is deep ITM, we can only estimate that the minimum upside breakeven point is $43.85. The downside breakeven point is approximately $36.15 (long $35 strike plus net debit). Again, we say approximately because if COST is at $36.15 at expiration of the short $40 Calls, the long $35 Call will still have time value left and may be worth more than its intrinsic value of $1.15.

Therefore, by rolling into the diagonal call ratio spread with COST at $37, you remove the initial risk of loss on your calendar spread of being assigned on your short call and roll into a bullish spread with an approximate profit zone between $36.15 and $43.85. Given the price of COST at $37, the adjustment is used only when you expect the stock to keep moving slightly higher or sideways until expiration of the short calls. If the short calls expire OTM, then you still have your long $35 Call and various choices for follow-up action (see Chapter 5).

Stock Moves Lower—Rolling into a Lower Strike Bull Call Spread Assume that you entered into a $35 Call calendar spread with COST at $35 for a net debit of $1.25. To better illustrate the steps presented in the following trade adjustment, we use specific expiration months for the long and short calls in the spread. Assume that your $35 call calendar spread consists of a short JUN $35 Call with 1 month to expiration and a long SEP $35 Call with 4 months to expiration. After opening the spread, COST slides lower to $32, and your short JUN $35 Call is almost worthless at $0.25 with just a few days left until expiration. Although COST has dropped in price in the short term, you do expect COST to recover and move somewhat higher by expiration of your SEP $35 Call. If you are confident that your short JUN $35 Call will expire worthless, you can leave it alone and roll your long SEP $35 Call into a lower strike bull call spread. Rolling your SEP $35 Call down into a lower strike bull call spread will lower your breakeven point and profit if COST moves higher.

Assume that your SEP $35 Call is now trading at $1.50 and a SEP $30 Call is trading at $3.00. The process of rolling your long SEP $35 into a lower strike SEP $30/$35 bull call spread is simply a matter of selling two SEP $35 Calls at $1.50 each for a total of $3.00 and using that $3.00 credit to purchase the SEP $30 Call. Your resulting position is a long SEP $30 Call and short SEP $35 Call for a bull call spread. Remember that you did not close the short JUN $35 Call. However, with COST at $32 and expiration a few days away, you expect that option to expire worthless. If you feel very confident about your short option expiring worthless, you can do nothing with it and simply roll the SEP $35 Call into the $30/$35 bull call spread.

Because your adjustment was done at no cost, your overall trade cost is still $1.25. Your new breakeven point on the SEP $30/$35 bull call spread is $31.25 (SEP $30 strike plus net debit). As long as COST stays sideways at its current price of $32 or moves higher by expiration of your SEP bull call spread, you will have a profit. Therefore, your adjustment allows you to turn a possibly losing position into a profitable one as long as COST does not move below $31.25 by expiration of your bull call spread.

If you are concerned about leaving your short JUN $35 Call uncovered despite the fact that it is deep OTM with expiration approaching, you can repurchase the JUN $35 Call to close it out. For example, if the short JUN $35 Call is trading at $0.30, it would require only a small additional capital outlay to close out your short JUN $35 Call. The additional $0.30 debit would be added to your overall trade cost of $1.25 (assuming you rolled your SEP $35 Call into a bull call spread at no cost). Therefore, repurchasing the short JUN $35 Call raises your trade cost to $1.55 and removes any assignment risk should COST suddenly surge higher in the last few days before expiration of the short call.

Rolling the long-term call into a bull call spread at a lower strike is a way to repair your call calendar spread if the stock has moved lower and you expect it to recover over the life of the long-term option. You are basically allowing your short call to expire worthless and repairing your long-term call with one of the call repair strategy adjustments discussed in Chapter 5.

Stock Moves Lower—Convert to a Calendar Strangle   As in the previous example, assume that after you open a $35 Call calendar spread with COST at $35, COST slides lower to $32 with a few weeks left to expiration of the short call. With your call calendar spread, you expect COST to move sideways until expiration of the short call, which will be OTM and expire worthless, and then move higher for significant profits on your long $35 Call. However, what if you still expect the large price movement after expiration of the short call but no longer feel confident that it will be higher?

One way to take the bullish bias out of your call calendar spread and still take advantage of the short-term sideways movement of COST is to convert it to a calendar strangle. With COST at $32, you have a $35 Call calendar spread with a short $35 Call and a long $35 Call at different expiration dates. To convert your position into a calendar strangle, purchase the long-term $30 Put with the same expiration as the long $35 Call and simultaneously sell the short-term $30 Put with the same expiration as your short $35 Call. Assume you can add this OTM $30 Put calendar spread for a net debit of $1.00.

Your new adjusted position will be a short-term short $30/$35 strangle and a long-term long $30/$35 strangle for a total net debit of $2.25 ($1.25 of initial call calendar spread plus $1.00 net debit in adding put calendar spread). You want COST to trade sideways between the strikes of the short

$30/$35 strangle until expiration so that your short $30/$35 strangle will expire worthless and what will remain is your long-term $30/$35 strangle at a reduced price. Because you expect COST to make a significant price movement after expiration of the short options, your long strangle will profit from such a move. With a trade cost of $2.25, the breakeven points on your long $30/$35 strangle are $27.75 and $37.25 (add the trade cost to the upper call strike and subtract it from the lower put strike). However, you will have a couple of months to expiration to wait and allow COST to make its significant move and turn a profit.

Put Calendar Spread

The types of adjustments that can be made to a put calendar spread are the same as those that can be made to a call calendar spread. Therefore, we briefly illustrate the different adjustments for put calendar spreads and recommend you read the previous section first to review the different situations where each adjustment is preferable.

Stock Moves Lower—Rolling into a Bear Put Spread Assume that you purchased a $35 put calendar spread with COST at $35 for a net debit of $1.50. COST moves lower to $33 before expiration of your short option, and you expect COST to keep moving lower. To profit from COST moving lower and avoid early assignment on your short $35 Put, you can close your short put and roll your long $35 Put into a bear put spread. Assume that with COST at $33, your short $35 Put is trading at $2.25 and a $30 Put with the same expiration as your long $35 Put is trading at $2.00.

To convert your $35 put calendar spread into a long-term bear put spread, repurchase your short $35 Put for $2.25 and sell the $30 Put for $2.00 for a net debit of $0.25. Your resulting position is a long $35 Put and a short $30 Put for a long-term bear put spread. Your original calendar spread cost $1.50, and the adjusted position requires an additional debit of $0.25. Therefore, your new bear put spread adjusted trade cost is $1.75, and your new breakeven point is $33.25 (long put strike at $35 minus net debit).

Rolling your put calendar spread into a bear put spread is appropriate when the underlying stock has moved below your strike price before expiration of the short $35 Put and you expect the stock to continue moving lower. By making the adjustment, you remove the potential of getting assigned on your short option and convert your position into a bearish one that will profit as the stock keeps moving lower.

Stock Moves Lower—Rolling into a Diagonal Ratio Spread If the underlying stock has moved below your put calendar strike price and you expect the stock to move sideways or slightly lower from its current price, you can convert your put calendar spread into a diagonal ratio spread to take advantage of the sideways movement and remove the risk of assignment of your short ITM put. Assume you purchase a COST $35 put calendar spread for a net debit of $1.50 with COST at $35. Soon thereafter, COST moves lower to $32, and you expect COST to move in a sideways pattern for an extended period of time and perhaps move lower but not by too much. To take advantage of this extended sideways movement and avoid assignment on your short $35 Put, you can roll your position into a diagonal put ratio spread. Remember that a diagonal ratio spread is the same as a regular put ratio spread except that the short puts have an earlier expiration date than the long put in the spread.

Assume that with COST at $32, your short $35 Put is worth $3.25 and the next month's $30 Put is trading at $1.75. To roll into a diagonal ratio spread, repurchase the short $35 Put of your put calendar spread for $3.25 and sell two of the next month's $30 Puts at $1.75 each, for a total of $3.50 and a net credit of $0.25. Remember that the expiration date of the two short $30 Puts is between the expiration dates of your short and your long $35 Puts in your calendar spread. Your new position is a long-term $35 Put and short two mid-term $30 Puts for a total debit of $1.25 (original calendar spread net debit of $1.50 minus trade adjustment net credit of $0.25), which is a $35/$30 diagonal put ratio spread.

The intent of the position is to have COST at $30, or as close to $30 as possible, by expiration of the short puts so that they will expire worthless. For example, if COST is at $30, your short $30 Puts will expire worthless, and your long $35 Put will be worth at least $5.00 (minimum of $5.00 because the $35 Put will also have some time value premium left). With your $35 Put worth a minimum of $5.00, your minimum profit at expiration of the short $30 Puts is $3.75 ($5.00 intrinsic value of $35 Put minus adjusted trade cost of $1.25).

If COST moves back above $35 by the expiration of the short $30 Puts, then your short puts will expire worthless and your $35 Put will have some time value premium left. If the stock is well above $35 at expiration of the short puts, the time value premium in the long $35 Put may have shrunk below your adjusted trade cost of $1.25 for a loss. You can choose to hold on to your long $35 Put if you expect the stock to move lower, close out your long $35 Put for a small loss, or make another trade adjustment to your long $35 Put (see Chapter 5 for long put trade adjustments).

If COST moves significantly lower than $30 at expiration of your short puts, then you can have significant losses due to the presence of the extra naked put in your diagonal ratio spread. The theoretical downside breakeven point is $26.25 at expiration of the short puts. At $26.25, the long $35 Put will be worth a minimum of $8.75 (plus any time value premium remaining), and the two $30 Puts will be worth a total of $7.50, for a profit of $1.25, which is offset by your initial trade cost of $1.25. Therefore, $26.25 is the estimated downside breakeven point at the expiration of the short puts. The breakeven point may be lower, given that the long $35 Put will be worth slightly more than its intrinsic value because of the additional time left to expiration of your long put.

Rolling your put calendar spread into a diagonal ratio spread removes the possibility of assignment on your short $35 Put in your put calendar spread after the stock has moved lower. You want the stock to move sideways or slightly lower by expiration of the short $30 Puts so that your ratio spread can possibly reach the maximum reward, which occurs when the stock is at the short strike at expiration. If the stock keeps moving lower, you will have the potential for substantial losses, and therefore this adjustment is not used if there is a good chance the stock will fall much further by the expiration of the short puts.

Stock Moves Higher—Rolling into a Higher Strike Bear Put Spread   As before, assume that you purchase a $35 put calendar spread with COST at $35 for a net debit of $1.50. With expiration approaching, COST is at $39 and your short $35 Put is practically worthless. Your long $35 Put also has shrunk in value, and although you expect COST to move lower, you are not sure whether it will move back below $35. However, you do expect a move back to $35. You therefore want to raise the breakeven point on your position so that if COST does move back toward $35, you can realize a profit.

Assume that with COST at $39, your long-term $35 Put is trading at $0.75, and the $40 Put with the same expiration date is trading at $2.00. To roll your $35 put calendar spread into a higher strike bear put spread, sell two long-term $35 Puts at $0.75 each for a total of $1.50 and use the $1.50 credit to purchase the $40 Put of the same expiration date for $2.00, for a net debit of $0.50. Your new position is a $40/$35 bear put spread for an adjusted trade cost of $2.00 (original calendar spread debit of $1.50 plus adjustment net debit of $0.50). Your breakeven point on your new bear put spread is $38 (long $40 strike minus net debit), and your maximum reward at expiration is $3.00 if COST is at or below $35 at expiration of the bear call spread.

Remember that you have not closed out your short $35 Put. With expiration approaching, that short $35 Put is close to worthless, and with COST at $39, it has a good chance of expiring OTM. However, you should still be aware that it does exist, and if COST suddenly drops sharply before expiration, you will have a loss on your remaining naked put. If you want to remove that risk, you can repurchase the short $35 Put for its current price to close out the position. Just remember to add that additional capital outlay, no matter how small, to your adjusted trade cost.

Stock Moves Higher—Rolling into a Calendar Strangle   You purchase a $35 put calendar spread for a net debit of $1.50 with COST at $35. Shortly thereafter, COST moves higher to $37. Your analysis is that COST will move sideways until expiration of the short $35 Put and thereafter will have a significant price move, but you are no longer sure about which direction. You can take advantage of this short-term sideways movement and the expected future price breakout by converting your put calendar spread into a calendar strangle.

With COST at $37, assume that a $40 call calendar spread with the same expiration dates as your $35 put calendar spread can be opened for a net debit of $1.25. By adding the $40 call calendar spread, you will have a short-term short strangle made up of the short $35 Put and the short $40 Call and a long-term strangle made up of the long $35 Put and the long $40 Call. Your new trade cost will be $2.75 when the costs of both calendar spreads are combined. If COST stays between the short strike prices by expiration of the short options—that is, moves sideways—then both the short call and the short put will expire worthless, and you will be left with a long-term $35/$40 strangle.

If COST makes a subsequent large price move as expected, then you will have a chance for a profit, given your long strangle position. Your new breakeven points with the $35/$40 strangle, calculated by adding the adjusted net debit to the call strike and subtracting it from the put strike, are $42.75 and $32.25. With COST at $37 when the adjustment was made, you need COST to make a large price move before expiration. This trade adjustment allows you to convert your directional put calendar spread into a nondirectional trade when you expect a large price swing in the future after the stock moves sideways for a short period of time.

Butterfly Spreads

Butterfly spreads are the most versatile of all the complex option strategies. With a butterfly spread, you can go short or long volatility, go market neutral or have a directional bias, and use time decay to your advantage, all while establishing a wide profit zone. Despite a wide profit zone and putting many Greeks to work for you, the underlying can still move against your expectations. However, the versatile butterfly spread is easy to adjust. For illustration purposes, the following example focuses on calls only, but all positions and adjustments can equally be done with puts.

Long Butterfly to Long Condor   Assume that with GOOG trading at $390, you open a 1-month to expiration long call butterfly using the $340/$390/$440 strikes for a net debit of $24.50. The position has expiration

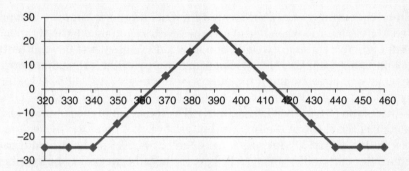

FIGURE 6.17 GOOG Butterfly Profit Profile

breakeven points of $364.50 and $415.50, and if GOOG is anywhere between those two prices at expiration, the position will produce a profit (Figure 6.17). This butterfly will have a maximum profit of $25.50 if GOOG is at $390 at expiration, and the profit potential decreases as it approaches the breakeven points.

The expectation is that GOOG will stay within the breakeven points as expiration approaches, but sometimes a stock can move and raise concerns that it might continue moving toward or even past the breakeven points. Assume that a week after entering this call butterfly, GOOG drifts higher to $420 and you feel that GOOG might continue to move up and down near this level but still stay somewhat range bound. The stock has moved past the upside breakeven point, and if the stock stays close to $420 at expiration, you will suffer a loss on your position. However, you can adjust the position to widen the profit zone and move the upside breakeven point higher so that you can still realize a profit if the underlying stays within the wider adjusted profit zone. The way to achieve this is to convert the long call butterfly into a long call condor.

The easiest way to shift the butterfly higher into a wide long condor is to add another same-strike-width call butterfly whose lower wing overlaps the body of the original butterfly and whose body overlaps the upper wing of the original butterfly. Let's use an example to illustrate this. We will use "+" or "−" to keep clear which strikes we are long and which strikes we are short. The original butterfly was a +1/−2/+1 butterfly with the $340/$390/$440 strikes. To overlap a new butterfly as described, you would select a +1/−2/+1 call butterfly with $390/$440/$490 strikes, which can be purchased for $20. Let's see what the net effect of these overlapping positions is.

The single $340 call strike from the original butterfly is left untouched after the adjustment. The new $390/$440/$490 butterfly is long one $390 Call, which offsets one of the two short $390 Calls from the original butterfly, leaving you net short one $390 Call. The new butterfly is short two $440 Calls, and when it is overlapped with the original butterfly's long $440 Call, you end up net short one $440 Call. Finally, the new butterfly has one long $490 Call that does not overlap with the original butterfly. If we now summarize all of the effects of the new $390/$440/$490 butterfly overlapping the original $340/$390/$440 butterfly, we are left with one +$340/–$390/–$440/+$490 long condor. The total cost of the resulting long condor is the debit of the original butterfly ($24.50) and the debit of the new butterfly ($20.00), for a total net debit of $44.50. This long condor has a maximum profit of $5.50, which is the distance between the short strikes ($50.00) minus the net debit ($44.50).

Figure 6.18 shows that the breakeven points of the new position are $384.50 and $445.50, compared with the original butterfly breakeven points of $364.50 and $415.50. As you can see, the adjustment of the long call butterfly has shifted the breakeven points higher, but this comes at a cost. As noted, the original butterfly has a debit of $24.50 and a maximum reward potential of $25.50 right at $390 at expiration, whereas the new long call condor has a net debit of $44.50 and a maximum profit of $5.50. The maximum profit of the adjusted position is smaller than the original, but there is an important distinction between the two positions. The long call butterfly has its maximum profit at one specific point at expiration (the middle strikes), and that drops off sharply as you approach the breakeven points. The long call condor, however, despite a lower maximum profit of $5.50, can realize that profit anywhere between $390 and $440 at expiration. This is one of the risk/reward trade-offs with condors versus butterflies; the condor has a smaller maximum profit potential, but you can achieve it over a wider zone at expiration.

This adjustment lets you stay with the position longer if the underlying happens to move away from the body of the original butterfly. Before

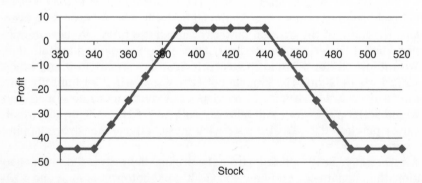

FIGURE 6.18 Long Condor Profit Profile

making the adjustment, you have to make sure that the cost of the additional butterfly does not turn the entire position into a guaranteed loss. Because of the cost of the adjustment, we recommend making only one adjustment along these lines and only if your assumptions have changed to where you are concerned that the underlying stock will not revert back toward the profit zone of the original butterfly.

Combinations

INTRODUCTION

A combination involves the purchase or sale of both calls and puts. The most popular forms of combinations that we cover in this chapter are straddles and strangles. Although these strategies are nondirectional, it is still possible to make adjustments to add a directional bias to the position, take advantage of short-term sideways movements while waiting for price breakouts on long combinations, or even to hedge the potentially unlimited losses that could occur on short combinations.

LONG STRADDLE

Long straddles are entered into when you expect a large price breakout in the underlying stock but are not sure about the direction. Usually straddles are entered into using a long time to expiration to give the underlying stock enough time to make the large move higher or lower and also to minimize the effects of time decay because you are long both a call and a put. We cover various possible trade adjustments to straddles that allow you to adjust to the movements of the underlying stock. Because a straddle is profitable whether the stock moves higher or lower (as long as it moves past the breakeven points), we present strategies to account for either upward or downward movement, where appropriate.

Straps/Strips

Although a long straddle consists of an equal number of calls and puts at the same strike price, you can also add different numbers of calls or puts to introduce a slight directional bias to your position, or you can add those additional calls and puts at different strikes to change the risk/reward profile of your position. Adding additional calls and puts at the same strike price of the straddle creates a position called either a *strap* or *strip*, depending on whether you add calls or puts, respectively.

A strap is a straddle with more calls than puts. Because you have more calls than puts in the position, the strategy has a bullish bias. Assume you purchase a 6-month COST $35 straddle for $6.00 when COST is at $35. This position is appropriate if you expect COST to make a significant move over the next couple of months or so but you are not sure in which direction. However, what if you do have a slight bias to the upside? You can still have a nondirectional trade and establish a bullish bias by adding an additional $35 Call to your position.

Assume that the $35 Call in your $35 straddle is trading at $3.00. To create the strap, you simply purchase an additional $35 Call, and your resulting position will be one $35 Put and two $35 Calls with the same expiration date. The addition of the extra $35 Call will raise your total trade cost from $6.00 to $9.00. On the original $35 straddle, your upside breakeven point is the strike price ($35) plus the trade cost ($6.00), which is $41. The strap has a higher cost ($9.00), but the presence of the additional call lowers your upside breakeven point at expiration from $41 to $39.50. At $39.50, each $35 Call will be worth $4.50 each, for a total of $9.00, which offsets your $35 strap trade cost.

The downside to adding the extra call and increasing your trade cost is that it lowers your breakeven point to the downside. Because your new trade cost is $9.00, your downside breakeven point at expiration moves from $29 ($35 strike minus $6.00 cost) to $26 ($35 strike minus $9.00 revised trade cost). If the stock moves lower instead of higher, it will have to make an even bigger move for the position to realize a profit. That is why the strap is only recommended with a bullish bias where you feel it is more likely than not that the expected move will be higher. However, if the move lower is significant, you can still realize a profit due to the presence of the $35 Put.

As Figure 7.1 indicates, the strap requires a larger move to the downside for the position to be profitable. However, the additional call lowers your upside breakeven point to reflect your bullish bias. Because the loss is larger if the underlying stock is right at the strike price at expiration with a strap, you should use this strategy only with stocks you feel are more likely to move away from your strike price by expiration.

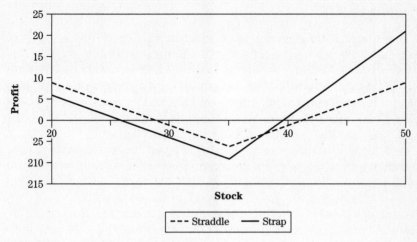

FIGURE 7.1 Straddle versus Strap

If your bias is bearish on your straddle, then you might consider a strip, which involves the purchase of an additional put at the same strike price and expiration date of your straddle. For example, assume that the $35 Put with the same expiration date as your $35 straddle is trading at $3.00. To introduce a bearish bias into your straddle, purchase the additional $35 Put for $3.00, which results in two $35 Puts and one $35 Call for a strip with a cost of $9.00 ($3.00 cost of $35 Put added to $6.00 cost of $35 straddle).

The strip has a higher downside breakeven point due to the presence of the additional put. Your original breakeven point of $29 (on the $35 straddle purchased for $6.00) is raised to $30.50. With COST at $30.50 at expiration, the two $35 Puts will be worth $4.50 each for a total of $9.00, which will offset the trade cost of $9.00. Although your downside breakeven point will be higher on your strip, so will your upside breakeven point. Your original upside breakeven point of $41 will be raised to $44 as a result of the higher strip cost. Therefore, the strip is only entered into when you want a nondirectional strategy with a bearish bias (Figure 7.2).

Remember, with strips and straps, you should give the position as much time to expiration as possible so that if the underlying stock does not move as expected, there is still time for the stock to move and produce a profit. Therefore, strips and straps should be established using options with as long a time to expiration as possible.

One suggestion we offer for you to experiment with is that if your bullish or bearish bias is only temporary—that is, you expect a significant move over the life of the straddle in either direction, but over the next

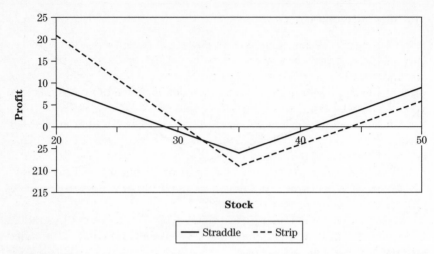

FIGURE 7.2 Straddle versus Strip

month or so you believe that the stock will move in one direction or the other based on technical analysis or unexpected news—you can add the directional bias to your straddle for the short term. The way you add such a short-term directional bias is to create a strip or strap using short-term options. We illustrate this position with an example.

Assume that you purchase a 6-month COST $35 straddle for $6.00 with COST at $35. In the next month or so, you see possible weakness in COST, and it could drift lower, but overall you still expect a significant move in either direction by expiration of your long straddle. You can try to take advantage of this short-term weakness by converting your $35 straddle to a time strip by using a short-term put. Assume that a 2-month $35 Put is trading at $1.25. If you add the 2-month $35 Put to your position, then your total trade cost will increase from $6.00 to $7.25, and you have a long $35 straddle and a 2-month $35 Put.

Assume that COST does move lower to $32 by expiration of the short-term $35 Put. The short-term $35 Put will be worth $3.00 at expiration for a profit of $1.75 because your cost was $1.25. You can apply that $1.75 profit to your original trade cost of $6.00 for a new reduced trade cost of $4.25. Because you reduced the cost of your $35 straddle, your breakeven points are now closer together and your risk is lower. If COST keeps moving lower or reverses and moves higher, you still have plenty of time left on your reduced cost $35 straddle to make a profit. Therefore, you can create time strips and time straps using short-term options to take advantage of short-term directional biases you have in the underlying stock and reduce your cost and risk.

Modified Straps/Strips

A modified strap is the same as a regular strap except the additional call is added at a strike price above or below the straddle strike price. Our recommendation of whether to add the call at the higher or lower strike price depends on where the underlying stock is at the time. Assume that you purchased a 6-month COST $35 straddle for $6.00 with COST at $35. Two months later, COST is at $30, you feel that COST could move back higher, and you want to take advantage of the large price swing in COST to reduce your risk and perhaps boost your profits somewhat. You still expect COST to continue to move from its current price, but if COST does move back higher instead, you could lose time value and any unrealized gain as COST slowly makes its way back higher.

Assume that a $30 Call with the same expiration as your $35 straddle is trading for $2.50. You can purchase the $30 Call and create a modified strap, which includes a $35 Put and a $35 Call as well as the $30 Call, for a total trade cost of $8.50 when the additional call premium is added. The question is, Why would you add more premium to your position? The answer is easily seen by looking at the risk/reward profile of the modified strap (Figure 7.3). If COST is between $30 and $35 at expiration, then the $35 Call will expire worthless, and the $30 Call and the $35 Put will combine for a total value of $5.00. For example, if COST is at $33, the $30 Call will be worth $3.00 and the $35 Put will be worth $2.00, for a total of $5.00. Because you paid $8.50 for the modified strap, your loss if COST is between $30 and $35 is $3.50.

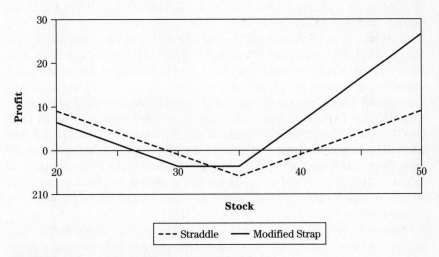

FIGURE 7.3 Long Straddle versus Modified Strap

If COST moves above $35 by expiration, then the addition of the $30 Call creates a bullish bias in your position. As COST moves higher, you have two calls to realize a profit. For example, if COST is at $37 at expiration, the put will expire worthless, but your $30 Call will be worth $7.00 and your $35 Call will be worth $2.00, for a combined value of $9.00 and a profit of $0.50. If you still had your $35 straddle for $6.00, your position would have a loss of $4.00. Therefore, the modified strap lowers your upside breakeven point and creates a bullish bias.

Like the regular strap, the modified strap lowers your downside breakeven point. Your original downside breakeven point on your $35 straddle was $29, and on the modified strap, the breakeven point is $26.50. At $26.50, your calls will expire worthless and the $35 Put will be worth $8.50, which offsets your higher cost.

The benefit of rolling into a modified strap after the underlying stock has moved lower is that you reduce your maximum loss at the original strike price. Your original $35 straddle has a loss of $6.00 at $35, whereas the modified strap has a loss of $3.50. The downside is that you are locked into this minimum loss over the range of stock prices between $30 and $35. It should come as no surprise that the picture of the risk/reward profile in Figure 7.3 looks like the risk/reward profile of a long strangle. The reason is that in effect your position has become a long (ITM) strangle with a $30 Call and a $35 Put. With the $35 Call, the position has a bullish bias. Therefore, you would achieve the same result if you purchased an ITM $30/$35 strangle for $6.00 and added a $35 Call for $2.50. The decision to convert to the modified strap depends on whether you feel that by expiration, the stock will move outside the $30/$35 strike prices, as with any strangle. Therefore, the trade adjustment lowers your overall risk at the strike price of the straddle and creates a bullish bias.

This example demonstrates adding the $30 Call after the stock has moved lower. If you add the $30 strike call initially or after the stock has moved higher, then you will be paying a high premium, given the intrinsic and time values built into that call. For example, with COST at $35 when you opened your 6-month $35 straddle, the ITM $30 Call might be worth $7.00. Adding the $30 Call will increase your total trade cost to $13.00. Therefore, COST will have to make a significant move down to hit the much lower breakeven point. Moreover, if COST stays right near the strike price, your maximum loss will be bigger than your loss on the unadjusted straddle. Therefore, we only recommend creating a modified strap with the lower strike call when the stock has moved to that strike price to reduce the cost.

You can also create a modified strap using the next higher strike call, that is, the $40 Call. If COST is below $40, then the (OTM) $40 Call will be cheaper, and therefore converting to the modified strap will not increase your overall trade cost by that much. For example, assume that with COST at $37 you want to convert your COST $35 straddle to a modified strap, and the $40 Call with the same expiration as your straddle is trading at $1.50. By adding the $40 Call to your $35 straddle, you increase your overall trade cost from $6.00 to $7.50. Your previous upside breakeven point on the $35 straddle was $41.00, and your modified strap will have a revised breakeven point of $41.25. With COST at $41.25 at expiration, your $35 Call will be worth $6.25 and the $40 Call will be worth $1.25, for a total of $7.50, which is offset by your higher trade cost of $7.50. Adding the higher strike call, therefore, raises your upside breakeven point and, because your overall cost is higher, also lowers your downside breakeven point.

Spreading out your breakeven points requires a bigger move from the underlying stock for your position to be profitable and raises your risk because of the increased cost. The benefit you receive is that your modified strap has the potential for bigger profits should COST continue to move higher as a result of the additional $40 Call. For example, if COST is at $45, your original $35 straddle will be worth $10.00 for a profit of $4.00, whereas your modified strap will have a value of $15.00 ($10.00 for the $35 Call and $5.00 for the $40 Call) for a profit of $7.50. Therefore, you get a profit boost on the upside despite the bigger move required from the underlying stock. We only recommend the modified strap using the higher strike call when you expect an exceptionally large move upward in the underlying stock and can purchase the upper strike OTM so that it is cheaper.

The modified strips follow the same structure and analysis as that for the modified straps. The use of the upper strike put for the modified strip will create a type of ITM strangle position using the $35 straddle and the $40 Put. For example, assume that after you purchase the COST $35 straddle for $6.00, COST moves to $40, and the $40 Put with the same expiration as your straddle is trading at $2.50. To convert your position into a modified strip, simply purchase the $40 Put, and your overall trade cost increases from $6.00 to $8.50. The calculation of the profit and loss in the modified strip is the same as with the modified strap, and the risk/reward profile is detailed in Figure 7.4.

Just as with modified straps, a modified strip using the upper strike put creates a bearish bias in your straddle position, reduces your potential loss right at the straddle strike price, and also affects your breakeven points (raises your lower and higher breakeven points). The reason for converting to a modified strip is that you expect the stock to reverse and make a significant move lower and you want a bearish bias in your position. However, you still make a profit if COST should continue to move higher.

Calendar Straddle

When you purchase a long straddle, your expectation is that the stock will make a significant move higher or lower by expiration. To give the

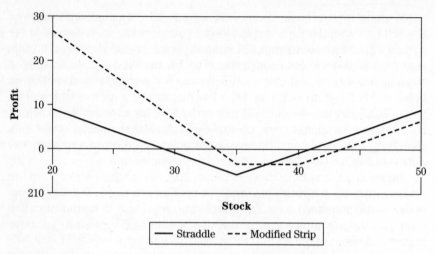

FIGURE 7.4 Long Straddle versus Modified Strip with Higher Strike Put

underlying stock as much time as possible, use long-term options—
4 months to expiration, for example. Sometimes when you purchase a
straddle, however, the stock will stay quiet for a period of time before moving in one direction or the other.

There is a trade adjustment that can help you take advantage of
these short-term quiet periods and reduce the trade cost and risk in your
long straddle. The adjustment is to convert your long straddle into a calendar straddle. Calendar spreads in general are meant to take advantage of
short-term sideways movement, reduce your long-term trade cost and risk,
and then profit from price breakouts in one direction or the other after expiration of the short-term option. You can get the same benefits by creating
a calendar straddle except that after the short options expire, you do not
need to pick a direction because you will profit from a price breakout in
either direction.

Assume that after you purchased a 6-month COST $35 straddle for
$6.00 with COST at $35, COST enters into a sideways trading pattern, and
you do not expect any price breakout in the next few weeks. You observe
that a 1-month COST $35 straddle is trading at $2.75. Because you expect
COST to trade around $35 until expiration of the 1-month straddle, you
can sell that straddle to collect the premium and benefit from the lack
of movement in the underlying stock and time decay. You will not have a
naked position because you already own the long $35 straddle. Therefore,
you can sell the short-term $35 straddle and collect $2.75 in premium. This
$2.75 in premium will reduce your long-term $35 straddle cost from $6.00
to $3.25.

Selling the short-term $35 straddle against your long-term $35 straddle is equivalent to buying a $35 call calendar spread and a $35 put calendar spread. Therefore, your risk is limited to your net debit, which in this case is $3.25. The best scenario would be if COST is right at $35 at expiration of the short $35 straddle. At $35, the short put and short call will expire worthless, you keep the entire premium collected ($2.75), and you still have the long $35 straddle at a reduced price of $3.25. This reduced price brings your breakeven points closer to your straddle strike price and reduces your risk. Therefore, if COST does make a significant move by expiration of the long $35 straddle, you will have increased profits as a result of the reduced cost.

The worst-case scenario occurs if COST makes a significant move in either direction before expiration of the short-term $35 straddle. If COST makes a large move higher or lower, then one side of your short straddle could be assigned. Moreover, the spread between the two straddles will shrink to zero, just as in regular calendar spreads, and your maximum loss will be the adjusted debit of $3.25. Between these best- and worst-case scenarios is what you most likely expect to happen, that COST will be close to $35 at expiration. If COST is very near $35, then you can close out your short options before you are assigned and lock in a profit. For example, if COST is at $34 during the week of expiration, your short-term $35 straddle is probably trading at $1.50. You can close out the position for a profit of $1.25 and avoid assignment on your short put.

The $1.25 profit on your short straddle reduces the original $6.00 cost of your COST $35 straddle to $4.75. Your breakeven points are now $39.75 and $30.25. The calendar straddle adjustment allowed you to take advantage of the sideways movement of COST in the short term and reduce your overall trade cost. If, after expiration of the short straddle, you still feel that COST will move sideways, you can sell the next 1-month straddle to bring in more premium and lower your adjusted trade cost even more.

Rolling a Long Straddle into an Iron Butterfly

An iron butterfly involves the purchase of a straddle and the sale of an OTM strangle. The sale of the OTM strangle reduces the cost of your long straddle but also limits your maximum profit. If you break down the position into pieces, you will see that it is also the combination of a bull call spread and a bear put spread with the long options at the same strike price. The iron butterfly is useful as an initial adjustment or to take advantage of relatively expensive options in short-term expiration months to create a diagonal iron butterfly. In both cases, the idea behind the adjustment is that the premium taken in from the sale of the OTM strangle reduces your trade cost and thus reduces your risk.

Assume you purchase a 3-month COST $35 straddle for $4.00 with COST at $35. You expect COST to make a large move higher or lower but feel that the breakeven points of your straddle might be at the edges of where COST is expected to move. In other words, you expect COST to make a move, but you are not sure whether it will move far enough past the breakeven points to make the position profitable. To reduce the cost of the straddle, you can sell the OTM strangle of the same expiration date. You observe that the $30/$40 strangle is trading for $1.25. To create the iron butterfly, sell the OTM strangle for $1.25, which reduces the cost of your long straddle from $4.00 to $2.75.

Your maximum loss on the adjusted iron butterfly is limited to the debit paid ($2.75). The upside and downside breakeven points are calculated by subtracting and adding the debit paid from the straddle strike of $35, which results in $32.25 and $37.75, respectively. Your maximum reward is also limited because you now have a short $30 Put and a short $40 Call to go with your long $35 straddle. The reward is limited to the difference between the straddle strike and one of the strangle strikes minus the debit paid. For example, if COST is at $29 at expiration, the calls will expire worthless and the remaining long $35 Put and short $30 Put will be worth a combined $5.00, for a profit of $2.25.

As the risk/reward profile demonstrates in Figure 7.5, the iron butterfly reduces the overall trade risk as well as your potential profit on the upside and the downside. However, if you expect a smaller move in the price of the underlying stock but are not sure of the direction, then the iron butterfly will allow you to create a nondirectional position at a lower cost than the outright purchase of a straddle.

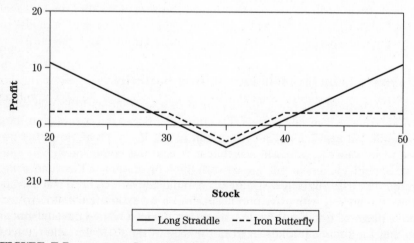

FIGURE 7.5 Iron Butterfly versus Long Straddle

Diagonal Iron Butterfly

The calendar straddle described in the previous section explained how to take advantage of short-term sideways movement when you own a long-term straddle. You can also take advantage of short-term sideways movement in the underlying stock by selling a short-term strangle instead of a short-term straddle. The short-term strangle will bring in less premium but allows more room for the stock to move in the short term before the short options are ITM.

Assume you purchase a 3-month COST $35 straddle for $4.00 with COST at $35 and you expect the stock to move sideways in the first month or so. You observe that a 1-month OTM $30/$40 strangle is trading at $0.75. To take advantage of the sideways movement of COST in the next couple of weeks, you could sell the short strangle and collect $0.75 of premium to create a diagonal iron butterfly. The $0.75 in premium collected reduces the cost of your long $35 straddle from $4.00 to $3.25.

In the short term, you want COST to be between the short strikes of your strangle ($30 and $40) so that it expires worthless and you can keep the entire premium collected. If COST is between $30 and $40 at expiration of the short strangle, then you will keep the $0.75 in premium and have a reduced trade cost for your long straddle, which lowers your risk and narrows the spread on your breakeven points.

Your position will still produce a profit if COST makes a large price swing prior to expiration of the short strangle. Because the difference between the strangle strikes and the straddle strikes is $5.00 and your trade cost is $3.25, you will still realize a profit if COST moves outside the short strangle strike prices. For example, if COST is at $42 at expiration of the short strangle, the puts will expire worthless and the long $35 Call and the short $40 Call will combine for a value of $5.00, for a profit of $1.75.

If the short strangle expires worthless, you still have your long $35 straddle at a reduced cost of $3.25. You can decide to sell the next 1-month strangle short to bring in more premium and further reduce your trade cost and risk. As long as COST stays between the two strike prices of the short strangle by expiration, you can keep rolling forward to the next month and bring in more and more premium.

Partial Iron Butterfly

The iron butterfly involves the sale of both the OTM call and the OTM put in conjunction with your purchase of a long straddle. However, you can also introduce a bias to your iron butterfly position by selling only one of the OTM options of the strangle if you expect a potentially larger move in one direction or the other. For example, assume you expect a large move in COST and purchase a 3-month $35 straddle for $4.00 with COST at $35. You do have a slight bias and feel that the potential move in COST could be higher rather than lower, and you do not want to cut off your potential profits to the upside. However, you do want to reduce your trade cost if possible.

Assume that the OTM $30 Put with the same expiration as your long straddle is trading at $1.00. You can sell the $30 Put, collect $1.00 in premium, and reduce your overall trade cost from $4.00 to $3.00. The reduced trade cost reduces your risk but also moves the breakeven points closer to the strike price of the long $35 straddle. If COST moves higher, your potential profit is unlimited as long as COST moves above the upside breakeven point of $38 (straddle strike of $35 plus reduced debit of $3.00). On the downside, no matter how far COST moves below $30, your position value is limited to $5.00, which is the difference between the long $35 Put and the short $30 Put. With a maximum value of $5.00, your maximum reward is $2.00.

As the risk/reward profile demonstrates in Figure 7.6, the partial iron butterfly with the short $30 Put has an upward bias with unlimited profit potential if COST moves higher. On the downside, the potential profit is limited but still significant, given the reduced trade cost of $3.00. Therefore, the bullish partial iron butterfly is used when you want to open a nondirectional position but with a bullish bias without the additional cost of the straps or modified straps covered in the earlier section. To create a bearish modified iron butterfly, simply sell the $40 Call to reduce your trade cost, and the risk/reward profile is similar to Figure 7.6, except that

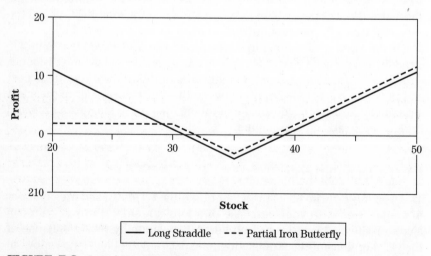

FIGURE 7.6 Partial Iron Butterfly versus Long Straddle

the limited profits occur if COST moves above $40, whereas the potential for significant profits exists to the downside.

Long Call/Long Put Adjustments

Remember that a straddle is made up of a long call and a long put at the same strike price. If the stock makes a significant move in any direction, either the call or the put will be ITM, increases in value, and produces a profit for the position if the stock moves past the straddle breakeven points. Therefore, any of the possible adjustments covered in Chapter 5 can be added to the long straddle to adjust either the long call or the long put portion of the position. For example, you can use protective calls and puts or call and put replacement strategies to hedge your risk or boost your profits. Therefore, you should review many of the strategies in Chapter 5 and see how they can be applied to either the long call or the long put of your long straddle position.

LONG STRANGLE

A long strangle involves the purchase of an OTM put and an OTM call and is also a nondirectional strategy. By using OTM options, the position cost is less than that of the long straddle, but the underlying stock has to make a large move for the position to be profitable. Just as with the long straddle, there are a few trade adjustments that can be made to reduce your overall risk and perhaps boost your profits.

Diagonal Iron Butterfly

A strangle requires a very large move in the underlying stock for the position to be profitable. Therefore, a long time to expiration is preferred to give the stock more than enough time to make the required move. However, in the meantime, the stock may move sideways or not at all while you wait for the large anticipated move. You can take advantage of this sideways movement by converting your position into a diagonal iron butterfly by selling the front-month straddle at the strike price between your strangle strikes. As the stock moves sideways, the premiums in the short straddle will decrease because of time decay, and you will be able to close out your short straddle for a profit. Any profit you earn from the short straddle sale will reduce the overall cost of your long strangle and narrow the spread between the breakeven points.

Assume that you purchase a 3-month COST $30/$40 strangle for $1.00 with COST at $35. You expect a large price breakout by expiration, but in the short term you feel that the stock will go sideways and you want to take advantage of this movement. You observe that the 1-month $35 straddle is trading at $2.50, and because you expect COST to hover around $35 for the next few weeks, you can sell the $35 straddle and collect $2.50 in premium. Because you have a long $30/$40 strangle, your short straddle is covered. However, there will be a small margin requirement because the combination of the short straddle and the long-term strangle creates two credit spreads ($35/$30 bull put spread and $35/$40 bear call spread).

The best scenario would be if COST is right at $35 at the expiration of the short straddle. If COST is at $35, the short straddle would expire worthless, and you would keep the entire $2.50 in premium collected. Because you originally paid $1.00 for the long strangle, the premium received will cover the cost of your trade and provide a net credit of $1.50. Therefore, you will end up with a free long strangle plus a guaranteed profit of $1.50.

If COST is just slightly above or below $35, then your short straddle will still have a profit if the value of the short straddle is less than credit you received, $2.50. Therefore, if COST is between $32.50 and $37.50, you can close out the short straddle at expiration for a profit, which will reduce the cost of your long strangle. You are taking advantage of the short-term sideways movement of the stock to generate a profit on the short straddle to lower your strangle cost or to own the long strangle for free.

The potential for a temporary loss in the position occurs if COST moves outside the profit range of $32.50 to $37.50. For example, if COST is at $30 at expiration, the short $35 Call will expire worthless, and the short $35 Put will be worth $5.00, for a loss of $2.50. The maximum loss on your short straddle is $2.50 no matter how far COST moves above or below $35 because your long $30 Put and long $40 Call can be used to cover your short straddle and limit your loss. You could also close your short straddle and keep your strangle in place. Any loss realized on closing your straddle is added to the cost of your strangle. In the foregoing example, the loss of $2.50 combines with your original debit of $1.00 for an overall trade cost of $3.50. Your long $30/$40 strangle will still have time value premium and will increase in value if COST keeps moving lower. Therefore, your position still has a chance to cover your loss and produce a profit.

If you can achieve a profit in closing the short straddle, you will reduce your long strangle cost. If you feel that COST will continue to move sideways for another month, you can sell the next month's $35 straddle and use the profits from that position to either reduce your trade cost even more or end up owning the long strangle for free with a guaranteed net credit.

Calendar Strangle

If you want to take advantage of the short-term sideways movement of the underlying stock but do not want the larger, albeit limited, risk of the short straddle in the diagonal iron butterfly, you can convert your long strangle into a calendar strangle. A calendar strangle involves the purchase of a long-term strangle and the sale of a short-term strangle with the same strike prices. You want the stock to be between the short strangle strike prices at expiration so that the short-term strangle expires worthless and the premium collected reduces the price of your long-term strangle. As long as the stock stays between the strike prices at expiration, you can continue to sell the next month's short strangle with the same strike prices to reduce the cost of your position or possibly own a long strangle for free.

Assume that you purchased a long-term COST $30/$40 strangle for $1.00 with COST at $35. You expect COST to move sideways in the short term and therefore sell a 1-month $30/$40 strangle for $0.40. The short-term strangle and the long-term strangle create a calendar strangle for a net debit of $0.60. If the stock stays between the short strangle strikes by the expiration of the short strangle, then you keep the $0.40 premium collected and reduce your overall trade cost from $1.00 to $0.60. You can then hold on to your reduced-cost strangle or sell the next month's short strangle to bring in more credit and further reduce the cost of your overall position. If COST stays sideways the whole time to expiration of your long strangle, rolling the short strangles month to month until expiration of the long strangle will take advantage of this sideways movement and allow you to reduce the cost of your trade. If you take in enough credit by rolling each month, you may be able to own the long-term strangle for free or collect a net credit for a guaranteed profit.

The maximum loss on your calendar strangle is limited to the net debit paid of $0.60. If COST makes a significant move higher or lower by the expiration of the short strangle, then you can cover the position with the corresponding long option in the long-term strangle. For example, if COST jumps to $42 by the expiration of the short strangle, you can cover the short $40 Call with your long $40 Call. Therefore, the calendar strangle has limited risk and the potential for unlimited rewards if the stock makes a significant move after expiration of the short strangle. Even if you roll your short strangle from month to month, you can keep taking advantage of the sideways movement and reduce your potential risk.

Long Call/Long Put Adjustments

Just as with the long straddle, the long strangle is made up of a long call and a long put. If the stock makes a significant move in one direction or the other, one of the long options will be ITM and potentially produce a profit. At that point, you can hedge your risk, lock in a profit, or even boost your returns by using one of the adjustments covered in Chapter 5 regarding calls and puts. Although your original position is a long strangle, once the stock makes a significant move, the position becomes more focused on the side of the position that is ITM. Therefore, using some of the strategies from Chapter 5, you could add protective calls or puts, roll into bull call or bear put spreads, or use other strategies from that chapter to adjust either the long call or the long put side of your long strangle. Because the overall cost of the long strangle is very low, you may be able to make various adjustments that will significantly improve the performance of your strangle position.

SHORT STRADDLE/SHORT STRANGLE

Short straddles and short strangles are extremely risky positions with the potential for unlimited risk if the stock makes a significant move higher or lower before expiration. In Chapter 1, we told the story of Nick Leeson, who sold naked strangles on the Japanese Nikkei index and wiped out an established banking institution as a result of more than $1 billion in losses. We usually do not recommend naked straddles or strangles to beginners or intermediate traders because the credit received might not be worth the substantial risk. Many traders are enamored with the idea of collecting premium from the sale of these positions, but it takes only one bad position to wipe out a successful trader. We do feel these strategies can be appropriate in certain situations for those traders who are fully aware of the significant risks and can use these positions responsibly. Therefore, even though we do not recommend these strategies for most traders, we do discuss some adjustments that can be made to limit the risk on these naked positions. Although limiting your risk will reduce the premium you collect and your maximum reward, the significant reduction of risk will at least allow you to earn small profits without the fear of being wiped out from a stock that gaps up or down past your breakeven points and keeps moving.

Short Straddle

The best way to limit your risk right from the start while selling short straddles is to create iron butterflies. Remember, an iron butterfly consists of a short straddle and a long OTM strangle with strike prices surrounding your short straddle strike. The sale of the short straddle will take advantage of the sideways movement of the stock and bring in premium, which you get to keep if the stock is right at the short strike at expiration. The purchase of the long strangle surrounding the short straddle will limit your risk because the OTM call and put in the strangle can be used to cover and limit your losses on the short call and short put of your short straddle.

Assume that with COST at $35, you want to sell a straddle to take advantage of expected sideways movement. You observe the 1-month $35 straddle trading at $3.25, which you sell for $3.25 in premium. You also observe the $30/$40 strangle with the same expiration trading at $0.50. To limit the risk on your short straddle, you purchase the long $30/$40 strangle for $0.50 and reduce the amount of premium you took on the sale of the short straddle from $3.25 to $2.75.

Your maximum reward on the iron butterfly is the net credit received, which in this case is $2.75. If COST is right at $35 at expiration, all the options will expire worthless and you keep the $2.75 credit received. The upside and downside breakeven points are calculated by adding the net credit to the straddle strike price ($37.75) and subtracting it from the straddle strike price ($32.25). If COST is anywhere between $32.25 and $37.75, you will realize a profit on your short straddle.

The existence of the long strangle in the iron butterfly will limit your risk in case COST moves well above or below the $35 strike price. The maximum risk in the iron butterfly is the difference between the straddle strike and one of the strangle strikes ($5.00) minus the net credit ($2.75), which is $2.25. The iron butterfly has a lower maximum profit than a naked straddle, but the limited risk is worth it because you will not suffer significant losses (Figure 7.7).

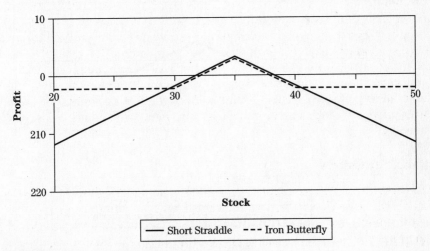

FIGURE 7.7 Iron Butterfly versus Short Straddle

If you want to sell the straddle because you expect the stock to move sideways and you are concerned about a large move in the underlying stock in one direction, then instead of adding the strangle to create an iron butterfly, you can simply add an OTM call or OTM put, depending on which direction you are concerned with. For example, assume you sell the 1-month COST $35 straddle for $3.25 expecting COST to hover around $35 by expiration. Your major concern is that COST could move significantly above $35.

To hedge against such a move without reducing your credit received by too much, you can simply add the OTM $40 Call with the same expiration for $0.25 (assumed price). Your new net credit is $3.00, and your breakeven points are $32 and $38. On the upside, your risk is limited to $2.00 due to the existence of the $40 Call. On the downside, your risk is substantial because you have no protection at all. Therefore, your position is a half-iron butterfly with an upward risk limitation, as indicated in Figure 7.8. If your concern was about a move lower, then instead of the long $40 Call, you would add the long $30 Put, and the risk/reward profile for this position would simply be the reverse of the one in Figure 7.8.

If you are willing to move out a little in time with your short straddle but do not want to cut into your premium received by also buying the longer term strangle, then you can sell a 2-month straddle and purchase a 1-month strangle to create a diagonal short iron butterfly. For example, if the 2-month COST $35 straddle is selling for $3.75 and the 1-month COST $30/$40 strangle is selling for $0.50, you can create a diagonal short iron butterfly by selling the straddle and purchasing the strangle for a net credit

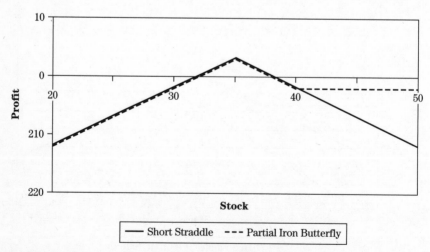

FIGURE 7.8 Partial Iron Butterfly versus Short Straddle

of $3.25. The breakeven points, calculated by adding and subtracting the net credit to the straddle strike price, are $31.75 and $38.25, respectively. With a net credit of $3.25, the maximum loss on the diagonal short iron butterfly is $1.75 at expiration of the long strangle.

We highly recommend that the position be closed out at the expiration of the short strangle after the first month. Once the short strangle expires, you will be left with the naked straddle, and the limited-risk benefit of the diagonal iron butterfly will disappear. Because the short straddle will still have some time value at expiration of the long strangle, it is hard to estimate the exact position values, but the risk will still be limited by the presence of the long call and put.

Rolling Short Straddle into Iron Butterfly

The adjustments suggested previously are based on removing a significant amount of the short option risk of short straddles by placing the adjustment at the same time as the trade. However, those who are willing to assume higher risk can sell the short straddle and later, if the right circumstances exist, adjust into an iron butterfly by purchasing the OTM strangle. This adjustment works best when you enter the short straddle, time passes, and your position has an unrealized profit as a result of either time decay or a decrease in volatility. If you feel the underlying will stay range bound close to your short strikes and want to maintain the position to increase your potential profits, then moving into the iron butterfly is a good adjustment to consider.

Let us walk through an example using some historical option quotes. On April 24, 2009, the NASDAQ-100 index (NDX) was at 1374. Assume that you expect the index to trade in a range-bound pattern over the next few

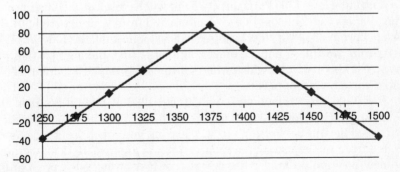

FIGURE 7.9 NDX Short Straddle Profit Profile

weeks as MAY expiration approaches, so you decide to sell the NDX MAY 1375 straddle, which is trading at $88.00. Figure 7.9 shows the profit profile of the short NDX MAY 1375 straddle. As indicated in the graph, as long as NDX continues to trade in a range close to 1375, the position will have a profit. The upside and downside breakeven points are 1463 and 1287, respectively.

About two weeks later, on May 7, 2009, with MAY expiration about a week away, the NDX is trading at 1390, and your short straddle is worth $57. The NDX has basically gone sideways for two weeks, and due to time decay and possible changes in volatility, your short straddle position now has an unrealized profit of $31.00. At this point, you can close the position for a nice profit, which is never a bad decision, but what if you expect NDX to continue to move sideways for the next week and want to really take advantage of the increasing time decay with expiration so close? The big concern is that holding on to the short straddle into expiration still exposes you to significant risks and margin requirements as the NDX could have an explosive move in the next week and not only reduce your unrealized gain but also turn it into a significant loss. Therefore, if you want to stay in the position and eliminate a lot of the risks of the short straddle position, you can adjust it into an iron butterfly by adding an OTM strangle.

With your NDX straddle trading at $57.00 on May 7, 2009, the MAY NDX 1400 Call/1350 Put long strangle is trading at $35.00. If you purchase the 1400 Call/1350 Put long strangle, then your original credit of $88 received from the short straddle is reduced to $53. You now have an iron butterfly consisting of calls and puts with strikes of 1350/1375/1400 for a net credit of $53.00. Let's look at the profit profile of this adjusted position. If NDX is at 1375 at expiration, then the adjusted position will have a maximum profit of the net credit received ($53) as all options will expire worthless. If NDX is below 1350, then the 1375 and 1400 Calls will expire worthless, and the remaining long 1350 Put/short 1375 Put will have a loss of $25 since it is a bull Put spread. The loss of $25 is subtracted from your net credit of $53 for a net profit of $28. If NDX is above 1400 at expiration, the 1350 and 1375 Puts expire worthless, and the remaining short 1375 Call/long 1400 Call will have a net loss of $25.00, which when subtracted from the net credit of $53 leaves you a net profit of $28.

If NDX is anywhere between 1350 and 1400 at expiration, then the OTM long call and long put will expire worthless, and the remaining short 1375 straddle will be worth $0 to $25, leaving you a net profit when subtracted from the adjusted net credit of $53. As Figure 7.10 demonstrates, the new position no longer has any risk of loss at any NDX price at expiration. You have turned your significantly risky short straddle with an

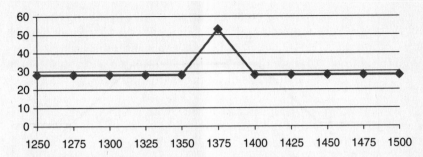

FIGURE 7.10   NDX Adjusted Straddle into Iron Butterfly

unrealized gain of $31 into an iron butterfly with a locked-in profit rang-
ing from $28 to a maximum of $53. Now you can let the position run to
expiration with no possible losses and give it a chance to earn even more
money. More importantly, the margin requirement of the short straddle
in your portfolio is drastically reduced since you are no longer short any
naked options.

Short Strangle

A short strangle has wider breakeven points due to the distance between
the strike prices. The maximum reward on a short strangle is lower than
that of a short straddle because the premium collected is lower, but the
position still has the potential for unlimited risk. The only benefit of choosing a short strangle over a short straddle is that the separate strikes give
the stock some room to move before the short options are ITM. Regard-
less, the only trade adjustment we truly recommend is one that limits the
risk on the short strangle. Because the strike prices are spread apart, it is
harder to diagonalize the spreads or create an iron butterfly. However, you
can create an iron condor by purchasing an even further OTM strangle to
go with your short strangle.

Assume that with COST at $35, you sell a 2-month COST $30/$40 stran-
gle for $0.95. Because the short strikes are spread apart, you can use
2-month expiration options; you have wide breakeven points and can absorb more stock movement over the 2 months. To limit your risk on the
naked position, simultaneously purchase the further OTM $25/$45 strangle, which is trading at $0.20. The long $25 Put and the long $45 Call will
limit your risk on the short strangle. Your maximum reward is limited to
the net credit received for establishing the iron condor, which is $0.75. The
maximum risk, which occurs if COST moves below $25 or above $45, is

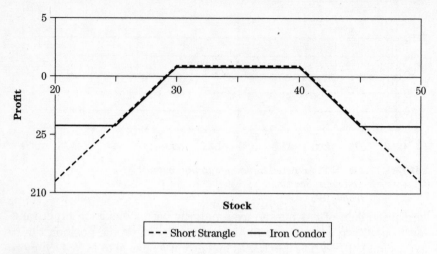

FIGURE 7.11   Iron Condor versus Short Strangle

the difference between the two strangle strikes ($5.00) minus the credit received ($0.75), which is $4.25.

As Figure 7.11 demonstrates, the short strangle has unlimited risk and very small rewards. The small potential rewards of short strangles do not make the strategy very appealing. The iron condor also has limited rewards but significantly reduces your risk. Therefore, the iron condor is preferred over the short strangle.

Index